THE CRYPTO CONTROVERSY

Law and Electronic Commerce

Volume 6

The Crypto Controversy

A Key Conflict in the Information Society

by

Bert-Jaap Koops
Tilburg University
Eindhoven University of Technology

KLUWER LAW INTERNATIONAL
THE HAGUE / LONDON / BOSTON

A C.I.P. Catalogue record for this book is available from the Library of Congress.

ISBN 90-411-1143-3

Published by Kluwer Law International,
P.O. Box 85889, 2508 CN The Hague, The Netherlands.

Sold and distributed in North, Central and South America
by Kluwer Law International,
675 Massachusetts Avenue, Cambridge, MA 02139, U.S.A.

In all other countries, sold and distributed
by Kluwer Law International, Distribution Centre,
P.O. Box 322, 3300 AH Dordrecht, The Netherlands.

Printed on acid-free paper

Kluwer Law International incorporates the publishing programmes of
Graham & Trotman Ltd, Kluwer Law and Taxation Publishers,
and Martinus Nijhoff Publishers.

Printed in the Netherlands.

ILLUSTRATIE LOUIS RADSTAAK

The crypto controversy: a key conflict in the information society

Only connect...

(E.M. Forster)

Table of contents

Acknowledgements

This book is the result of a Ph.D. research project financed by the Co-operation Centre Tilburg and Eindhoven Universities. I am grateful for their support. The staff of the Co-operation Centre, in particular Karen Leurs, Els van Loon, and Marianne Wagemans, have been helpful in providing excellent working conditions.

My supervisors have supported and stimulated me from the start. Marc Groenhuijsen has been the best supervisor I could have wished, stimulating and valuing my work, and carefully correcting what errors I was apt to make. Our discussions were without exception inspiring and thought-provoking. Jan Smits is a living example of the integration of IT and law, and he has transferred his fascination for this research field to me in many discussions, which were all the more relevant and agreeable for not always being to the point. Henk van Tilborg improved my knowledge of cryptography and provided helpful feedback on the technological sections of this book. Paul Wiemans, the instigator of the project, has cheerfully guided me into the research topic as well as into the university, and his careful analysis of legal issues has several times provoked me to reconsider an immature conclusion. Finally, Corien Prins, as head of the IT-law section of the Tilburg University law faculty, created an inspiring environment for research, and her judicious proofreading of the book helped me to improve it in various ways. To all, I am grateful for their support, for their inspiration, and for their confidence in my individual way of working.

Several people have commented on parts of this book. Thanks are due to Wibren van der Burg, Petrus van Duyne, Simone van der Hof, Bert Kroese, Elisabetta Manunza, Christian Meyn, Bart Streumer, Anton Vedder, and Eric Verheul for offering their expertise on particular subjects in criticizing relevant chapters. Besides, Eric Verheul has helped me gain a better knowledge of applied cryptography, and our joint work on an article proved beneficial to this book as well. I have had helpful discussions with Henk Algra, Ronald de Bruin, Hans Henselaar, Cees Jansen, Jan Koers, Dick Komen, Ronald Prins, and Henk van Rossum on the larger issues of this research. Marianne Sanders proved an excellent as well as entertaining teacher who gave me the courage and tools to write this book in English. I thank Jean-Marc van Tol, Bastiaan Geleijnse, and John Reid for their illustrations, and I hope this book may help Fokke and Sukke to travel abroad more frequently.

I also thank the many people I met on the electronic highway, in particular all those who provided information for my online Crypto Law Survey. The people discussing on several mailing lists, notably on cypherpunks, Perry's cryptography, ukcrypto, and krypto, helped me to gain an understanding of a wide range of issues related to my research, and – even with their occasionally less ideal signal-to-noise ratios – they have been a wonderful source of information.

Quite less virtual but equally stimulating have been my colleagues, in particular of the penal-law department and the IT-law section of Tilburg University, and of the law and technology section of Eindhoven University of Technology. The secretaries, especially Vivian Carter, Marian de Jong, and Paula Verheij, have also helped to make my work agreeable and efficient. Finally, I thank Karin van Tuijn, my invaluable room mate of early days, for our discussions on numerous vital and trivial subjects.

I am grateful to my parents for their continuous support of my personal development, my studies, and my other activities. This book is the result of the combination of all these, and my parents deserve credit for at least the good parts of this book. Last and foremost, Ad van der Meer has supported me in more ways than I can express gratitude for. Throughout this research project, he has been the most scrupulous proofreader of my writings, and he has made my life a happy one. I will only be able to return all he has done for me once he starts writing his Ph.D. thesis.

Bert-Jaap Koops
August 1998

Chapter 1. Introduction

"No," Ernie said. "We do speak Guugu Yimidirrh, mate."
"That's good."
"Yes. It is good to have a language. Now listen. I can say" – he spoke some words quickly, a muttered rumbling that sounded like worrojool gangaral – "and you wouldn't know."
As he had spoken, Gladys jerked her head out of her grandson's hands, and blinked hard, and looked away.
"What wouldn't I know?"
"I said, 'Kill that white man,'" Ernie said, looking pleased, "and, see, you didn't know what I said."
(Paul Theroux, The Happy Isles of Oceania)

1.1. A problem without a solution

Before I started the research that led to this book, I – like the vast majority of the Dutch – had never heard of cryptography, the digitized and automated sister of secret writing. Then, in March 1994, as I braced myself for the job by hiking the Himalayas, cryptography made headlines for a brief period in Dutch newspapers. A pre-draft law had been concocted in the dark recesses of the Dutch Ministries of Justice and Internal Affairs, which would have effectively outlawed cryptography. Someone envisioning a consequent economic disaster leaked it to the press, and the resulting outcry was heard all over the world, reinforced by the Internet community. Its echoes even reached the dark recesses of the Ministries themselves. This pre-draft law was not a Good Thing, they realized. But how then should they address the rapidly spreading use of encoding programs which protect stored data and communications? After all, knowledgeable criminals would be sure to seize the opportunities offered them by uncrackable codes, and leave wiretapping and searching police empty-handed.

Since early 1994, cryptography has indeed spread widely, spurred by explosive growth of the Internet, electronic banking, and electronic transactions. By mid-1998, it has become a common technology that many people use without knowing (in GSM phones, for instance) and that an increasing, though still rather small, number of people use explicitly (in e-mail, for example, or when ordering books online). Cryptography has proved itself a primary tool in information security. Actually, criminals are also – albeit slowly – discovering the potential of cryptography to elude law-enforcement's scrutiny (many still rely on more traditional tricks, such as using a bunch of mobile phones with untraceable prepaid cards).

With the increasing need in the information society to employ cryptography on the one hand, and with the increasing concern that criminals can effectively escape justice by using

National studies on the crypto controversy

Australia: the Walsh report was released in early 1997 after considerable pressure from Electronic Frontiers Australia; although several sections were not available for national security concerns, the published part is a thorough, consistent, and broad analysis of the issue in the Australian context [Walsh].

Canada: the Task Force on Electronic Commerce issues a discussion paper *A Cryptography Policy Framework for Electronic Commerce* in February 1998, listing several options to address encryption of stored data, encryption of real-time communications, and export controls [TFEC].

Denmark: one of the earliest national reports to appear, the 1995 collection of articles by the Technology Council, *A Danish crypto policy. How to keep digital information secret?*, aptly termed the issue a Gordian knot that badly needed cutting (without suggesting how) [Stripp]. The more elaborate *Report by the Expert Committee on Cryptography*, released in April 1997, by representatives of seven ministries, recommended not to introduce regulation of cryptography in Denmark; however, having only considered mandatory options, they recommended studying the possibilities and consequences of introducing incentive schemes [ECC]. As a result, the Expert Committee continued its work, and in June 1998 released a report recommending – for the time being – not to limit crypto use by incentive schemes either, but to continue to monitor international developments [Fsk].

Sweden: the October 1997 report from the Cabinet Office Reference Group for Cryptographic Issues, *Crypto Policy: Possible Courses of Action for Sweden*, is a broad inventory of digital signature and encryption issues; it recommends free use of cryptography, but is rather optimistic (or pessimistic, depending on your point of view) on the option of voluntary deposit of crypto keys (cf. Chapter 7), apparently assuming that many countries are considering such schemes [Cabinet].

United States: the 1994 Association for Computing Machinery's *Codes, Keys, and Conflicts, Issues in U.S. Crypto Policy* was the first major study of the issue to appear; it is still a valuable analysis of the issues at stake [ACM]. In 1996, the National Research Council, with government, business, and academic members, published its visionarily titled 'Cryptography's Role In Securing the Information Society' (mark the acronym). The extensive and in-depth analysis of all aspects of the crypto conflict and its many informative appendices make it the best report available. The report contains several partial recommendations, among others, not to bar domestic manufacture or use of encryption, and to progressively relax (but not abolish) export controls. [NRC]

cryptography on the other, the *crypto controversy* has emerged as a major problem for governments: how should they balance the conflicting interests of privacy and information security on the one hand with the interests of law enforcement and national security on the other?

Thus, the crypto controversy has become one of the major policy debates of the information society. There are lively discussions on the Internet (special mailing lists have been set up to discuss the issue, such as 'ukcrypto' and the German 'krypto', while other mailing lists and news groups have discussed it extensively, e.g., cypherpunks, cryptography@c2.net, talk.politics.crypto, and sci.crypt). In the parliaments (notably in the US and Germany), and increasingly in national newspapers, the debate is continuing in wider public circles. These discussions show the fairly broad interest in the topic, as well as the extreme positions some lobby groups take in this debate. Often, the discussion has not led the two lobbies of the privacy community ("no regulation whatsoever!") on the one hand and the law-enforcement community ("give us the keys!") on the other to come any closer. Rather, most have repeated well-known arguments and insisted upon their own conclusion being the right one to balance the conflicting interests. The 'middle way' everyone is looking for keeps disappearing across the horizon.

The Dutch government has racked its brains on how to balance the conflicting interests of cybersecurity and cryptocriminals. Tentative suggestions for (partial) solutions are still being discussed. Indeed, many countries have assigned study groups to develop a discussion or position paper on the issue (see sidebar). The most notable of these are the Australian

Walsh report and the US NRC report.

If there is one thing these reports have in common, it is that they acknowledge the complexity and importance of the problem while not really knowing how to solve it. I share this common denominator: one thing I will not do in this book is give *the* solution to *the* problem. Instead, I will present a dynamic approach which indicates in what way governments, and in particular the Dutch government, could and should address the problem.

Instead of 'solutions to the crypto problem', I will talk of 'ways to address the crypto problem'. For lack of a simpler term, I will refer to these ways as 'optional directions'. This indicates that, if one is to resolve the problem, one can look in several directions which may at least provide a way to live with the problem, even if none of them truly solves it.

1.2. What this book is not about

This book is not about *national security and intelligence*. National security agencies have the same problems as law enforcement if their objects of surveillance use cryptography.[1] However, their methods of surveillance, although perhaps the same in practice, differ from those of law enforcement in that, at least in the Netherlands, they are supervised through political procedures, not by legal authorities according to legal procedures. Their use is obscure, as is their effect. Criminal investigation, on the other hand, is, in principle,[2] subject to court scrutiny, which results in more public data on the use and effectiveness of the investigation measures. I have therefore confined myself in this book to looking at the problems that *law enforcement* faces in the *investigation of crimes*. Although this means that the analysis covers only part of the problem that governments have to address (nefarious use of cryptography), it is – I believe increasingly – felt to be the more important and more urgent part of the problem. Until the mid-1990s, the crypto debate centered for a large part around national security and intelligence, but over the last three years, the debate has gradually shifted towards law-enforcement interests.

This book is not about *export controls*. As a consequence of leaving aside national security problems, I disregard the debate about crypto export controls. These are, after all, targeted at keeping uncrackable cryptography out of the hands of foreign crooks and terrorists – potential objects of intelligence surveillance, but not of law enforcement. Export controls do not see to domestic use of cryptography by criminals (although they may have served in the US as a domestic policy instrument, cf. 5.1.2). A large part of the crypto debate

1 A nice example of cryptography's use in a plot threatening national security is provided by Mary, Queen of Scots. As Babington, a former page of Mary's, conspired to kill Queen Elizabeth of England, he needed the approval of Mary, who was then held under house arrest. The correspondence between them, faithfully encrypted with nomenclators, was exchanged through a double-agent, who forwarded all letters to England's state cryptanalyst, Phelippes. Once Mary had written an incriminating message, approving of the assassination plot, her fate was sealed, and she was executed shortly afterwards. [Kahn, 121-124]

2 The qualification is needed after IRT-gate, in which InterRegional Teams investigating serious crime turned out to have bypassed court scrutiny to a degree unheard of in Dutch society.

in the United States has revolved around the export controls, but since a few years, it also focuses on domestic regulations, following the Clipper fiasco and the SAFE coup in Congress (see 5.3.8). In the Netherlands, domestic controls have always been the focus of the crypto controversy.

This book is also not about *tapping*. Although wiretapping is an important subject in this book – much of the crypto debate discusses safeguarding the future of wiretapping – it is subordinate to the crypto problem. That is, I take as a starting point that wiretapping is allowed under certain conditions, and that the law requires telecom providers to make their networks tappable (see 4.3.1) and to facilitate specific wiretaps. Wiretapping as such is not questioned. Note that in considerable parts of the crypto debate, particularly in the US, and also in the UK, this starting point has itself been challenged: in many discussions, opponents of crypto regulations have argued against wiretapping capabilities as such rather than against regulating cryptography for wiretapping's sake.[3] As a consequence of not discussing wiretapping as such, I will not analyze to what extent wiretapping is technically feasible regardless of cryptography. The development of the information and communications infrastructure is posing several technical problems to wiretapping; despite the ardent wish of the legislature to maintain the technical capacity to wiretap, these technical problems may turn out to be a significant obstacle for continuing current-level wiretapping. This is outside the scope of this book. I shall assume here that wiretapping is technically possible, in order to analyze the problems of crypto use for wiretapping. (Note that if the emerging communications infrastructure will turn out to make wiretapping technically difficult as such, the analysis of the crypto problem will have to be reassessed.)

Finally, this book is not about *digital signatures*. A large (and probably the most important) part of the information-security need of the information society concerns the authenticity and integrity of communications and transactions. Digital signatures can fulfill these objectives, and cryptography is a key technology for digital signatures. Policies and (probably) legislation to facilitate the use of digital signatures are called for, and so, a considerable part of the overall crypto policy debate should address this need. Digital signatures as such do not, however, pose a problem for law enforcement. Therefore, I will only deal with digital signatures when this touches upon the law-enforcement problem, notably in section 7.3 when discussing technologies that separate authentication-only from confidentiality cryptography.

1.3. What this book is about

This book is about the mid- concern with cryptocriminals. The central question I answer in this book is:

---

3 See, for instance, the summary of responses to the 1997 UK consultation document on crypto policy: the "issue of access to keys for law enforcement purposes attracted by far the most comment – particularly from individuals. Much of it was fundamentally opposed to the whole concept of lawful access, and either explicitly or implicitly also rejected the existing powers for lawful access to traffic under the Interception of Communications Act". [Roche]

How can and should the Dutch government address the problem that the use of strong cryptography by criminals poses to law enforcement, taking into account the legitimate needs to use cryptography in the information society?

1.3.1. Focus on the Netherlands

In a globalized and networked society, one should not look for national solutions to international problems in the field of information and communication technologies (ICT). The information society is global by nature. Moreover, crime, especially organized crime, is increasingly crossing borders and forcing law enforcement to cooperate internationally. Both developments suggest that to address the crypto conflict, one should choose an option which is valid throughout the information society.

I will not do so. Given the complexity and precarious nature of the issue, addressing the problem from the perspective of a single state is difficult; addressing it from an international perspective is impossible. An option has to acknowledge national concerns, legal cultures, the specifics of constitutional protection. It is unrealistic to choose international or even supranational options to address the crypto conflict. The failing effort of the OECD to achieve just that, an international direction of crypto policies, underlines this. The OECD 'guidelines', after all, do not guide. They leave it to every single state to strike a balance somewhere; virtually any balance, packed in proper rhetorics, will satisfy the OECD principles. A compromise between cybersecurity and law-enforcement interests cannot apparently itself be compromised on an international level. States, then, must do it themselves.

This effectively leaves the crypto conflict at a dead end. While national options are not appropriate, international options are not viable. The only way out seems to me to focus on nationally-based options that take the international context as one of their preconditions. I shall look for options that can be implemented in the Netherlands, whether or not other countries implement similar or contrary policies. This, of course, is a major constraint, but it is an inevitable one.

Analyzing the crypto conflict from a Dutch perspective has several advantages. I can give a more detailed and in-depth description of the context in which the problem should be seen, and I can better argue whether particular options fit the legal system and legal culture. Moreover, the Netherlands is a particularly interesting case given 'IRT-gate': the practice of some investigation agencies (IRTs) exploring and increasingly crossing the legal margins of investigation powers. When things had really gotten out of hand, by 1993, a parliamentary inquest had to set things straight and bring Dutch justice back to order. The report of the inquest, usually referred to after its chairman as the Van Traa report, provoked a rethinking of criminal investigation and led to several legislature proposals on investigation measures. This rethinking of investigation law and practice is a felicitous context for the crypto debate, as this is closely linked to one of the central needs of criminal investigation: gathering information.

The national focus does not mean that this book is of interest to Dutch readers only. On the contrary, much of the material covered is equally valid for other countries - it is the details that vary, not the outline. I sometimes illustrate this variation for other countries in sidebars and sections, in order to provide a wider context for the analysis; this is illustrative

A wide gap

The crypto debate features two sides with opposing interests. The privacy lobby and the law-enforcement lobby have discussed the issue extensively, but they do not seem to have come much closer to each other.

Alan McDonald, senior counsel with the FBI, has said that "privacy activists had fought any balance in proposed encryption legislation." He called the extreme privacy positions "ultimately elitist and nondemocratic in that they presumed the views of a knowing privacy cognoscenti should pre-empt the views of the nation's elected officials and the Supreme Court" [quoted in Braun].

Two of the constraints that Mike Nelson formulated for finding an encryption policy that makes everyone happy (or equally unhappy) [Nelson] are particularly telling in this respect:

- Any solution the U.S. government endorses is immediately suspect.
- No one trusts anyone.

On the other side of the debate stands the FBI, as described by Stewart Baker: "the FBI is not too troubled by the bad press it's getting over encryption, or by the privacy and industry complaints – or even by the Congressional harrumphing. (...) in the end, the Bureau believes that Congress will have to mandate crypto controls just as it had to mandate wiretap requirements." [Baker 98a]

rather than systematic. In particular, I often indicate the situation in the US – not to provide a final analysis of the US conflict, but to show the ingredients one can use to transpose my analysis of the Netherlands to the US.

Moreover, one of my major concerns in this book is the methodological issue of how to balance conflicting interests. I value not so much the outcome of this procedure (the particular balance I propose for the Netherlands), but the procedure itself. For other countries, filling in the particulars will vary, but the procedure I follow to reach an outcome can, I suggest, be equally valuable in other Western countries (and, who knows, in South American countries and South-East Asian (former) tigers).

1.3.2. Outline

The first part of this book defines the context of the crypto conflict. Chapter 2 features the information society and its need for information security. Here, I am lavish with quotes from government policy documents on the importance of information security, in order to provide a counter-weight to the bold law-enforcement statements that will follow later. In Chapter 3, I argue that cryptography is a key technology to provide information security. After a primer on cryptography, I illustrate the importance of encryption by listing many applications, including its benefits for governments themselves. Chapter 4 provides the context of investigation, focusing on the kinds of criminals at issue and their information-management practices, the investigation measures hampered by cryptocriminals, an assessment of the cracking opportunities for the police, and a guesstimate to what extent crypto has obstructed law enforcement to date. In Chapter 5, I survey what laws and regulations have been enacted or planned to deal with the issue. Together, these chapters define the problem and the context in which options will have to be found.

Part II provides a framework to address the crypto conflict. Chapter 6 defines the principles which will guide the procedure of balancing interests. These principles are applied in Chapters 6½-10 to the four directions that options can be looked for (and to one non-direction: banning cryptography or mandating law-enforcement access to keys, Chapter 6½):

- voluntary crypto systems which provide law-enforcement access to keys, including non-confidentiality systems, key escrow, and key recovery (Chapter 7);

- requiring people to provide decryption; the central issues here are to what extent the privilege against self-incrimination and the presumption of innocence allow suspects to be ordered to decrypt, and how such a decryption command can be enforced (Chapter 8);
- alternative investigation measures. Conceptually, once law enforcement cannot access keys or plaintext if the options of accessing keys beforehand (Chapter 7) or afterwards (Chapter 8) do not work, they will have to leave the encrypted data aside and find other ways to gather information. Chapter 9 describes (not exhaustively) possible alternatives to wiretaps and computer searches: direct eavesdropping, intercepting electromagnetic radiation, infiltration, crown witnesses, and data mining;
- doing nothing, which is the only logical thing to do if all possible alternatives turn out to have more negative than positive effects; note that doing nothing is a conscious decision in this respect (Chapter 10).

Chapter 11, finally, is the synthesis of the previous chapters. Taking as input the principles from Chapter 6 and the viable options that emerge from Chapters 7-10, I provide a procedure to address the crypto conflict, inspired by John Rawls' theory of justice. The major interested parties (except the criminals, of course) will match the various options with the principles at stake, and decide which (partial) option or options best balance the conflicting interests in the Dutch context.

The analysis in this book is, in principle, a conceptual one. This does not mean that I disregard details or the way things work out in practice; rather, I have tried to provide an overall, abstracted analysis of the issues at stake. More detailed descriptions of options serve as illustrations and show the pros and cons of the options. The descriptions are far from exhaustive, and often (notably in Chapters 7 and 9), I have chosen a sample of options which may have left other, equally valid, examples unmentioned. Also, in arguing over the real value of a particular option, I have tried to keep reality in mind and not lose myself in long arguments over counter-examples. Particularly, cryptographers excel at inventing ways to subvert solutions and to offer patches for the gaps, inviting others to attack the patches and offer patches for bugs in the patches, and so on ad libitum. With the second round of counter-counterattacks, the debate has often moved far beyond a realistic assessment of real-world issues (which is not to say that these theoretical discussions are not useful). I have also abstracted from particular implementations, should one or the other option be chosen, with respect to the specific legal constraints under which the option could or should be implemented. I assume that the usual legal safeguards apply, such as proper warrants and the principles of subsidiarity and proportionality for investigation powers.

1.3.3. Aim

My overall aim with this book is to provide a conceptual analysis of the crypto problem for law enforcement. I analyze the issues at stake and the pros and cons of the various options to address the problem. By giving a broad overview of the many sides of the problem and of the many valid (and occasionally invalid) arguments, I hope to clarify the debate, to show the nature of the problem (a conflict of interests), and to show how it can be addressed (justifying the choice of particular options by open and argued reasoning in an explicit procedure).

Indeed, the issue of *how* to balance conflicting interests is central to the framework I choose. All too often, people list options and criteria, and jump to the conclusion that one or other option best balances the interests, essentially leaving hidden the process of arriving at this conclusion. A second aim of this book, then, is to bring to light the methodological issue of how to balance interests; I shall do this mainly by making explicit the assumptions I make and by clearly describing the procedure of choosing an option.

Through the conceptual analysis of the problem, I hope this book will help to bridge the gap, still particularly wide in this debate, between technology and law, between cryptographers and lawyers, between privacy activists and governments. Underlying this book is the sense that the two research fields, ICT and law, cannot do without each other. Each has to understand what the other area is about, how it functions, and – perhaps most importantly – how people reason in the other field. Although the crypto problem is essentially a legal problem, addressing it requires knowledge of the technology involved. Moreover, if the resulting policy is to bridge the gap between the two fields, the reasoning must be consistent with the accepted practices of both technology and law. Therefore, the thrust of the argument in this book should be acceptable to specialists in both fields. I have refrained from giving detailed legal or cryptographic analyses and focused instead on combining the two fields in a readable book. If I have succeeded in making the two parties that have so often taken sides against each other in the crypto debate gain some understanding of the other side of the debate, it is sufficient justification for this book.

1.4. How to read this book

I have tried throughout this book to make it readable for everyone interested in the subject, be they lawyers, ICT specialists, cryptographers, cypherpunks, e-merchants, or interested information citizens. I explain terminology and introduce basic concepts of both ICT and law, assuming only a basic knowledge of computers and the Internet. An extensive glossary and abbreviation list of technical and legal terms should help the reader in understanding the text. This does not mean it is always easy to follow (lawyers may require considerable effort to grasp Chapters 3 and 7, whereas ICT specialists may need time for the subtleties of Chapters 4 and 8), but everyone willing to invest time and brain activity should be able to read the book throughout.

Readers can, in principle, skip certain chapters if they wish. For instance, cryptographers will be familiar with most of Chapter 3, and frequent visitors of my online Crypto Law

Survey need not read Chapter 5. Those well-versed in the crypto debate may skim through Part I to see which areas I cover, and move on to Part II. However, readers must bear in mind that the reasoning in Part II is based on the entire context outlined in Part I, and that I do not always explicitly refer back to assumptions and distinctions I have made earlier.

I have tried to make this a reader-friendly book, with illustrations, quotations, and sidebars enlivening the text. The contents of the sidebars and footnotes are usually not essential to the argument, but should not be regarded as less important than the main text[4] (one of the (few) nice achievements of postmodernism is the blurring of center and margin). Where it does not affect the thrust of the argument, I have occasionally valued readability and understandability over (technical or legal) correctness.

In cryptographic literature, the technology is commonly illustrated by crypto characters Alice and Bob, the friendly personifications of the blank A and B so often encountered in technical texts. I have taken the liberty of extending the crypto family with a few law-enforcement characters, which seemed a good way of illustrating the various options at work.

I use American English, with two exceptions: I Do Not Capitalize Titles, and I use the more consistent British way of indicating dates (dd Month yyyy). All translations are mine.

I use references only to substantiate the text, not to suggest further reading. The references are indicated in the text with square brackets [Fokke & Sukke] and can be found in the bibliography, except the references to newspapers and magazines, which are in italics [*China Daily*, 29 October 1997]. Where useful, I refer to page numbers [Rawls, 121], partly to facilitate looking up the reference, and partly out of nostalgia that there are still page numbers to refer to. With longer electronic documents, I refer to sections [Walsh, 3.2.1]. Dutch legislation proposals are referred to as [25880, nrs 1-2, 197]: parliamentary document series 25880 (*Legislation for the electronic highway*, the title is mentioned in the bibliography), numbers 1-2, page 197. EU and EC documents are referred to by their number [COM(94) 347, 96/C329/01]. These are separately referenced in the bibliography. Case law is referred to by the Court name (e.g., HR = Dutch Supreme Court) and date or (mostly with European and US cases) by their (nick)name; the full references can be found in the case-law section of the bibliography.

The research of this book was finalized on 1 July 1998. Later developments that are important to the overall reasoning of this book (notably, enacting of legislation that is still at the drafting stage when this book goes to print), I will update on my homepage <http://cwis.kub.nl/~frw/people/koops/thesis/update.htm>.

---

4 Cf. Anthony Grafton, *The footnote. A curious history*, London: Faber and Faber, 1997.

Part I

Problem and context

Chapter 2. An information society needs information security

The future had arrived. There was a generation waiting to inherit the earth, caring nothing for old-timers' concerns: dedicated to the pursuit of the new, speaking the future's strange, binart, affectless speech – quite a change from our melodramatic garam-masala exclamations.
(Salman Rushdie, The Moor's Last Sigh)

At the threshold of a new millennium, a new society is emerging: the information society. As more and more people rely on information for their work, entertainment, and daily life, information and communication technologies conquer large parts of society. The protection of these areas of life must be redefined, then, in terms of information security. Particularly the confidentiality, integrity, and availability of information should be safeguarded. In this chapter, I will sketch the outlines of the information society – (inter)national policies, the infrastructure, and the problems confronting it (2.1). Then, I will describe the role of information security therein (2.2). I will pay particular attention to the role of governments in establishing information security.

2.1. The information society

Europe's citizens and consumers can look forward to a more caring European society with a significantly higher quality of life. Thus spoke the Bangemann Report on *Europe and the global information society* [Bangemann 94]. The information revolution will profoundly change the way we live and work.[1]

2.1.1. Developments

Several developments contribute to the emergence of this information-based society. First, information is increasingly being digitized through the enhancement of information technol-

---

1 Information and communication technologies are affecting almost all professions. For instance, a farmer nowadays relies on computers for his increasingly complex paperwork and for production planning, while he uses telecommunications to increase his action radius. A well-known example is the Texas rancher who gave his cows pagers rather than bells, and they would gather at the right place when beeped. [*Telemanagement*, February 1995] The issue of the changes in work through information and telecommunication technologies (teleworking, employment shifts, and changing job profiles) is specifically addressed in the report *Building the European information society for us all* of January 1996, by a high-level group of senior experts of the European Union which investigates the social and societal aspects of the information society.

ogies. As the cost-performance ratio of these technologies is dropping, the advantages of digitizing information are rapidly becoming clear. It can be processed at astounding speeds, reproduced without any effort, and spread over large distances in an instant. Moreover, interfaces for information processing have become much more user-friendly; for instance, the Internet really started to be used on a large scale after the advent of its graphic interface, the World Wide Web (WWW).

A second development is the increasing integration of different media. Whereas, for instance, telephones and computers used to perform different functions, information technologies and telecommunications technologies nowadays increasingly interoperate; thus, one speaks of information and communication technologies (ICT). Telephone lines are being used for facsimile traffic, electronic data interchange, and e-mail, and Internet technology can be used for making cheap long-distance phone calls. The market for telematics, the combination of telecommunications and information technology, is soaring. Television cable networks have a huge potential for carrying all kinds of information, with the possibility of interactive communications – a great advance over the one-way broadcasting of television programs. Ultimately, an integration of computer, television, telephone, and facsimile might be expected.

A third and related development is the convergence of sectors. Where formerly the sectors of telecommunications infrastructure, telecom services, and content were clearly separated, increasingly companies occupy themselves with several segments of the ICT market at one and the same time. For instance, telephone companies offer network and value-added services. Cable network operators merge with service providers and busy themselves with providing content. Some operating-systems producers even want to have a say in every ICT market segment. Thus, in the information society, a new infrastructure is emerging, with new segments and blurred borderlines.

Increasing liberalization of the telecommunications sector contributes to the growing attractiveness of telecommunications. Once the telecom market has been fully liberalized (in the European Union, this was largely the case in January 1998), users can choose from a range of providers and services, which providers will gear to their needs in order to survive in the competitive market. A good illustration is the fast-growing market of mobile phones, where fierce competition has lured numerous people into buying a mobile phone. Apparently, more and more people consider a mobile phone vital[2] (for their status if not for their needs).

Moreover, the information society is primarily demand-driven [23900, nr 20, 2.1]. Due to the proliferation of services, customers can pick and choose what kind of information they want and how and when they want to receive it. Video-on-demand is an example (albeit a slowly developing one); in the near future, knowbots (information agents) may roam the information superhighway to collect specific bits of information their masters are interested in.

The youngest development of the information society is electronic commerce. Industry

---

2 A Swede perished on Midsummer eve 1995 when he dived from a ferry to save his mobile phone [*Volkskrant*, 20 June 1996].

and governments are beginning to realize the potential of the online economy – ordering, paying, and, with intangible products, delivering through electronic networks. Although everyone recognizes the importance of this development, electronic commerce is yet in its infancy. Lack of consumer trust (in payment systems and the protection of personal data, for instance) and the uncertainty over the legal implications and obligations are among the main obstacles for e-commerce to fully bud and bloom.[3]

Overarching all these developments is the increasingly global nature of the information society. Globalization (or, if you perceive the information society as a global village, glocalization) permeates the information revolution, which causes traditional frontier-based distinctions to be increasingly obsolete. Territoriality gives way to borderless cyberspace. The physical constraints of volume, time, and space are fading, as electronic media displace material applications.

These developments lead to a society that is increasingly dependent on information. An estimated two thirds of the economy in Western countries rely on information-related work,[4] and many functions of the network economy (communication, information management, transactions) rely to a large extent on electronic information exchange [WRR, 7]. This development is so profound that some speak of "a new industrial revolution already as significant and far-reaching as those of the past." [Bangemann 94, 4n]

2.1.2. Information society policy

The rise of the information society has been noticed at government levels. Politicians see a huge potential for the information infrastructure, provided certain conditions are met. They have launched initiatives to set down these conditions and to make sure they are met.

United States

US vice-president Gore in 1993 launched the National Information Infrastructure (NII) initiative, which "captures the vision of a nationwide, invisible, seamless, dynamic web of transmission mechanisms, information appliances, content, and people", in the words of [NIIAC]. Private investment, competition, open access, universal service, and flexible governmental action were seen as key issues. An Information Infrastructure Task Force (IITF) was established, with three committees, on telecommunications policy, information policy, and applications and technology – each divided into working groups that investigate and report on specific subjects. Moreover, an NII Security Issues Forum was established, which coordinates security-related efforts in NII policy. In early 1994, the NII Advisory Council (NIIAC) was set up to advise the administration on a national strategy for promoting the development of the NII and the Global Information Infrastructure (GII). Its first report,

---

3 According to GVU's 8th WWW User Survey (endorsed by the World Wide Web Consortium), "security remains the number one reason Web users report for not purchasing over the Web". [GVU]

4 "Individual, corporate and national wealth expresses itself increasingly in the form of information. The growth and performance of an estimated 2/3 of the economy relies on manufacturing or services heavily dependent on information technology, telecommunications and broadcasting." [DG XIII, section 1] "[I]nformation is one of America's most critical economic resources, for both service and manufacturing industries, for both economic and national security. This is not surprising, considering the fact that almost two-thirds of US workers have information-related jobs." [Bekkers, 11-12]

Common Ground: Fundamental Principles for the NII of March 1995, presented overall principles for furthering the NII, covering universal access and services, privacy and security, intellectual property, education and lifelong learning, and electronic commerce. It envisioned an improvement of the quality of life, for instance, through strengthening education, improving healthcare, increasing entertainment options, and enhancing participatory democracy, provided the NII is grounded in a unified vision. The 1995 *GII: Agenda For Cooperation* extended the vision of the NII to a global level. [Brown]

Electronic commerce is increasingly seen as a central development in the information society. On 1 July 1997, president Clinton and vice-president Gore presented *A Framework For Global Electronic Commerce*, which suggested a set of principles and presented a series of policies to articulate "the Administration's vision for the emergence of the GII as a vibrant global marketplace" [Clinton, 3]. The main principles stressed the central starting-point of a non-regulatory, market-oriented approach by governments: the private sector should lead, governments should avoid undue restrictions, and government involvement must aim for a predictable, minimalist, consistent, and simple legal environment. Moreover, electronic commerce over the Internet should be facilitated on a global basis. The 'non-bureaucratic' facilitating approach is echoed in the report *The Emerging Digital Economy* of April 1998, one of the elaborations of the Framework [Margherio].

European Union

The May 1994 Bangemann Report *Europe and the global information society – Recommendations to the European Council* confronted the challenge of establishing an information society. Much of it is still as topical today as when it was published. It stressed the need for private investment for developing the information infrastructure, while governments should focus on creating a stimulating and balanced regulatory environment, covering the issues of liberalization,[5] interconnection, universal service, protecting privacy and intellectual property rights, and ensuring free movement in the Internal Market. Furthermore, ten application projects were defined for, among others, teleworking, distance learning, and road-traffic management. The recommendations were elaborated in an action plan by the European Commission, *Europe's Way to the Information Society* [COM(94) 347], which serves as a reference framework for the EU's activities on the information society. In 1996, the framework was incorporated into a *Rolling Action Plan* [COM(96) 607].

Three recent EU initiatives relate to the regulation of the information society and specifically of electronic commerce. The EC Communication *A European Initiative in Electronic Commerce* of early 1997 aims to provide a coherent policy framework for Community action in the area of electronic commerce, to encourage "the vigorous growth of electronic commerce in Europe" [COM(97)157]. It calls for a predictable legal and institutional framework to support trust-building technologies, such as digital signatures and electronic payment mechanisms. This was elaborated in the Communication *Ensuring*

5 To encourage private investment in the information infrastructure, the telecommunications market was liberalized, a process that started in the 1980s and was completed in early 1998 with the liberalization of the voice telephony market. See [96/19/EC].

security and trust in electronic communication – Towards a European framework for digital signatures and encryption of 10 October 1997 [COM(97)503]. The second initiative is the EC Green Paper on convergence of December 1997, which is a discussion paper on the many issues facing the regulatory environment of the information society in view of the increasing convergence of technologies and sectors. It "represents a key element of the overall framework put in place to support the development of an Information Society" [COM(97) 623]. On the basis of comments on this Green Paper, the Commission intends to produce a Communication by the end of 1998. The third and most encompassing (and consequently rather vague) initiative is Bangemann's call for an 'International Charter' to coordinate world-wide policies regarding the information society [Bangemann 97, further developed in COM(98) 50]. The European Commission argues that the global electronic marketplace requires strengthened international coordination in creating an enabling framework that covers technical, commercial, and legal aspects. The envisaged international charter would not be a detailed document outlining rules on specific topics, but would rather establish a "sustained method of coordination in which public and private sector interests are adequately represented" [COM (98) 50]. The Charter is scheduled to be discussed at a ministerial conference in early 1999.

Europe-wide, at the Bonn conference of 6-8 July 1997, ministers agreed on a reticent role of governments in regulating the information society. A host of representatives from the EU, the EFTA, Central and Eastern Europe, and guests from the US, Canada, Japan, and Russia discussed barriers and solutions to the development of Global Information Networks. The joint declaration affirms that the expansion of global information networks must essentially be market-led. Governments have two major roles: providing a clear and balanced regulatory framework, and stimulating new services. [Bonn]

The Netherlands

National initiatives have followed up and elaborated on the European action plan. The Dutch National Action Plan *Electronic highways: from metaphor to action* [23900, nr 20] of December 1994 and its follow-up reports [24565] stressed the need for additional national activities, in order to strengthen the Netherlands' position of 'Gateway to Europe'. The policy was based on two main tiers: liberalizing the telecommunications and media markets to stimulate the private investment needed for establishing a Dutch electronic highway, and redefining the state's role in the public domain, which changes significantly through the rise of ICT. According to the National Action Plan, the preconditions for a well-functioning information infrastructure should be optimized by addressing such issues as intellectual-property rights, privacy, security, law-enforcement wiretapping, and standardization.

The Dutch government further outlined the issues at stake in regulating the information society in the hefty and somewhat diffuse policy document *Legislation for the electronic highway* of February 1998 [25880, nrs 1-2]. It concluded that the transition to the information society brings far-reaching changes, but does not constitute a radical rupture with the past: offline rules will generally also hold online. The document presents a touchstone for the legislature as well as several suggestions for adapting legislation and regulation. The government defines its main roles as safeguarding fundamental moral values and facilitating electronic traffic. The government notices one major problem "that is not really solvable":

the international character of the electronic highway. They argue, however, that the problem can be reduced significantly by a 'pragmatic multi-track approach'. Such an approach is similar, one may suppose, to the 'open approach' advocated by the Scientific Council for Government Policy [WRR]. In its 1998 report *State without a territory*, the Council advises to flexibly strike new balances between fundamental points of departure, given the fact that ICT penetration makes obsolete the self-evidence that a state should regulate things based on territoriality. The changes the information society will bring about must not be met in terms of the existing capacity to act and with the customary concepts. 'More-of-the-same' legislation is unlikely to prove sufficient, the report states. (Admittedly, the Council remains somewhat vague about just what new concepts are required in the 'open approach'.)

The touchstone of *Legislation for the electronic highway* lists principles for government intervention. Regulation should preferably be global and involve as many countries as possible, or else be agreed upon in supranational fora such as the OECD, the Council of Europe, or the European Union. National regulation can be considered to protect moral values, if an international approach is not feasible. However, the legislature should first examine whether self-regulation is possible, provided the government can ensure that the conditions for self-regulation (such as sufficient enforcement) are met. Government intervention is called for where fundamental moral values are at stake, notably fundamental citizen rights and the prevention and investigation of serious breaches of the rule of law and national security. The government should expressly choose between instruments of action: self-regulation, leaving issues for the courts to decide, administrative measures, and formal legislation. [25880, nrs 1-2, 12-14]

The *Electronic Commerce Action Plan* of March 1998 [EZ] is one of the new policy initiatives emerging from the reassessment of the National Action Plan. Noting that the Netherlands has a good potential basis for becoming one of the leading countries in e-commerce, it aims at addressing the barriers that obstruct e-commerce. Among these barriers are legal uncertainties, and the Action Plan consequently sets the government the target of ensuring a clear and coherent legal framework. Moreover, the government should enhance trust and security in electronic transactions. Thus, a national Trusted Third Parties (TTP) project aims at stimulating the development of a reliable TTP infrastructure, which will facilitate and build trust in electronic commerce [KPMG 98].

In all, many countries have taken steps to anticipate the advent of a global information infrastructure (GII). One noteworthy aspect of these steps is that they are being shaped by the interaction of public and private sectors: all actors in the information society are defending their interests in policy debates that often have to build consensus out of conflicting interests. Government-business fora are increasingly being held in this policy-making process.

Not only Western countries, but also countries in Asia, Latin America, and Eastern Europe have recognized the importance of ICT for their economic growth and development. At a GII meeting in July 1994, chairman Brown of the US IITF envisaged the GII "as a web of interconnected local, national and regional networks that would 'substantially further economic growth and job creation, infrastructure improvements, and broad based social discourse within and between and among all countries.'" [quoted in Saxby, 228]

2.1.3. Building blocks and participants

The backbone of the information society is the information infrastructure. It consists of several networks and services with providers and users – all interrelated and interconnected. To see how the information infrastructure is built up, one should distinguish between information production and use (which are content-sensitive) on the one hand, and information transport (which is content-neutral) on the other. Again, one can divide the facilities serving information transport into transport networks and transport services. The information infrastructure can thus be modeled as in figure 2.1.

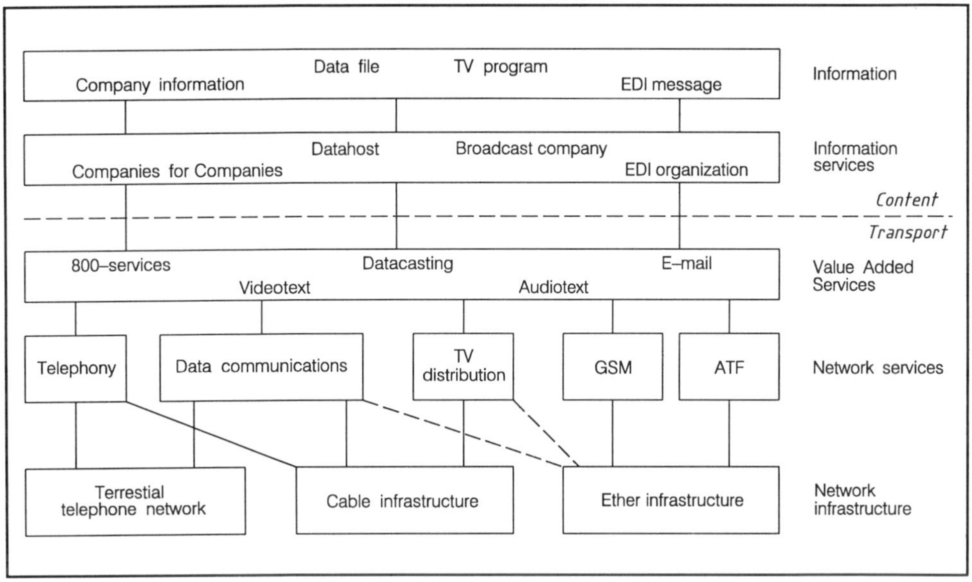

Figure 2.1. The layer model of the information infrastructure [based on Smits and on Arnbak]

The infrastructure providers (also called network operators or network providers) operate the infrastructure: telephone, cable, and the electromagnetic spectrum. They provide capacity to the network service providers, or sometimes directly to end users (as with rental lines, which can, for instance, be used for intranets[6]). Networks can be interconnected – for example, phone calls on the GSM system for mobile communications run partly across the ether and partly across the terrestrial telephone network.[7]

6 Intranets are a quickly developing market for companies desiring a private network for internal communications. Their functioning and use are often similar to the Internet, but they are not connected to wider, external networks (except, perhaps, through a firewall). A recent development is the restricted opening of intranets to third parties, effectively making the intranet an 'extranet'.

7 Analogous mobile networks (such as ATF and NMT) are quickly yielding ground to digital networks, the most important of which are GSM and DCS-1800. A standard for a Universal Mobile Telecommunications System (UMTS) is being developed, which will incorporate Internet access and video-conferencing services. Besides mobile communications through the ether and the terrestrial networks, satellite personal communications are also gaining ground.

Network services are the basic services that open up the infrastructure to users. They route information from information providers to end users, using the capacity of one or more infrastructural networks. Basic network services are voice telephony (both mobile and stationary), data transport, and radio and television distribution.

On top of these basic services are value-added services (VAS). These add a certain value to the basic service – additional facilities, user interfaces, access to data bases, et cetera. Well-known VAS are the dial-800-services, directory services, e-mail services, Internet access-provider services, data casting,[8] and caller-ID.

The data and information that are transported through these layers come from content providers – artists, program makers, data-base makers, enthusiastic WWW users, and the like. Sometimes, this information is managed through information services that mediate between the makers and the consumers of the information – broadcast companies, electronic publishers, information brokers, or data-base managers.

Figure 2.1 also indicates connections that have just been or will shortly be realized. For instance, cable network providers offer voice telephony services,[9] and ether network providers can offer data transmission services through mobile data terminals. So, the traditional borders between the various networks are disappearing. As the traditional distinction between voice, sound, and text is blurring through digitization and multimedia, the core terrestrial networks of telephone lines and TV cable as well as the air networks of satellite and radiographic transmissions can – depending on their bandwidth – all transport various kinds of data, be they voice, sound, text, or image.

From this model, one can see that the participants in the information society are providers (of networks, services, and content) and users. A third participant is the government, which plays a role not only as an end user but also as a regulator.

2.1.4. Problems

All participants have something to gain in the information society. Providers have great commercial opportunities for new services and for marketing. End users profit from a wide range of interesting and useful applications tailored to their needs. For the government, the information infrastructure offers new opportunities, for instance, raising the general education level, better involving the public in its governing, and opening up its public information through an easily accessible and cheap medium.[10]

However, the information infrastructure is not a *deus ex machina* that provides instant happiness for all. Several problems inhibit the full realization of the opportunities it offers. I mention some of the challenges the information society faces, in particular those that are

---

8 Data casting is the process of sending data to a specified group of users along with radio or television transmissions.

9 In April 1996, cable provider Edon started offering telecommunications services in the north and east of the Netherlands via its cable infrastructure. The largest cable network operator in the Netherlands, Casema, is offering telephony via the cable since 1997.

10 Some governments may also use it as yet another medium for propaganda. For instance, the China Internet News Centre launched a video documentary on the Internet <www.China.or.cn>, "which exposes the true colour of the 14th Dalai Lama (...) engaged in activities directed at splitting China." [*China Daily*, 29 October 1997]

directly or indirectly related to the crypto problem.

Network providers face a hard task of interconnecting the several backbones that lie spread across the world. Interconnection and interoperability are primary conditions for establishing an infrastructure that is suited to the needs of the global information society. Yet the disparity of national infrastructures as well as the incompatibility of some of the technologies used hamper the interconnection of all networks into one global information infrastructure.

A second concern is intellectual-property rights. Current legislation is based on traditional media and is widely believed to be inadequate for protecting intellectual-property rights in the information age. The present protection is felt to be interpreted too broadly (particularly by the European Commission) to cover situations in electronic media for which it is not appropriate, whereas the enforcement of intellectual-property law in electronic surroundings is insufficient. These problems have to be addressed, if the still increasing demand for online entertainment as well as for online cultural and educational information is to be met.[11]

A third major problem is the keeping in order of the information infrastructure. Governments on the one hand are liberalizing the telecommunications market, presuming that market competition will enhance technologies and reduce costs for customers. On the other hand, they see the advent of a new medium, perhaps of a new society, in which they have to safeguard at least the basic citizens rights and duties that pertain to the present society. As a medium built bottom-up and belonging to its users, electronic highways can hardly be regulated, but as they are taking over parts of traditional life, governments' desire to somehow regulate them is becoming more compelling. Besides, jurisdiction presents great problems, as the information infrastructure is essentially an international undertaking which does not tolerate nationally-based rules.

Finally, the users of the information infrastructure do not really jump at the potential the providers so alluringly offer them. Two of their main concerns, privacy and security, are insufficiently safeguarded.[12] As long as consumers are diffident that their privacy is being

---

11 The value of intellectual-property rights-related products in the Netherlands was estimated at twenty billion guilders (USD 10 billion) in 1994, according to the National Action Plan [23900, nr 20, 2.2]. The European Parliament is "concerned that the total availability of knowledge, or of the products of the creative process which the term information society conjures up, risks being an illusion if intellectual property rights as a whole are not guaranteed, particularly artists' rights, at the same time as the rights of access and use at reasonable cost for individuals" [*European Parliament Resolution*, 30 November 1994]. See also the third principle of the [NIIAC] document.

12 According to GVU's 8th WWW User Survey, Internet users consider privacy the number one most important issue facing the Internet; for European respondents, privacy is the third most important issue, after navigation and censorship. Although electronic commerce is taking off, "security remains the number one reason Web

The Internet

The Internet, the mother of all networks, is a network that connects all kinds of networks worldwide. Over 100 million users are guesstimated to have access to its treasures. Most of them are located in North America (around 60 per cent) and Europe (around 20 per cent).

The Internet comprises tens of thousands of mailing lists, which forward e-mail messages to subscribers, and the World Wide Web (WWW), a graphic interface that allows people to create and read homepages with attractive graphics, sound bites, and video fragments. Besides, Usenet serves over 25,000 globally available news groups: gigantic notice boards where everyone can post and respond to messages. FTP (file transfer protocol) services allow people to download documents, and with Telnet, people can login remotely on open servers.

To pin down the significance of the Internet, people have coined many metaphors. Each metaphor emphasizes some aspects, but none covers it satisfactorily. The 'information superhighway' stresses the technological potential of the Internet (opening up the hinterland to new technologies) but fails to incorporate its variety of users and applications (and is somewhat misleading as to the speed of information transfer). The (world wide) 'web' catches the structure of a network with many interconnected nodes, but lacks an innovative sound. The 'never-ending worldwide conversation' and 'a kind of chaos' (as US judge Dalzell worded it) fail to catch the many forms of offering information and the increase in commercial applications. Perhaps the most attractive simile is the Internet as a 'community' – a separate society with its own people and its own values, habits, and culture. It suggests, however, that the Internet is somehow 'disconnected' from the rest of the world: a distinction between 'the Internet' and 'the real world' that is misleading if anything. The Internet, after all, is as real as television, school, or the pub.

The volatile, ungraspable character of the Internet is caused by its variety of manifestations, its ever changing and diverse population, and its focus on technical rather than legal regulation. Started in the 1960s as the ARPAnet, a research network with defensive components, the Internet has gradually evolved into an international network linking universities, government institutions, businesses, and individuals, only to fully emerge in the 1990s as the prime banner-bearer of the information society. Especially since the advent of the WWW, its growth has been exponential, the end of which is not yet near.

The Internet was built up by its users and is said to belong to its users. They will not hear of control or regulation; their own 'rules' – or lack thereof – are sufficient to keep everything in order. Netiquette, the do's and don'ts of Internet communications, is the main set of rules to take into account. This self-regulation works, the Internetters say. Governments increasingly disagree and – with visions of the four horsemen of terrorists, child pornographers, drug dealers, and money launderers – argue that some control is inevitable. But how do you control a web-like virtual supercommunity?

threatened by the unlimited collection of personal data, they will be reluctant to engage widely in electronic transactions. Moreover, generally accepted and secure systems for electronic payment are required before electronic commerce can really take off.

These problems have to be addressed before a global information infrastructure can really emerge. That it *will* emerge in the end, few people doubt, but just *how* it will take shape depends on the solutions that will be chosen to address the problems.[13]

---

users report for not purchasing over the Web". [GVU] A report by INRA (Europe) of January 1997 polled the EU member states; they found that two thirds of the respondents worry about leaving tracks of personal information on information networks by using them. [INRA] "Without the legal security of a Union-wide approach, lack of consumer confidence will certainly undermine rapid development of the information society. (...) INTERNET is so big, and growing so fast, that it cannot be ignored. Nevertheless, it has its flaws, notably serious security problems." [Bangemann 94, 18-23]

13 The hopeful visions of future benefits of a global information infrastructure can become reality, but it may take a generation or so to take full effect. As a sensible report of the International Telecommunication Union words it: "Our children are the ones that will really benefit from the global information infrastructure." [quoted in *CLSR*, March-April 1996]

2.2. Information security

In the information society, information is of primary importance. People and enterprises are increasingly growing dependent on information. The protection of information from loss, unauthorized altering, or disclosure is therefore a major concern. According to the EU *Green Book on the Security of Information Systems*, "2/3 of the economy (...) depends critically on the accuracy, security and trustworthiness of information" [DG XIII, section 1].

Several developments have contributed to the growing importance of information security. Where information-processing systems used to be sparse, confined to well-defined, guarded buildings, and so complex that only a few people knew how to handle them, nowadays computers are all-pervasive and often linked over insecure networks, and ever more people know how to operate them.

Businesses attach increasing importance to the reliability of their information-processing systems, not only because the integrity or confidentiality of the information is essential for the company's manufacturing or services, but also because customers are making more demands on the reliability of the enterprise. With the globalization and deregulation of the economy, competition gets fiercer. A company's image is crucial to its viability, and computer security-related incidents can be fatal as the public loses confidence in the company's reliability. Moreover, industrial espionage is a major concern for larger enterprises who depend on the secrecy of their manufacturing processes, research and development, or contract negotiations.[14]

The advances in computer technology have also contributed to the growing importance of information security. A vast number of new applications and an enormous increase in computing power are causing entire areas of life to be digitized. So, alternatives have to be found for the traditional ways of protecting these areas and of securing privacy.

Most importantly, computers are being interconnected in ever larger networks, not only via the Internet, but also in private networks (intranets and extranets) and Local Area Networks. Where physical control used to suffice to protect single computers stored in guarded buildings, networks need a different kind of protection.

This section deals with information and communications security objectives, threats, and measures, and with the role of governments in facilitating information security. As a case study, I will sketch the (lack of) information security within the Dutch government.

14 In 1993, a German consortium led by Siemens lost a major order for a high-speed train in South Korea to the British-French GEC-Alsthom. Information intercepted through the global surveillance system Echelon was thought to have given GEC-Alsthom a crucial advantage. In January 1994, French Airbus lost a six-billion-dollar order in Saudi Arabia to Boeing and McDonnell Douglas, because Clinton had offered to meet the constraints that king Fahd had asked the French for in vain; American security agents boasted afterwards they had won the order through their interception capabilities. Also in 1994, US Raytheon outsmarted French competition in a Brazilian radar order. The fact that Raytheon met the Brazilian demands in all respects just a little better than the French inevitably suggested they had used signals intelligence. [Brouwer] In mid-1996, the US intelligence service was rumored to have hacked into the computers of the European Parliament and the European Commission in order to obtain economic information. [*Sunday Times*, August 1996]

2.2.1. Objectives

The three basic objectives of information security are confidentiality, integrity, and availability: the CIA of information security. An additional objective is non-repudiation.

Confidentiality is the requirement that information is kept secret from people who are not authorized to access it. In communications security, it can include the requirement that traffic analysis be prevented, that is, that information about who communicates with whom when, how often, and from where is kept secret. Confidentiality is sometimes referred to as exclusiveness.

Integrity is the requirement that information is unaltered and complete, or, in the ITSEC definition, that information "is modified only by those users who have the right to do so." [ITSEC] A similar requirement, sometimes understood as a part of integrity, is *authenticity*, the certainty that the message indeed originates from the purported sender. In practice, these two objectives are closely interrelated: safeguarding authenticity usually implies safeguarding integrity (and often vice versa). I shall handle integrity and authenticity as distinct but related objectives.

Availability is the requirement that information and information and communications systems are available to their users at the right time.

Non-repudiation means that the sender or receiver of a message cannot deny having sent or received the message. This is particularly important in situations where sending or receiving a document constitutes a legal act. For instance, in business transactions, it can be essential to invoke liability rules, and in sending electronic appeals to a court, it can constitute the difference between conviction and acquittal.

2.2.2. Threats

Information and information systems are threatened from all sides. Natural disasters, such as earthquakes or floods can destroy information facilities as well as (backup) information. Animals like (kamikaze) squirrels or raccoons electrocute themselves in power generators, putting down entire systems for days [Neumann, 85].

People threaten information in a variety of ways. *Unintentional* incidents, such as password loss, infecting the corporate system with a home-copied virus, or spilling coffee over a keyboard are typical examples. A widespread security flaw is weak password protection. Many people choose easily guessable passwords, and others are careless with their passwords.[15] A study estimates that 80 per cent of security-related incidents in the Internet have to do with improper use of access codes and passwords [Fraser]. Many of these are made possible by the neglect of authorized users – or they are perpetrated by them.

Although it does not necessarily cause more damage than carelessness, *intentional*

---

15 Former French president Mitterand, on his first day in office, put the paper with the code for launching the atomic weapon in a suit pocket (contrary to Pompidou and Giscard, who wore it engraved in a necklace). He forgot all about it, and the code was only saved just before the suit was brought to the dry cleaner's. [*Volkskrant*, 18 May 1995]

computer misuse has received by far the most attention.[16] Especially external threats from hackers and virus producers are notorious.

Hackers can cause extreme (real or symbolic) damage, such as the Dutch hackers who retrieved hundreds of US military secrets which they offered to Saddam Hussein during the Gulf war.[17] They are by definition hard to trace, and likely a great number of hacks remain undiscovered. Still, as computer-security expert William Cheswick has noted, "the fact that so many security holes have gone unused for so long could mean that there are far fewer malicious hackers on the Internet than the din of dire public pronouncements would have people think" [Wallich].

Over 10,000 viruses roam computer networks and personal computers to do their malicious (or sometimes beneficent) jobs. Anti-virus software protects against the bulk of known viruses, but new viruses appear all the time – an estimated six a day [Kephart]. Most recently, the new family of macro viruses appeared on the stage: small programs which automatically execute some action in a word-processing or spreadsheet program. Macro viruses spread from document to document, and so, they travel frequently as attachments to e-mail messages.[18] Some viruses are resistant against most anti-virus software by masquerading or transforming themselves proteanly every time they copy themselves onto another system (some use cryptography to do this). Viruses remain a serious threat and are more pervasive than hackers.

Political viruses

Viruses can have political implications. A virus spread around China in the early 1990s asked the computer user whether Li Peng was a good prime minister. If you answered no, the virus did nothing, but if you affirmed the leadership qualities of Li Peng, the virus erased the entire hard disk. [Kristof, 279] The Dutch green-left party GroenLinks considered launching a virus in a voting campaign. The virus would pop up a slogan inciting to vote for GroenLinks. In the end, the party decided not to spread it – perhaps unfortunately, as the virus would have immunized computers against the much more harmful Jerusalem virus [Sophos, 135].

US government intelligence experts (the Moynihan Commission) showed their ignorance in a report on protecting government secrecy, when they warned against the virus Penpal Greetings "that could infect the hard drive and destroy all data present". [*Crypt newsletter*, April-May 1997] In reality, Penpal Greetings is a hoax virus: a message continually being sent around the Internet that warns against a non-existent virus. Penpal is a little brother of the notorious GoodTimes 'virus'.

Despite the publicity given to intentional break-ins from the outside, the vast majority (an estimated 80 per cent) of computer security-related incidents are caused by internal users [Wright 95].[19] Studies of computer-related crime regularly find that a high percentage of the perpetrators are employees who have regular access to corporate information and

16 Although most of these threats attack the confidentiality or integrity, some attacks harm the availability of ICT. For instance, stealing communications lines can "seriously disrupt the national system" (in the words of the Chinese *Legal Daily*) – but executing nineteen people for this seems somewhat out of proportion, even by Chinese standards [*The Independent*, 17 July 1996].

17 According to intelligence experts, this could have potentially changed the course of the war, had not the data been ignored by Iraq – probably because they feared a hoax. [Reid]

18 "Since the first macro virus appeared in the wild in July 1995, the speed of its spread and the scale of infections have probably surprised even the gloomiest doom merchant." [Hruska]

19 "Survey after survey over the past years has shown that the greatest threat to computers is to be found not from the sophisticated attack perpetrated by a highly motivated outsider, but from the simple error, omission, or malicious action of an employee." [Smith, 418]

information systems. Notably computer fraud, data diddling, and placing logic bombs are popular with them. Well-known cases of computer fraud include a Rotterdam municipal official who embezzled six million guilders (at the time about USD 3 million) by adding pay orders to the daily pay file after the automated check-up had taken place. Several cases are known of disgruntled employees who placed logic bombs in the corporate system to destroy key information or block all access, for ransom or out of spite.[20]

The number and variety of threats to information security are growing along with computer technology [Neumann, 168].[21] Since security technologies are also advancing, threats and protection remain more or less balanced, and so, the general level of security threats remains roughly the same [Neumann, 178].

2.2.3. Measures

The implementation of an information-security policy varies with the situation. No single security measure provides full security (if 'full security' exists at all), and so, a combination of physical, technological, and organizational measures may be called for to achieve the desired level of security.

Physical security measures, such as isolating key information and vital information systems in closely guarded rooms, are important, but they can be impractical. *Technical* measures include hardware and software protection of networks and of data themselves. With a connection to a larger network, such as the Internet, a firewall can shield a local network from intrusions.[22] Cryptography is the main way to shield information itself. *Procedural* measures, such as responsibility division or the regular changing of passwords, are necessary to back up the physical and technical measures. *Inspection and auditing* have to assure detection and tracing of security violations; they can be regarded as the final piece

---

20 For instance, after his dismissal, an employee of Omega Engineering Inc. allegedly activated a computer 'bomb' which permanently wiped out the company's critical design and production programs, causing an alleged loss of USD 10 million. [*ECLR*, 25 February 1998]

21 The *Code of Practise for Information Security Management* voices the expectation that the threats to information security will continue to increase and grow ever more serious and refined. [BSI]

22 Even firewalls do not provide complete protection (see Ch. 3, note 45). The computer language Java allows small applications (applets) to be downloaded to run on the downloader's system. This can undermine the firewall's protection against outside threats. "If a Java program can access users' files to help bring order to their electronic life, it can also easily wreak disorder (...) and bring the Net to its collective knees. (...) In theory, strict cryptographic safeguards should prevent mischief, but the system has yet to be thoroughly tested." [Steven Cheswick, quoted in Wallich]

of an information-security policy.[23]

Security measures, however, can severely limit the convenience of information processes. In general, a trade-off has to be struck between security, ease of use, and costs. Because information security costs money without yielding obvious gains, it is not evident to give it wide attention, and businesses and institutions may fail to fully realize the importance of the confidentiality, integrity, and availability of their information.

Information-security policy

Given the variety of threats information is exposed to, and the fact that security objectives vary with each situation, no general rules can be given for implementing information security. Each enterprise or institution has to make its own policy, based on an internal risk analysis that takes into account the particular circumstances of the environment.

The risk analysis has to include an analysis of possible security incidents, the damages these might cause, and an estimate of the likelihood that such incidents occur. It is vital that all aspects of information security are taken into account, because security is only as strong as its weakest link. It is useless to implement secure mechanisms such as encryption or firewalls, if confidential information can be found in the waste-paper basket ('dumpster diving') or if employees can easily be lured with bribery without risking discovery.

An overall policy, therefore, is essential in information security. One of the main theses of the *Code of Practise for Information Security Management* [BSI] is that this policy needs the backing of the management in order to assure that all measures are followed in practice. Only an integral policy can effect the level of security called for.

2.2.4. Governments' role in information security

The importance of information security has been recognized in several government initiatives and reports. The 1992 OECD *Guidelines for the security of information systems* provides a framework for private and public bodies to implement a consistent and adequate program for protecting their information systems.

In 1992, the European Council adopted a *Council decision in the field of the security of information systems* [92/242/EEC], which comprised the development of overall strategies for information security (an action plan), and the setting up of a Senior Officials Group (SOG-IS) to advise the Commission. As an intermediate step to formulating the Action Plan, in October 1993, the Commission published a *Green Book on the Security of Information Systems* (the draft of which was never officially adopted) [DG XIII]. The INFOSEC program has subsequently been investigating several policy areas in information security, most recently within the framework of the European Trusted Services (ETS) framework [ETS].

The 1997 EC Communication *Ensuring security and trust in electronic commerce* provides a policy framework for information security, focusing on integrity and authentication services (digital signatures) and confidentiality services (encryption). This should lead to, among others, a European framework for digital (or, broader, electronic) signatures [COM(98) 297], and the integration of cryptography within the framework of other European policies, such as privacy protection and intellectual-property rights.

---

23 The *Computer Security Handbook* lists as minimum requirements for communications and network security: employee awareness and vigilance, password and access supervision, hard-copy control, encryption, and frequent log monitoring [Hutt, 17.21].

In the United States, the (sadly deceased) Office of Technology Assessment published *Information Security and Privacy in Network Environments* [OTA]. This study addressed policy issues in the areas of cryptography policy, safeguarding unclassified information in federal agencies, and legal issues and information security, including electronic commerce, privacy, and intellectual property. The NII Security Issues Forum released a draft report *NII Security: The Federal Role* [NIISIF], calling for a government role in supporting a secure NII by facilitating private-sector activity, ensuring public safety by protecting against abuses, and supporting research and development. It stressed, however, that much of the responsibility lies with the private sector. Security is also one of the issues in the *Framework For Global Electronic Commerce.* For a secure GII, a range of technologies, supported by trustworthy infrastructures, are required, and the US government, in partnership with industry, is taking steps to promote such technologies [Clinton, 20-21].

All of these documents stress the importance of information security – it is a vital issue in the present information society. With the increasing importance of information and information-processing systems, protecting the confidentiality, integrity, and availability of information needs full attention.[24] Governments should ensure that measures to enhance information security are developed and that their use is stimulated, while there is a primary role for the private sector to see to the shaping and implementation of these measures.

2.2.5. Information security in Dutch government

Considering their information-security policy documents and regulations, one expects governments to be careful with information protection. They handle sensitive, privacy-related, and confidential information. However, significant parts of the Dutch administration seem to be rather unmindful of information security.

For instance, the justice department of The Hague district discarded computers, selling them to a Nijmegen company. A student in Nijmegen bought one of them, and found confidential information – psychiatric reports, interrogation reports, correspondence – from judges, prosecution officers, and court clerks. She forwarded it to the regional newspaper. [*ANP*, 8 December 1995] A new system was installed at the Central Criminal Intelligence Agency in The Hague; shortly afterwards, "[c]riminals were set free, and innocent people were arrested. The computer system was taken out of service. Unfortunately, the back-up system had been decommissioned. The vendor blamed the police for using the system incorrectly." [Neumann, 175-176] The police in Southern Limburg lost documents on contentious investigation practices, due to a convenient computer crash [*De Limburger*, 3 November 1997].[25]

More importantly, law-enforcement agencies increasingly face counter-strategies by criminals attacking their information resources. In August 1994, prosecution officer Valente had taken home some fifty diskettes with investigation and prosecution information. The

---

24 "There is an urgent need to address requirements and options for action in the field of security of information systems at national, Community and international level in close collaboration with sector actors and national governments. Any action must take into account both national and international commercial, legal and technical developments." [DG XIII, section 1]

25 Losing important files is not only caused by computer incidents. A theft case stranded at the Dutch Supreme Court because the "documents had been lost" [HR 29 October 1996, nr 103.446].

Information security in EU and Dutch law

In some situations, information security is mandatory. Many countries have data-protection laws which require processors of personal data to adequately protect the data from unauthorized access or altering. The 1995 European *Directive on the protection of privacy with regard to the processing of personal data and on the free movement of such data* states that "the controller must implement appropriate technical and organizational measures to protect personal data against accidental or unlawful destruction or accidental loss and against unauthorized disclosure or access, in particular where the processing involves the transmission of data over a network, and against all other unlawful forms of processing." [95/46/EC, art. 17a para. 1]

In addition to this general Data Protection Directive, the *Directive concerning the processing of personal data and the protection of privacy in the telecommunications sector* requires that the "provider of a publicly available telecommunications service (...) take appropriate technical and organisational measures to safeguard security of its services, if necessary in conjunction with the provider of the public telecommunications network with respect to network security. Having regard to the state of the art and the cost of their implementation, these measures shall ensure a level of security appropriate to the risk presented." [97/66/EC, art. 4]

The Dutch Data Registries Act requires holders of personal data registries to take "the necessary technical and organizational measures to protect a personal registry against loss of or damage to the data and unauthorized cognizance, alteration or supply thereof" (art. 8). Following the EU Data Protection Directive, the Data Registries Act is to be replaced by a new Data Protection Act. Article 13 of this draft DPA requires proper technical and organizational measures to protect against loss or any kind of unauthorized processing of personal data. The measures should guarantee an adequate level of protection, taking into account the state of the art of technology, costs, the risks, and the kind of data involved. The Police Registries Act of 21 June 1990 has a similar requirement as the Data Registries Act on the security of police registries. According to the Dutch Act on Municipal Basic Registries of 1 October 1994, the State is responsible for assuring the security of the network of municipal basic registries; the protection of the registries themselves will be regulated by implementing order. Possibly, municipalities will be required to encrypt their registries [Schönfeld, 24].

In the Netherlands, hacking is punishable only if security measures have been infringed (art. 138a DCC). This serves as an injunction to computer users to take security measures. In 1993, the Dutch Civil Code was expanded with an obligation of the accountant to include in his report to the board of commissioners his findings on the reliability and the continuity of the company's automated data processing (art. 2:393, para. 4).

Information security in departments is the subject of several guidelines, such as the *Decree on government-department information-security instructions 1994*. The *Governments Accounts Act* charges the departmental accountant with the care for information security.

diskettes were stolen, and the unprotected information was leaked to the press, causing significant embarrassment. [Traa, 187] After a burglary at two police agents' homes in Almere, information on a murder case from stolen diskettes was published by a tabloid [*Volkskrant*, 1 June 1996]. A businessman from Amersfoort claimed having bought his police file for USD 200 – within an hour, someone had cracked the police computer system for him and delivered the file on diskette, with the codes for decoding and all [*Volkskrant*, 16 June 1995]. Thieves entering the Zeist office of the National Police Services Force in December 1996 stole some portable computers; the suitcase containing the portable computers also contained a hand-written note with the access codes [25208, nr 1].

Also, communications among law-enforcement agents are regularly being monitored.[26] The same criminal organization that stole diskettes at Valente's home was suspected of recording his telephone conversations [Traa, 187]. Indeed, many cases were reported of scanner-freaks who were constantly locating police teams; they eavesdropped on telephone lines and walkie-talkies, for example, of Valente and police officer Woelders [Traa, 67]. Even

26 Warrington police agents were fed up with their mobile phones being monitored. They reported over the police radio that a UFO had crashed on a nearby field, and told how to reach that field. Within minutes, people came nosing around – to be arrested on the spot. [*London Times*, 23 March 1994]

despite being encrypted, mobile-phone conversations were sometimes recorded and cracked: the Amsterdam police found tapes during a search with the decryption of encoded conversations [*Volkskrant*, 3 May 1996].

Following such incidents, security measures have been taken. The Minister of Justice in 1993 confirmed that to protect police radio conversations from being monitored, "indeed a larger spread of encryption equipment was intended." [23047, nr 12, 1] The Valente incidents led the Public Prosecutor in 1994 to order better protection for courts and sensitive information [OM 94]. In 1996, the Brabant-Zuidoost police adopted a secure crypto system for their radio communications [*ANP*, 21 March 1996]. The Van Traa committee accorded addressing the threat of counter-strategies a high priority in order to prevent these activities from influencing the maintenance of law and order [Traa, 71]. Consequently, in April 1997, a *Police Information Security Regulation* took effect, requiring police-force managers to implement information-security policies.

Other parts of government also handle sensitive information, but security policies are sometimes lacking. For instance, the Chamber of Audit found that the information security within the Dutch Internal Revenue Service, although improved, was still seriously flawed in 1997. The access to its automated systems was not adequately protected. For example, officials were careless with their passwords, and too many people had access to confidential information. [25290, nrs 1-2] Municipalities have widely varying information security policies – if they have one at all. A 1996 study concluded that only 30 per cent of Dutch municipalities have a worked-out security plan. Only 20 per cent conform to the data-protection guidelines of the Data Protection Authority. Of the municipalities connected to the Internet, 63 per cent had not taken additional security measures. In 1997, the municipal audit department of Amsterdam found that the security of computer registries of personal data was functioning badly, making municipal services vulnerable to fraud and corruption [*Het Parool*, 15 October 1997]. The Chamber of Audit found in 1995 that of all Dutch ministries, only four had an adequate policy on information security. The central authorities still ran risks of loss, unintentional disclosure, and unauthorized alteration of data, and the ministries themselves had insufficient understanding of the scope of these risks [24175, nrs 1-2]. With the *Decree on government-department information-security instructions 1994* that came into force in January 1995, one may hope the departments are now better implementing information-security policies.

The lack of good information-security measures in government is all the more pressing, as more and more areas of the administration are being digitized and interconnected. For instance, the 'Government Office 2000' initiative plans to offer a one-stop-shop service for citizens: they can access all relevant government information from a single, public terminal. This calls for the highest security level, as interconnecting all kinds of data bases renders the system extremely vulnerable.

2.3. Conclusion

The information society is in the making. Information and communications technologies are shaping the information infrastructures, and all parties involved – providers, users, and the government – have a lot to gain. The establishment of the information society is for a large part the task of private investors, while governments focus on stimulating the development of a national (and global) information infrastructure, providing a motivating and balanced regulatory environment, and giving citizens transparent access to government information.

Governments must address several problems which currently inhibit the information society from fully developing. One of these problems is information security, a major interest in the information society. "Democratic societies engaged in the global economy need to provide for appropriate levels of information security." [SOG-IS][27] Governments have recognized the importance of information security: although it is up to the private sector to establish adequate security measures, governments are committed to stimulating the development and putting into practice of good security policies. The fact that information security is not yet fully incorporated into all sectors of government, as security breaches within the Dutch government show, indicates that governments should also safeguard the implementation of adequate security measures for themselves.

27 In a way, the need for information security can be compared to the public need of traffic safety: "Establishing security for information and communications technologies can be regarded as a society task in line with the treatment of traffic safety on the public roads." [Stripp, 60]

Chapter 3. Cryptography, a key technology for information security

During these days he had noticed a tapping code scratched into the wall of his cell, and had begun, eagerly, to send messages to whoever might be on the other side of the wall. After an hour or so of tapping, however, the door to his cell burst open, and an amused guard sauntered in to tell him, in filthy, broken English, that his neighbour wanted him to 'shot the fock op,' because, alas, 'nobody give to him the focking code.'
(Salman Rushdie, The Moor's Last Sigh)

In information security, cryptography – the art of secret writing – plays a vital part. It is nearly as old as the art of writing itself. "The multiple human needs and desires that demand privacy among two or more people in the midst of social life must inevitably lead to cryptology wherever men thrive and wherever they write." [Kahn, 84][1] As a tool for keeping communications secret, it has been widely used in intelligence, diplomacy, and wars. Revolutionary advances in cryptography have boosted its use in recent decades, opening up an amazing array of applications. It can be used to authenticate computer users, ensure the integrity and confidentiality of electronic communications, and keep sensitive information safely stored. From a secretive military technology, cryptography has emerged a key technology for all participants in the information society concerned about information security.

This chapter gives an overview of cryptography and its applications. I will sketch the history of cryptography (3.1.1) and introduce the crypto family (3.1.2), focusing on the recent developments in symmetric and public-key cryptography (3.1.3). Then, I will detail attacks on crypto systems (3.1.4) and the consequences this has for key length (3.1.5) and key management (3.1.6). Also relevant for the rest of this book are some further distinctions (3.1.7) and the technology of steganography (3.1.8). Finally, some special protocols extend the potential of cryptography (3.1.9). In the second part of this chapter, I outline the many applications of encryption, as used by providers (3.2.1), governments (3.2.2), and other users (3.2.3). I conclude with an indication of the extent cryptography is being used today (3.2.4) and a general assessment of the importance of cryptography in the information society (3.3).

---

1 The historiograph of cryptography, David Kahn, opens his account nearly 4,000 years ago, with an Egyptian scribe carving an inscription with hieroglyphic substitutions about 1900 B.C.

3.1. Cryptography

3.1.1. History

Cryptography is of all times and of all cultures. In its long history, the two basic forms that have prevailed are codes and ciphers. *Codes* are lists of words, names, etc. coupled with an encrypted form, e.g., letters or numbers – comparable to a dictionary. *Ciphers* are methods to change each letter (or group of letters) into other letters, numbers, or symbols. Generally, codes work on words, whereas ciphers work on letters. For a long period, a combination of codes and ciphers in the form of nomenclators (a sort of secret dictionaries) was used. Nowadays, only ciphers avail.

Two of the cryptographic systems used in Antiquity illustrate the basic methods of ciphers that are still being used today: transposition and substitution. The Spartans used a staff of wood around which a strip of papyrus or parchment was wrapped. The message was written vertically on the staff, so that after the strip of papyrus was unwrapped, all the letters of the message were mixed up. The message could be decrypted by winding the strip around a staff of the same thickness. This process of mixing letters together is called *transposition.*

Another basic method is *substituting* letters by other letters or symbols. Julius Caesar invented a system in which each letter was substituted by the letter three places further down the alphabet (jumping from z again to a). Decrypting was done by substituting each letter by its third predecessor. The system of replacing each letter by a letter a fixed number of places down the alphabet is called a Caesar cipher. Another kind of substitution cipher is the Hebrew system of Atbash.

Whereas the operations of substitution and transposition used to be done by hand, from the First World War onwards, machines were developed to encrypt and decrypt messages automatically. These machines were widely in use during the Second World War. The British, for instance, employed tens of thousands of people to crack the German machine. A like number of US cryptanalysts managed to build a replica of the Japanese machine, so that they were able to read almost any message encrypted with it. (It was not enough to prevent Pearl Harbor, although they came close [see Kahn, Chapter 1].)

During and after the World Wars, cryptology was very much an intelligence issue. The invention and breaking of systems were reserved to military and security institutions. The world's best cryptographers were employed by the US National Security Agency, which sur-

Atbash

Atbash is a Hebrew encryption system based on substitution. Each letter is replaced by the one below or above it in the other row.

א	ב	ג	ד	ה	ו	ז	ח	ט	י	ך /כ
aleph	bet	gimel	dalet	heh	wav	zayin	chet	tet	jod	kaf
ת	ש	ר	ק	צ	פ	ע	ס	נ	מ	ל
tav	shin	resh	qof	tsade	pe	ayin	samekh	nun	mem	lamed

Thus, Babel (בבל) becomes Sheshach (ששך), an encryption used in Jeremiah 25:26: "and all the kings of the north, near and far, one after the other – all the kingdoms on the face of the earth. And after all of them, the king of Sheshach will drink it too." [Kahn, 77-8] rounded the field with an aura of utmost secrecy (the agency commonly being known as 'No Such Agency'). Although citizens and scientists were working on cryptology, results were largely classified and publications were sparse. This only changed in the 1970s, with two simultaneous developments that meant a breakthrough in cryptography.

> **Terminology**
>
> *Encryption* is the automated process of hiding data so that no unauthorized people can access them; this is done by means of a procedure (algorithm) and a key. *Decryption* is the reverse process. A *crypto system* is an implementation of an encryption scheme or algorithm. The making of crypto systems is called *cryptography*, the breaking of them is called *cryptanalysis*. *Cryptology* is the science that studies both aspects. Cryptography also includes making authentication or *digital signature* schemes that use an algorithm and a key.
>
> A clear message is called a *plaintext* message, which is transformed by cryptography into a *ciphertext* message.
>
> In *symmetric* crypto systems, both sender and receiver use the same key. In *asymmetric* or *public-key* cryptography, they use different keys. Symmetric keys are called *secret keys*, whereas public-key encryption uses pairs consisting of one *private* and one *public* key.

3.1.2. Intermezzo – dramatis personae

Alice and Bob have been corresponding secretly for many years, since the advent of modern cryptography. They are now the main characters in the ongoing story of cryptography literature. Their communications security is threatened by Eve, an eavesdropper who listens in on them, and Mallet, a malicious interceptor who can alter and fabricate messages. Criminal Carol is also an avid user of cryptography. Occasionally, Alice and Bob attract the attention of Leah, a law-enforcement agent, who together with policewoman Polly is monitoring Carol. Alice and Bob sometimes use the trustworthy services of Trent, a Trusted Third Party, or of Dorothy, a Key Escrow Agent who holds private keys in deposit.

3.1.3. Symmetric and public-key cryptography

In the early 1970s, in response to a request for ciphers by the US National Bureau of Standards, IBM submitted a recently developed crypto system called Lucifer. A weaker version[2] was developed into a new system, the Data Encryption Standard (DES), that has remained a standard to the present day. It is a conventional crypto system, using many alternating rounds of substitutions and transpositions, with a 56-bit key. It is a *symmetric* system, in that both encryption and decryption use the same key.

DES has proved a strong system. Despite doubts about the key length, its US status of Federal Information Processing Standard (FIPS) has been extended each five years; it was last recertified in 1993. Since the middle of the 1990s, DES can be cracked, but at considerable cost;[3] it is still secure for most purposes. For maximum security, triple-DES is

---

2 The initial submission of IBM, Lucifer, contained a 112-bit key. This was reduced to 56 bits, allegedly under pressure of the NSA. When in the 1990s a new cryptanalytic method, differential cryptanalysis, was invented, DES was found to be so designed that it was optimized against this attack, a significant improvement on Lucifer. Apparently, the developers of DES already knew about differential cryptanalysis at the time they made it, fifteen years before it was reinvented. A longer key than 56 bits would not have significantly improved the strength of DES against differential cryptanalysis, and so the reduction to 56 bits turned out to be not really a weakening. [Wayner 95, 77-80].

3 Already in the 1970s, it was thought a special computer could be built at a cost of several million dollars to crack DES in a day. In 1993, it was estimated that a USD 1 million machine could crack DES in an average of 3.5 hours. [Schneier, 283-284] The Electronic Frontier Foundation built a DES cracker in 1998 at the cost

used to encrypt the message three times, using two 56-bit keys (yielding an effective key-length of 112 bits). Since DES is no longer completely reliable, the US National Institute for Standards and Technology is developing a new symmetric standard, the Advanced Encryption Standard, which can serve as a FIPS for the next decades; the AES should offer significant advantages over triple-DES.[4]

Today, many other strong symmetric systems exist, such as IDEA (developed in the 1990s and considered a strong symmetric cipher), RC4 and RC5, Blowfish, and Khufu. There is one symmetric crypto system that is provably and unconditionally secure. This is the One-Time Pad (OTP).[5] Although it is the only provably uncrackable crypto system,[6] it is not in wide use. Not only is it difficult to generate a truly random string of bits, but, more importantly, the key can be used only once (there is an easy method of attack if it is used twice), which makes it impracticable. Moreover, the key must be as long as the message and must be exchanged securely between sender and receiver; this pays off only for small and highly confidential messages (and for storage of information). Its main application has been (or is?) in the red line between Moscow and Washington.

The drawback of symmetric crypto systems is that one has to first distribute the secret key securely – you cannot use conventional cryptography for this because you need a common key first. Besides, you need a lot of keys, one for each pair of persons communicating with each other. With large groups, the required number of secret keys becomes enormous (for 100 people, you need almost 5,000 keys). The thought of solving these problems triggered the development of a new kind of crypto system: one in which you can communicate securely before first having to exchange secret keys.

The idea of these crypto systems was launched in 1976 by Diffie and Hellman [Diffie].[7] They proposed a *public-key* crypto system, in which each user has a pair of keys, one private and one public. A message encrypted with the public key can be decrypted only with the corresponding private key, and vice versa. Either key of the pair can not be derived from the other. The private keys are kept secret by the users, but the public keys are widely published. If Alice wants to send a message to Bob, she looks up his public key in a key directory,

---

of USD 250,000; it cracked the message in RSA's DES Challenge II in less than three days. [EFF] Compare the sidebar in 3.1.5.

4 The AES should specify an unclassified, publicly-disclosed, royalty-free encryption algorithm, providing strong security for twenty to thirty years. Submissions to the AES selection process include RC6, Rijndael, Serpent, and Twofish. In August 1998, the first Candidate Conference was held, initiating the Round 1 Evaluation and Analysis period. The process of adopting the FIPS will take at least two years, and likely much more. [NIST 98]

5 The One-Time Pad consists of a truly random string of bits that is used only once as a key. The ciphertext is the addition (XOR) of the plaintext and the key (XOR means 'exclusive or': 0+0=0, 0+1=1, 1+0=0, 1+1=0). Since the key is completely random, the ciphertext does not contain any information on the plaintext. With a different random key, it decrypts to a different plaintext, and without knowledge of the key, one has no way of knowing what the real plaintext was.

6 All other systems are said to be computationally secure: they have withstood public scrutiny for a long time, in that ciphertexts can not be deciphered in a reasonable time. This is the best one can say of these systems: they have good reason to be *thought* strong. The OTP is the only system that is *known* to be strong.

7 Actually, this was the second invention of public-key cryptography. As was revealed only in 1997, James Ellis and Malcolm Williamson of the UK Communications-Electronics Security Group had invented the same concept, 'non-secret cryptography', in 1970. CESG had kept it secret all the while. [Ellis]

encrypts the message with it, and sends it to Bob. He can decrypt it with his private key – and no-one else can, since he is the only one who knows his private key. The great advantage of this system is that you do not first have to exchange keys in a secure manner. (There is, however, another problem: you have to be sure that the public key you use is the right one; see below.)

There is another property of public-key crypto systems which makes them attractive. They can be used to authenticate messages and to prove their integrity. To do this, Bob uses his private key to 'encrypt' (or 'sign') the digest of a message to Alice, which he sends along with the message. Now Alice (or anyone else) can check the authenticity and integrity of the message (or 'undo the signature') by using Bob's public key to decrypt the digest. If her own digest of the message as received matches the decrypted digest, the message cannot have been tampered with and must have been sent by Bob, since only could have signed the digest with his private key. This does not provide for confidentiality, since the message is sent in the clear. Secrecy can be established, however, by encrypting the message, after signing, with Alice's public key. Then, only Alice can decrypt it with her private key, and subsequently undo the signature with Bob's public key.

An important implementation of a public-key crypto system is RSA, named after its inventors Rivest, Shamir, and Adleman [RSA]. It was developed in the late 1970s, and counts as the best-known public-key crypto system.

The working of public-key cryptography

Public-key cryptography is based on one-way trapdoor functions. A *one-way function* is a mathematical operation that is easy to do in one way, but difficult or impossible to reverse. An everyday example is the throwing of an antique vase into thousands of pieces: easy enough to do, but almost impossible to reverse. A *trapdoor* one-way function means that there is a trick (i.e., secret information) with which it is easy to reverse the otherwise one-way operation. In public-key cryptography, you use the trapdoor one-way function to encrypt a message, and use the trapdoor to decrypt it. The pair of public and private keys consists of two numbers computed by using the trapdoor.

An analogy may clarify this. Bob has settled on translation into Kwakiutl as his crypto system. His public key is the English-Kwakiutl dictionary, which he publishes widely (say on the Internet). As private key, he uses the Kwakiutl-English dictionary, which he keeps secret. To send a message to Bob, Alice uses the English-Kwakiutl dictionary to translate her message into Kwakiutl. Now Eve, who eavesdrops on the message, has access only to the English-Kwakiutl dictionary; to translate back a single word, she has to leaf through the entire dictionary to see which English word it matches. Bob, on the other hand, can use the Kwakiutl-English dictionary to conveniently translate the message.

With this system, Bob can also sign messages. For this, he has another key pair, say Xhosa. He now publishes the Xhosa-English dictionary, while keeping secret the English-Xhosa one. To sign a message, he translates it into Xhosa. Anyone can subsequently translate it back into English, using the public Xhosa-English dictionary. Thus, they can check the signature, for Bob is the only one who 'knows' Xhosa.

Mathematically, this is done through exponentiation with numbers (typically of about two hundred digits), modulo a certain large number, the product of two prime numbers (arithmetic 'modulo k' means reducing all numbers to a number below k, which is what you do when you say it is 7 o'clock when it is 19:00 hours: you count modulo 12). The public key is used for exponentiating the message (digitized into bits). For decryption, Eve can try to compute the inverse of the exponentiation, but this is (probably) a so-called 'hard' mathematical problem, meaning that it takes too much time to be computationally feasible.[8] Bob, who has got the private key, uses this to make another exponentiation – the private key is chosen in such a way that the two exponentiations neutralize each other.[9]

Because the mathematical implementation of public-key cryptography uses numbers, both encrypting to keep the message secret (Kwakiutl) and encrypting for signing messages (Xhosa) can be done by the same key pair. This property makes public-key cryptography a convenient, multifunctional system.

There is one drawback. Public-key systems are slow – much slower than conventional, symmetric crypto systems. RSA is about ten times slower than symmetric systems such as DES or IDEA, making it inefficient for encrypting large messages.[10] Therefore, in most applications, a combination is used to exploit the advantages of both systems. First, Alice uses RSA to send a, say, DES key to Bob; she can do this by looking up his public key. After Bob has decrypted this message with his private key, he and Alice both have got the same DES key, so now they can use the fast DES to communicate securely. The combination of a symmetric and a public key system is called a hybrid crypto system.

Authenticity, integrity, and non-repudiation

Authenticity and integrity (without confidentiality) can also be safeguarded by hash functions and message authentication codes. A *one-way hash function* is a one-way function, without a trapdoor: it can only be used to transform a message into a digest, which cannot be reversed. The digest, or hash, is usually a short, fixed-length block (typically 128 to 160 bits) (for an analogy, one can think of a mincing machine outputting a very concentrated piece of minced meat). To show that a message has not been tampered with, Alice can use

---

8 A 'hard' problem is a problem that can not be solved in polynomial time. This means that as the numbers involved get larger, it quickly becomes too time-assuming to solve the problem. For sufficiently large numbers, the problem is too complicated to be solved – even with supercomputers. For example, presently, 200-digit numbers are beyond factoring.

9 There is another class of public-key crypto systems (such as Diffie-Hellman and ElGamal), which are based on another mathematical problem: discrete logarithms. For convenience's sake, I restrict the description here to public-key systems based on the factoring problem, such as RSA.

10 Elliptic-curve crypto systems, which have been developed in recent years, speed up public-key cryptography significantly. However, certain elliptic curves can be cracked relatively easily, and it is not yet certain whether implementations can ensure that users avoid choosing these weak curves.

a *message authentication code* (MAC). This is a key-dependent one-way hash function (it can also be a one-way hash function that uses a symmetric crypto system to encrypt the resulting hash). With the input of the secret key, the MAC computes a hash, which is sent along with the message. Bob, who also has the secret key, can then verify the message's integrity: he also computes the hash on the received message with the secret key, and compares this with the received hash. Only if these two match can he be sure the message has not been tampered with. Mallet, if he intercepted the message, can not have altered the message and computed a new digest to send along with it, since he does not know the key Alice and Bob use. Note that a MAC does not provide for confidentiality, as the message itself is sent in the clear.

If instead of a symmetric system (with a secret key known only to Bob and Alice) Alice uses a public key system with a hash function, the result is usually called a *digital signature*. Alice signs the hash with her private key, and sends the message and the signed hash to Bob. He, upon receiving Alice's message, undoes Alice's signature of the hash, computes a digest of the message himself, and checks whether these match. If they do, only Alice could have sent the message, since she signed the hash. Moreover, the message has not been tampered with, or it would have yielded a different digest.

Besides safeguarding confidentiality, integrity, and authenticity, public-key cryptography can also be used for a fourth objective, non-repudiation. Assuming her private key has not been compromised, Alice can not repudiate messages signed with her key (in a common-sense understanding, that is – legally, she can always repudiate anything, and with a good lawyer, she might convince a court that someone else used her key). She can only repudiate signatures if she has notified a key compromise within a reasonable period after noticing the compromise. Messages will have to have been time-stamped in order to see which messages Alice can not repudiate. Non-repudiation of the receiver can in general not be effected, except by more complex protocols and procedural agreements.

Table 3.1 summarizes the objectives the various forms of cryptography can serve.

objective / ***crypto system***	**confidentiality**	**integrity and authenticity**	**non-repudiation**
symmetric	yes	yes/no[11]	no
public key	yes	yes	(yes)
hash functions	no	no	no
message authentication codes	no	yes/no[11]	no

Table 3.1. Cryptography and security objectives

11 Symmetric crypto systems and MACs can provide for integrity and authenticity between communicating parties. However, they cannot prove this to others: there is no way Bob can prove a message came from Alice, as he could have encrypted it with their common key himself.

3.1.4. Cryptanalysis and the strength of crypto systems

The art of breaking encoded messages and crypto systems is called cryptanalysis. It is the counterpart of cryptography, the art of making crypto systems. Cryptanalysis can attack any part of the process of encryption, for example, the algorithm used, its implementation, the key management, carelessness of the user, or the waste-paper basket.

A cryptanalyst's attack depends on the information at his disposal. The most basic is a ciphertext-only attack, where the cryptanalyst has only got a ciphertext to decipher. A known-plaintext attack is easier, as the cryptanalyst has got a ciphertext and a corresponding plaintext, for example, because he has found it somewhere or because he can guess the contents of a standard message. Still more powerful is a chosen-plaintext attack: the cryptanalyst can choose plaintexts and have them encrypted (for instance, by testing how a stolen smart card encrypts plaintexts). If the crypto system can resist a chosen-plaintext attack, it is strong indeed. In developing new systems, devisers often assume a cryptanalyst to be able to commit a chosen-plaintext attack; the system should be devised in such a way that it resists this.

Still, it is difficult to assess the strength of a crypto system. Crypto systems are always under attack, from all angles. Although one can argue that a certain algorithm is theoretically sound, and one can study an implementation to see if it contains any trapdoors, still one does not know whether the system does not yield to an attack unthought of. New attacks appear every so often. For instance, in November 1995, Paul Kocher announced a timing attack that cryptanalyzes by means of closely timing the processor's cryptographic operations [Kocher]. Against a computer, this is essentially an academic attack (someone who is powerful enough to measure to the microsecond what your computer is doing is likely also able to look over your shoulder at the screen), but it may work against smart cards. Another attack, developed in 1997 by Biham and Shamir (extending an attack developed in 1996 by Bellcore researchers), uses a micro-wave oven to trigger minor errors in the processor of a smart card; the results can be exploited for cryptanalysis through 'differential fault analysis'. [Biham]

Even the mathematical security of an algorithm can not be proven. Public key crypto systems rely on problems that are thought to be 'hard', such as taking discrete logarithms (Diffie-Hellman) or factoring large numbers (RSA). However, there is no proof that these problems are indeed hard – there could be a solution as yet unthought of to factor large numbers in reasonable time.

There is an argument in favor, though, of assessing the problem as 'hard': the problem of factoring has been studied by many specialists for decades, precisely because it has such great implications in the field of cryptography. It had already been studied for a long time before, and the fact that it has large implications in cryptography has only added to its appeal as a research object. This makes it unlikely that someone comes up with a new and easy method of factoring large numbers. The more people are attacking the problem and the longer they take, the more likely it is that the problem is indeed 'hard', even though it has not been mathematically proved.

The same argument holds for assessing the strength of a crypto system. If a crypto system has been published for a long time, has been studied by many cryptanalysts around the world, and still resists cracking, then it can be assumed to be strong. So, DES and RSA, which both were published in the 1970s, are good crypto systems which are unlikely to be broken all of a sudden.[12] This can not be said of unpublished crypto systems: they have not been intensively scrutinized, and there might be a backdoor cracking method that its devisers overlooked.[13]

This is why most cryptologists argue that crypto systems should be published: the system will be widely studied and analyzed, so that any flaws it contains will likely be found. This way, for instance, the implementations of public key cryptography based on the 'knapsack' problem[14] were found insecure, even though the mathematical problem was 'hard'. Crypto systems that rely on secrecy are generally viewed with scepticism by experts (who call such systems 'snake oil') – they know the complexity of devising a crypto system, and only trust it when it has been studied by experts in the field. As the fundamental tenet of cryptography says: "If lots of smart people have failed to solve a problem, then it probably won't be solved (soon)." [Kaufman, 40]

Apart from attacking the crypto system itself, the cryptanalyst will try any other possible attack. "There are numerous practical attacks that don't involve cryptanalysis, that can expose the contents of a PGP encrypted message as easy as peeling a banana. These attacks are cheap, efficient, sometimes difficult to detect, and may be elegantly simple." [McNamara 97] For instance, someone may have used weak keys or weak passphrases (which can be automatically cracked by, e.g., PGPCrack). Attacks often benefit from design errors. Many designers focus on theoretic attacks, resulting in products so complex that they lead to implementation blunders and consequent security failures. According to cryptanalyst Ross Anderson, almost "all security failures are in fact due to implementation and management errors." [Anderson 94]

Even if the system and implementation are secure, someone can attack the key management by bribing someone. If the persons involved are beyond corruption, he may use a TEMPEST device to intercept the electromagnetic radiation your computer emits. If you prevent a TEMPEST attack by building a Faraday cage, he will infiltrate your favorite pizza-catering service and look over your shoulder while you type in your key. Crypto use is only as strong as its weakest link: it pays to use strong systems only if you take into account all feasible attacks. Indeed, most attacks do not seem to use cryptanalysis at all, but merely involve "crooked employees, clever sting operations, stupid implementations, integration blunders, and random idiocies." [Schneier, 214]

---

12 Of course, Eve might have cracked the system and have kept silent. After cracking a few sensitive corporate messages to do profitable business on the stock market, and after selling some nuclear-technology secrets to a backwater country, she could have retired to Puka-Puka, and no-one is the wiser.

13 For instance, Bruce Schneier, John Kelsey, and David Wagner announced on 20 March 1997 that they had discovered a flaw in the privately designed Cellular Message Encryption Algorithm used in digital cellular phones, allowing an attack to succeed within minutes on a conventional personal computer. [Counterpane]

14 The knapsack problem is the task of exactly filling up a knapsack with a selection of boxes from a given collection of boxes. In mathematics, this comes down to the following exercise: given a set of integers, find a subset of these integers that add up to a given large integer.

Distributed attacks

Several efforts have shown the vulnerability of crypto systems to major, concerted attacks. Over the past two years, several cracking contests have tested the strength of symmetric crypto systems with varying key lengths. All contests except the last one were won by the combined computing power of many computers testing keys in their spare time (e.g., at night, or in the form of a screen saver), facilitated by lively discussions and software exchange over the Internet. The results show the power of networking, with more and more people participating in combined attacks.

date of crack	system and key length	time spent	number of computers involved	key space searched	cracker
28.1.97	RC-5 40 bits	3.5 hours	250	32%	Ian Goldberg
10.2.97	RC-5 48 bits	13 days	3500	58%	Germano Caronni and others
17.6.97	DES 56 bits	120 days	70,000	25%	Rocke Verser, Michael Sanders, and others
19.10.97	RC-5 56 bits	250 days	500,000	47%	David McNett and others, distributed.net
23.2.98	DES 56 bits	39 days	no information available	90%	David McNett and others, distributed.net
15.7.98	DES 56 bits	2.5 days	1	25%	EFF DES Cracker

3.1.5. Key length

A good working assumption in cryptology is that the strength of a crypto system relies entirely on the keys.[15] That is, the system should be so strong that the only way to crack it is to try every possible key: a *brute-force attack*. Therefore, keys should be of sufficient length to resist a brute-force attack. Trying every possible key to see which one fits can be done in parallel, on many computers at the same time. Also, one can build special hardware for cracking algorithms; although this hardware can be used for cracking only one system, it is much quicker than general-purpose software. Brute-force attack is a trade-off between cost and time: the more money you spend on computing power, the quicker you will find the key.

The number of keys to be tried rises exponentially with their length. Every bit added to a key doubles the number of possible keys. If you are not sure how much computation capacity the attacker has got, it is wise to add a few key bits to be on the safe side – it does not cost much to use a somewhat longer key, but it makes the cryptanalyst's work of brute-forcing the key space a lot harder. A rule of thumb known as Moore's law says that the computing capacity of computers doubles about every eighteen months. To keep abreast of advances in computer technology, it therefore suffices to raise the key length by one bit every year and a half, or to add six bits every ten years.

15 Sooner or later, someone will find out how the system works (like the American cryptanalysts building a replica of the Japanese encoding machine in WWII). Cryptography experts hold that 'security through obscurity' does not work: a good crypto system relies on the secrecy of its keys, not on its own secrecy.

The required length for symmetric keys and for asymmetric keys differs due to the variety in attack. Strong symmetric systems can be attacked only through brute force (trying every possible key), whereas public key systems are attacked by trying to factor the large numbers they are based on. Symmetric keys are usually 64 to 128 bits long. DES, with its 56 bits, is crackable, although at considerable cost; to be on the safe side, triple-DES is used, with an effective key length of 112 bits. A panel of acknowledged experts in 1996 suggested a minimum symmetric key length of 75 bits for keeping messages secure for some time to come.[16] Adequate asymmetric keys vary from 768 to 2048 bits in length.

Apart from using a large enough key, one can also thwart brute-force attacks by compressing a message before encryption. With a robust compression system, you can remove most information redundancy from the data. This makes it difficult, if not impossible, for a brute-force attacker to recognize the original message when he tries the right key.

Developments that may shake the field

Computer power advances rather steadily. Moore's law (computer power doubles every eighteen months) of the 1960s still holds today. This means that cryptography users can rely on current estimates of how much time and money it costs to break a crypto system. However, there are several developments that might change this outlook.

First, biotechnology can be used to solve mathematical problems. DNA has solved the 'hard' problem of the traveling salesman (find a travel path that visits a specified number of cities exactly once). With smartly chosen strings of DNA, each representing a city or a road between two cities, a (liquid) solution containing these DNA strings and an enzyme to link them together, a (problem-solving) solution was found. Although a modest project, the attempt shows that traditional computers do not have a monopoly in problem solving. Efforts are made to use biochemics for cracking crypto systems. [Leutwyler] However, it is uncertain whether such solutions scale well. According to Donald Beaver, for factoring a 1000-bit number, "far more than (...) 10^{200000} liters of solution would be needed, an amount that perhaps would have unsettled the biblical Noah." [Beaver]

Second, efforts are being made to develop quantum computers. These would rely on quantum properties of photons to represent bits of information. The uncertainty principle means that one bit could have different values at the same time, a revolution in computing. A quantum computer might factor a large number in polynomial time, possibly leading to the downfall of factoring-based public key cryptography. However, due to physical problems, it is as yet uncertain whether such computers will ever be feasible.

Apart from revolutions in computing, thermodynamics places limits on computing power. A certain amount of energy is needed to represent information: each operation involves a minimum amount of energy. According to Bruce Schneier, there is not enough energy in space to brute-force attack a 256-bit symmetric key ("until computers are built from something other than matter and occupy something other than space"). [Schneier, 158]

For the time being, one can rely on conventional computer technology and cryptography to safeguard information security. It can do no harm, though, to keep an eye on developments elsewhere in science – some application might appear to shake the present-day crypto field.

3.1.6. Key management

As the security of encryption lies mainly in its keys, not only do they have to be of sufficient length, but they also have to be kept well. Symmetric keys and private keys have to remain secret, whereas public keys require a proof of integrity. Key management is the most

16 "[K]eys used to protect data today should be at least 75 bits long. To protect information adequately for the next 20 years in the face of expected advances in computer power, keys in newly-deployed systems should be at least 90 bits long." [Blaze 96]

significant part of using encryption. Just as it is useless to have the best safe for your valuables if you stick a paper on top of it with the code, it does not help to use a strong crypto algorithm if you are careless with your keys.

Good cryptographic keys are random (or random-looking) strings of numbers of at least eight characters: they are more like *%p8@CO,hq* than like *topsecret*. Except mnemonic wizards, people have to store the keys, which usually happens immediately after generation, under protection of a password (or, ideally, a passphrase). A good option is to store the keys on magnetic or smart cards – these tokens can serve as conventional keys to be inserted in a lock in the computer or communications device. Alternatively, the keys may be encrypted by a master key, which is closely guarded by a trusted person.

Once you lose a key, you lose the information, as the system is (supposed to be) uncrackable (or you need not have used it in the first place). Also, employees can suddenly die or be bribed by the competition. It is therefore prudent to keep back-up keys somewhere, even though this might diminish security. Often, back-up keys are stored centrally with a security employee or the management. Sometimes, a key-escrow agent may be found outside the company – this is usually a Trusted Third Party (TTP).

Especially private keys, which have a lifetime of several years, should be guarded from disclosure. Once a private key has been compromised, all users should be notified, lest they rely on the corresponding public key that is no longer valid. For this, key-distribution centers or Certification Agencies maintain lists of compromised keys. To solve liability questions that may arise in case of a key compromise, a key certificate can be issued with a limited time-span, and agreements can be made on the time limit to notify the key center of a key compromise. Because the idea of using digital signatures is useless if people can sign a message and subsequently deny having signed it ("Oh, sorry, I lost my key before this message was signed."), it is advisable to have a TTP *time-stamp* transactions. If the key center has not been notified of a key compromise before the time-stamp, the signature can be considered valid and the holder of the corresponding private key is accountable for the signature.

In public-key crypto systems, one must rely on the correctness of the public key. Mallet can issue a public key in Bob's name. He can then read any message Alice sends to 'Bob'. Therefore, Alice must have a way of knowing that a public key really belongs to Bob. The reliability of public keys is usually ascertained by the digital signature of a Certification Authority (CA). This CA issues key certificates containing the public key, identifying information, a time-span, and the signature of the CA.

Two systems for communications security, Pretty Good Privacy (PGP) and Privacy Enhanced Mail (PEM), illustrate potential key-certification structures. PGP has a flat, horizontal structure, with users certifying each other: if you trust someone, you sign his key. If someone's key is signed by (someone whose key is signed by) someone you trust, you will accept his public key. So, PGP relies on a web of trust. In PEM, on the other hand, certification is hierarchic: a top certification center certifies national certification centers, which certify local or corporate certification authorities, which certify users. The trust of PEM depends on faith in the top certification center.

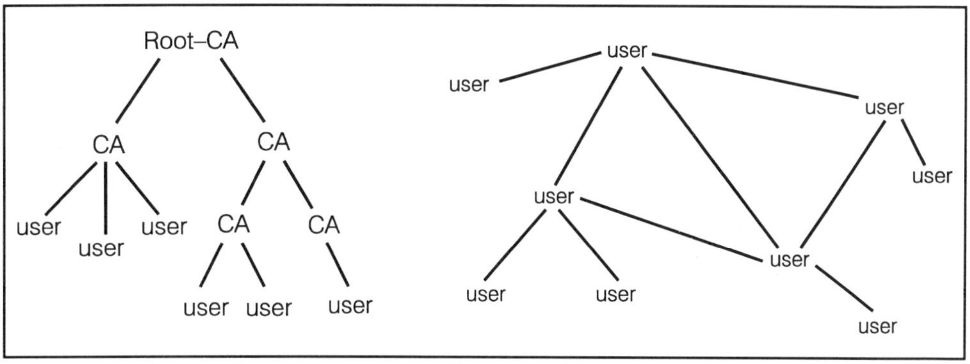

Figure 2.2. The certification structures of PEM (left) and PGP (right).

The framework for key-management services (such as key recovery, certification of public keys, and time-stamping messages) is called a Public Key Infrastructure (PKI). The establishment of a PKI is important to ensure that cryptography can be used well in the information society. People are often required to use cryptography for communicating with unknown people, and so, they must have a way of ensuring that the keys they use are valid. Trust is essential, and this can almost only be established through a certification infrastructure that has a firm basis in law (formulating requirements for CAs, for instance) as well as in practice.

Today, PKIs are beginning to emerge, oriented either more vertically or more horizontally, depending on their context. An intra-organization PKI, for instance of a multinational, will usually be hierarchic, but it may have a cross-certification relationship with PKIs of fellow multinationals. These could all be hierarchically incorporated in a Chamber of Commerce PKI, which could in its turn cross-certify an international NGO PKI. At the national and international levels, all sorts of PKIs are conceivable, and time will tell which PKIs will emerge where. (See further 7.1.)

3.1.7. More distinctions

Apart from the difference between 'weak' and 'strong' crypto systems,[17] some more distinctions are useful in describing the field of cryptography. Cryptography can be used for protecting either *communications* or data *storage*. This influences the choice of cryptography. In general, for communications security one needs - usually short-term - confidentiality or integrity and authenticity, or all of these. For storage, only confidentiality or integrity are needed, but for a longer period. In communications, session keys can be discarded directly after the conversation; for storage, the keys obviously have to remain valid and secret for as long as the information needs to be stored. Therefore, the management of keys also varies with the application.

The Spartan and Caesar ciphers show that cryptography can be implemented in *hardware*

17 "There are two kinds of cryptography: one that keeps your little sister from reading a message, and one that keeps the government from reading a message." [Schneier, xix]

(the Spartan staff) or *software* (the Caesar algorithm). Often, modern cryptography is implemented in (tamper-proof) hardware.[18] This is mainly for efficiency reasons: software implementations are slower and more vulnerable to attacks. The drawback of hardware is that it is less fit for distribution and upgrading; software implementations can be easily transmitted and upgraded. As processing speeds continue to advance, more cryptography may be implemented in software, although for specific purposes hardware solutions will probably remain preferred.

In networks, cryptography can be used link-by-link or end-to-end. *Link-by-link* encryption means that each node in the network decrypts incoming messages and encrypts outgoing messages; in the node itself, the message is in the clear. In *end-to-end* encryption, on the other hand, a message is encrypted at the start and decrypted only after arrival at its destination. The advantage of link-by-link encryption is that the sender only needs to know the key of the first node, regardless of the addressee. With end-to-end encryption, every user should know the keys of all the people he might want to communicate with. However, in link-by-link encryption, the message can be read at every node, so the overall security is only as strong as the weakest node, and all nodes have to be trusted. End-to-end encryption safeguards security over an insecure network.

3.1.8. Hiding cryptography

Just as messages can be hidden by cryptography, the use of cryptography can itself be hidden. This is called *steganography* (hidden writing). For instance, a message can be tattooed on the scalp of a courier, who – once his hair has sufficiently grown – runs to the addressee, who shaves his hair and reads the message (as Histiaeus did with a slave to urge his son-in-law to revolt against Persia, according to Herodotus [Kahn, 81]). Quicker is an ancient Chinese method of hiding a message written on very thin silk in a ball of wax which the courier hides or swallows [Kahn, 73].

More elegant forms of steganography hide messages in messages – seemingly innocent texts that contain secret messages underneath. Naive people 'hide' their PIN codes in their address book, writing it as a postal code[19] – usually to no avail, as it is easy to detect fake postal codes. Another example is 'Yuan Xiao', a poem by a Chinese student in the US, which was published in the Chinese official newspaper *Renmin Ribao* (People's Daily) in March 1991. Seemingly an innocent poem, it escaped the notice of the severe Chinese Communist Party's censors, but most of the readers noticed the hidden message: the diagonal was a call for Prime Minister Li Peng to be replaced.[20] More practical than Chinese is the use of digital signatures to send subliminal messages: hiding data in the signature attached to the message. In fact, "[a]ny signature scheme can be converted into a subliminal channel" [Schneier, 536] (see also 7.3.2).

---

18 Note that claims of tamper-resistance should be viewed with some caution. [Anderson 96].

19 Dutch postal codes have the form *1234 AB*, which can 'hide' the PIN 1234.

20 Subsequently, Chinese officials have become more cautious. Public-security officers withheld a letter written by dissident Wang Dan in prison. They did not understand the poem it contained, and suspected that it contained secret signals to outsiders. Consequently, they required Wang Dan to write another letter. [*Ming Pao*, 26 August 1997]

Most methods of steganography tend to significantly enlarge the message size. A system (mockingly) proposed by a Dutch professor, in reaction to the Dutch plans to restrict crypto use, would multiply a message's size seventy times [Mulder]. Moreover, systems that hide messages in normal-language texts are hard to automate. However, efficient programs exist to hide messages in digitized images (for instance Stego, Hide and Seek). These images consist of many (usually 256) shades of white to black (or color)[21]; in the least significant bit of each byte of a pixel, a bit of the message can be hidden. This hardly alters the appearance of the image, as the subtle shade differences are unnoticeable to the human eye. Thus, you can store a 64 kilobyte message in a 1024 x 1024 grey-scale picture [Schneier, 10]. This process is also possible with digitized sounds.

Another way to 'hide' cryptography is to use a 'duress' code, which can apply two different keys to the same ciphertext: one decrypts it to its original (real) plaintext, the other decrypts it into another, innocent message.[22] Some password systems use this method of duress codes: if a bank employee is forced at gunpoint to get money from the safe, he can type in a password that opens the safe but at the same time triggers a silent alarm.

Detecting cryptography

How do you distinguish, in E.M. Forster's phrase, 'mystery' from 'muddle', or cryptography from nonsense? If you have a random-looking stream of bits, how do you know whether it is an encrypted message, a picture hiding a message, or just plain nonsense? If you can transform it into something meaningful by means of a decryption algorithm, you can reasonably assume that the string was indeed the encryption of that message. Failing this, there is no real method of distinguishing between the two. Checking the pattern of the random-looking string can help, as good crypto systems transform a message into a ciphertext that satisfies the main properties of randomness. The context can give more evidence. E.g., the least significant bits of digital images have patterns not necessarily similar to those of ciphertexts, so the pattern may indicate that an image hides a message.[23]

---

21 According to Peter Wayner, if colors are defined by 8 bits, the effects of hiding data in them can be quite significant, but with 24-bit colors the result is much better. [Wayner 96, 159-160]

22 Say you want to send the message: "twelve tons of dope" using a Vigenere system (addition of letters: A+B=B, C+D=F, et cetera). With Hamlet's monologue as a key, this yields the ciphertext:

```
plaintext:     twelvetonsofdope
key:           TOBEORNOTTOBETHA
ciphertext:    MKFPJVGCGLCGHHWE
```

When forced to decrypt, you might – instead of giving the real key – use the key BWSJ YNLY NEGQ NDSR, which decrypts the message as follows:

```
ciphertext:    MKFPJVGCGLCGHHWE
key:           BWSJYNLYNEGQNDSR
plaintext:     longlivethequeen
```

This way you can decrypt the ciphertext to any plaintext you choose: from the ciphertext and the desired plaintext, you can compute the key you need to 'decrypt' to the desired plaintext.

23 One could prevent detection through this kind of analysis by building an image around the (cipher)text to be hidden, instead of hiding the text in an existing image. Computer graphics or fractals are possible candidates to compose images from (random-looking) texts.

3.1.9. Protocols

Apart from cryptographic algorithms, a large number of cryptographic protocols are being developed. These are a series of steps, involving two or more parties, designed to accomplish a task using cryptography [Schneier, 21]. They can be used for a wider variety of objectives than simple crypto systems. Indeed, it is amazing what can be accomplished through cryptographic protocols: mutually distrustful parties can do a great variety of things over a network without being able to cheat. For instance, they can fairly toss a coin or play poker over the telephone, or sign a contract simultaneously over a network.

Suppose you are a carpet dealer in Baghdad. One day, Ali Baba comes and steals a carpet. You run after him, but he flees into a tunnel in the rock. At a junction, you are at a loss; as you cannot wait all day, you choose left. Wrong: at the end there is a blank wall, but no carpet robber. Bad luck. The next day, the same happens, and this time, you go right at the junction – wrong again. The stars must be against you. By the tenth carpet you lose this way, though, you will doubt whether it is only bad luck – the chance of your choosing wrong ten consecutive times is less than one in a thousand. There must be a catch: Ali Baba knows a secret passageway connecting the two tunnel ends, so that he can escape no matter which way you go. You do not know where this secret passage is, but you are convinced it must be there. Ali Baba has used a *zero-knowledge protocol* to convince you that he knows a secret, without giving it away.

Zero-knowledge protocols have interesting applications, for instance in authentication procedures: you can authenticate yourself by showing you know a secret (for instance, a PIN code), without giving any information about the secret itself.

Other cryptographic protocols that have a great potential are secret-sharing protocols. With these, you can divide a secret among a number of people, so that they can reproduce the secret only when a certain number of them are together; still, each single holder does not have any clue to the secret. The protocol can be sophisticated into any detail desired: you can give certain (groups of) people priorities or veto rights. Secret sharing can be used for taking major decisions, such as launching a missile attack, or for sharing a vital company secret among the board.

3.2. Applications

Cryptography is used to safeguard information-security objectives: integrity, authenticity, confidentiality, and (within limits) non-repudiation. In the information society, many applications call for these objectives. Often, cryptography is virtually the only way to effectively safeguard information. This section will show to what uses cryptography can be put by the various participants in the information society.

3.2.1. Providers

Network providers can incorporate cryptography in their networks, to make sure all information transfers are secured from altering and eavesdropping. Link-by-link encryption will ensure that in between nodes all information is enciphered. The new version of the Internet Protocol (IP – the basic protocol that determines transmissions over the Internet),

IPv6, is to incorporate DES in the network layer. At the transport layer, network providers can incorporate the Secure Sockets Layer (SSL) to facilitate secure communications between communicating parties over the Internet. The ISDN protocol includes the capability of incorporating encryption. Even if built-in encryption is not always viable for large, public networks (for instance, because of lack of interoperability), network encryption can be efficient for local area networks or intranets.

The major network to incorporate cryptography is SWIFT, the international financial network. Because of the enormous value of its transactions, protection is paramount. It is estimated that daily half the world's Gross Domestic Product travels over the network. This calls for maximum transmission security safeguarding both integrity and confidentiality.[24]

For service providers, cryptography is a good feature in new services to enlarge consumer trust. For instance, the WWW browser Netscape has a cryptography feature that allows subscribers to communicate securely: users that obtain a signed certificate are assured that all their communications are automatically encrypted (as long as, of course, the other party also has a certificate). It can also serve to authenticate clients and servers. Internet Service Providers will be required to protect the privacy of their clients (at least by providing adequate security of stored unread e-mail), and perhaps to provide their clients with means, including cryptography, to protect their online activities.

Other services that can profit from cryptography are teleconferencing, for which generally confidentiality should be safeguarded.[25] Still more important is the protection of mobile telecommunications, one of the fastest growing markets. As radio communications are easier to intercept than wire communications, they should be better protected. GSM has incorporated the encryption algorithm A5 to automatically encode all communications between the mobile phone and the base station.[26] Software developers can use Message Authentication Codes to serve as proof of correctness of software [Hueske]; especially for critical company operations, users need to be sure the software has not been tampered with.

For service providers and content providers, protecting intellectual-property rights will be a major crypto application, although the technology is yet in an early stage. Major market shares of the information society will consist of conditional-access services and payable services on demand. Pay-TV and (near) video-on-demand are quickly gaining ground. They rely on the possibility to shield transmitted information from unauthorized use. Conventional (analogue) scramblers used for encoding programs on a broadcasting net are traditionally

---

24 "In such business, confidentiality is paramount – consequently, security is a fundamental aspect of the entire S.W.I.F.T. system and is rigorously implemented throughout in order to address the full spectrum of risk." [SWIFT, 8]

25 The EC *Council resolution on the use of videoconference and videophone techniques for intergovernmental applications* of 9 June 1986 [86/C160/01] calls confidentiality one of the problems specific to the use of videoconference facilities by governments. Likewise, most company meetings contain sensitive information, and private video-conferencing may be privacy-sensitive.

26 Encryption can also be used to prevent the cloning of mobile phones: the reprogramming of a stolen analogue phone to resemble a legitimate phone, causing the calls to be billed to the legitimate owner. Fraudulent use of stolen mobile phones by cloning rose by 500 per cent in 1995. Newer systems, such as GSM, use encryption to prevent cloning. [*CLSR*, January-February 1996]

easily breakable.[27] For video-on-demand to really take off, better encoding schemes are called for, relying on good crypto systems to prevent unauthorized decoding. Likewise, Digital Versatile Disks (DVDs, the next-generation compact disk) will incorporate encryption to prevent piracy of the movies stored on them.

Also, for the online distribution of copyrighted works, such as books, compact discs, or digitized art works,[28] encrypted distribution and electronic copyright-management systems are necessary.[29] Such protection may include 'locking' products (publishing a product of which the main part is cryptographically locked; users can download it and pay a fee to receive the decoding key), fingerprinting (adding buyer-specific data to each sold copy),[30] and watermarking (marking the source and copyright information with steganographic methods, so that the watermark will be preserved when the product is copied or altered),[31] all of which measures require some form of cryptography. Since it is impossible to prevent authorized users from redistributing the product (they, after all, have legitimate access to the product as it is), mechanisms to track unauthorized re-use, such as watermarks, may be even more important than secure distribution to authorized users. Cryptography can help tracing the source of leaks, when 'traitors' (authorized recipients) allow non-authorized parties to obtain the data [Chor].

The technical protection for conditional-access services and for copyright-management schemes is being supplemented by legal protection. First, the European Commission has presented a draft *Directive on legal protection of conditional access services* in July 1997 [COM (97) 356], which covers all broadcasting and online services offered on a conditional-access basis. The draft requires member states to prohibit commercial activities that facilitate unauthorized access to pay services.[32] Second, the WIPO Copyright Treaty requires legislation to prohibit the circumvention of technological copyright-management information.[33] The European Union and the US are taking steps to implement these requirements.

---

27 For instance, illegal decoders were publicly marketed for decoding European Broadcasting Union transmissions of the European Championships soccer in 1996. [*Volkskrant*, 29 February 1996]

28 Marketing digitized art constitutes an emerging market, but museums worry about losing control of their collections. "Some computer-literate museum employees are starting to think about ways to encrypt such images so that only authorized users can look at them." [Powell]

29 "Technologies developed for securing information hold promise for monitoring the use of protected information, and provide a means for collecting and compensating the owners of intellectual property." [OTA]

30 Such fingerprinting can also be done anonymously. [Pfitzmann]

31 For instance, Playboy is watermarking its online photos to track use of its images on the Web. [Lazarus]

32 The scope of the draft directive is broader than the original *Green Paper on the legal protection of encrypted services in the internal market* of July 1996, which covered only illegal decoding of broadcast services. Amendments to the draft directive raised concerns within the cryptographers community in early 1998, as they appeared to also prohibit cryptanalytic research. However, the final proposal for the Directive [COM(98) 332] implemented these amendments.

33 Article 11, 'Obligations concerning Technological Measures', of the WIPO Copyright Treaty, adopted 20 December 1996, reads: "Contracting Parties shall provide adequate legal protection and effective legal remedies against the circumvention of effective technological measures that are used by authors in connection with the exercise of their rights under this Treaty or the Berne Convention and that restrict acts, in respect of their works, which are not authorized by the authors concerned or permitted by law." The WIPO Performances and Phonograms Treaty of the same dat contains a similar requirement.

The Dutch government likewise recognizes that criminal law should protect against infringements of technical measures, such as encryption, that protect information [25880, nrs 1-2, 6].

Cryptography also facilitates new business processes for content providers. For instance, record companies welcome the option of recording music at different places at the same time - vocals in New York, the band in London. They can efficiently exchange the recordings over the Internet in a secured, confidential way, and mix the recordings.

3.2.2. Government

Traditionally, governments have been the main users (and breakers) of cryptography. They employ it in diplomatic services, intelligence gathering, military affairs, internal memoranda, et cetera. The 'black chambers' of the eighteenth century, which deciphered virtually all diplomatic correspondence [Kahn, 157-188], have a modern counterpart in intelligence agencies that employ a large number of mathematically trained cryptanalysts.

Yet cryptography is not only used for intelligence purposes. It shields personal registries maintained by the government, such as municipal, social-security, and police registries. Equally important, it protects intra-government communications. Some examples of government networks requiring high levels of information security are a trans-European public administration network called for by the Bangemann report, OB2000 (a Dutch network for electronic messages within (local) governments and for communication between government and citizens), and C2000 (a Dutch single, high-grade network for mobile voice and data communications between police, fire brigades, ambulances, and military constabulary). More specific applications also call for encryption, such as the information interchange between the Central Criminal Intelligence Agency and Interpol [Hendriks], and the online checking of license-number information by traffic wardens [*Telecommagazine*, September 1996].

As government information is increasingly published electronically to facilitate access to public-sector information, the concern for integrity is growing. In many cases, for instance, in applying for a subsidy or in setting up a business, people must be able to rely on the correctness of the electronic administrative information.

Also, cryptography opens up new ways for improving the relationship between citizen and administration.[34] For instance, online tax declaration is a client-friendly and expedient medium. Electronic elections and referendums may be held, with large efficiency gains. The reliability and unforgeability of votes can only be safeguarded by cryptography, such as digital signatures with private keys issued by an election Certification Authority. Electronic toll collection or road-pricing schemes can be implemented. The data used in these projects must not only be correct, but also confidential, as information on traveling behavior can be privacy-threatening.

34 Indeed, in less democratic countries, cryptography may even enhance the democratic value of parliamentary decisions itself. In early 1998, China's National People's Congress put into use a new electronic voting system that "is designed to make it impossible to track down any individual deputy's voting options" [*Xinhua*, 4 March 1998]. This might help in transforming the traditional applause machine into a more critical legislative body.

One of the most important uses of cryptography in this context is that it helps to prevent crime. Cryptography protects against computer crime, fraud, and industrial espionage. In the words of James Fotis, Executive Director of the Law Enforcement Alliance of America, "the threat to public safety comes from the lack of encryption; files that are not secure are ripe for theft and misuse. (...) [B]y using encryption we can reduce computer theft crimes and lower economic espionage." [Fotis]

Last, a quaint application has been proposed in the draft Dutch Computer Crime Act II. Cryptography can be used for 'seizing' or 'attaching' information that the judiciary wants to bring out of someone's power (for instance, because it is child pornography), comparable to the traditional seizure of property. If the seizure of the information carrier is disproportionate, the 'cybersheriff' could encrypt the information on the owner's disk, so that the information would get out of reach of the person involved (provided he does not have a copy somewhere). Only when the judge grants replevin, the information would be decrypted and thus 'returned to the owner'.[35]

3.2.3. Other users

Besides the government, the other users of the information society – both individual and corporate – can gain much from new ICT applications. In many cases, integrity, authenticity, or confidentiality are called for.

Financial applications

First, financial transactions have to be secure. Home banking is an increasingly popular activity, which relies on the integrity, authenticity, and confidentiality of transmitted requests and orders. For online payment, transmitting credit-card numbers over networks is, to say the least, risky. Losses through the interception of credit-card numbers have occurred repeatedly. Information that is directly valuable should be encrypted before being sent online, if not before being typed at all – packet sniffers can intrude in terminals and record information to be downloaded later by the initiator of the sniffer (which can even bypass firewalls). It is wiser to use a zero-knowledge protocol to give the credit-card number,[36] for instance, by challenged signed response: the server gives the client a random number, which he types into a personal calculator containing a chip with the credit-card number. Inside, the chip computes a hash from the random number and the credit-card number, which the client send to the server. The server can then verify the correctness of the credit-card number by computing the same hash.

Other methods are being developed for online payment. Electronic cash (e-cash) systems

---

35 First suggested by Ministry of Justice official Alexander Patijn [Patijn, 805], it was incorporated in the draft Computer Crime Act II, proposed article 125o. Another way to 'seize' data would be to copy them and delete the 'original' data.

36 "An Internet user should not be required to type in a password or reveal any personal characteristics that someone else could copy. Instead users should be asked to provide answers that depend on their knowledge of some secret without revealing it." [Beth]

have been proposed and are being tested in practice.[37] An electronic coin or note is a (large) number digitally signed by the issuing bank. An (electronic) shop-owner can verify the bank's signature and send it to the bank to add to his account. All e-cash systems incorporate a feature to prevent or to detect and trace double spending. Anonymity is a disputed feature: it is desirable from a privacy point of view (normal cash, after all, is anonymous), but it creates opportunities for illegal purposes, like money laundering, tax evasion, and cashing a ransom anonymously with no risk of being traced [Solms].

A particular use for electronic cash is micropayment: paying very small fees for very small services, like viewing a WWW page. Such a feature might stimulate the development of good web pages: page makers would be rewarded for their efforts, and competition would ensure that the web does not perish in a chaos of infinitely many web pages where no-one can find his way. Micropayment could be a feature implemented in browsers: each user has a stack of electronic coins (each, say, of tens of a cent), of which the browser would automatically transfer one to the holder of the requested web page, while transferring the page to the user.

Digital money will increasingly be stored on smart cards. Altogether, smart cards hold great promise, not only for storing digital money (in Dutch the 'chipknip' or 'chipper'), but also for membership cards, medical-insurance cards, museum cards, and public-traffic permits. To protect the information on smart cards, which can have direct financial value or be privacy-sensitive, cryptography should be used to guarantee authorized use only of the information stored.[38]

Privacy and sensitive data

Cryptography will also ensure that on multi-functional smart cards, people can only read the sections they are allowed to access – an important feature to prevent the making of privacy-threatening personal profiles. More in general, cryptography serves to protect personal data files, as required by data-protection laws.[39] Moreover, for many purposes, Privacy Enhancing Technologies (PET) can be used to protect personal information from unnecessary disclosure: pseudonymous data often suffice for the purposes of collecting personal data. A Norwegian report thus recommends 'pseudonimizing' health registries, so that data can be gathered for research purposes without threatening personal privacy [NOU]. A joint report of the Dutch and Ontarian data protection registrars strongly recommends the use of PET in a variety of applications. Often, it is not necessary to know the identity of the people involved: a *pseudo-identity* suffices. Only for authorizing and billing is it necessary

---

37 DigiCash has developed *ecash*™, a digital equivalent of cash which was accepted as currency by Mark Twain Bank (until September 1998) and by some other banks on an experimental basis. Contrary to the 'cash' of DigiCash, other online-payment systems rely on encrypted transmission of credit-card numbers or account information (CyberCash, First Virtual, Netscape's built-in encryption software developed with MasterCard and Visa) or on smart cards (Mondex).

38 "Smart cards have been technologically demonstrated. Whether the business and personal privacy issues they raise can be settled is another matter. Companies in a wide variety of businesses see uses for smart cards, but each has an interest in controlling the personal information that will be stored on them." [Zysman]

39 According to the Dutch Data Protection Authority, encryption is one of the most powerful tools to protect data bases and data supply as required by the Data Registries Act. [Registratiekamer 94]

to know the name and address of the users of the service. [Registratiekamer 95] Cryptography will help implement the 'identity protector' used in privacy-enhancing technologies. Similarly, cryptography can protect data bases, so that it is easy to find the data of a single person but hard to extract an entire mailing list from the data base [Schneier, 73-4].

In general, storage will require encryption to shield sensitive information in a variety of situations, from keeping a secret diary[40] or shielding adult material from your kids to outlining plans you do not want others to know of – both in private and business surroundings.

Aside from the protection of stored personal data, data security often also requires communications safety. Business communications need to be protected, both from eavesdropping and from altering. Many intra-enterprise communications are confidential, such as annual figures, research and development information, personnel mutations, and travel information of high corporate officials who run a risk of being taken hostage. Many (larger) companies use private networks or intranets, where the security risk is lower. Still, even private networks are vulnerable to hacking and eavesdropping, so that sensitive information should be protected additionally by cryptography. Also, cryptography is a good means of shielding information from unauthorized users within a company (especially important since the larger part of security threats comes from employees) .

Also for private use, cryptography will be required for communications security. As the use of e-mail is soaring, increasingly people are sending confidential information across public networks. One of the principles of the US NII Task Force reads: "Individuals should be able to safeguard their own privacy by having (...) the opportunity to use appropriate technical controls, such as encryption, to protect the confidentiality and integrity of communications and transactions". [NIITF] The use of e-mail encryption will likely be a major application of cryptography in the near future. Examples are electronic private letters, electronic confessions,[41] online psychological help,[42] or escaping from government scrutiny. Lawyers and their clients will often want to communicate confidentially through encryption.[43]

Human rights

Cryptography can be life-saving for political and human-rights activists who fear persecution from human rights violating governments. The US State Department report on human-rights practices lists quite a number of countries whose governments illegally monitor the

---

40 In 1996, an employee of Emmen municipality was suspended when his diary, which he kept at work on his hard disk, was found to contain rather unkind statements about his colleagues. Although the diary had been erased from the hard disk, two colleagues managed to unearth it with undelete utilities while he was on holiday. Cryptography would have helped the employee to keep his diary secret – and his job.

41 In 1996, an Austrian priest went online to offer a confession service. He encouraged people who wanted to confess to use PGP. [Cf. Landwehr]

42 Psychologist Robert Wilson expects 40 per cent of psychological help to take place online within a few years, especially since it is decidedly cheaper. [*Intermediair*, 25 September 1997]

43 The Iowa Supreme Court Board of Professional Ethics and Conduct has stated that e-mail containing sensitive material must be encrypted, or else the lawyer must obtain written acknowledgment from the client that he consents to the risk. [*EPLR* 1996, 515]

communications and illegally search the houses of its citizens, notably of dissidents.[44] Phil Zimmerman, maker of PGP, received several messages from a Central European human-rights activist who thanked him for writing PGP. "Without PGP we would not be able to function and protect our client group. Thanks to PGP I can sleep at night knowing that no amount of prying will compromise our clients. (...) There is no Constitution, enforced by capable courts in this part of the world able to protect us from such abuses, so we must have the right to protect ourselves from abuse" [Zimmerman 96]. Human Rights Watch has called on governments to allow "users of the GII to encrypt their communications and information without restriction." [HRW] When Hong Kong had been handed over to China in 1997, Amnesty International called on its China coordinators to encrypt all communications with Amnesty's Hong Kong Regional Office. After the 1996 publication of Nicky Hager's book on the global surveillance system Echelon (see sidebar in 4.3.2), a project was started in the Pacific to promote and supply publicly-available encryption software to democracy movements in countries with repressive governments. [Hager]

Public and private networks

Encryption is important in connections with the outside world. More and more individuals and companies connect to public electronic networks. Security is a major concern, especially when connecting to the Internet. Firewalls generally protect internal systems from outside threats, but some sophisticated attacks can bypass even firewall protection. Sensitive information has to be additionally protected with cryptography from spoofing attacks.[45] In connections with the outside world, virus protection is paramount. Cryptographic integrity checks (for instance, a signed hash) can serve to assure that a software program has not been altered by a virus. Each time the program is invoked, the computer first checks the hash to see if the program is still the same.

Through external connections, communicating with other parties, for instance, in distance selling, negotiating mergers, exchanging marketing information, and tendering, is increasingly done online. Electronic Data Interchange (EDI) uses standardized communication formats, for instance for insurance contracts, court pleadings, bills of sale, and shipping documents. Production and sale chains can be set up for just-in-time order and delivery; in consequence, the stock can be much smaller and efficiency is enhanced. The factories and companies in the chain have to rely on the integrity and authenticity of the orders; these objectives can be effected through digital signatures and message authentication codes.

Cryptography is essential for electronic commerce. Digital signatures and Certification Authorities can address the need for non-repudiation, integrity, and authenticity of requests

44 For instance, on China, the report states: "In practice, however, authorities frequently monitor telephone conversations, fax transmissions, electronic mail, and Internet communications of foreign visitors, businessmen, diplomats, residents, and journalists as well as Chinese dissidents, activists, and others. Authorities also open and censor domestic and international mail. (...) Government security organs monitor and sometimes restrict contact between foreigners and citizens, particularly dissidents." [DoS]

45 In a spoofing attack, TCP/IP packets are faked so that a server is fooled into believing they come from an authorized user; this way, one can even bypass firewalls. The only real method of protecting information against these sophisticated attacks is to use cryptographic authentication.

and delivery (provided international legal recognition and liability issues are solved). Often, confidentiality may be called for. "The use of strong encryption which ensures the confidentiality of both sensitive commercial and of personal data is one of the foundation stones of electronic commerce." [COM(97)157, at 50] The Bonn conference likewise recognizes "the importance of the availability of strong encryption technology for electronic commerce." [Bonn, at 35]

Another option created by electronic networks is teleworking. If employees work at home, they may save commuting time and child-care costs. Access to the company's network and automation facilities can be established through telephone-modem connections, but the openness of the public telephone network warrants encrypting all communications between the company and home.

Other applications

Besides confidentiality, integrity of communications is often necessary. R&D information, annual returns, and the like must be relied on. Integrity is also paramount in safety-critical processes. For instance, in automated medical procedures, such as the administering of medicine or computer-supported operations, the integrity of the data used is a matter of life and death.[46] As a result of a nurse altering data in the data base of a British hospital, a child with meningitis received medication for a heart disease [Breed, 17]. Several cases are known of factory robots having killed people [Neumann, 65]. In safety-critical applications, both the integrity of information input and of the software used must be ensured; cryptographic checks play a significant part in this.

A secret-sharing protocol (3.1.9) can help to protect key company secrets, such as the recipe of the company's product or the combination to the safe. It is dangerous to have a single person keep secrets (what happens if he debauches, defects, or dies?), so the secret should be shared among, say, five company officials and employees, in such a way that each three of them can decrypt the secret. A secret-sharing protocol ensures that the secret is divided among them, without any single person having knowledge of the secret: it is only with a minimum number of them that they can reconstruct it. So, if any one holder defects to a competing company, he can give away no information, and the secret can still be reconstructed. The chances of the competition bribing a number of employees is significantly smaller than the chance of a single employee being corrupt.

Last, the advent of public-key cryptography creates a curious possibility: you can prove you have made an invention without making known how it works. You simply make a hash of the document describing your invention, sign it with your private key, and publish it in the New York Times. Later, by the time you want to market your invention, you can patent it; the published and signed hash serves as proof that you made the invention at the time of publishing, which invalidates claims of others that made the same invention after you. Delaying marketing of a new invention gives you more time to sophisticate it or to do market research; with traditional patent claims, time runs against the inventor.

46 A woman who had been told she and her children had incurable syphilis killed her daughter and tried to kill her son and herself. The medical information turned out to be based on a computer error. [Neumann, 71]

3.2.4. Cryptography in practice

Cryptography is widely available. A worldwide survey of cryptographic products by Trusted Information Systems found 1619 products as of December 1997 (rising from 1393 in December 1996). Of these, 656 non-US products were identified from 29 countries (43 per cent using DES), mostly in Europe, but also in Argentina, India, Iran, Mexico, and Russia. These products were produced and distributed by 949 companies (475 US, 474 non-US) in at least 68 countries. [TIS]

Although the potential applications for cryptography are abundant, its present use is confined to a few major areas. It protects the integrity of valuable information, it authenticates people who engage in transactions, and it shields confidential information from unauthorized access. It is mainly used in financial areas (bank transactions, home banking, smart cards, e-cash), in privacy protection (personal registries, smart cards, government registries, sensitive information storage), and communications security (e-mail, facsimile, the air interface of GSM).

A survey of business cryptography use, ordered by the Dutch government in 1994 when it prepared its hapless law to restrict crypto use, concluded that cryptography is mainly used by large organizations. Of the 97 respondents, 18 organizations indicated they used cryptography, and ten expected to start using it within the next ten years – a total of 29 per cent. Cryptography was mainly used in business provision of services (notably banks) and in telecommunications. The researchers expected that future cryptography spread would be larger than the results indicated, given the fast growth of the number of computers and modern applications like home banking and EDI. [KPMG 94, 6-7] In the US, the Chamber of Commerce estimated that 17 per cent of companies used encryption for confidentiality in 1995. They expected the figure to rise to 60 per cent by 2000 [mentioned in Denning 97b].

So, in practice, cryptography is still mainly used by large entities: banks, great enterprises, administrations. Individuals and small and medium-sized enterprises are starting to use it, but in general they lag behind, possibly through a failure to recognize the importance of information security, and through a lack of standardized, user-friendly cryptography products. It is commonly expected, however, that crypto use will rise significantly in the near future, as more and more areas of life are digitized and as encryption technologies become more widespread and user-friendly.[47]

3.3. Conclusion – the importance of cryptography

"Cryptographic technologies are nowadays widely recognised as the essential tool for security and trust in electronic communication. (...) Encryption of data is very often the only effective and cost-efficient way of meeting these requirements." [COM(97) 503]

---

47 "The market for encryption in distributed computation, databases, and electronic mail is beginning to expand exponentially as the U.S. and other countries develop and popularize electronic commerce, public networks, and distributed processing. (...) Less technologically advanced countries, where demand for encryption software is reportedly negligible, will soon undergo widespread development and computerization leading to increased demand for encryption software within the next 10 years." [DoC]

Through the advent of public-key encryption, a whole range of crypto applications has opened up to secure information. Some of these are exotic, but many applications are basic and will be essential in the information society – for providers, for users, and, not least, for governments. The confidentiality and integrity of communications and stored information will often have to be safeguarded through encryption.

The importance of cryptography is widely recognized by governments. For instance, the Dutch Ministry of Economic Affairs stated: "It is undisputed that for businesses and government alike cryptography forms an indispensable and useful instrument for the reliability and security of message traffic and of the infrastructure and telecommunications services used for this." [24565, nr 1, 5] Likewise, the German Ministry of Economic Affairs found that "effective information protection requires secure encryption methods (...) A reliable protection of [confidential] information from unauthorized access is often only to be effected through the deployment of secure encryption methods." [BfW] The Australian Walsh Report found that the "ready availability of strong encryption (...) is the most effective safeguard of individual privacy." [Walsh, finding 1.2.39]

Most importantly, even proponents of restricting cryptography in view of cryptocriminals recognize the need for strong cryptography. "Practically everyone agrees that cryptography is an essential information security tool, and that it should be readily available to users. I take this as a starting assumption and, in this respect, have no disagreement with the crypto anarchists" [Denning 96] (written when professor Denning still advocated systems with built-in law-enforcement access to keys). Even the director of the FBI, Louis Freeh, agrees: "We see encryption as a public safety issue, and we are (...) absolutely committed to the development of encryption technology. In order to do all of the things we want to do in public safety – as well as in commerce and for national security – we must be strong proponents of encryption." [Freeh 95b]

Chapter 4. Cryptocriminals, a public concern

Communications, not easy at the best of times in Pakistan, were, quite literally, bugged. I eventually got through from Islamabad to speak to Jamila in Peshawar on the phone, only to be cut off after just a few words. When I redialled, the phone had gone completely dead. I asked the advice of the English journalist whose phone it was.
'Oh,' he said, not at all surprised, 'I know what it is. You were speaking French. The man listening in wasn't able to understand, so he's cut the line off and gone to find a colleague who can. Give him a few minutes to do so and you'll get through with no trouble.'
I followed his advise and he was perfectly right.
(Nick Danziger, Danziger's Travels)

Cryptography has a wide range of applications. As it can satisfy many good, even essential, needs in the information society, so it can be put to less noble purposes in the crime society. This chapter deals with the nefarious uses of cryptography: it will define in which ways encryption hampers law enforcement.

For a good understanding of the law-enforcement problems, one must analyze the context in which investigation takes place. Therefore, I will sketch some developments in crime (4.1) as well as in substantive criminal and criminal-procedure law (4.2), concentrating on the developments that are particularly relevant to ICT-related investigation. Then, I will describe relevant investigation methods, concentrating on gathering information in transport (tapping and traffic analysis, 4.3) and in storage (e.g., search and seizure procedures, 4.4). This will define the place of today's crime and crime-fighting in society, which enables me to analyze just what problems cryptography poses to law-enforcement (4.5). I conclude with an assessment of the essence and scope of the crypto-problems for law enforcement (4.6).

Obviously, law enforcement and cryptocriminals are issues society at large faces all over the world. With an increase in international crime and with the advent of the information society, cryptocriminals will more and more become an international problem. However, international or multinational investigation and cooperation is yet in its infancy - investigation continues to be very much a domestic issue. Problems and procedures differ in each country, perhaps not in essence, but at least in emphasis. I will describe the Dutch situation, and provide occasional side-steps to other countries that can serve as indications of how those countries would deal with these problems. The analysis in this chapter will serve as a case study, which may be transposed to other countries' systems and cultures as appropriate.

4.1. The crime society

In the 1950s, crime was not a prime issue in the Netherlands. Ordinary crimes such as theft and robbery prevailed. Two decades later, society was confronted with hijackers, psycho-rapists, and terrorist groups. Still, crime was mainly restricted to small groups operating on their own.

Then, in the 1980s, the Netherlands discovered a new phenomenon: organized crime.[1] Criminal organizations and organized criminals seemed to threaten society in ways and on a scale beyond imagination. They were supposed to penetrate the legal realms of society, they seemed to gain incredible profits which they invested in legal activities, and they began to spy on the police rather than suffer to be spied upon.

At the same time, with the rise of the information society, computer crime became more pervasive. Hackers hacked their way into Pentagons, viruses spread like a disease, and computer fraud rose significantly.

Society's answer to these new types of crime was to intensify investigation and to try and find new ways to combat modern crime. 'Crime-fighting' and the 'war on drugs' became buzz words in policy documents, as the legislator called for adequate measures to react to organized and computer crime. Laying bare the communicative patterns of criminals appeared to be one of the best methods of investigation.

This section deals with the criminal part of present-day society. It starts with a description of the new, serious forms of crime confronting society: organized crime, business crime, computer crime, and other forms of serious crime. I use these categories mainly because one can distinguish between typical perpetrators of these crimes. How and when these categories of criminals use information and communication technologies is of particular relevance to the crypto problem. I will outline the information behavior and the use cryptography of these various categories.

4.1.1. Organized crime

They plan the overthrow of something,
Maybe by bomb, or gun, or spoken word.
That something exists. It modifies the words
Of the conspirators
(Howard Nemerov, Portrait of three conspirators)

One can speak of organized crime when there are groups of persons who

- are primarily focused on illegal financial gain,
- commit crimes systematically with serious consequences for society, and

---

1 It is a misconception that criminal organizations only came into being in the past few decades. As far back as the 17th and 18th centuries, criminal groups roamed the country; they would fit most present definitions of a criminal organization. [Duyne] Still, the 1985 parliamentary memorandum *Society and crime* stated that the Netherlands had in the past largely remained free from organized crime [18995, nrs 1-2, 47].

- are able to relatively effectively shield these crimes, in particular through showing willingness to use physical violence or corruption [Traa, 25].[2]

Organized crime is to be distinguished from business crime (or somewhat broader: organizational crime), which indicates members of a legal organization (primarily businesses) participating in committing offenses, while the organization does not as such function as a criminal organization (see 4.1.2).[3]

Contrary to what the term suggests, criminal organizations are not always well-structured and hierarchical. Rather, they operate in network structures or worldwide webs. One could speak of 'disorganized crime' [Duyne, 6], since the behavior of the organization is not ruled by market or company rules, but rather by the need to keep its activities secret from the judiciary. One could also speak of organiz*ing* crime, to stress the dynamic, ever-changing character of the criminal groups [Duyne, 18]. Flexibility and international cooperation[4] are notable characteristics.

Activities

Criminal organizations engage in a range of illegal activities. Most specialize in particular areas, but some organizations are active in diverse markets. Besides financial crimes, the core activity of criminal organizations is trade in forbidden goods and services – formerly prostitution, gambling, and arms, nowadays mainly drug trafficking. The gains in this area are so high that at least part of the gain has to be reinvested in the 'upper world' (the legal realms of society). Money laundering is therefore an activity which any criminal organization somehow has to take part in; some specialize in laundering profits for other criminal organizations. Thus, modern crime is much more intertwined with the legal economy.

Apart from the main area of drugs, new areas of crime include trafficking in waste material ('waste crime'), nuclear materials, arms, and people (women, refugees, illegal immigrants). These require more specialist knowledge or have smaller markets, and are served by more specialized criminal organizations.

Another area that forms a great potential for organized crime is the area of taxes and subsidies. Especially in the European Union, the economy is being regulated through a complex system of taxes and subsidies, leading to large 'price wedges' between the costs of manufacture and of sale. This creates opportunities for organized fraud schemes. [22838, nr 2, 2]

---

2 Interestingly, the FBI definition is quite similar, except for the final part: "Any group having some manner of formalized structure and whose primary objective is to obtain money through illegal activities. Such groups maintain their position through the use of violence or threats of violence, corrupt public officials, graft, or extortion, and generally have a significant impact on the people in their locales or region of the country." [Abadinsky, 3] The "significant impact on local people" is US-centric, being largely inspired by Italian-style mafia and South American-style drug cartels.

3 I disregard the academic debate over the definitions of organized crime and business crime. Although the two overlap significantly (in many cases, business crime verges on organized crime, and the two are often interdependent), for the purposes of this book, it is useful to distinguish between (purely) criminal organizations and business criminals (who operate largely within a lawful context).

4 A survey by the German Federal Criminal Bureau (*Bundeskriminalamt*) found 67.5 per cent of the criminal organizations to cooperate with different nationalities. [Duyne, 24]

Seriousness

The past few years have witnessed an enormous increase in political attention for the problem of organized crime. Reading the reports and statements of policy makers, one gets the impression that society is shaking to its foundations. The 1992 memorandum on organized crime in the Netherlands reads: "The threat to Dutch society emanating from present-day criminal organizations must in our opinion be taken very seriously, given the far-reaching economic and moral implications." [22838, nr 2, 6] In discussing this memorandum, the Minister of Justice and the parliament were of the opinion that the seriousness of organized crime can hardly be overestimated [23047, nr 6, 3]. UN Secretary-General Boutros-Ghali, addressing a 1994 UN conference, warned against the destabilizing effects: "Transnational crime, however, undermines the very foundations of the international democratic order. Transnational crime poisons the business climate, corrupts political leaders and undermines human rights. It weakens the effectiveness and credibility of institutions and thus undermines democratic life." [Boutros-Ghali]

The financial gains and turnover of organized crime cause significant losses to the economy, as well as serious damage to the environment. Moreover, the potential interweaving of criminals in the upper world could form a serious threat to the stability and integrity of the entire society – and to its functioning as a democratic constitutional state.[5] However, there are no indications that organized crime has systematically infiltrated specific sectors or free professional groups, such as attorneys, notaries, or accountants [Traa, 50, 56].

Organized crime takes place in the dark recesses of society, and it is difficult to assess its real extent and threat. There is no method to assess the 'how-badness', and therefore one may easily create spooks [Duyne, 193].[6] One *can* say, though, that there has been an increase in organized crime over the past few decades, to such an extent that organized crime is a significant part of today's society. The potential threats to the economy and the integrity of our society are obvious, but it is difficult to estimate the scope of these threats.

Information behavior

Criminal organizations must communicate in order to plan and perform their activities. They have a high need for communication.[7] As the organization is larger and its operating field is bigger – often covering several countries – the criminals must use telecommunications to discuss their plans, give orders, convey information on where and when to operate, and warn each other against pursuing police agents.

---

5 According to the Dutch criminologist Hoogenboom, society might suffer more damage in the future through the offenses committed by legal corporations, and sometimes also by administration, than by organized crime. [*Staatscourant* 4 April 1996]

6 One might wonder what caused the sudden government attention for organized crime. Schmid suggests three reasons: 1. The government needs a new enemy after the collapse of the Eastern bloc. 2. Ministries need more money, and so they create problems to combat. 3. There is really something amiss. After some consideration, Schmid opts for the third reason. [Schmid, 7]

7 "Organized crime is characterised by, among others, the fact that the criminal behavior is thoroughly planned and presupposes the cooperation of several perpetrators, who particularly in the planning phase have a large communication need." [Thiesen, 49]. "Especially criminal organizations, with a view to executing their actions, often have to rely on intensive communication." [23047, nr 3, 2]

In general, criminal organizations have enough money to use the newest technologies. The telephone has been used since its invention to commit crimes.[8] Lately, facsimile machines, mobile communications, and computer networks have proved welcome additions to make communications easier and more flexible. With mobile data terminals, one can exchange any message around the world from any place within seconds.

Of course, criminals are aware that their communications are being monitored. Although this does not always keep them from using communication means which they know to be tappable, criminal organizations are sophisticated enough to take efforts to prevent the police from hearing them. They are aware of police activities and anticipate new investigative methods.[9] Increasingly, criminal organizations are shielding themselves from police scrutiny [Traa, 28]. For instance, a criminal group that operated a drugs line on Morocco and ripped drug consignments from other criminal organizations "did all possible to keep the internal communications secret" [Traa, 36]. An effective criminal must be a good information manager.

Criminals exploit legal and technical gaps in the police's monitoring capabilities. Today, for instance, the police has difficulty in tapping certain mobile phones and data communications. Consequently, criminal organizations regularly use mobile phones, often a large number of them at the same time, and they use prepaid or stolen phone cards, which makes it difficult for the police to trace the right number to tap. "Some leaders of a criminal organization had an entire battery of pocket or car telephones at their disposal. None of these were registered on their own name. Others let themselves be beeped, after which they held their conversations only in public phone booths." [Duyne, 174][10]

A good example of information behavior is the group of Henk R., which imported and exported soft and hard drugs and produced XTC. The organization used modern communications equipment, such as pagers, mobile and car phones, and facsimile machines. The organization feared that the police was listening in on them and therefore did not use home telephone connections. Henk R. made sure all his people were continuously reachable by mobile or car phones. Furthermore, Henk R. had an interest in a telecommunications company in Amsterdam. This enabled him and the members of his organization to change mobile or car phones or connection numbers at any moment. This happened regularly, in particular when a drug consignment had been confiscated or when members of the organization were held by the police. The group also had unregistered phones at their disposal. Besides, telephones were purchased with false papers, and phones were registered on names of people who were not involved in the organization or who were even completely ignorant. [Traa, 193-194]

---

8 "The period since the Second World War has seen a democratisation of the telephone and a consequent increase in the number of offences committed with its assistance." [CoE 82, 5]

9 Cf. the Second World War, when the phone was a relatively unfamiliar medium. People had the idea that the occupying forces could eavesdrop on all phone calls, which led them to largely refrain from using the phone for communications. Interestingly, as most telephone exchanges had been automated, the possibility of phone tapping was rather limited. [Hogesteeger, 32-33]

10 "The members of the organization communicate among themselves almost exclusively through car phones that can only be tapped with difficulty. In their houses and offices, several mobile phones are available for that purpose." [22838, nr 2, 4]

Another common way of trying to thwart telephone taps is talking in codes. Instead of talking about drugs or consignments, people will use codes and seemingly talk about everyday affairs. Thus, one can hear: "I'll come and sell 10,000 sheep." [Duyne, 174] Whether this really hampers investigation is to be seen, especially when such diverse things are being ordered as "batches of jackets, stuff, young piglets, pure earth, milk, rooms", when it appears possible to order half a cassette or half a movie, and when a request is made to bring a pair of scales [Traa, 254]. Such 'codes' are easily crackable.

Use of cryptography

Not many cases are known of criminal organizations using encrypted communications. An example of the pre-automated era are the rumrunners shipping liquor to the dry US in the 1930s. Although they used increasingly complex codes, cryptanalysts cracked message after incriminating radio message, culminating in leading cryptanalyst Elizebeth Friedman's cracking of the Consolidated Exporters Corporation radio traffic. The prosecutor acknowledged her worth: "Mrs. Friedman was summoned as an expert witness to testify as to the meaning of certain intercepted radio code messages.... Without their translations, I do not believe that this very important case could have been won." [Kahn, 802ff]

As, currently, tapping mobile phones can be made difficult by easy measures (such as using prepaid cards or various unregistered SIM cards), there is not yet a real need for criminals to use cryptophones. A Dallas detective noted "that the big drug dealers were not encrypting phone calls. Instead, they were swapping phones (using cloned phones) to stay ahead of law enforcement." [Denning 97d] The use of codes, however translucent, may indicate, though, that technologically advanced criminals could start using cryptography as the modern equivalent of these codes.[11]

Some cases indicate that criminal organizations do use encrypted data transmission. The Danish police has, to a limited extent, encountered encrypted data transmission among suspects [Thiesen, 49]. A German jurisdiction leader stated that "hot business such as arms and drug trade is not any more done by telephone, but is being settled in encrypted form on the worldwide data networks." [*Der Spiegel*, 25 March 1996] And a White House official claimed that "organized crime members are some of the most advanced users of computer systems and of strong encryption." [*EPLR*, 13 September 1996] The Cali cartel allegedly used sophisticated

11 On the other hand, criminals may also turn to other communications means: "The current practice shows that suspects aware of the danger of being monitored shift to other ways of communication rather than send encrypted messages." [E. Schmidt-Jortzig, quoted in Moeller]

encryption for their telephone conversations [Denning 97d]. However, even if they will use encryption among themselves, criminals will have to communicate with the upper world in the clear - the more the organization tries to enter the legal realm, the more plaintext communications they will have to make.[12]

In general, criminal organizations are much more dependent on data communications than on data storage. They do not need to keep records of their transactions, and they can quickly destroy most of the incriminating information they have on paper or disk. If they have to keep data stored, it is probable they will try to shield these data, and cryptography is a likely means of doing so. Almost all of the organized crime and terrorist cases listed by Denning and Baugh in their directory of cryptocriminals involve stored encrypted files, not encrypted communications; the Walsh report found the same [Walsh, 3.2.1]. For instance, the Japanese religious sect Aum Shinrikyo, which committed a gas assault on a Tokyo subway station in 1995, had encrypted some of its computer files with RSA; the authorities were able to decrypt the files after they found the key on a diskette [Denning 97d]. In another case, Dutch police captured a PC with an encrypted partition they were unable to decrypt at the time. There was enough other evidence to convict the organized crime member, and when the disk was eventually decrypted, it was found to be of little interest. [Denning 97d]

But overall, it seems few criminal organizations presently use cryptography. The Dallas detective investigating a national drug ring said that "in the ten years he had been working drug cases, this was the only time he had encountered encryption, and that he rarely even encountered computers. He noted that the Ecstasy dealers were into computers more than other types of drug dealers, most likely because they are younger and better educated. They are using the Internet for sales, but they are not encrypting electronic mail." [Denning 97d]

4.1.2. Business crime

Business crime can be defined as offenses committed by organizations that mainly rely on legal activities for their income; business fraud is the main example of business crime. In contrast to organized crime, business crime takes place for a large part in the upper world. Organizations that perform legal activities can commit fraud or waste dumping, but they have to maintain a legal basis. Whereas criminal organizations can easily give up front stores and start new ones without hampering their main activities, legal organizations depend on the legality of their main activity. The types of business crime committed are mainly financial offenses, such as tax fraud, money laundering, bribery, and forgery.

Seriousness

Business crime may involve large sums of money, and the interweaving of legal institutions and crime poses a threat to the long-term credibility of the rule of law. Therefore, business crime is an important issue for criminal investigation. The increasing importance of financial investigation to curb money laundering and large-scale fraud underlines this.

---

12 The Australian Federal Police stated that "much valuable telecommunications interception evidence and intelligence comes from targets talking to people who are not part of a criminal activity and who would not use encryption (arranging hotel, shipping or airline bookings is one obvious example.)" [quoted in Orlowski]

Information behavior and use of cryptography

The main goal of corporations committing business crime is not to make as much money as illegally possible, but to assure the survival of the company. Consequently, the corporation needs to conform to legal rules, and keep accounts and suffer tax investigations. This means that their reliance on information storage is much greater than is the case with criminal organizations. In the case of tax fraud, which is often assisted by forgery, a double account may need to be kept,[13] and the 'black account' will need to be hidden. Cryptography may be a useful tool for hiding these kinds of activities. In practice, investigators found that in business crime cases, if cryptography is used, it is generally ready-at-hand systems, such as those in WordPerfect or Lotus. "Encryption in these cases was used mainly to conceal financial, procurement, and other business records. It was generally broken." [Denning 97d]

Apart from crooked businesses, fraudulent employees will also be a target for investigation. Their fraud often concerns deceiving the business itself in order to make money. This usually involves forgery, not secret data to be hidden in double books or to be shielded by cryptography. Occasionally, their computers may contain encrypted diaries or fraud-enabling software. Fraudsters operating on an individual basis or with one associate, a study on VAT fraud concluded, "tended to take no, or less sophisticated measures to protect their operation from exposure." [Aronowitz, 99]

When it comes to communications, the perpetrators of business crime will usually use common means of communication, such as the phone or the company's e-mail system. They often are less prepared for being tapped, and they will not likely use cryptography on the phone – unless this be a common feature of the company's communications policy. E-mail will often be in the clear, unless the company's policy is to regularly encrypt outgoing mail. On intranets, however, such regular encryption is more common.

4.1.3. Computer crime

Computer crime refers to all punishable acts in which the computer plays a significant part (cf. 2.2.2). Thus, hacking is a form of computer crime, as it can not be perpetrated without a computer. Destroying a computer is generally not regarded as computer crime, unless it be a computer that contains the only copy of a nearly finished dissertation – in that case, the fact that it is a computer rather than a ping-pong ball being destroyed *is* significant.

This definition refers to intrinsically computer-related crime. As I treat the problems of (computer-related) cryptography for judicial investigation, I will use a broader definition: computer crime refers to all punishable activities of which the perpetration or investigation requires knowledge of computers. Thus, a fraud committed with a computer – which could equally well have been committed on paper – falls within this broader meaning of computer crime: the police must have knowledge of computers to be able to investigate this fraud.

The main forms of computer crime are: fraud, forgery, computer sabotage, software piracy, and hacking [OECD 86]. A more extensive list, compiled by the Council of Europe [CoE 90], includes:

---

13 For instance, in 1985, a municipal fish market implemented a 'Roundabout System' (*BuitenOm Systeem*) to keep the sales of 'gray' fish out of the regular records [Charbon, 34-35].

- unauthorized access
- unauthorized interception
- unauthorized use of a computer ('joycomputing')
- alteration of or damage to computer data or computer programs
- computer sabotage
- computer espionage
- unauthorized use or reproduction of a protected computer program ('software piracy')
- unauthorized reproduction of a topography ('chips piracy')
- computer forgery
- computer fraud.

The Internet facilitates new forms of bad deeds which do not fall under these headings, such as spamming or unfair competition by abusing HTML metatags.

Computer-related crimes differ from traditional crimes, in that they are generally quickly executable, invisible, automatically and endlessly repeatable, and borderless, and they potentially involve high damages. Thus, computer crime can be at the same time highly profitable and hard to trace, making it alluring for criminals and 'respectable people' alike. Computer crime for a large part takes place in business surroundings, as the main perpetrators of computer crime are regular employees (see 2.2.2).

Apart from computer-related crimes 'proper', a number of traditional offenses are committed with computers, and therefore fall within the scope of the wider definition: they require computer knowledge to investigate them. The main offenses at issue are fraud and 'information crimes': hate crimes (such as calumny or propagating racism) and child pornography. Increasingly, perpetrators of these crimes exploit the potential of computer networks. As with other types of computer crime, they are hard to track down, especially in an international context.

Seriousness

It is difficult to assess the incidence of computer crime. There is a high dark number of unreported and – perhaps – undetected incidents. It is estimated that only a few per cent of all computer-related offenses are reported. The reasons for this obscurity lie mainly in the invisibility of computer crime itself and in the unwillingness of many companies to report computer crime incidents. Enterprises fear loss of respect and customer trust if it is known that their information security is flawed. Besides, they often prefer to handle incidents internally rather than have the police obstruct the continuity of the corporate network by its investigation. Moreover, most companies would be unhappy if the prosecution details the information-security flaws as evidence in a public trial.

Despite the difficulty of estimating the incidence of computer crime, one can say something about its development. Over the past decade, computer crime has risen, and there are various reasons to estimate that it will rise significantly in the near future. As the information society is taking shape, more and more areas of society are being computerized, creating new opportunities for computer crime. Moreover, the present young generation is growing up with computers integrated into their education, upbringing, and leisure activities. They will be familiar with computers to an extent only a small part of present-day society is.[14] If the level of security gaps remains the same (see 2.2.2), a lot more potential malefactors will attack the all-pervasive computer systems.

In a study on the future of high-technology crime, traditional experts (with law-enforcement backgrounds) and non-traditional experts (hackers) were asked about their assessment of future computer crime. "Child pornography, property crimes, data manipulation, and the criminal use of cryptology are some key areas of importance identified by [the traditional experts]. (...) Both groups agree that the focus of new criminal activity will include attacks on computer systems and the use of computers to commit fraud and manipulate data. These activities are likely to come in the form of counterfeiting, financial fraud, and software piracy. Advancements in computer technology itself will assist in the commission of these types of crimes." [Coutorie, 26]

Information behavior and use of cryptography

Most computer criminals have considerable knowledge of modern technologies, and so, they are likely to use cryptography to facilitate or hide their activities. Computer fraud will be hidden in encrypted files, virus makers will use encryption techniques to make their viruses more persistent and obscure – or to encrypt and extort[15], and hackers will store their bounty in encrypted form. For instance, the Danish hacker 'Macronite' encrypted his hard disks just before being arrested; as he refused to surrender the key, the investigation was stuck [Harbou]. Hacker Kevin Poulson used multiple-DES to encrypt files documenting his feats. These were cracked; allegedly, it took a Department of Energy supercomputer several months. In several cases, pedophiles and child pornographers were found to have encrypted e-mail and files; often, the culprits used PGP, likely because they generally are educated, technically advanced, and experienced Internet users. [Denning 97d]

As computer crime is mainly committed by individuals rather than by groups (excepting, perhaps, computer fraud by businesses), communication is less important an issue. Consequently, computer criminals will less likely use cryptography to shield their communications (a notable exception is closed groups of people exchanging child porn electronically). However, they may often use data transport, for instance in hacking, and here they can use cryptography or anonymous remailers to hide their activities. Warez user communities, who share illegally copied or cracked software, often use cryptography to exchange passwords needed for downloading – a journalist investigating the practice encountered a high number of PGP keys, and noticed that almost all warez sites contained cracked crypto software [*Computable*, 10 January 1997].

4.1.4. Other types of serious crime

Other types of serious crime relevant to the crypto problem are serious forms of non-organized, 'traditional' crimes. One can think of terrorism, kidnaping, murder, and armed robbery.

---

14 "Our society is about to feel the impact of the first generation of children who have grown up using computers. The increasing sophistication of hackers suggests that computer crime will soar as members of this new generation are tempted to commit more serious offenses." [Kenneth Rosenblatt, quoted in Coutorie]

15 Cryptoviruses encrypting critical files were used to extort at least nine businesses in London. [Denning 97d]

In these cases, preparation of the crime can involve communication between perpetrators, or storage of data relevant to the crime. Although less likely than with criminal organizations or computer criminals, offenders may use cryptography to hide their activities from investigation, as in the case of Aum Shinrikyo's gas attack on the Tokyo subway.

Petty crimes are not a real issue in the cryptography debate. Usually, investigative powers such as tapping can only be used in serious crimes punishable with several years of imprisonment. Moreover, the police will be less dependent on automated information in investigating petty offenses, as these usually do not involve information transport or storage.

4.2. Investigation

Investigation used to be defined as all examination intended to clear up a presumably committed offense and to prepare the possibility of imposing a related criminal sanction [Corstens, 237]. It includes fact-finding, as well as measures taken to assure that the potential sanction can be executed, such as seizure to confiscate property. In this understanding, investigation can only take place when there is probable cause that a particular offense has been committed.

However, because increasingly, the investigation of particularly organized crime takes place in the context of laying bare networks of criminal groups rather than in the context of specific offenses, a broader definition has been proposed by the Van Traa committee. Investigation is: collecting, registering, and processing data and information

- on the basis of a reasonable presumption that punishable acts will be committed that, given their nature or the organized context in which they are committed, are a serious infringement of the rule of law, or
- on the basis of at least clear indications that punishable acts have been committed

in order to arrive at a criminal sanction. [Traa, 455]

Dutch criminal and criminal-procedure law have been significantly changed to meet developments in the field of crime, particularly of organized crime. Moreover, several organizational measures have changed the outlook of investigation practice, and the stages in which criminal investigation takes place have gradually shifted. This section deals with these developments, to outline the context in which the investigation of organized crime, business crime, and computer crime takes place.

4.2.1. Developments in criminal investigation

Roughly speaking, the developments in criminal investigation come down to increasing attention for the informational and financial behavior of criminal groups, and to a general broadening of investigative powers.

In *criminal law*, three major topics are relevant. First, the 'loot-targeted' approach has been significantly extended in 1993. To attack criminal organizations where it hurts them most (money and fast cars), a convict can be dispossessed of his illegally acquired gains. To enhance the feasibility of executing this sanction, the police can seize property, such as bars of gold or Ferrari's, in anticipation of a court decision. The law, commonly referred to as 'Strip 'em', has yet to prove its value in practice; often, the loot tends to be untraceable.

Second, certain preparatory activities were penalized in 1994: acts in preparation of serious crimes to be committed in conjunction with others. Potentially, the law has a very broad scope. For instance, in theory, a lawyer who corresponds with a notorious drug syndicate leader on tax issues might be accused of activities in preparation of the offense of participating in a criminal organization (art. 140 DCC). The effect is that, especially where organized crime is concerned, investigation can take place in a very early stage, even before the (presumed) criminal organization has committed any offenses.

The third topic is computer crime. In 1993, the Computer Crime Act (CCA) extended the Dutch Criminal Code with several computer-related offenses, the most important being hacking, manipulating or damaging data (including spreading viruses), forging credit cards, and committing fraud with telecommunications services (such as phone freaking). In 1998, a follow-up Computer Crime Act II was proposed, to deal with liability of service providers, unauthorized access of protected e-mail, the power to demand decryption, and some more or less cosmetic improvements of the wording of the CCA provisions.

In the area of *criminal-procedure law*, the police has gradually acquired more powers. Since the introduction of tapping telephone conversations in 1971, the developments in telecommunications have forced the legislature to broaden the scope of this power to the tapping of all telecommunications traffic. The Computer Crime Act, along with the penalization of computer-related offenses, introduced new measures in 1993 to enable the police to investigate computer crime (referred to as investigating in 'automated surroundings') (see 4.3 and 4.4). The draft Computer Crime Act II revises the wiretap conditions and introduces some guidelines for Internet investigation, notably to allow pseudo-purchases via the Internet of data (read: child porn).

Recognizing that ICT will be an essential part of everyday life in the information society, the Policy Advisory Group on Computer Crime has proposed that *digital investigation* (investigating punishable acts committed with the help of any kind of ICT) be incorporated into everyday police work. Its June 1996 report [Beleidsadviesgroep] recommends that the ICT knowledge of the basic police staff be enhanced through education, so that they will know how to act when they encounter ICT in the course of an investigation. They should be supported by the more specialist investigation knowledge of the computer-crime teams. International cooperation and the development of the Internet are among the urgent issues to be addressed.

The stress on investigating the financial behavior of suspects has led to the introduction of a specific type of investigation: the *criminal financial inquest*, aimed at determining the illegally acquired gains. Such an inquest will help the judge 'strip' the suspect. Moreover, banks and exchange offices are obliged to notify the police of large and unusual financial transactions. Increasingly, financial investigation is seen as an outstanding means for investigating organized crime.[16] One can assume that financial investigation and digital investigation will be major tools for future criminal investigation.

---

16 "Financial investigation is an entire way of working. From all activities within a criminal organization, you bring out all activities in the financial field. You look via those financial lines, who actually belongs to the criminal group. In practice, it appears you get a good overview indeed of who is really involved." [G.J.C.M. Bakker, team leader customs investigation FIID, quoted in Traa, 280]

Another development has been a gradual broadening of the scope of investigational powers, not through legislation but through case law. Consequently, procedural safeguards for suspects have been somewhat reduced – what safeguards were introduced are mainly due to European Court case law. For instance, whereas evidence resulting from an unlawful tap can not be used in court, the Supreme Court has allowed such evidence to be used in a trial against a different suspect who only later had become known. [HR 14 April 1987]

As the courts perhaps slowly slacked the restrictions on coercive powers, the police perhaps did more than was technically allowed, arguing: "What is not explicitly forbidden is allowed." New methods of investigation – unregulated in the Code of Criminal Procedure – were put into practice, such as 'peeping operations' (breaking into sheds and garages to see whether an official search might be useful), the placing of direction transmitters, infiltration, and 'controlled delivery' of drugs. Eventually, there were so many signs that some police teams were operating on the verge of illegality, that a major parliamentary inquest was held into criminal investigation by the Van Traa committee.

IRT-gate

It was a voyage of discovery, prosecutor Van der Veen felt, like Columbus. Bruinsma and, after his liquidation in 1991, his three ('Delta') heirs were top criminals that escaped traditional crime-fighting methods. To knock-out the number one criminal organization of the Netherlands, new ways of investigation had to be explored. So, the InterRegional Team (IRT) of North Holland and Utrecht introduced the 'Delta method': delivering soft drugs under the secret direction of the police. Thus, an informer facilitating these shipments could grow into a civil infiltrator and gradually climb higher in the criminal organization, as he gained the confidence of Bruinsma and his heirs that he was a trustworthy criminal.

By September 1993, the police considered directing the marketing of a trial shipment of 100 kilograms of cocaine, in order to provoke a megashipment of 5000 kilos of cocaine. Then, the police would strike, and catch the Delta bosses. It never came to that. The supervision of the IRT had been transferred to the Amsterdam authorities in July 1993. In September, Van Kastel became the new IRT leader, and by the end of October, he discovered that the IRT was involved in the innovative Delta method of controlled drug delivery, for which he did not want to bear responsibility.

From then on, things went fast. Van Kastel discussed the affair with the relevant Amsterdam authorities, who informed the responsible ministers, and they decided to stop the Delta method. A press release of 7 December 1993 announced that the IRT had been dissolved, apparently because the Amsterdam authorities considered it the only way to stop the method from continuing. Many who had worked hard to set up the IRT cried out loud, arguing in public that other causes (corruption?) must have been the real reason for the dissolution of the IRT. A controversy was born. Feuds ensued between the Amsterdam crime fighters and their interregional colleagues (or competitors), between proponents and opponents of the Delta method, and between prosecutors and lawyers who eagerly took advantage of the increasingly available amount of information on illegal investigation practices. The police had 'directed' at least 100 tons of soft drugs to be marketed, and besides, several secret and unsupervised investigation methods came to light, such as 'peeping operations' that explored the usefulness of an official search or that placed cameras and direction transmitters. The supervision of these measures turned out to be seriously flawed (perhaps partly because some policemen would go 'prosecutor-shopping' to find a prosecutor who would give them the freedom they desired). People spoke of a breakdown of investigation authority. The press eagerly published all sordid details of the affair, and it became apparent that something was really rotten in investigation practice at large.

By the end of 1994, a parliamentary inquest chaired by Maarten van Traa had to set things straight. Its task was to find out what had really happened, and to suggest adequate regulations for investigation methods and for effective supervision to keep investigation within its proper limits. The Van Traa committee did a thorough job and in early 1996 published its ten-volume report *Regarding investigation*. Their golden rule 'No power without responsibility, and no responsibility without giving account' prompted new legislation that would precisely define the contents and limits of investigation powers.

Meanwhile, long after the dissolution of the IRT, the Delta method lived on in North Holland and Utrecht. After all, one could not risk stopping the activities of the infiltrator all of a sudden – he had to be 'reduced' slowly...

[Source: 24072, nr 14, Chapter 7]

The Van Traa report concluded that in several ways, criminal investigation had gotten out of hand. The 'crisis in investigation' was to be addressed by a thorough rethinking and reordering of investigation, with legislation detailing which powers can be used in which circumstances. The recommendations and parliamentary discussions were followed by a reshuffling of police officials, clearer controls on investigation practices, and legislature proposals regulating investigation powers, in which a balance was sought to define investigation powers in enough detail to be clear without becoming a straight-jacket. The draft legislation targeted special investigation powers, police registries, and pledges to criminal witnesses.

Draft legislation

As of 1 July 1998, the Dutch legislature is considering several legislation proposals in criminal procedure law. The following are relevant to the crypto debate.

Special investigation powers
Resulting from the IRT-gate debate, the draft law on special investigation powers [25403, nrs 1-2] is a major proposal to redefine investigation powers and to introduce several new ones. It aims at laying down strict conditions under which the investigation powers can be used, and to check their use in practice by sufficient supervision measures. With the introduction of a new 'suspicion criterion' – the reasonable presumption that someone is involved in the scheming or committing of organized crimes – it extends the scope of investigation (which, so far, targets only specific crimes that have been committed) with cases that center on organized crime in general. Moreover, some of the investigation measures (such as infiltration and pseudo-purchase) can also be performed by civilians. The investigation measures dealt with in the draft are: observation, infiltration, pseudo-purchase and pseudo-provision of services, systematic information retrieval, 'recording' a private place (largely, a 'peeping operation'), 'direct eavesdropping', wiretapping, and gathering telecom traffic data. Having been introduced in June 1997, the proposal still awaited discussion in the Second Chamber as of July 1998.

Crown witnesses
Another result of IRT-gate is a draft law to regulate 'pledges to witnesses in criminal cases', which would allow the Public Prosecutor to bargain with criminals and give them some judiciary reward in return for their testimony in a serious case against another criminal. This crown-witness legislation was drafted in 1997 and sent to the Council of State for advice after approval by the Council of Ministers in April 1998. It is to be submitted to parliament by the end of 1998.

Telecommunications Act
To meet the effects of the liberalization of the telecommunications market, the Telecommunications Facilities Act is to be replaced by a Telecommunications Act [25533, nr 309]. It aims at strengthening the Netherlands' competitiveness, safeguarding the quality and accessibility of the telecom infrastructure, and protecting the public interests in accessing and using telecom facilities. Thus, it includes, for instance, provisions on liability, universal service, number policy, interconnection, and privacy. Also, it requires telecom providers to ensure that their networks and services are tappable from the start. Having been approved by the Second Chamber in April 1998, the proposal was scheduled to be approved by the First Chamber in late 1998.

Computer crime II
In some respects, the 1993 Computer Crime Act (CCA) is felt to be inadequate to deal with computer crime. An update law is being drafted, the Computer Crime Act II, which contains four major items: the liability of telecommunication providers, the power to read 'closed' electronic messages stored with a telecom provider for later distribution, the power to seize and confiscate data, and an extension of the power to demand people to decrypt. (Initially, the draft contained a provision to demand suspects to decrypt as well, but this was removed after protests from the legal community.) Besides, several textual improvements of the CCA provisions are proposed, and the terminology is adapted to the liberalization of the telecom market. The January 1998 draft had not been submitted to parliament by July 1998.

4.2.2. The organization of criminal investigation

In the Netherlands, the people involved in criminal investigation fall into three categories: the police,[17] the public prosecutor, and the examining judge. Roughly, the public prosecutor leads the investigation process, while the police executes the investigation. In case of an inquest, the examining judge takes over the leadership of the investigation, in consultation with the public prosecutor.

The police, after a recent reorganization, operate in 25 regional forces and one national force, the National Police Services Force. The regional forces have the tasks of maintaining public order and giving help to the needful (under supervision of the regional mayors) and maintaining the rule of law (under supervision of the public prosecutor). In this last capacity, they investigate crimes.

The National Police Services Force consists of a great number of specific services. It includes the Central Criminal Intelligence Agency, which coordinates national and international investigation, and the Payment Traffic Detective Service, which coordinates and executes investigations into money and securities-traffic offenses.

With a view to combating organized crime, six special interregional teams (IRTs) were established in the early 1990s. They were each to investigate a special type of organized crime, such as heroin trade from Turkey or the production of synthetic drugs. Due to IRT-gate (see sidebar) and a lack of clarity regarding their position, their work has not yet fully budded.[18] One national team with a similar task, the National Detective Team has been formed.

Similarly, in 1991, special teams were formed to investigate computer crime. The Computer Crime Teams conduct specific investigations and collect and analyze information on computer crime. They assist police teams with activities involving computers, such as searching a company with a large automated system, and examining seized computers. Their work is supplemented by the forensic computer-investigation division of the Forensic Laboratory, which aids in examining, among others, pagers, computers, computer files, and smart cards.

A number of specialist investigation services and teams perform additional investigative tasks. The most important ones are the Economic Surveillance Department, which investigates economic crimes such as illegal imports or stock-trade fraud, and the Fiscal Intelligence and Investigation Department, which investigates (serious) tax-fraud cases.

---

17 More precisely, law-enforcement agencies, such as police detective teams and special investigation services. I shall often refer to this collectivity as 'the police', using the common notion of police as 'crime fighters'.

18 Since IRT-gate, the teams are usually referred to as 'core teams', to not associate them with the past excesses of certain IRTs.

The special investigation services generally have a restricted task and limited powers in investigating crime. On the other hand, they have inspection competence. Thus, regardless of a suspicion of criminal activity, they can wield certain powers to check whether pertaining regulations are being complied with.

Of the other two parties in criminal investigation, the public prosecutor is closest to the police, leading the investigation. He decides to start an investigation, to start an inquest to be able to execute certain coercive powers, to close an investigation, and whether or not to start a prosecution. Once an inquest is opened, the supervision is referred to the examining judge, who can order coercive powers to be performed. In general, the execution of coercive powers, such as search, seizure, and phone tapping, lies with the examining judge, the public prosecutor, or police agents, depending on the gravity of the corresponding infringement of constitutional rights (the graver the breach, the higher the official needed to perform it), and on the urgency involved to perform the measure - in certain cases, lower officials can execute the coercive power if there is no time to wait for the higher official.

4.2.3. The stages of criminal investigation

The investigation process consists of several stages. The 'pro-active' stage is the stage when there is no indication yet that an offense has taken place. Once there is probable cause that a (specific) crime has been committed, the stage of investigation proper starts.[19] When the public prosecutor wants to exercise certain powers, he can demand the examining judge to open an inquest. As soon as enough evidence has been gathered, the inquest is closed and a prosecution against the suspect is started. In this prosecution, the evidence gathered during the investigation is presented in court and examined by the judge.

The 'pro-active' stage was regularly not counted as belonging to investigation, but changes in the field have made it a significant part of investigating organized crime, where the focus of the investigation is on the criminal group rather than on a specific crime already committed, and where the investigation may also target the planning of crimes. The draft law on special investigation powers provides a basis to perform coercive powers when there is not a concrete suspicion of a specific crime. (Formerly, this was generally not possible,[20] as coercive powers require a warrant which can only be given in the stage of investigation proper or during an inquest.) The law does not speak of the 'pro-active stage', but refers to another 'suspicion criterion': investigation can also take place when there is a suspicion that serious crimes are being schemed or committed in an organized context (this is limited to crimes for which pre-trial detention is allowed or which form a serious breach of the rule of law) (proposed art. 132a DCCP).

During the inquest, grave coercive powers can be used, but the (impartial) judge allows

---

19 One should bear in mind, though, that in practice, "in the investigation of organized crime, a distinction can hardly be made between investigation of offenses already committed and the investigation focused on laying bare criminal networks." [23047, nr 6, 4]

20 The inspection powers of special investigation services can be used to gather information in this stage, but these powers may not be used primarily for investigation's sake (which would be *détournement de pouvoir*, that is, abuse of power). If the special services find evidence of crimes while inspecting a case, they can proceed to investigate this (which, as continued application of their inspection power, is not *détournement*).

them only if they are necessary for the investigation, taking into account the rights of the suspect and others whose constitutional rights may be infringed by the measures. Sometimes, the rights of the suspect can hamper the investigation. For example, a suspect's right to know that an investigation is taking place will render a telephone tap useless. A major revision has taken place of the inquest stage, in order to better anticipate such practical and legal problems. The drift of the change is to limit the inquest to investigation powers which directly require the personal involvement of the examining judge.[21]

At the trial, the information gathered during the investigation may serve as evidence. The only admissible sources of evidence are the observation of the judge during trial, statements of the suspect, of witnesses, and of experts during trial, and (written) records. The judge will use the evidence according to his personal conviction: he has a discretionary power to use evidence as he sees fit (as long as he complies with the minimum rules of evidence). According to the exclusionary rule, 'contaminated' evidence (resulting, for instance, from improper or unlawful investigation activities) will be laid aside. Sometimes, if the improper activities of the police have seriously breached the rights of the defendant, the judge can rule the public prosecutor to be dismissed in his prosecution. Also, the judge will need to be convinced of the truth and reliability of the evidence, and so, the police must act systematically and carefully when gathering evidence, following guidelines and accounting their acts. Particularly with computer-related evidence, special care must be taken to assure its integrity and authenticity.

4.3. Gathering data in transport

In the process of investigation, the police sometimes need to violate people's rights. For instance, in investigating the scene of a crime, they have to trespass into someone's home. Because of their gravity, infringements of constitutional rights require an explicit legal basis, and they have to be as restricted as possible. The ways in which the police can breach fundamental people's rights are called coercive powers. These can only be introduced through an Act of Parliament: the constitution requires that infringements of fundamental rights by law-enforcement agencies can only take place if they are embodied in national laws and if they are necessary in a democratic society for the sake of, among others, national security or the prevention of offenses.[22]

The coercive powers that involve ICT-related information retrieval can be divided into powers that gather data in transport (4.3) and those that gather stored data (4.4). Gathering data in transport concerns retrieving the data *themselves*: tapping (4.3.1-4.3.2) and gathering information *about* the data: traffic analysis (4.3.3).

---

21 In the early 1990s, the Moons Committee proposed several changes in the rules governing the inquest. Some of these are being implemented in the draft law on the revision of the inquest [23251].

22 The European Court of Human Rights requires infringements of fundamental rights to be established by 'substantive' law, which may be an Act of Parliament or settled case law [*Kruslin, Huvig*].

4.3.1. Tapping

Telephone tapping is eavesdropping (monitoring or recording) public telecommunications as part of criminal proceedings or as part of national security [24679, nr 1, 4], or, broader, "clandestine interference with the telephone system in order to intercept a conversation." [CoE 82, 5]

The power to tap phones was introduced in 1971, because "in the preparation and execution of the operations of criminal gangs, the telephone plays an important part." [Lensing, 1011] Since then, it has become an increasingly popular means of gathering information, especially in the investigation of organized crime. It is not used so much as to gather evidence, but rather to get a clear view of the criminal organization concerned, so that the police can better and sooner intervene. Apparently, tapping is particularly useful where first offenders are concerned, or people in the periphery of a criminal organization, as they usually do not reckon with the possibility of being tapped [Reijne, 35-36].[23] Even with criminals aware of the danger of being tapped, the police will gain information on contacts and appointments.

Often, real-time interception is crucial, to prevent crimes or to act quickly on intercepted plans – notably to follow suspects or to intercept deliveries on the spot, and so to gain evidence. "Law enforcement agencies require a real-time, fulltime monitoring capability for the interception of telecommunications." [96/C329/01] [24]

Despite the costs, which can be prohibitive, the use of telephone taps has increased significantly over the past decades. The reasons for this are the rise in attention paid to organized crime, the apparent success in quickly gaining information on criminal organizations, the high density of phones, and an easing of judges' willingness to give allowance.[25] Whereas in 1986, 1,088 taps were executed, by 1994, the number of taps had risen to 3,284 [Reijne, 19].[26] One should realize that one allowance of tapping may involve several connections being monitored, often for a longer period. Thus, one tap warrant can lead to over 80,000 conversations being heard.[27]

Conditions

The legal conditions for applying a tap are as follows. The investigation must urgently require a tap (a consequence of art. 8 para. 2 ECHR). The case must involve a crime for which pre-trial detention is allowed (usually, an offense punishable with at least four years

23 Another example of the use of a tap is the case of the 'Exportteam', where the phone of a civil infiltrator was tapped to see whether the information he gave was correct. [Traa, 272] Sometimes, to enhance the effectiveness of a tap, the police apparently consider leaking 'disinformation' to the press, to provoke suspects into discussing the 'news'. [Traa, 287]

24 Likewise, the Walsh report concludes that "the availability of real-time decrypted communications is central to the investigative capability of law enforcement agencies" [Walsh, 1.1.9].

25 From interviews with four examining judges, it appeared that: "There is a clear increase. (...) The boundaries have shifted. (...) All in all, these things lead in certain views to a quicker application of [tapping]." [Breuil, 47-48]

26 The figures are inaccurate due to incomplete reports by the courts and, perhaps, differing definitions of what constitutes 'a tap'.

27 In the Laundry case, which involved both the tapping of normal and car phones and of facsimile machines, 88,424 conversations were heard. [Traa, 226]

of imprisonment).[28] The draft law on special investigation powers contains a revision of the tapping provisions. It includes a new power to tap in the not-so-called 'pro-active' stage, that is, when there is a suspicion that serious, organized crimes are being schemed (see 4.2.3).

Another condition is that there is a reasonable expectation that the suspect will participate in the conversation. Thus, not only suspects' phones can be tapped, but also, for instance, relatives' phones. This condition is somewhat peculiar, as in practice a large number of taps are so-called 'NN taps', being part of an inquest in which the suspect is not yet (formally) known. This allows a broader tapping of phones, since there is no suspect expected to talk over specific phones. In practice, NN taps can continue long past the moment at which the suspect really becomes known to facilitate this broader tapping, making the condition that the suspect should likely participate in the tapped conversations a parody rather than a safeguard. Moreover, it is sometimes useful to continue a tap even when the suspect has been taken into custody, and conversations from third parties (such as relatives) can also be important for ascertaining the truth. Therefore, the draft law on special investigation powers suggests dropping the condition.

If one of the participants to a conversation is someone who has a professional right of non-disclosure (mainly, lawyers, notaries, doctors, and clergy), the police can not monitor or record it (unless the professional himself is suspected).

Only the 'public infrastructure' may be tapped (home connections as well as mobile phones). Private networks (for example, a corporate or campus phone network) are beyond scrutiny. However, the forthcoming Telecommunications Act allows non-public networks and rented lines which are open to third parties to be tapped by decree; thus, intranets - say, a worldwide network of a multinational, consisting of rented lines - can be tapped. Wiretaps may also include in-house conversations overheard if the receiver has not been put down well [HR 21 March 1989].[29] Radio communications can readily be intercepted if this does not involve a 'special effort' on the part of the police. For intercepting radio communications that does involve a 'special effort', such as the use of advanced devices, or systematic and sustained interception, a warrant is required.

There is not a specific formal term for which the tap allowance can be given. Guidelines recommend a term of four weeks, to be extended each time with four weeks. The draft law on special investigation powers formalizes this term - one of the consequences of the *Kruslin* and *Huvig* verdicts of the European Court, in which the court judged that tapping must be "based on a 'law' that is particularly precise. It is essential to have clear, detailed

---

28 Tapping can not be used in the case of simple hacking, as traffic analysis will suffice (see below). In the case of 'onward hacking' (from one hacked site to another), the source from which the hack is perpetrated can not be recovered from traffic analysis, but this offense has been penalized with four years in order to allow content tapping.

29 Technically, the police could also listen in on conversations within a house even if the receiver is *on* the hook. By blowing up the capacitor of the phone with an electric surge over the phone line, the phone is automatically taken 'off hook'. This is still possible with many phones. Consequently, the police can claim that the in-house conversations thus recorded took place while the receiver was off the hook, and, referring to this court decision, use the recordings as evidence. According to Statewatch, the new UK telephone ISDN network uses a protocol with a built-in facility to take a phone 'off hook' and listen to conversations near the phone without the user being aware [*Statewatch bulletin*, March-April 1995].

The effectiveness of tapping

A 1996 study by the WODC (an academic, advisory center to the Ministry of Justice) investigated the practice and efficacy of tapping in the Netherlands. The study showed the following results on the effectiveness of tapping [Reijne, 35-44].

The goals of tapping – gathering evidence, tracking perpetrators, and uncovering criminal networks – are achieved in one half of the cases. Examining judges were of the opinion that in 70 per cent of the cases, the same results could absolutely not have been reached without a tap. Indeed, many interviewees indicated sometimes not to know how to fight organized crime without tapping. Examining judges particularly value tapping in cases of drugs, theft, and fraud.

With criminal organizations, tapping yields useful information on networks and financial gains. As the persons tend to be more wary of speaking overtly (considering the frequent use of codes), tapping does not often provide direct evidence. With business crime, however, evidence often results directly from facsimile tapping. On the other hand, some interviewees think tapping does not offer much for investigating business crime. With individual crimes, especially serious offenses against people, tapping generally provides direct evidence. Computer crime is not mentioned in the study. The study found that in 41 out of 91 cases, the tap did not yield any evidence. In 21 cases, the tap furnished direct evidence, in 15 cases, indirect evidence, and in 14 cases both.

One caveat in evaluating the effectiveness of tapping is the influence of interpreters, some of whom are considered unreliable; many interpreters select conversations without fully knowing the particulars of the case under investigation. It is also worth noting that the costs for interpreters have risen sharply, and now exceed the costs for tapping and printing [Reijne, 71].

The ultimate evaluation shows that two thirds of the interviewees consider tapping a reasonably to extremely effective means of investigation. Some, however, think the expectations of tapping too high, and consider tapping to often cost more than it yields.

A comparative study on wiretapping in Germany and the US is one of the few studies with figures on effectiveness in other countries [Böttger]. Based on the US wiretap reports of 1987-1989, the study found that in 95 per cent of the cases in which wiretaps were employed, incriminating conversations were recorded. Arrests were made in 47 per cent of the cases, whereas in 33 per cent of the cases, someone was convicted. In the cases in which at least one person was convicted, on average, another 8 to 15 persons were convicted as well, which the authors perceive as an indication that wiretaps are indeed efficacious in laying bare structures of criminal organizations. The figures suggest that wiretaps are less productive in yielding decisive evidence, since the incriminating conversations have not led to arrests or convictions in many cases. Or perhaps there are long-term effects the study could not incorporate. According to the 1997 yearly report of the Administrative Office of the US Courts, 20 per cent of all conversations intercepted in 1997 produced incriminating evidence (it does not say in which percentage of cases), leading to the arrest of 3,086 persons and the conviction of 542 persons, a conviction rate of 18 per cent of all persons arrested. The cumulative figures show that in 1997, the wiretaps completed in previous years led to 1,762 more arrests and to 2,352 more convictions. The number of convictions resulting from the 1988 intercepts, for example, increased from 543 in 1988 to 1,192 in 1989, and then decreased through 400 in 1990 to 57 in 1993 and 11 in 1996. [OA] The effects of wiretaps may therefore be slow but sure.

rules on the subject, especially as the technology available for use is continually becoming more sophisticated."

Legal problems

One of the main legal problems with tapping is the requirement to notify a suspect that a criminal investigation is taking place against him. Naturally, once a suspect has been notified, the tap is useless. For this reason, the notification is usually postponed until the latest possible moment, just before the inquest is closed and when an indictment is near. The judges allow this postponement with a view to the efficacy of tapping. This point might also be an argument for public prosecutors to open an NN tap, even if they have enough reason to suspect someone in particular. The contradiction between the requirement of internal openness (the right of the defendant to know the activities of the prosecution) and the requirement of effective investigation has led the draft law on special investigation powers to disconnect the telephone tap from the inquest. Tapping would also become possible in investigating the 'scheming of crimes'.

A related problem is the current requirement to destroy information and material that are no longer relevant to the investigation. Although intended to protect the suspect's privacy, the obligation leads to a situation in which the defendant can not check whether conversations have been transcribed (or translated) correctly, and he has no opportunity of demanding disculpatory information to be added to the file. Therefore, the draft law on special investigation powers requires the prosecutor to keep the original recordings until two months after the case has ended.

Technical problems

The rapid developments in the communications infrastructure are posing major challenges to the technical feasibility of wiretapping, through the introduction both of new networks and of new services.

New networks usually have different technologies, and so, tappability is not self-evident. For instance, ISDN seems difficult to tap. More importantly, the police has difficulty in tapping certain mobile phones. Although analogue car phones can be intercepted by scanning the spectrum,[30] with the advent of digital and satellite communications, tapping has become increasingly difficult. For instance, GSM uses encryption for the air interface, making scanning useless. Therefore, tapping GSM happens at the terrestrial infrastructure, which initially required considerable effort.[31] Now, GSM and other digital mobile telephony, such as DCS-1800, are being tapped regularly. Satellite-based mobile phones are currently out of tapping's reach.[32] The EU is working on a treaty to ensure interception capabilities of mobile satellite communications.

Still more problematic is tapping electronic messages. The main problem is the packet switching technology. As the messages are divided by, e.g., the TCP/IP protocol into many small packets, which are all routed over the network depending on the availability of capacity, it is virtually impossible to intercept all parts of a specific message along the way, unless the tap is placed close to the house connection of the sender or recipient. "This technology makes tapping complicated." [Dijk]

Like new networks, *new services* often rely on new technologies. Sometimes, these do not pose technical problems. Facsimile machines can be easily tapped, and this happens

30 This requires a judicial warrant, as scanning the spectrum and selecting the conversations of targeted suspects involves a special effort. In the case of Henk R. (see 4.1.1), the police listened in on Henk's car phones with mobile scanners; they had a warrant to eavesdrop for four weeks on all car phone conversations in which he participated. [Traa, 198] Pagers can be intercepted through scanning, like analogue mobile phones. Strangely enough, the Amsterdam court has considered the scanning of pagers to involve no special effort, so it would not require a court warrant. [Rb. Amsterdam, *A.D.*]

31 "GSM differs thus fundamentally in complexity from other services, and is estimated to be relatively difficult to monitor." [Nielsen, 37] According to the *Tapping GSM* regulation, GSM should have been tappable in the Netherlands by 1 January 1996 [24108, nr 5, 3], which was rather optimistic.

32 Satellite-based mobile digital telephones are "presenting prosecuting authorities throughout Europe with a problem. (..) [These are] seeking European co-operation in setting up a system to monitor international telephone calls made on this type of mobile phone." [Nash]

regularly.[33] For example, in the Tanker Cleaning Rotterdam case, phones and company facsimile machines were tapped for six weeks [Traa, 204].[34] Other services, however, make tapping more difficult, for instance because it is harder to find the right point to tap. Thus, a recent problem with intercepting mobile communications is the use of prepaid cards, which can prevent customer identification; this is one of the main problems today for tracing the user of a mobile phone.[35] Also, the *21 switch-based call-forwarding service has made wiretapping as such more difficult.[36] Likewise, calling houses which offer cheaper phone calls through international lines give criminals yet another opportunity of using more or less anonymous phones. The advent of Internet telephony adds considerably to the difficulty of tapping phones, because criminals can use this technology which, for the time being, is hard to tap. And the rise of mobile data terminals may make these things worse yet for the police.

A more general problem is the increasing variety of protocols and formats. Whereas formerly, only analogue conversations were transmitted over telephone lines, nowadays a telephone tap can also record digital signals. So, the police must first distinguish the communication protocol used, and subsequently identify the format in which the contents are transmitted (is it compressed digitized speech, a compressed image or video file, or perhaps a MIME-encoded WordStar text file?).

Finally, a technical problem is knowing which numbers to tap. With the liberalization of the telecoms market and the enormous growth in applications and services, people can have several telecommunication subscriptions with different providers (say, Internet access through XS4ALL over an ISDN line belonging to Telfort, a Libertel subscription for the telephone that uses the old telephone line belonging to KPN, and a mobile phone from Dutchtone). Thus, it is increasingly difficult to quickly have access to the subscriber information necessary to know where to tap. To address this, the government proposes to set up an information center which will collect the required data. [25533, nr 5, 133]

Maintaining tappability

With the implementation of the Computer Crime Act in 1993, all kinds of telecommunications can *legally* be tapped, including facsimile messages, electronic data transfers, mobile phones, and satellite communications. The *technical* feasibility of tapping all forms of telecommunications, however, is still dubious. Thus, as US FBI director Freeh stated: "Merely maintaining without expanding the ability of law enforcement to conduct court-ordered wiretaps is the single most important problem law enforcement faces today." [Freeh 95c]

---

33 Before 1993, the tap competence included only telephone *conversations* [HR 26 May 1992], and so, facsimile messages or data messages were not allowed to be tapped.

34 The fact that facsimile machines are regularly being tapped in China became apparent when a New Zealand tourist was expelled from the Tibet Autonomous Region. The Chinese authorities accused him of trying to subvert the government and split the country, because he had sent a facsimile message from the Lhasa Holiday Inn, in which he had mentioned having heard a bomb explode near his hotel. [TIN]

35 The government seems to hope that this may be redressed by technical solutions [25533, nr 8, 10-12], but this does not seem quite feasible. Registering the people that buy prepaid cards may ensure traceability, but this poses a significant privacy threat.

36 "With the currently available tap facilities, the judiciary can not listen in on conversations held through *21." [Dijk]

The authorities worry that this valuable investigation method is becoming powerless, and they want to assure its continued efficacy in the future. Thus, the Dutch government requires telecom providers through article 64a TFA to take the necessary technical measures to assure that their infrastructure is tappable. The cost for tappability is theirs, while tapping is paid by the judiciary. The main action line of the government is to oblige all telecom operators to make sure their systems are fit for judicial taps from the start: "All public telecommunications networks and services (..) should be tappable from the moment of their introduction." [24679, nr 1, repeated in 25533, nr 3, 43] The draft Telecommunications Act, which is to replace the TFA shortly, incorporates this in article 13. In fact, it is internationally a common requirement: the EU and the US both require telecom providers to ensure tappability of all forms of telecommunications.[37]

The government may ardently wish to maintain tapping capability, but at the moment, tappability is far from being the case when it comes to mobile phones and electronic data transfers. It will likely take several years before the police can tap all mobile phones, Internet telephony, and e-mail. The authorities are aware that – even with the guideline of mandatory tappability – the potential for intercepting telecommunications may decrease, and they are looking for alternatives, such as direct eavesdropping.[38]

4.3.2. Tapping in other countries

Although regulations and practices differ, almost all countries allow judicial taps. In the European Union, all countries have a legal regulation for law-enforcement tapping – Belgium was the last to introduce legislation, in 1991 (see [CoE 82] and [Huybrechts]). Moreover, like the 1995 EU Council resolution, the 1995 Council of Europe *Recommendation Concerning Problems of Criminal Procedure Law Connected with Information Technology* recommends states to impose obligations on network operators to "avail themselves of all necessary technical measures that enable the interception of telecommunications by the investigating authorities." [CoE 95]

In *Germany*, the wiretap regulations have recently been adapted. The 1996 Telecommunications Act requires network providers to ensure technical tappability (paying the costs themselves), and to provide yearly tapping statistics to the regulation authority. The Accompanying Law to the Telecommunications Act of December 1997 covers the personnel consequences of liberalization and aims at ensuring future tappability by requiring all employees of telecom providers to cooperate in tapping. The Accompanying Law would also extend this cooperation requirement to operators of corporate networks [Wuermeling]. The number of taps has risen from 1,805 in 1987 to 3,499 in 1992 and 3,667 in 1995. [*CR* 1996 nr 4, 256] There was a sharp increase in 1996, with 6,428 telephone connections and 1,911

---

37 The EU Council Resolution of 17 January 1995 calls "upon the Ministers responsible for telecommunications (...) to cooperate with the Ministers responsible for Justice and Home Affairs with the aim of implementing the Requirements in relation to network operators and service providers." The first requirement reads: "Law enforcement agencies require access to the entire telecommunications transmitted, or caused to be transmitted, to and from the number or other identifier of the target service used by the interception subject." [96/C329/01] For the United States, see 4.3.2.

38 "The present competence proposed [direct eavesdropping] can to a certain extent replace the decreasing possibilities to intercept telecommunications." [23047, nr 3, 2-3] See further 9.1.

Echelon

Even before the body of former Iranian prime minister Shahpour Bakhtiar had been found in Paris, his murderers were stopped by Swiss customs. On 7 August 1991, a day before the body was found, Teheran sent an (encrypted) message to its diplomatic missions in London, Paris, Bonn, and Geneva asking "Is Bakhtiar dead?" Then, French authorities monitored all communications from public phone booths on the Paris-Geneva highway, and intercepted a call from the perpetrators to the Iranian diplomatic mission in Geneva, essentially solving the murder before its discovery.

The interception of the Iranian communications was part of a US-led global surveillance system that has been operated since at least the early 1980s. Designed by the US National Security Agency, the ECHELON system regularly intercepts e-mail, fax, telex, and telephone communications around the world. The countries of the UKUSA signals intelligence agreement – the US, the UK, Canada, Australia, and New Zealand – operate an extensive network of stations that intercept the communications carried by Intelsat and other satellites, as well as those transported over land-based microwave networks. The intelligence agencies of the countries each scan the intercepts for key words, organized in a wide range of categories, that include names, addresses, and places of interests. (Although it may not yet be feasible to thus scan all spoken messages, high-volume voice-recognition technology may soon be capable of processing most telephone conversations as efficiently as written messages can be scanned nowadays.) Subsequently, with 'intelligent' agents based on statistical methods and neural networks, key words and their combinations are looked for to select the most interesting messages. These are forwarded to the headquarters, where specialists read them and act accordingly.

Despite earlier publications – as early as 1988, Duncan Campbell reported on ECHELON in the *New Statesman* – ECHELON only gained publicity in 1996 with the publication of extensive details by Nicky Hager, who had interviewed many New Zealand intelligence staff members. With the publication of a European Parliament document in early 1998, in which Hager's findings were repeated (along with a frightening number of other surveillance and control technologies), the global surveillance system seemed to receive wider attention by the institutions that safeguard democracy. So far, however, UKUSA governments seem to simply and happily continue global monitoring.

Although since the end of the Cold War, the global surveillance systems have often been justified by the need to fight terrorism and to facilitate economic intelligence, according to Nicky Hager, "by far, the main priorities of the intelligence alliance continue to be political and military intelligence to assist the larger allies to pursue their interests around the world. Anyone and anything the particular governments are concerned about can become a target." Thus, for instance, GCHQ, the UK intelligence agency, intercepted the communications of Amnesty International and Christian Aid.

Incidentally, one might expect ECHELON to suffer from large-scale encryption by governments, who in diplomacy and state secrets after all are well-known users of robust cryptography. Of course, the NSA had reckoned with that. A report by Wayne Madsen of 1998 revealed that for decades, the US government had routinely decrypted top-secret messages of 120 countries through a secret agreement with Swiss crypto producer Crypto AG. Their machines had been manipulated so that the secret key would be automatically and clandestinely transmitted with each message. The Iranian authorities, after the Bakhtiar killing, felt that their encryption scheme had been cracked, and they arrested Hans Buehler, Crypto AG's marketing representative in Teheran. He was questioned for five hours a day for nine months, but he apparently did not know the equipment was bugged. In 1994, two Iranians were convicted for Bakhtiar's murder, but the third, Zeynold Abedine Sarhadi, was acquitted. Madsen suggests one of the reasons may have been a tacit agreement to spare Sarhadi in order to avoid having to use the intercepted and decrypted communications as evidence.

[Sources: Hager, Madsen, Wright 98]

mobile phone connections being tapped [DB].

In the *United Kingdom*, the power to tap evolved from the 17th-century power of government officials to intercept and open mail [Kahn, 172]. It was given an explicit basis only in 1985, with the Interception of Communications Act 1985 defining the conditions for law-enforcement, intelligence, and security wiretapping. Although it authorizes interception by warrant, it does not allow use of direct wiretap evidence in a criminal prosecution [LAB]. Still, during 1996 and 1997, "interception of communications played a part – often the crucial part – in operations by police and HM Customs which led to 1,200 arrests" [Roche]. The wiretap figures (for Great Britain) have risen from 522 in 1989 to 1,047 in 1994

[Statewatch]; in 1997, there were 1,647 wiretaps [EPIC Alert 5.11].

In the *United States*, tapping is regarded as essential by law-enforcement agencies, but it is controversial with civil-liberties organizations. Part of the crypto debate has centered on the ability to tap at all rather than on regulating cryptography to maintain wiretappability. A Supreme Court decision (*Katz* v. *United States*) in 1967 that wiretaps were searches requiring warrants under the Fourth Amendment, led to the enactment of the Omnibus Crime Control and Safe Streets Act of 1968, which together with the Electronic Communications Privacy Act of 1986 today regulates the interception of telecommunications. The conditions for intercepting electronic communications (such as e-mail) are less stringent than for intercepting voice communications; the exclusionary rule (which rules out illegally acquired information as evidence) does not hold for electronic interceptions. [NRC, 84-86]

To meet the challenge of continued tapping capabilities, the 1994 Communications Assistance for Law Enforcement Act (CALEA) was enacted. This requires telecom providers to make their networks tappable. Especially the requirement to facilitate a maximum number of simultaneous taps has raised fierce discussions. After two earlier trials, the FBI published final wiretap capacity figures in March 1998, requiring the simultaneous tapping of over 57,000 lines nationwide [see FBI]. However, the CALEA deadline for meeting the tappability requirements, 28 October 1998, was considered unrealistic by the telecoms industry, especially since negotiations by industry and the FBI on technical wiretap standards stranded, allegedly because the FBI insisted on far-reaching capabilities extending beyond CALEA. For instance, the FBI was seeking enhanced ability to track geographical locations of cell phones, and the ability to separate out content from signaling data of packet-based communications [*EPIC Alert* 4.15]. In mid-1998, the deadline for CALEA implementation was postponed until 30 June 2000.

In the US, the number of (both federal and state) taps has varied between 634 and 1,100 in the period 1984-1997. In 1997, 1,094 taps were placed. The majority of US interceptions involved drug investigations (73 per cent), followed by gambling and racketeering (both 8 per cent). [OA]

The efficacy of wiretapping is disputed in the US, as only few cases use intercepted communications as evidence. [Böttger, 12] The FBI, on the other hand, claims that "[c]ourt-ordered wiretapping is the single most effective investigative technique used by law enforcement to combat illegal drugs, terrorism, violent crime, espionage and organized crime. The majority of wiretapping is conducted by state and local law enforcement. Last year there were 1,154 wiretap court orders nationwide for all of law enforcement but these court-ordered wiretaps are critical to saving lives and solving the very worst crimes suffered by the public. Moreover, that number is not expected to increase in any significant manner when the law already passed by Congress [CALEA] is fully implemented. (...) '[T]here is no intention to expand the number of wiretaps or the extent of wiretapping.'" [Freeh 95c]

In short, Germany, the UK, and the US have recently adapted their telecommunications regulations to ensure future tappability in the light of technical and regulatory developments. All have experienced a significant increase in wiretaps over recent years, comparable to the Netherlands. The figures show that wiretapping is used extensively in the Netherlands and in Germany (although less than in the Netherlands). The UK and the US are tapping relatively little.[39]

4.3.3. Traffic analysis

Besides tapping phones to get at the content, the police can gain information from telecom operators about the communications as well. Not only can the content of conversations be useful for investigation, also the knowledge of who called whom when, how often, for how long, and from where is of interest. These traffic data can give a good indication of communications patterns and lay bare the structures of criminals participating in joint activities.

As traffic information is less privacy-sensitive than the contents of conversations, the competence to demand traffic data is less grave and, consequently, to be preferred to tapping if it suffices to gather the required information.

The public prosecutor and the examining judge have the competence to command people working with a public telecommunications operator to give information on conversations that have taken place, in which – presumably – the suspect participated (art. 125f DCCP). Although this suggests that the power can only be applied to *past* conversations, in practice, permission is usually given for requiring information on *future* conversations, so that the operator can take measures to be able to comply with this request. The application is only possible with offenses for which pre-trial detention is possible, as well as hacking[40]; the draft law on special investigation powers would also allow traffic analysis when there is a suspicion that serious, organized crimes are being schemed. The conditions may be revised when the results of a study into the law-enforcement need for business data will be available.

The digitization of telephone exchanges has enabled better and broader traffic analysis, as more data are stored automatically [23047, nr 6, 20]. Traffic analysis can be an important tool in investigation, although its usefulness must not be overestimated. It supplements the

---

39 There are several reasons why tapping is used less frequently in the US than in the Netherlands. For one thing, in the US, the judge supervises the application of wiretaps more closely, and he has to openly account for his considering the tap necessary. In the Netherlands, the examining judge authorizes the tap, but he does not need to openly motivate his decision. More importantly, the application of the subsidiarity principle differs. In the US, wiretapping is considered a last resort, more intrusive and graver than, for instance, undercover operations. In the Netherlands, wiretapping, although considered a grave measure, is found convenient in many more cases, and preferable over employing undercover agents. This difference may be partially due to a different conception of privacy. [Cf. 25403, nr 5]

40 Although only punishable with six months' imprisonment, hacking was added here, because traffic analysis is virtually the only way of tracing a hacker.

content scrutiny of tapping, but it can not serve as an alternative, because for many purposes, it is necessary to be aware of what is being said rather than that something is being said.

4.4. Data storage

The most common method of finding evidence is looking for it. One can of course first kindly ask people to hand over data (4.4.1), but if they refuse, the police can use graver measures. They can search for the information itself, and look for computers and data carriers for search and seizure (4.4.2); they can also use computers to search for data over a network (4.4.3). If the computer is access-protected, the police should be able to undo the protection (4.4.4).

4.4.1. Handing over data

As the competence to search and seize property is a grave measure, the police should first try other effective means to achieve the goal of evidence gathering (according to the principle of subsidiarity). Rather than seizing things by force, they can ask the keeper to hand over the (seizable) objects needed. The police should specify which objects should be handed over. The competence is limited when it comes to letters and people with a right not to give evidence because of their profession, and the command for handing over can not be given to a suspect.

As data are not 'property',[41] the police need an additional power to command the handing over of data that may serve the investigation. This competence was introduced in 1993 with the Computer Crime Act. It authorizes the examining judge to command someone to hand over specific (automated) data relating to the crime or to the suspect. The suspect can not be given this command. The addressee can comply with the order by recording the data, bringing them to the court registry, or giving access to the examining judge (for instance, through an online connection). The way in which data are to be handed over is to be determined by the examining judge. In the case of encrypted files, this formulation, however vague, can not be supposed to include the

Criminal financial inquest

For the estimation of illegally acquired gains, a criminal financial inquest can be opened in order to allow certain measures; the offense concerned must be punishable with a fine of the fifth category (NLG 100,000). During the financial inquest, the examining judge can use the same powers as during an inquest. Thus, he can have phones tapped, request traffic information, investigate computers, and search and seize (this includes the power to search and seize letters and other writings, so it is likely he can investigate e-mail messages). For instance, in the Henk R. case, the financial inquest was focused on investigating the seized administration and tapping phones [Traa, 240]. The police has a general competence to command someone to give documents or data for inspection, although this command may not be given to the person who is the target of the investigation, and people with a right to non-disclosure can remain silent.

41 Despite two rulings by the district court of Arnhem, data are not considered 'property' in the sense of criminal law, as they are multiple and the product of mental rather than physical labor, and as copying them does not take them away out of someone's power of disposal. Moreover, special laws address immaterial values, such as intellectual-property law.

competence to order that the data should be handed over in unencrypted form; this would imply that the keeper should first modify the data, and this is contrary to the intention of the article, which presupposes the integrity of the surrendered data.

Apart from the police which investigates crimes, special investigation services also have coercive powers. These services inspect compliance with special regulatory laws, such as tax or environment laws. Their competence differs from that of law enforcement. For instance, the Fiscal Intelligence and Investigation Department (FIID) can command people to show them relevant documents and files. The addressee has to comply with such a command, under penalty of six months' or – if denied wilfully – four years' imprisonment. The subject of an investigation provides the investigation agent with books, records, or other data-storage devices, or the contents thereof. The data must be provided clearly and without restriction, and copies can be made (art. 49 State Taxes Act). The wording of the article seems to imply that the data handed over must be in the clear, and so, decryption may be commanded.

4.4.2. Search and seizure

If necessary, the police can look for evidence contrary to people's will: with a search warrant, they can turn a house upside-down to recover pieces of evidence. These pieces can be photographed or otherwise recorded, or they can be seized to serve as evidence in court.

The ability to search and seize property includes the competence to search in computers and to copy data. After all, a house search is the gravest possible coercive power to dig up evidence. The *Cocaine in kitchen cupboard* case has interpreted it as a 'focused and systematic investigation,'[42] in which closets may be opened (with force, if needs be), floors may be broken up, and clocks may be searched (taking into account the principles of subsidiarity (first try the least infringing measure) and proportionality (use as little force as is necessary)). Therefore, also computers can be subjected to a search. Analogously to the taking of finger prints, copies can be made of data stored in the computer. Thus, investigating stored data can regularly be executed. It can only be done during a house search, though, as looking in a computer to see if there is incriminating evidence can only be done through a 'systematic' investigation. Therefore, the police[43] can only look for electronic evidence in more serious cases – those for which pre-trial detention is possible (or in *in flagrante delicto* situations).

Another option for investigating computers is to seize them and subsequently investigate the seized object. This is a useful competence for stand-alones, laptops, diskettes, and personal digital assistants, which can be seized both in a search (e.g., when the police lacks the time to exhaustively investigate the computer on the spot) and while arresting or stopping someone, or in an *in flagrante delicto* situation. The seizure competence includes all objects that can serve to ascertain the truth or the illegally acquired gains. The search and

---

42 Such a 'focused and systematic investigation' can only be executed in case of a house search with a corresponding warrant; other ways of intruding in homes to look for evidence are restricted to 'casual' looking.

43 A house search should be executed by the examining judge, or, if his arrival can not be awaited, by the public prosecutor or, again in case of urgency, by an assistant prosecutor.

> **International investigation**
>
> As organized crime and computer crime take place in a largely international context, international cooperation in investigation is an increasingly important issue. Investigating criminal organizations operating in various countries requires legal assistance, notably for wiretapping and searching in other countries. Computer crime often involves online international investigation, for instance, because evidence is stored abroad or because the crime has effects in several countries.
>
> International cooperation in investigation takes place on two levels. First, legal assistance is given by states based on a mutual agreement, usually a (bilateral or multilateral) treaty. Thus, foreign states can request the Netherlands to find evidence in a certain case. The examining judge can then use certain powers he has during an inquest, for instance, tap a phone or conduct a search. As the procedure for requesting legal assistance takes some time, this will often be inadequate to investigate computer crime. In 1995, the Council of Europe recommended adapting criminal-procedure laws to enhance the international investigation of computer crime. [CoE 95] For instance, the possibility to search online in computers abroad would greatly improve evidence-gathering in computer-related cases.
>
> Second, joint investigation is called for in international cases. As many of today's criminal organizations operate internationally, state-bound investigation and the slow provision of legal assistance are insufficient. Joint investigation teams could serve the task of investigating organized cross-border crime. The EU Maastricht and Amsterdam Treaties call for closer police and judicial cooperation, including operational cooperation in investigating crimes. Such joint teams may be supported by members of Europol, the facilitating investigation service of the EU. The main task of Europol will be to assist member countries in investigation, mainly through facilitating information exchange, education, and research.

seizure of letters or other writings is limited: there must be a clear connection with the offense or the suspect, or the court must authorize it. For seizing letters entrusted to the postal or telegraph service, the examining judge can order the contents to be made known to the police, as far as they are apparently intended for the suspect or originate from him. There is hardly any case law yet to indicate whether this competence could be used to seize e-mail messages stored with a service provider.

Whereas special investigation services have more powers than the police to command information to be given, they have less powers to search for it if the subjects do not cooperate: they can not, e.g., as such conduct a house search or tap phones.[44] They can, however, seize property. Thus, the FIID can seize books, including computers and diskettes.

4.4.3. Searching elsewhere

While conducting a search in a computer, it is possible that the police find that data are not stored in the computer, but elsewhere in a network to which the computer is connected. If this other place of storage is beyond the limits of the search warrant – a likely case with networked computer systems, searching in the computer system elsewhere requires another warrant. Because requesting other warrants for the location where the other computer is located is both impractical and detrimental to the investigation (a suspect could easily destroy the information in the meantime), a specific power to search elsewhere in computers while conducting a search was introduced with the 1993 Computer Crime Act. The competence stops at the national border, as national sovereignty prohibits investigating in other countries (safe when specific treaties create a competence for cross-border invest-

44 "In other words: according to general criminal proceedings, the suspect does not have to cooperate with the seizure, and the judiciary can look themselves; in special criminal proceedings, the judiciary may not look themselves, but the suspect must cooperate." [Buruma, 218]

igation). Moreover, the power must involve data that are reasonably necessary for ascertaining the truth, and the computer systems located elsewhere must be legally accessible to the regular occupants of the location being searched. Again, letters and personal writings are protected analogously, so that probably e-mail messages stored elsewhere can not be read.

4.4.4. Providing access

Many computers are protected against unauthorized access. Therefore, the police will have difficulty searching a computer if they can not remove its protection. Article 125k paragraph 1 DCCP authorizes them, during a search, to request someone who is likely to know the means of protection to provide access to the computer, or to provide the knowledge of the protection. As the command can not be given to suspects, the police will have to address a system manager or, in case of a home personal computer, housemates.[45]

With the introduction of the Computer Crime Act, it was already recognized that not only access to the computer could be protected, but also access to files – through encryption. Therefore, article 125k paragraph 2 DCCP was introduced, declaring article 125k paragraph 1 analogously applicable. Thus, the police can require someone likely to know the means of encryption (i.e, the key) to surrender the key or to decrypt. As usual, the suspect can not be addressed. I will further describe the potential and limitations of this competence in Chapter 8, when analyzing the option of commanding a suspect to decrypt. Note that usually the suspect is the only one with knowledge of the key, which makes the present competence virtually useless in practice. This is all the more so, because the police always copies the encrypted data for later investigation at the office – and then the power to demand decryption can no longer be given, the house search having ended. The draft Computer Crime Act II addresses this latter issue by allowing the command to be given when the search has ended, but leaves the former problem unaddressed.[46]

4.5. Problems through encryption

Inevitably, cryptography will be used by criminals to hamper investigation. In this section, I will use the applications of cryptography detailed in section 3.2 to assess how criminal use of encryption may thwart the information-gathering powers of law enforcement. From this analysis, I will define the main problems to be handled in the second part of this book.

Encryption for the sake of integrity and authenticity will not hamper evidence-finding, as this leaves the original text in the clear.[47] Only encryption for confidentiality purposes renders the message unreadable. Also note that whereas cryptography hampers tapping, it does not obstruct traffic analysis. I will therefore restrict myself to confidentiality encryption hampering the retrieval of the contents of data.

---

45 Since family members to the third degree and spouses can remain silent, this will often be ineffective.

46 Initially, the draft proposal contained a provision to demand suspects to decrypt, under strict conditions. After protests from the legal community against this infringement of the privilege against self-incrimination, the provision was removed from the draft.

47 If, as is usual, a signed hash is used. If the entire message is encrypted with a private key, the police can use the public key to decrypt. Cf. 7.3.

4.5.1. Main crypto-problems

If *network providers* use encryption to secure their network, the communications transferred over their infrastructure will be out of reach of police tapping. However, the obligation for providers to assure the technical tappability of telecommunications infrastructure (art. 64a TFA; art. 13 draft Telecommunications Act) can be interpreted as prohibiting unconditional use of encryption by network providers. That is, if they use encryption as a standard feature of the telecommunications infrastructure, they should offer wiretapping officials the original signal as it entered their network. Naturally, providing the original signal will still leave the police empty-handed if the users encrypt themselves. Traffic analysis will in any case still be possible if network operators use encryption, as they are required to cooperate and to give these data to law-enforcement officers.

Encryption use by *service providers* will generally not hamper investigation. Telecommerce using encrypted (pay) services, such as video-on-demand, is not part of criminal organizations' communication patterns, and taps are not hampered by these.[48]

The main problem for law enforcement will be encryption by *end users*. They will use encryption for securing both information transport and storage. As far as *transport* is concerned, financial transactions, teleworking, video conferencing, and other types of communications will increasingly be encrypted for confidentiality. Supposing that mobile phones and data communications can in the future regularly be tapped, criminal organizations and computer criminals, with their knowledge of computer technologies, are likely to shift to encryption in order to remain outside the reach of wiretaps. Then, encryption for escaping law enforcement will be used on a larger - or even large - scale. After all, robust encryption software and hardware is available around the world, sometimes even online and as freeware or shareware, such as the widely used PGP.

Moreover, as voice communications will increasingly be performed on digital networks, even across the Internet, encrypted conversations will be common. For Internet telephony, the program PGPfone is available from the Internet free of charge; it can be used for secure (voice) conversations on the Internet. Especially when encryption programs will be incorporated in general services, for example, in Internet protocols (IPv6), mail programs (Pegasus, Eudora), web browsers (Netscape Navigator, Internet Explorer), or operating systems (Linux, Windows), the use of cryptography will become common and all-pervasive. Then, also 'traditional' criminals, such as minor frauds, child pornographers, and individual serious criminals, will widely use encryption to thwart law enforcement.

So, cryptophones, cryptofaxes, and the encryption of e-mail, data transfers, and voice communications over digital networks make tapping ineffective: the clear text is only recoverable at both ends, and currently the police has no means to trace this.

In fact, encryption is only a threat to tapping if tapping is possible at all. Conceptually, tapping causes three potential problems. First, the signal must be intercepted and recorded, which is largely a physical and technical matter. For most of the communications, this is

---

48 The information on who is using which services will be interesting to law enforcement, as this can assist the making of perpetrator profiles. The present powers to request information or, if the service provider will not cooperate, to search and seize the provider's administration - including the power to request decryption (art. 125k para. 2 DCCP) - are probably sufficient for getting this information.

possible, although it may be difficult with the Internet packet-switching protocol to intercept all packets. Then, the signal must be interpreted, which is a logical problem: what do the bits and bytes signify, what kind of information is it, and what format is it in. Third, once this is done, only then does encryption come into view. If the file is interpretable as a certain type of file, the text, image, or sound may turn out to be encrypted. Supposing that the first two stages can be addressed through technological sophistication, encryption may gradually turn out to be the main problem for wiretapping. Encryption of data transport, then, is likely to be one of the main future problems for law enforcement, hampering the tracing of perpetrators, the uncovering of networks of criminal organizations, evidence-gathering in fraud cases, and, to a lesser extent, catching computer criminals. FBI director Freeh, in a speech meant to incite the US Congress to restrict encryption, stated that "drug cartels are buying sophisticated communications equipment. Unless the issue of encryption is resolved soon, criminal conversations over the telephone and other communications devices will become indecipherable for law enforcement. This, as much as any issue, jeopardizes the public safety and national security of this country. Drug cartels, terrorists, and kidnappers will use telephones and other communications media with impunity knowing that their conversations are immune from our most valued investigative technique." [Freeh 95a] One should bear in mind, though, that such statements are aimed at convincing others of the necessity of restricting cryptography, and may not be unbiased. Privacy advocates often point out that "the FBI has not been able to point to a single case to date where encryption has hampered their investigation of a case." [Hoffman 94] But then again, that may be because the police wants to let sleeping dogs lie.

Likewise, the use of cryptography for securing information *storage* (for instance, of accounts, e-mail folders, and villainous plans) is a threat to law enforcement's ability to investigate. The current search and seizure procedures are widely inadequate to cope with encrypted files. Only in a small number of cases can the police require the decryption of enciphered data, namely, during a search when a non-suspect person knows the means of encryption (which will rarely be the case), and when tax officials require to see the books. Even then, faced with a demand to decrypt, the addressee might use a duress code to thwart the demand: he will produce innocent data rather than the original incriminating plaintext. Thus, the use of encryption for securing data storage is another main problem for law enforcement, especially relevant in investigating organized crime (think, for instance, of laptop computers or personal digital assistants containing address lists), organizational and business crime (especially if the books are encrypted), and computer-related crime.

4.5.2. Cryptocriminals in practice

There is little reliable information on cases in which cryptography has hampered investigations in practice. Most policy documents and statements by police officials confine themselves to stating the potential (imagined?) gravity of the problem and giving one or two notorious examples. The only extensive (public-domain) study of cryptocriminals was undertaken by Dorothy Denning and William Baugh in 1997. A world-wide query to submit cases of cryptocriminals resulted in a list of examples of terrorism, organized-crime, espionage, and child-pornography cases involving cryptography. Their findings suggest "that the total number of criminal cases involving encryption world-wide is at least 500, with an annual growth rate of 50-100%." [Denning 97a] In a considerable part of these cases, the police were able to retrieve the information, or they were able to convict the criminals regardless of the encrypted data. FBI director Freeh claimed that the FBI has seen the number of cases involving encryption or password protection increase from 2 to 7 per cent. [Freeh 98] In 1996, a bill was adopted by US Congress, the NII Protection Act, which requires the Sentencing Commission to report annually on the use of computer encryption to facilitate or conceal criminal activity, and so more definite figures for the US may be available in the future.

Some examples of cryptocriminals, apart from those already mentioned in section 4.1, are the terrorist group responsible for bombing the World Trade Center in 1994 and a Manila Air airliner in 1995. The laptop of member Ramsey Yousef contained encrypted files on further plans, which were successfully decrypted; however, much of the information was also available in unencrypted documents, and decryption was not essential to prevent the planned attacks. [Denning 97d] A gambling enterprise operating multiple sites linked by a computer system encrypted four years of accounts; the codeword was cracked by exploiting weaknesses in the crypto system, resulting in a plea of guilty. [Denning 97d] The police in Sacramento, California, found a number of large encrypted files with a person suspected of involvement in child pornography. The suspect refused to surrender the key. [Wayner 93] At a 1996 OECD meeting discussing crypto policies, "the Italian representative said he was unaware of any criminal probes defeated by use of encryption, but he reported that the Mafia was thought to be seeking access to strong U.S. encryption for its communications. This led Austria to ask whether anyone knew of cases of crooks using encryption. Denmark reported one case. Holland reported a case of suspected terrorists using high-grade encryption; when pressed for information about how the case turned out, the Dutch representative simply said, 'The encryption gave us a lot of trouble.'" [Baker 96] One of the five computer crime teams in the Netherlands encountered encryption in about ten cases, involving, for example, hacking, money laundering, and drugs; in one of the cases, the encryption obstructed the investigation beyond repair [Komen].

4.5.3. Cracking evidence

So, that twenty-first century kid, that fast-track Infobahni, that arriviste crooning I-did-it-I-way, proved to be not only a scheming usurper, but a moron – who thought himself uncatchable, and therefore got caught with laughable ease.
(Salman Rushdie, The Moor's Last Sigh)

If the police encounter encrypted data, what are their chances of decrypting? Where encrypted *communications* are concerned, the chances are slim indeed. If the police can record and distinguish an entire encrypted communication at all (which is not always easy, as they should know just where the communication begins and where it ends; or, with digital networks, they must select all packets of the message), they will likely not be able to cryptanalyze it. They only have a chance if they know how the communication is encrypted, and if the crypto system is weak enough to allow a brute-force attack. If the data are compressed before encryption, a brute-force attack becomes very difficult even with weak systems. Also, given the high number of conversations recorded in a single wiretap, many messages would have to be cryptanalyzed (remark that selecting relevant messages is impossible). Perhaps most importantly, cracking communications through a brute-force attack cannot be done real-time; it will usually require at least several days and often weeks or months. This significantly limits the efficacy of the wiretap (cf. 4.3.1); and then, the police may be reluctant to use decrypted intercepts in court, as this will give criminals insight into their cryptanalytic skills and capacity – it could "provide a tutorial to criminal elements bent on eluding law enforcement" [US].

There are much better chances with *stored* encrypted files (cf. 3.1.4-3.1.5). It is easier to see or guess with which system the file has been encrypted (for instance, because the encryption program is stored on the same computer, or because a Crypto User Handbook features on the bookshelf), and so, a cryptanalytic attack can be better focused and more efficient. In practice, some criminals use easy-to-crack crypto systems provided with general software packages, and only the more technologically advanced use strong crypto systems such as PGP. More importantly, many criminals use weak passwords or passphrases, which can be fairly easily guessed with automated password-guessing programs, such as PGPCrack. Sometimes, the key may simply be found stored on a diskette, as the police found in the Aum Shinrikyo case [Denning 97d]. Since the time pressure is smaller than with wiretaps (the search alerts the suspects that an investigation is taking place anyway), and the number of encrypted files may be limited, a brute-force attack may be a good last resort if the stakes are high enough. (Indeed, the police could perform distributed attacks (see sidebar in 3.1.5) to use the idle computer power of all police offices, for instance with a screen saver program, to crack the most important files.)

That there is a reasonable chance of success is indicated by the fact that data recovery is often used by businesses who need to decrypt files encrypted by disgruntled or careless employees. Specialist companies provide such data-recovery services. For example, the US company AccessData "specializes in data recovery and decrypting information utilizing brute force as well as 'smarter' attacks. Regular clients include the FBI and other law enforcement agencies as well as corporations." [Ad Hoc][49] AccessData took twelve hours to crack the custom-encrypted files in a Bolivian terrorism case; AccessData software[50] also enabled the decryption of encrypted files in the Aldrich Ames spy case [Denning 97d]. Another possibility is that the manufacturer of the hardware or software has a master key.[51] This way, the police may recover a certain part of stored encrypted files.

Indeed, the Denning-Baugh survey found that in organized-crime and business-crime cases, the encryption of stored data was generally broken [Denning 97d].

---

49 "AccessData (...) reports receiving about a dozen and a half calls a day from companies with inaccessible data. About one-half dozen of these calls result from disgruntled employees (...) another half-dozen result from employees who died or (...) forgot to leave their keys." [Denning 96]

50 Phil Zimmermann reported a conversation with the author of the AccessData package that cracks many built-in encryption schemes in general products: "he said his program only takes a split second to crack them, but he put in some delay loops to slow it down so it doesn't look so easy to the customer." [Zimmermann 94, 105]

51 Cf. [HR 29 March 1994], in which the Japanese manufacturer of a pocket computer recovered the data from the protected secret memory.

4.5.4. Further crypto-problems

An additional problem is caused by the possibility of hiding encryption.[52] The use of steganography to communicate without anyone noticing the exchange of information, e.g., through posting a message in a digital image to a news group, can be called the ultimate way to prevent the police from investigating communications patterns. Although impractical in cases of urgency or when two-way feedback is needed, it is a viable option for exchanging shorter messages when there is no urgency.

More damaging to law enforcement will be the use of steganography to hide information in computers.[53] Files can be stored hidden in images or sounds. The police may search the computer's contents, but may easily overlook the incriminating evidence. Indeed, to really hide incriminating files, smart criminals may even "concoct some mildly incriminating dummy messages to take the place of the really incriminating real messages. A pair of Israeli spies once did this." [Schneier, 228] One should not overestimate the possibilities of steganography, though. In many cases, the pattern of the image, sound, or text file will show that it is not an ordinary file. Moreover, there is bound to be some header information for the stegano program to be able to recognize the file as containing a stealth message.

Problems in proof

Apart from potential crypto problems for evidence gathering, cryptography may also cause problems in court. As computer-related evidence may result from highly technical procedures, a smart lawyer can cast doubt on the reliability of the evidence. A judge without a degree in maths will find cryptology abracadabra, and so, he will have to rely on the statements of experts.

Suppose the prosecution uses evidence resulting from encrypted information, obtained through either cryptanalysis or through decryption with the proper key (found somewhere or given by someone). The police will have to prove that the resulting clear text is indeed the original plaintext. The defending attorney may try to discredit this, saying there is no mathematical certainty that the given text is the right plaintext. However, as it is virtually impossible that a given ciphertext decrypts to two meaningful plaintexts, an expert witness will likely convince the judge of the reliability of the cryptanalysis or decryption. (Compare the *pocket computer* decision, where the appeal court stated: "The proposition, that in Japan the secret memories of the pagers may have been tampered with, has not become plausible. The expert heard in appeal Professor Kaspersen did state that manipulation was not entirely to be excluded, but he added that he considered this a purely theoretical possibility. There is nothing that indicated this possibility." This statement was not challenged in cassation.) The judge must be convinced, however, that the police (or the Forensic Laboratory) has acted properly in obtaining the plaintext: after all, they might have XOR-ed the ciphertext with a conveniently incriminating plaintext to obtain a One-Time Pad key which yields – behold! – the incriminating, but false, plaintext. So, in the process of cryptanalysis or decryption with an obtained key, the police must act carefully and systematically, and must make official reports of all activities to ensure that the process can be checked by neutral experts. The defense might claim a right to a counter-check [cf. Buruma, 228-237]. It would be wise to have standard procedures for handling encrypted data, comparable to, for instance, the initial proposal for direct eavesdropping, which contained a prescription for the (automated) recording of each step in the process of treating the recordings to enhance their clarity. A similar procedure should be developed for crypt-analysis and, in general, the handling of encrypted evidence.

Perhaps the biggest challenge will be to find expert witnesses who can clearly explain to the judge how encryption and cryptanalysis work. The gap between the legal and mathematical jargons (not to say: world views) looms so big, that a judge might be hard to convince that this magic really works.

---

52 Cf. section 7.3 on stealth messages in digital signatures.

53 Although the presence of stegano-software would indicate that there are files hidden somewhere. A search on the images with a dictionary attack might render incriminating plaintexts (compare Illustration 4.1).

[illegible]
AND CHILD. I HURT ME. AS YOU SHOULD COMING IN A MISERABLY
SITUATION. WHILE I HAVE THE POSSIBLY CHANCE TO ESCAPED FROM
PRISON. IN DECEMBER TEGEN DIE TIJD LAAT IK JE WEL WETEN HOE JE EEN
SINTERKLAASPAKKETJE MOET VERSIEREN. O. SORRY. NOG STEEDS DANK
VOOR HET VORIGE!.. B. VEEL DANK JOH. EN HET BESTE, IMMER MET MOED! [illegible]

Illustration 4.1. UV-scan of a letter written in urine by a detainee. The revealed text appeared to contain very incriminating evidence. [source: Stapel & De Koning, 216]

One other problem deserves mentioning, as it involves cryptography-related technologies. Electronic cash can be used for sending large amounts of money around the world in a very short period, as often as is desirable. This is a great opportunity for money laundering, as tracing all these transactions is virtually impossible. Since financial investigation has become an important part of investigating organized crime, e-cash poses a serious problem to laying bare the financial patterns of a criminal organization. This problem, however, is outside the scope of this book.

4.5.5. Scope of the problem

The publicly available information, in particular the Denning-Baugh survey, suggests that cryptography is encountered in only a few criminal cases. Where encryption is encountered, it often does not block the investigation, either because the police can crack it or because there is sufficient other evidence.

In *telecommunications*, end-to-end cryptography is used little by criminals.[54] If they do, investigation usually stands powerless. Encryption is used more often in protecting *stored* criminal data, but in quite a few of the crypto-cases to date, the investigators were able to crack the encryption or the encrypted data were not necessary for a conviction. Only a small group of criminals use robust cryptography which cannot be cracked, and where practical attacks do not work. The Walsh report on Australian crypto policy corroborates this: "For the present, the investigative capability of the agencies is not significantly affected." [Walsh, 1.2.11] The threat, then, of cryptocriminals to law enforcement is presently a minor one.

The general expectation, however, is that the cryptocriminal threat will grow significantly in the near to middle future.[55] The central claim of the Denning-Baugh study is "that the impact of encryption on crime and terrorism is at its early stages." [Denning 97a] As cryptography becomes familiar to ever wider groups of users, also less technologically advanced criminals will start to use robust cryptography. The profoundest impact will likely result from incorporating strong cryptography in general software programs, such as word-processing, browsing, and e-mail software. US export controls still curb this development, but it seems inevitable that the information infrastructure and the primary information services will incorporate strong cryptography in the near future. Then, investigation will still benefit from practical attacks exploiting weaknesses in the use of cryptography, but cracking or brute-forcing of weak crypto systems employed by criminals will be a thing of the past.

4.6. Conclusion

Developments in crime show that organized crime and computer crime have become serious threats to society. Both are dependent on information-processing: criminal organizations rely heavily on communications, and computer criminals often use data storage. Both criminal

54 "As far as the committee has been able to determine, criminal use of digitally encrypted voice communications has not presented a significant problem to law enforcement to date." [NRC, 90]

55 For instance, [COM (97) 503, III.3(I)], [Denning 97a], [Australia, 6], [Norway, 2], and Interpol expert Takizawa in [Ghosh].

organizations and computer criminals use modern technologies, and are likely to use these to shield their activities from police scrutiny. Business crime, including large-scale fraud, also relies on data storage and may use encryption to hide incriminating evidence. Other forms of serious crime can also involve data transport or storage.

To counter the threats of serious crime, states investigate crime and prosecute the perpetrators. To assure the safety of citizens and the integrity of society as a whole, investigation and prosecution are of great concern. The Dutch Minister of Justice has called fighting organized crime and other serious forms of crime a "pressing social need" [23047, nr 3, 3].

In investigating these types of crime, information-gathering has a central place. Wiretaps and traffic analysis are primary tools for revealing structures of criminal organizations and for tracing hackers. Technological developments are making tapping more difficult, in particular of mobile phones and electronic data transfers. The obligation for telecom operators to make their networks tappable may require several years to take full effect. Search and seizure, including specific powers for investigating in automated surroundings, are main methods of gathering evidence and tracing computer crime and business crime.

Currently, encryption is used very little by criminals in *telecommunications*; if they do, however, it is generally impossible for the police to retrieve the contents of the communications. At present, the technical problems of tapping all forms of communications are more serious than the use of cryptography, but once tapping all telecommunications is widely possible, cryptography is bound to render taps useless. Wiretaps will become illusory if criminals regularly encrypt end-to-end. The extent to which criminals will do this is hard to predict, but one can safely assume that it will rise, especially where communications via the computer (e-mail, Internet telephony) are concerned. Gathering information *about* the communications data is not hampered by cryptography, and so, traffic analysis will remain an important tool for investigation.

Cryptocriminals today are using cryptography oftener in *data storage*. So far, this usually does not hamper the investigation, because the police can crack the ciphertext or because there is sufficient other evidence. However, with the developing information infrastructure, robust cryptography will come within the easy reach of more criminals (in particular, of less-automated organized criminals and of business and computer criminals who currently do not use encryption, or who use it insecurely). Although significant opportunities may remain for the police to crack encryption by exploiting weaknesses in crypto use if not in crypto systems, overall, searches in computers will become ever less effective.

I conclude that the threat of cryptography to law enforcement, and therewith to society at large, is currently low, as there are few real cryptocriminals to date. The threat, however, will increase in the near to middle future. Therefore, there is a significant public concern to address the crypto problems for law enforcement.

The main crypto problems for law enforcement

Problem 1: criminals' use of strong confidentiality encryption for voice and data transport
Problem 1a: criminals' use of steganography to hide communications

Problem 2: criminals' use of strong confidentiality encryption for data storage
Problem 2a: criminals' use of steganography to hide data in storage
Problem 2b: criminals' use of duress codes to decrypt to a different message

Chapter 5. A survey of cryptography laws and regulations

So far key escrow products are enjoying less than stellar sales.
(Bruce Schneier, Applied Cryptography)

Governments increasingly worry about the threat of criminals using cryptography to thwart law enforcement. Several governments have taken steps to address this issue; many are still studying potential lines of action. In this chapter, I describe the various existing and envisaged laws and regulations on cryptography in several countries, focusing on cryptography used for confidentiality purposes.[1] I will briefly go into export regulations in general (5.1); since these are not intended to safeguard law enforcement (they are targeted at hostile foreign powers and terrorists), the details fall outside the scope of this book. After a description of the major international initiatives on crypto policy (5.2), I will outline the encryption policies of Belgium, Denmark, Germany, France, the Netherlands, the Russian Federation, the United Kingdom, and the United States (5.3). Together, they cover the full spectrum of crypto regulations to date (5.4), and so, they provide a good source to look for directions on how to address the crypto conflict.

5.1. Export and import controls

5.1.1. COCOM and Wassenaar Arrangement

The export of cryptography has long been restricted. Evidently, governments have wanted to avoid strong cryptography from falling into the hands of foreign powers, which would have thwarted their ability to do intelligence work. Cryptography has long been regarded as a weapon, and it is still featuring on lists that control the export of munitions. The main international agreement on export controls, the treaty of COCOM,[2] the Coordinating Committee for Multilateral Export Controls, was replaced by the Wassenaar Arrangement in 1996.

---

1 For this survey, I have made use of several studies, including [Chandler] and [Kuner]. This chapter covers the state of affairs as of 1 July 1998; for a more elaborate and up-to-date overview, see my online Crypto Law Survey [Koops]. Most of the documents I refer to in this chapter are available online and can be found through a link from this website, so I have not added the references here. See also [Baker 98b].

2 The 17 COCOM members were Australia, Belgium, Canada, Denmark, France, Germany, Greece, Italy, Japan, Luxemburg, the Netherlands, Norway, Portugal, Spain, Turkey, United Kingdom and the United States. Cooperating members included Austria, Finland, Hungary, Ireland, New Zealand, Poland, Singapore, South Korea, Sweden, Switzerland, and Taiwan.

COCOM was an international organization for the mutual control of the export of strategic products and technical data from country members to proscribed destinations. It maintained, among others, the International Industrial List and the International Munitions List, regulating all kinds of cryptography. In 1989, COCOM decontrolled password and authentication-only cryptography. In 1991, COCOM decided to allow export of mass-market cryptographic software (including public-domain software). Most member countries of COCOM followed its regulations, but others, such as the United States, maintained separate regulations.

The main goal of the COCOM regulations was to prevent cryptography from being exported to 'dangerous' countries – usually, the countries thought to maintain friendly ties with terrorists, such as Libya, Iraq, Iran, and North Korea. Exports to other countries were usually allowed, although states often required a license for these.

COCOM was dissolved in March 1994. In 1995, 28 countries decided to establish a follow-up to COCOM, the *Wassenaar Arrangement on Export Controls for Conventional Arms and Dual-Use Goods and Technologies*. The negotiations on the treaty were finished in July 1996, and the agreement was signed by 33 countries.[3] The Wassenaar Arrangement controls the export of weapons and of dual-use goods, that is, goods that can be used both for a military and for a civil purpose; cryptography is such a dual-use good. The provisions are largely the same as COCOM regulations. The General Software Note excepts mass-market and public-domain crypto software from the controls; five countries (Australia, France, New Zealand, Russia, and the US) deviate from the GSN and control the export of mass-market and public-domain crypto software. Export via the Internet does not seem to be covered by the regulations. The Wassenaar Arrangement is scheduled to be revised in late 1998.

5.1.2. United States

The United States of America has restricted cryptography export more severely than COCOM and Wassenaar. Crypto exports were controlled under the International Traffic in Arms Regulation (ITAR) until 1996; at the end of that year, they were transferred to the Department of Commerce under the Export Administration Regulations (EAR). ITAR restricted export of 'dual-use' cryptography by placing it on the Munitions List. For (relatively strong) products that can encipher data, an export license is usually issued only for use by foreign branches of American enterprises and for use by financial institutions. 'Weak' cryptography (e.g., with a certain maximum key-length, currently 40 bits for symmetric crypto) can also be exported.

In June 1996, the National Research Council released a long-awaited study on cryptography policy [NRC]. It recommended that export controls be relaxed, but not eliminated. Export of 56-bit symmetric encryption products (such as DES) should be allowed, whereas export of cryptography using more than 56 bits should be exportable if the

---

3 Initially, Argentina, Australia, Austria, Belgium, Canada, the Czech Republic, Denmark, Finland, France, Germany, Greece, Hungary, Ireland, Italy, Japan, Luxembourg, the Netherlands, New Zealand, Norway, Poland, Portugal, Romania, the Russian Federation, Slovakia, South Korea, Spain, Sweden, Switzerland, Turkey, the United Kingdom, and the United States. Later, Bulgaria and Ukraine also signed the treaty.

users agree to provide the US government access to decoded information. The NRC recommendations have not (or not yet?) been implemented. Although exports for financial institutions have been gradually relaxed, the export controls remain largely as they are. To promote the administration's key-recovery policy (see 5.3), export of 56-bit crypto is allowed if the producer pledges to incorporate key recovery in its products within two years.

The restrictions on cryptography hamper US enterprises, not only those that make crypto products, but also those that make products in which cryptography is a tool, such as web browsers or e-mail programs. Because for some businesses it is inefficient or impractical to make two versions of their products, the export restrictions may also have had the effect of weakening domestic crypto products, as producers may have chosen to make a single, exportable product. Many people feel the EAR rules to be outdated. Strong crypto products incorporating US-made cryptography (or derivatives thereof) are widely available around the world, often online, and sometimes as shareware [TIS]. Several initiatives have been taken to relax the export controls, both in court and in Congress, but they have to date not been successful, with the exception of the *Bernstein* decision. In this case, Daniel Bernstein sought the ability to export his encryption algorithm; the district and federal courts judged the export regulations to be too restrictive. They found the licensing system an unconstitutional prior restraint on free speech (having ruled earlier that crypto source code was protected by the First Amendment). The decision is on appeal. Another case, *Junger* v. *Daley*, rejected this reasoning and held that encryption export is not protected under the First Amendment.

5.1.3. Import restrictions

As the main goal of export restrictions is to prevent foreign rogues and spies from obtaining cryptography, they usually have no pendant in import restrictions – the more strong cryptography imported, the better. On the other hand, countries with restrictions on *domestic* crypto use generally do apply import restrictions, to prevent the internal market regulation from being disrupted by foreign cryptography. The most notable countries that have import restrictions are France and the Russian Federation. Other countries restricting cryptography import include China, India, Kazakhstan, and South Korea.

5.2. International developments

5.2.1. OECD

The OECD (Organisation for Economic Co-operation and Development) have developed 'guidelines' for a crypto policy, after extensive discussions throughout 1996. The OECD started discussing and drafting policy 'guidelines' in December 1995 with an Ad-hoc Meeting of Experts on Cryptography Policy. The 'guidelines' were discussed and revised in several meetings in 1996, leading to the adoption of the *Recommendation of the Council concerning Guidelines for Cryptography Policy* on 27 March 1997 [OECD 97]. The 'guidelines' are non-binding recommendations to Member governments, meaning that they are not part of international law. The 'guidelines' provide principles which states should take into account and balance in developing a national crypto policy.

The principles are:

1. *Trust in cryptographic methods*: market forces and government regulation should foster user trust in cryptographic methods.
2. *Choice of cryptographic methods*: users should have the right to choose any cryptographic method, subject to applicable law.
3. *Market-driven development of cryptographic methods*: the market should determine the development and provision of cryptographic methods, including international standards.
4. *Standards for cryptographic methods*: international and interoperable standards for cryptographic methods should be developed; national standards should be consistent with international ones.
5. *Protection of privacy and personal data*: national cryptography policies and the implementation and use of cryptographic methods should respect the fundamental rights of individuals to privacy, including secrecy of communications and protection of personal data.
6. *Lawful access*: national cryptography policies may allow lawful access to plaintext or cryptographic keys.
7. *Liability*: the liability of crypto users and of crypto service providers should be clearly stated.
8. *International cooperation*: governments should cooperate to coordinate cryptography policies; governments should remove, or avoid creating, unjustified obstacles to trade.

The principles should be seen as "interdependent and should be implemented as a whole so as to balance the various interests at stake. No principle should be implemented in isolation from the rest." The balance basically has to be struck between the first five (crypto-friendly) principles and the sixth (police-friendly) principle, lawful access. This crucial and most controversial principle reads: "National cryptography policies may allow lawful access to plaintext, or cryptographic keys, of encrypted data. These policies must respect the other principles contained in the guidelines to the greatest extent possible." Interestingly, the most crypto-friendly principle, free choice, was adapted at the final stage. Where the earlier version read that crypto users should have a right to choose any crypto method, this was extended with the restriction "subject to applicable law", thus opening the door for a prohibition of cryptography.

Some have welcomed the OECD principles as a victory for privacy over US-pushed key recovery, while others object to certain points as being too inflexible or too vague. Although the 'guidelines' do not endorse key recovery, they do not prohibit it either. In fact, the 'guidelines' are vague enough to allow a broad range of interpretation, and states will be able to choose a privacy-oriented or a law-enforcement-driven policy line as they see fit. While the 'guidelines' recommend states to cooperate to coordinate their crypto policies, one may be skeptical about the chances of governments coming to an agreement. After all, within the OECD, states have not been able to agree, and they have left individual states with the task of finding a balance themselves between, roughly speaking, information security/ privacy and law enforcement/ national security – a balance the OECD could not find.

Terminology

Several governments are studying crypto systems that involve some form of law-enforcement access to keys (LEAK). I will explain these systems in 7.4 and 7.5, but I will already use the terminology here.

data recovery	all-encompassing term for retrieving the plaintext of encrypted data if the key for decryption is not available, through key escrow, key recovery, or plaintext recovery; the TTP providing data recovery can give private keys, session keys, or plaintexts
KEA	Key Escrow Agent, TTP which provides key-escrow services
key escrow	generic term for crypto systems that provide government (and authorized-user) access to keys by having people deposit their private (or supersymmetric) keys with a TTP
key recovery	originally a term for a crypto system which provides LEAK by having people tag along to messages a recoverable session key rather than deposit their private keys; is increasingly used, irrespective of the technology, as a generic term for LEAK and a replacement for 'key escrow' which has become a too negative term; I use it in the original sense: recovering session keys
LEAK	Law-Enforcement Access to Keys, a generic term for key escrow and key recovery for law-enforcement purposes
TTP	Trusted Third Party; a trusted, independent organization which offers cryptography-based services that enhance the reliability of electronic data interchange and storage, such as key certification, distribution, revocation, and time-stamping; the term includes Certification Authorities, Key Escrow Agents, and Data Recovery Agencies

5.2.2. European Union

The 1993 draft *Green Book on the Security of Information Systems* [DG XIII], which has not been officially adopted by the European Council, posed a case for the provision of 'Public Confidentiality Services' (which would somehow offer Law-Enforcement Access to Keys).

Since 1996, the European Commission has been working on the establishment of a Europe-wide network of Trusted Third Party Services [ETS]. The network would be established for providing certification services by private TTPs. Although primarily meant for establishing an infrastructure for the use of public-key encryption, the initial proposal also tried to address the legal-access problem, e.g., through key escrow. The studies conducted did not address data recovery in-depth, but concentrated on issues related to establishing a public-key infrastructure for digital signatures. The report on the results of the 1995 TTP projects said that data-recovery systems "can potentially provide at least part of the answer to the problems raised by confidentiality functions." These "should be investigated as a matter of priority, in order to complete the picture of TTP functionality."

With the release of the Communication *Towards A European Framework for Digital Signatures And Encryption* [COM (97) 503], however, the European Commission has chosen a direction away from data recovery. Building on its April 1997 *Communication on Electronic Commerce*, this communication aims at creating a reliable European framework for digital signatures. It also addresses confidentiality crypto policy, although it is much less explicit here than it is on digital-signatures policy. It stresses the economic and societal importance of cryptography: "the public needs to have access to technical tools allowing effective protection of the confidentiality of data and communication against arbitrary intrusions. Encryption of data is very often the only effective and cost-efficient way of meeting these requirements." The Commission is concerned that restrictions on encryption affect the right to privacy, its effective exercise and the harmonization of data-protection laws in the Internal Market. Also, "divergence between regulatory schemes might result in obstacles to the functioning of the Internal Market."

The Commission is wary of data-recovery issues. "Key escrow or key recovery raise a number of practical and complex questions that policy makers would need to solve, in particular issues of privacy, vulnerability, effectiveness and costs. If at all required, regulation should be limited to what is absolutely necessary. Regulation would also need to distinguish between a multitude of possible key types (storage keys, session keys, authentication keys, etc.)." The Commission will examine whether national restrictions are totally or partially justified, notably whether they are proportionate, taking into account the provisions on the free circulation of goods in the Internal Market, and the requirements of the Data Protection Directive. Also, regulations should distinguish authentication services from confidentiality services. An EU expert meeting was organized in Copenhagen, on 23-24 April 1998, to initiate a broader debate on encryption issues; the meeting exuded a reserved attitude towards data recovery.

At the RSA Data Security Conference of January 1998, Detlef Eckhert of the European Commission (DGXIII) said that no regulation is planned for the EU.

ETSI (the European Telecommunications Standardisation Institute) is developing a standard for Trusted Third Parties. Part of the standard would relate to lawful access to encrypted data. Great Britain has pushed here for its Royal Holloway key-escrow scheme (see 7.4.3) to be used as a basis for the standard, but this was not adopted, as several EU countries opposed the mandatory key-escrow approach.

5.2.3. Other European initiatives

On 11 September 1995, the Council of Europe[4] issued a *Recommendation Concerning Problems of Criminal Procedure Law Connected with Information Technology*, which stated that "measures should be considered to minimise the negative effects of the use of cryptography on the investigation of criminal offenses, without affecting its legitimate use more than is strictly necessary." [CoE 95] The recommendation itself does not state *which* measures should be taken or *how* the "balance must be found" in the "conflict of interests between the needs of the users and law enforcement". Although some have interpreted the recommendation as leading to mandatory key escrow, the text does not imply this at all.

The 6-8 July 1997 Global Information Networks Conference Bonn Ministerial Declaration of European Ministers (from the European Union, EFTA, Central and Eastern Europe, and Cyprus) echoes the OECD 'guidelines'. It recognizes the importance of strong cryptography, and declares that crypto products should be available internationally and that users should have free choice, subject to applicable law. Measures to safeguard lawful access should be proportionate and effective. Like the OECD 'guidelines', this leaves ample room for interpretation (pro or con data recovery).

---

4 The Council of Europe is a 40-member intergovernmental organization (not to be confused with the European Council, which is a body of the 15-member European Union). Its treaties are not directly applicable in national law, but its recommendations induce members to adapt their legislation accordingly.

5.3. Domestic crypto laws per country

5.3.1. Belgium

In January 1996, Belgium all of a sudden discovered that it had a law which some interpreted as prohibiting the use of unescrowed encryption. The law had been passed in December 1994 as part of a larger law and had gone unnoticed at the time. The law adds a condition under which telecoms equipment may be seized, namely when end equipment renders tapping ineffective.

According to this law, crypto systems had to be agreed by the Belgian Institute for Posts and Telecommunications (BIPT), and the law could be interpreted as allowing a phone to be disconnected when it uses cryptography. It could also enable the establishment of a system of mandatory key deposits at BIPT, where the judiciary could access them. [Clerk]

Two legislation proposals were submitted in June 1996 to drop the contentious provisions of the 1994 law. One of these, by Mmes. Bribosia and Maximus, additionally tried to solve the law-enforcement problem by requiring everyone who would be able to help in decrypting to do this, provided the help was necessary for the investigation.

The law was amended on 19 December 1997 to clear the confusion. A new article states explicitly that the use of encryption is free. The provision of indicated encryption services to the public is subject to prior notification (four weeks in advance) to the BIPT. The explanatory note states that the explicit mention that crypto use is free was needed to indicate the difference with the former law which wanted to subject encryption to key deposits. The new law does not mean that the government has abandoned every desire to gain access to coded messages in the future: "this problem will be reviewed later, having regard to the development of the technology or of potential abuse of encryption by mafia organizations or terrorists".

5.3.2. Denmark

The Danish Technology Council, in an October 1995 report [Stripp], discussed several options for cryptography policy, varying from doing nothing to prohibiting cryptography, without really taking a stand itself. According to the report, the issue is a Gordian knot, which the Danish government should cut expeditiously.

The Danish IT Security Council adopted a policy on encryption in June 1996. The Council recommended that no limitations on encryption use should be introduced. Only in the case of telecommunications companies providing encryption as an integral part of their services, the companies should be able to decrypt a communication through a court order. The Council was of the opinion that secure and inviolable communication should be promoted and that any encryption prohibition at present is an illusion in reality, given the spread of efficient cryptography through the Internet.

A departmental Expert Committee, appointed in the summer of 1996 in preparation for a final decision on the crypto issue by the government, released its *Report by the Expert Committee on Cryptography* in April 1997 [ECC]. The Committee, under pressure of time, rather unrealistically restricted its study to a regulation of the sale of cryptography (not its manufacture, use or import). The Committee recommended that no regulation of cryptography (sale) should be introduced presently. It further recommended that it continue its work, in order to carry out an analysis of the possibilities and consequences of introducing incentive schemes to induce people to use key-recovery crypto. The Committee was allowed to continue its work, and in June 1998, it recommended that the government should refrain from restrictions on crypto use, including incentive schemes to induce people to use key recovery. If, however, international developments should lead to other countries generally favoring key recovery, the government should reconsider this position. On the basis of the Committee's recommendations, the government was supposed to take a stand on the crypto issue after the summer holidays.

5.3.3. France

France has long restricted the import, export, use and marketing of cryptography. The regulation distinguishes between cryptography that can be used *only* for authentication, and cryptography that can (also) be used for confidentiality purposes.

Before 1996, delivery, export, and use of cryptography were subject to:

- previous declaration if the cryptography could have no other object than authenticating communications or assuring the integrity of transmitted messages;
- previous authorization by the Prime Minister in all other cases.

Simplified procedures existed for certain cryptography products or services or certain user categories. For authorization, a dossier containing technical details and administrative data had to be submitted. Authorization could be subjected to certain conditions in order to reserve the use of particular types of cryptography to defined user or application categories.

On 18 June 1996, France passed a law slightly liberalizing these restrictions. The law was published on 27 July 1996 and is referred to as the 26th July law. Decrees on the application of the law (which had to be promulgated for the law to be applicable) were delayed significantly, to be published only in February and March 1998. They covered, among others, the conditions of declarations and authorizations, and the conditions for key-escrow agencies.

Cryptography that does not provide for confidentiality can be used without restriction (the previous requirement of declaration is canceled); supply of authentication-only cryptography still has to be declared. Use and supply of confidentiality cryptography require authorization. A decree specifies categories of cryptography which do not require declaration or authorization, or which require only prior declaration rather than authorization (e.g., cryptography for video-scramblers or ATMs, and cryptography with a key length of up to 40 bits). A supplier is exempted from the formalities for use exclusively for developing, validating or demonstrating cryptography, if he informs SCSSI (the government body responsible for crypto policy) at least two weeks in advance. No authorization is given for cryptography for use by radio amateurs. A supply authorization for collective use exempts users from acquiring a use authorization.

The law furthermore introduces Trusted Third Parties (TTPs), or rather, Key Escrow Agents (KEAs). If a KEA and its key-escrow scheme have been approved, users who escrow their keys with the KEA will be able to freely use the cryptography scheme with these keys. The KEAs will be required to hand over keys to law enforcement under certain conditions. Currently, the only approved KEA is (surprise!) SCSSI itself.

Decree 98-102 specifies the conditions for KEAs. It addresses, among others, the duration of a license to operate, the information the KEA has to provide to SCSSI, the information to register, user contract terms, a register of key requests by law enforcement and a separate (classified) one for key requests by security agencies, security measures, and how to handle when a KEA ceases its activity. KEA employees are required to have a French security clearance.

The action plan on Electronic Commerce, published 7 January 1998 by a task force led by Francis Lorentz, stated that the government was "resolutely oriented towards a liberal reading of the law" [Lorentz]. It urged a rapid implementation of the new law, and it proposed further to promote with its (especially European) partners the principles underlying the policy, to bring about an agreement with France's most important trading partners on the principles and establishment of TTPs and key deposits, and to regularly review the regulatory framework (in particular, the 40-bit limit should be reviewed rapidly), conducting a broad consultation on this before the end of 1998. Given the quite restrictive decrees published afterwards, however, one wonders whether the government as a whole is "committed to a liberal reading".

It is unclear to what extent the present regulation is being enforced in practice; it is rumored to be widely ignored. It seems difficult for individuals or enterprises to obtain authorization for 'strong' cryptography.

5.3.4. Germany

In the February 1996 policy document *Info 2000: Germany's Way into the Information Society* [BfW], the German government supported the European Commission's ETS initiative. A focal point is promoting encryption to protect confidential information by network operators. "In this respect the legal preconditions for the decryption by state bodies are to be examined." As regards the fight against crime, "dangerous gaps" in law-enforcement's ability through criminals' use of encryption should be stopped as soon as possible. "Where this should not be possible with the available methods, new forms also of technical information provision should be considered, to not let crime get a lead." The deployment of criminal law means should be considered only as an "ultima ratio".

Several politicians have expressed a desire to regulate cryptography (see [Moeller] for an overview). There have been many conflicting rumors on the imminence of a crypto regulation, while the government continued to state it was still forming its opinion.

The German federal government is, in fact, itself divided over the issue. Federal Interior Minister Kanther stated, in a speech on 28 April 1997, that he wants to control encryption by allowing only technologies whose manufacturers agree to provide keys to law enforcement (this seems a requirement for crypto providers to build in LEAK). In June 1997, however, the Interior Ministry seemed to favor a two-year voluntary key-escrow approach, in which the government would certify cryptography products which incorporate key escrow. Use of certified products would be voluntary. In October 1997, parliamentarian Tauss revealed that Kanther favors a crypto chip, comparable to the US Clipper chip, for use by the government, in order to create market pressure to push others to use the same technology. There is little support from industry for such an approach. The discussion over this 'Pluto chip' was downplayed in early 1998, when producer Siemens and commissioner BSI (the government agency for IT security) stated that the chip did not contain a backdoor.

Contrary to Kanther, the Minister of Economic Affairs Rexrodt opposes any restriction on crypto use. Likewise, the state Ministers of Economic Affairs, in a March 1997 conference in Eltville, spoke out against a ban on cryptography. Justice Minister Schmidt-Jortzig also opposes a restrictive crypto regulation. The initiative on Electronic Commerce, from 29 October 1997, declares: "The federal government does currently not intend to legally regulate the marketing or use of crypto products. In Germany, therefore, crypto systems can be freely chosen and used." Ulrich Sandl, from the Ministry of Foreign Affairs, said at the RSA Data Security Conference, 13 January 1998, that LEAK systems were ruled out until at least the end of the year; moreover, he implied that use of US key-recovery products may not be in accordance with German privacy law.

By mid-1998, it was generally expected that the issue would, if at all, be decided after the September 1998 elections. The recent government statements show that it is generally leaning towards a stimulating rather than a restrictive approach to cryptography.

5.3.5. The Netherlands

In the early 1990s, when the Netherlands discussed a Computer Crime Act, it was recognized that the power to search in computers would be useless if the files in the computer were encrypted. Therefore, a power was introduced to demand decryption (art. 125k para. 2 DCCP). If encrypted data are found in a computer during a house search, the police can order anyone who can reasonably be supposed to know the means of encryption to decrypt the data. The command cannot be given to suspects, respecting the privilege against self-incrimination.

In March 1994, a Dutch pre-draft law on cryptography leaked out, the drift of which was a prohibition of having, using, or trading strong cryptography. Those with a "legitimate concern" could apply for a user license or a trade authorization. One condition for granting a license was giving information to an administration agency; many interpreted this as a requirement to deposit keys with the agency. After many protests from those who would have been affected by the proposed regulation, the government somewhat sheepishly withdrew it.

As the power to demand decryption is rather useless in practice (in almost all situations, it is only the suspect who knows the key to the encrypted files, and the command can only be given *during* a search), the government has studied on additional means to solve the crypto problem for law enforcement. An envisaged legislative update, the draft Computer Crime Act II, proposes to extend the present decryption command to cover encrypted telecommunications as well. So, if the police encounters encryption in a wiretap, they could command the conversing parties to assist in decrypting. The draft Computer Crime Act II also proposes to extend the power of the police to demand decryption to be given after the search has ended, to allow the police to seize the hard disk for later analysis. Initially, the draft also proposed to give the command to suspects as well, in case of grave evidence against the suspect and if this is urgently necessary for finding the truth. The Explanatory Memorandum considered this in accordance with the privilege against self-incrimination as interpreted in European Court case law, but after protests from the legal community, the provision was removed. (See further Chapter 8 on this issue.)

The government is working on a Trusted Third Parties policy, intended to set preconditions for TTPs to operate. The final report on the TTP project, of March 1998, mentions lawful access to cryptographic keys as a desirable condition for TTPs offering authentication or confidentiality services.[5] However, since most current TTPs do not store private keys, and because of the risks involved in requiring TTPs to store keys, the report suggests that it should not be mandatory for TTPs to store private user keys, although it recommends TTPs to do so. If the TTP does (in effect becoming a KEA), the police can access the keys with a warrant. [KPMG 98]

The government's policy document *Legislation for the electronic highway* of 12 February 1998 [25880, nrs 1-2], affirms that one of the premises for establishing law-enforcement powers is that the use of cryptography will remain free.

5.3.6. Russian Federation

On 3 April 1995, president Yeltsin issued a decree prohibiting unauthorized encryption [Указ]. State organizations and enterprises need a license to use encryption (for both authentication and confidentiality, for storage as well as transmission). Non-state enterprises and organizations using uncertified cryptography do not receive state orders. The Central Bank takes measures against commercial banks that do not use certified cryptography when communicating with divisions of the Central Bank. The development, production, implementation, or operation of cryptography without a license is prohibited. Licenses are issued by FAPSI (a successor of the KGB) based on internal regulations.

5.3.7. United Kingdom

The Department of Trade and Industry (DTI) has been working on a crypto policy since 1996. It proposed legislation in early 1998 after a consultation process with interested parties. After publishing a paper on regulatory intent in June 1996, DTI launched a *Consultation Paper on Licensing of Trusted Third Parties for the Provision of Encryption Services* on 19 March 1997 for a two-month comment period. The department took its time in studying the 260 reactions, publishing a summary of the responses in April 1998, together

---

5 The report suggests that the condition of lawful access does not hold for TTPs offering authentication services, but only if the TTP ensures "that the TTP service and the keys in question *can only be used* for authenticity and integrity." [KPMG 98, 15-16, emphasis added] In several crypto systems, signature keys can also be used for confidentiality encryption, and in fact, an authentication service can always facilitate confidentiality encryption (see 7.7.1). Therefore, this would imply that authentication TTPs would also have to provide lawful access to keys – which they usually will not be able to do since they do not have access to secret or private keys.

with an indication of envisaged legislation. The general aim of the legislation process would be to engender trust in TTP services, while at the same time addressing the law-enforcement problems caused by cryptography. In general, the UK government seems to favor a large-scale implementation of the Royal Holloway scheme (see 7.4.3); although it is not explicitly mentioned, the language of the papers suggests inspiration by the Royal Holloway configuration.

The legislation proposed in the 1997 consultation paper would regulate the licensing by DTI of TTPs that offer cryptographic services - Certification Authorities, Key Escrow Agents, and other types. All cryptographic services offered (by organizations, not by individuals) to the public and businesses would fall under the regime (except for intra-company TTPs and except for encryption services which are an integral part of another service, such as pay-TV). Services offered from abroad would also require a license, including services via the Internet (this would require TTPs that offer online crypto services available in the UK either to get a license or to take measures to not render the service to UK citizens, e.g., by including an exception in the advertisement). The offering of services without a license would be prohibited.

TTPs would be required to render escrowed private encryption keys under a lawful warrant issued by the Secretary of State, under safeguards broadly similar to current wiretap warrants. Only confidentiality keys would have to be handed over, not signature keys (although the paper does not say how to distinguish between (dual-use) keys). The paper involves key escrow (not key recovery), and law enforcement would receive the private encryption key, not session keys; no explicit safeguards are mentioned to assure the agency will destroy the private key on expiry of the warrant. For legal access to keys stored with foreign TTPs, there would have to be agreements with other countries on the basis of dual legality. TTPs would be liable for the protection of the private keys, and there would be strict liability for TTPs for compromise or disclosure of private keys. The requirement for releasing private keys upon a lawful warrant only addressed licensed TTPs who are able to comply, i.e., Key Escrow Agents, not Certification Authorities (CAs).

The paper confirmed that use of licensed TTPs would be voluntary, and that there would be no restrictions on the use of cryptography. However, since users need CAs, and CAs fall under the licensing regime, it was not clear to what extent the government would allow a Public Key Infrastructure to be set up without requiring escrowing of private keys. If the licensing of CAs were restricted, there might be an effective regulation of encryption use after all. Moreover, the "Government recognise[d] that further legislation may be required in the future to enable the appropriate authorities to obtain private encryption keys other than those held by licensed TTPs."

On 27 April 1998, Barbara Roche, Parliamentary Under Secretary of State at DTI, announced the definitive policy proposal of DTI, based on the responses to the consultation document. The policy follows the consultation paper, with some major changes to meet concerns raised in the consultation process. The licensing of TTPs will be voluntary, and so, crypto service providers are free to seek or refrain from licensing. There is also a better policy differentiation between digital signatures and confidentiality encryption. Thus, the policy distinguishes Certification Authorities from Key Recovery Agents. Organizations providing confidentiality encryption services (such as key-recovery or key-management services) are encouraged to seek licenses. Licensed service providers will be required to make recovery of keys possible "through suitable storage arrangements", which indicates a key-escrow rather than a key-recovery technology. Legislation will be enacted to enable law-enforcement agencies to obtain a warrant for lawful access to encryption keys (which does not include keys used solely for digital signature purposes). The legislation to yield access to crypto keys will apply both to (licensed and unlicensed) crypto service providers holding keys and to crypto users. (The latter seems an implementation of the initial Labour policy intention to demand decryption under judicial warrant; see below.) Despite meeting several concerns raised in the consultation process, the final proposal still met with negative comments from UK citizens, notably on the mailing list ukcrypto. Legislation is scheduled for the 1998-1999 parliamentary session.

The new Labour government thus has not significantly altered the DTI policy proposals, contrary to prior hopes and expectations. After all, Labour had stated in its policy on the information superhighway, *Communicating Britain's Future*, that it did not approve of escrowed encryption: "attempts to control the use of encryption technology are wrong in principle, unworkable in practice, and damaging to the long-term economic value of the information networks." [Labour] Instead, Labour wanted authorities to have the power to demand decryption under judicial warrant.

5.3.8. United States of America

Escrowed Encryption Standard (Clipper)

In 1993, the Clinton Administration announced the Escrowed Encryption Standard (EES), usually referred to as Clipper, after its first implementation in the Clipper chip. In this initiative, law-enforcement agencies wiretapping communications encrypted with EES could decipher tapped messages by obtaining the two parts of the chip's master key deposited with two escrow agencies (National Institute of Standards and Technology and the Treasury Department's Automated Systems Division), provided they had a court order for the tapping. Following criticisms on the choice of escrow agents, the government came up with 'commercial key escrow' (soon dubbed 'Clipper II'), a scheme in which the escrow agents could be independent organizations chosen by cryptography users.

The EES was a voluntary standard to be used in telephone communications. Privacy advocates feared that the government would declare escrowed encryption mandatory once it had captured a sufficient portion of the market. Documents obtained by EPIC under the Freedom of Information Act show that already in 1993, federal agencies concluded that the Clipper initiative would only succeed if other crypto-systems were outlawed. FBI director Freeh stated in hearings on pro-crypto bills: "I believe that the [voluntary key-escrow] policy that is enunciated here is a doable policy, but there could come a point where that policy, the voluntary policy, is not a viable one. And then I would certainly look at more mandatory controls" [*EPIC Alert* 3.14, 1 August 1996].

The EES was generally rejected, though, and in March 1997, the Department of Defense announced that the NSA, developer of the Fortezza card (which contained the key-escrow system of the EES), would no longer implement the EES. Instead, it would work to adopt key recovery as promoted by the US government (see below). (See further 7.4.2 on Clipper.)

Key Management Infrastructure

In its May 1996 draft paper *Enabling Privacy, Commerce, Security and Public Safety in the GII* (referred to by opponents as Clipper III), the government proposed the establishment of a key-management infrastructure (KMI) that incorporates key escrow [IWGCP]. Participation in the KMI would be voluntary, and choice of encryption algorithms would be free. A Policy Approving Authority would certify CAs; it would also be responsible for setting CA performance criteria to meet law-enforcement's needs. Users should escrow keys with an Escrow Authority (either the CA or an independent Escrow Authority) in order to get a public-key certificate. Self-escrow would be considered an acceptable option, if the corporate CAs could meet necessary performance requirements, including independence from the rest of the organization and handing over keys to law enforcement.

Efforts to develop a Federal Information Processing Standard for a KMI have been slow. Despite ten meetings, the Technical Advisory Committee could ultimately not produce a definite FIPS recommendation due to conflicting requirements. [Davidson] The charter for the elegantly named TACDFIPSFKMI[6] was renewed in August 1998 to continue work on the requirements for key-recovery products.

NRC report

The June 1996 National Research Council CRISIS study *Cryptography's Role In Securing the Information Society* [NRC], which was requested by Congress, favors widespread encryption. It says the government should promote extensive commercial use of cryptography. The government can explore key-escrow systems for its own use, but it should not push others to use it. Even if the many questions regarding key escrow were resolved, adoption of escrowed encryption (or of any other standard) should be voluntary.

Broad Encryption Policy

On 1 October 1996, Vice President Gore made a statement on export controls, in which he also referred to domestic crypto use. Domestic use of key-escrow cryptography would be voluntary, and the choice of an encryption system would remain free. The government would, however, promote key-escrow crypto by expanding the purchase of key-escrow products for itself, promoting key escrow in international discussions, and stimulating the development of innovative key-escrow products and services. The Administration would also seek legislation to facilitate commercial key escrow, covering, among others, liability issues for releasing keys.

The 'special envoy for cryptography', ambassador Aaron, appointed in November 1996, promoted international cooperation and coordinated US contacts with foreign governments on encryption matters. The 'crypto czar' traveled extensively abroad to lobby (largely unsuccessfully, as it turns out) for the US-favored key-recovery approach.

---

6 Technical Advisory Committee to Develop a Federal Information Processing Standard for the Federal Key Management Infrastructure.

Draft key-recovery legislation

At the end of March 1997, a draft Key Recovery Legislation was published: the *Electronic Data Security Act of 1997*. The Act would promote a Public Key Infrastructure with key recovery by registering (private or (foreign) government) Certification Authorities and (private or government) Key Recovery Agencies (KRAs). A registered CA could only issue a public-key certificate if the user provides a registered KRA with sufficient information to allow timely plaintext recovery by law-enforcement or national security. KRAs – both registered and unregistered – would have to disclose recovery information to government agents under the same legal criteria as those for wiretapping. The use of encryption in furtherance of the commission of a criminal offense would be punished with six months' to five years' imprisonment (having used key recovery which is reasonably available to the government would be an affirmative defense). Finally, the President should conduct negotiations with other countries on the mutual recognition of registered KRAs. The draft legislation affirmed that use of any encryption would be lawful except as provided in the Act or other law (which means any encryption use is lawful except in furtherance of a crime), and that use of the key-recovery infrastructure would be voluntary. The government stopped seeking a sponsor for the draft bill when developments in Congress seemed to lead to similar legislation.

Congress bills

On 16 June 1997, Senators Kerrey, McCain, and Hollings introduced a bill largely similar to the government draft key-recovery legislation, the *Secure Public Networks Act*. It had similar provisions on registration of CAs and KRAs, on criminalization of encryption in furtherance of a criminal offense, on release of recovery information (under broader conditions than the government bill), on international negotiations, and on the voluntary nature of the infrastructure. Additionally, it would require government use and government funding of encryption products to be based on key-recovery crypto, establish an Information Security Board, and provide a waiver authority for the president in cases affecting national security.

An unofficial proposed amendment to the *Secure Public Networks Act*, circulating in the government by the end of August 1997, would have prohibited the manufacture, distribution, sale or import of non-key-recovery cryptography (not its use or possession). The draft amendment contained several other changes, e.g., dropping the requirement for CA registration that the CA ensure recovery information to have been escrowed. In a 3 September 1997 Senate subcommittee hearing, FBI Director Freeh backed this draft legislation, but at the same time, he said that key recovery should be mandatory, not voluntary; Commerce Undersecretary Reinsch commented that this was not the administration's policy. According to Jim Bidzos, President Clinton, at a private dinner, in September 1997 also stated not to support the domestic encryption controls being considered in Congress. In February 1998, Kerrey and McCain were said to circulate a somewhat revised version of their bill, which required a court order for law-enforcement access and which dropped the link between digital-signature key certification and key recovery.

Also in 1997, Representative Goodlatte's *Security And Freedom through Encryption Act* (SAFE) was heavily debated. While aiming at relaxing export controls, it was substantially amended by the House Permanent Select Committee on Intelligence, effectively imposing mandatory key escrow (the Goss-Dicks amendment), and making it a quite different bill. The only provision of the original bill on domestic use had been a penalization of crypto use in furtherance of a criminal offense. However, the House Commerce Committee rejected a similar amendment (Oxley- Manton); instead, it adopted an amendment by Markey and White to create a National Electronic Technologies (NET) Center, a federal information clearinghouse on encryption, which would assist law enforcement by examining techniques to facilitate the efficient access to plaintext. Also, the amendment doubled the penalty for using encryption in furtherance of a felony. Goodlatte's prohibition of the government mandating key escrow was maintained by the Commerce Committee. Given the many competing versions, the bill was not fit for voting, especially since the chair of the House Rules Committee, Solomon, had declared to only move the Act to the floor if it contained a mandatory key-escrow provision.

Senators Ashcroft and Leahy, in May 1998, introduced the E-PRIVACY Act, a creative acronym for Encryption Protects the Rights of Individuals from Violation and Abuse in CYberspace. The bill would also penalize using cryptography to conceal incriminating information in the commission of a federal felony with five to ten years' imprisonment. Like the Markey-White amendment to the SAFE act, the bill would create a NET Center to assist law enforcement. The bill would prohibit the government from mandating key escrow or key recovery.

Conclusion

The US government has been trying to establish some form of more or less mandatory key-escrow or key-recovery policy, although lately, they have increasingly stressed the voluntary nature of their proposals. Such a policy is heavily debated, and citizens, privacy lobby groups, and industry generally fiercely oppose this approach. This is reflected in Congress, where many competing (versions of) bills have been and are being discussed, none of which seems currently to carry sufficient support to be enacted. Therefore, despite the heated debate, the US still does not have any domestic regulation of cryptography.

5.4. Concluding remarks

The survey of cryptography laws shows that regulations differ widely. Some countries have virtually prohibited cryptography (Russia, France). Others are looking at LEAKy solutions (in particular the US and the UK), but they face fierce opposition by their citizens. Moreover, other countries and the European Commission are wary of this approach. Some countries are looking at commanding people to decrypt as a solution. The Netherlands has enacted a law to that effect, which is currently under revision to enable the police to give a decryption command in more situations.

Most countries leave cryptography as yet unregulated – if not by a conscious decision, then at least by a failure to develop a viable and broadly supported policy. The complexity of developing an acceptable crypto policy is also reflected in the international talks on the subject. Given the failure of the OECD 'guidelines' to steer international crypto policies, there is little hope that there will be an international or supranational agreement on addressing the crypto problem within the foreseeable future.

Failing international consensus, countries are thinking of taking steps on their own, driven by a growing concern for criminal crypto use. However, most governments are confused over the direction of a policy, and they seem to be looking at other countries to see what the emerging international direction will be. So, there is a general impasse in the crypto-controversy debate.

Part II

Framework and analysis

Chapter 6. Framework and set of principles

A conception of right is a set of principles, general in form and universal in application, that is to be publicly recognized as a final court of appeal for ordering the conflicting claims of moral persons.
(John Rawls, A Theory of Justice)

The crypto controversy is a problem of balance. We have legitimate interests of crypto users as well as legitimate interests of law enforcement, and they clash. Addressing the crypto problem for law enforcement means finding the right balance between all interests. But how is one to find a right balance?

Consider the following two statements. The "law enforcement community fully supports a balanced encryption policy (...) Key escrow is not just the only solution; it is, in fact, a very good solution because it effectively balances fundamental societal concerns involving privacy, information security, electronic commerce, public safety, and national security." Thus spoke FBI Director Freeh [Freeh 96]. The National Research Council found, however, that "on balance, the advantages of more widespread use of cryptography outweigh the disadvantages," [NRC, 300] and concluded that key escrow is not the right balance. Both claim to have carefully balanced the interests at stake, and yet they draw quite different conclusions.

Most statements, standpoints, and reports hardly give insight in the process of reaching a balance. Not even the extensive and well-researched NRC report makes clear how it arrives at its conclusion. (Perhaps it did not have to, since the report, being the product of a commission with representatives from all sides, can be seen as being balanced by definition – pure procedural justice in practice.) The OECD 'guidelines' for a crypto policy fail to give any indication *how* one is to balance all principles. By stating that all principles can only be implemented together as a whole, they only reiterate the problem (there are clashing interests) without indicating a solution. The OECD 'guidelines' thus leave it at the discretion of each government to develop a policy, and say that they have struck the right balance – which may result in such differing outcomes as those stated by Freeh and the National Research Council.[1] Their procedure is like conjuring a rabbit out of a hat, leaving the public with the feeling that a trick is being played.

I could do the same – present possible options to address the problem, describe pros and cons, analyze how the options affect the interests at stake, and conclude that this or that option is, in effect, the most balanced one. That is hardly an intellectually satisfying result.

---

1 Compare this to what Rawls remarks about the intuitionist approach: "they include no explicit method, no priority rules, for weighing these principles against one another: we are simply to strike a balance by intuition, by what seems to us most nearly right." [Rawls, 34]

One should clarify the process of arriving at the conclusion (and 'balancing' is the key to this process), if the conclusion is to have any claim to being well-founded. This sounds more self-explanatory than it is; in academic legal studies, *how* one balances is often seen as a factual process, escaping rational explanation, just as a judge's intuitive decision whether someone is guilty or not is considered a factual and largely internal process.[2]

I will aim at doing more than just saying I have carefully balanced the interests. By posing a framework for balancing the various interests, I hope to make clear how one can address the crypto conflict. Into this framework, I will input assumptions largely based on the Dutch situation on which I focus. This, essentially, amounts to showing the rabbit before the conjuring starts, and to be open in the way I conjure with it, instead of conjuring up the rabbit at the final conclusion to the public's surprise. The framework I choose will make it clear which assumptions I make and which procedure I follow. Other people favoring different assumptions and coping with other national situations can use different rabbits. It is really the conjuring that matters, not the rabbit.

6.1. Choosing a framework

So for the purposes of this book, the views of the reader and the author are the only ones that count. The opinions of others are used only to clear our own heads.
(Rawls, A Theory of Justice)

For my framework, I choose elements from *A Theory of Justice* by John Rawls. I was led to Rawls by the fierce opposition in the crypto debate between the various pressure groups, each of which has been hard put to imagine that the 'other side' had a legitimate interest as well. This one-sidedness of both sides made me long for the 'veil of ignorance' that Rawls uses in developing his theory of social justice. He addresses the problem of choosing a just structure for the major institutions of society by having people choose principles behind a veil of ignorance, which prohibits them from seeing which position in society they really have. That, surely, would be a great procedure to follow here, if the police, privacy lobby groups, businesses, and citizens could discuss a crypto policy without knowing which of these groups they belong to in real life.

Whereas Rawls stands firmly on the shoulders of giant political philosophers, I have no intention of embedding my argument in legal or political theory. I use Rawls as a source of inspiration, mainly because of his lucid style of writing, his sense of justice, and his choice

---

2 "There is a need for methods to balance interests, to provide for the democratic legitimization of balancing interests, and not to do again the balancing of interests for every single case, but to generalize it as much as possible. At least in private law, there is yet but little research in which these methods are being developed." [Barendrecht, 713]. Compare also what Jan Leijten has said about the 'myth of the scales': "the particular nature of the pair of scales is lacking in the administration of justice. The concrete identification of the value of the weights. I myself, in a long life as a lawyer, will also have occasionally committed the sin of expressing that I had come to the decision after and through a careful weighing of the mutual interests. But it remains a phrase that in itself is saying nothing, because we do measure or weigh two things, but only after having first identified the weight of these things ourselves" [Leijten].

of metaphors to argue his case. I have taken the liberty of pulling Rawls' metaphors out of the context of their original position, and transposed them to my crypto problem, thus altering their original meaning. So, Rawls does not serve as a methodological basis, but he gives me useful metaphors to construct a convincing (or so I hope) argument – nothing less.

Besides the veil of ignorance, the elements of Rawls I find useful in this context are his ways of simplifying the problem – which is one of the major challenges of addressing any complex problem. Rawls defines representative groups that hold the various social positions relevant to the problem; this clarifies the analysis. Then, by choosing the perspective of a least advantaged group from which to judge the problem, one can effectively simplify the decision making in a way that satisfies our intuitive sense of justice. Finally, another useful simplification is Rawls' handling of the ordering problem. If you have several principles, there must be a way of comparing these: you must identify meta-rules. Rawls greatly simplifies the problem by postulating a serial ordering, which means that the first principle should be met before the next principle can be taken into account.

Of course, Rawls' framework cannot be transposed directly to other problems. His problem, *social* justice, is quite different from the crypto problem, which is a subset of *criminal* justice. I will therefore use the framework as a source of inspiration which allows me to describe the problem and the reconciliation of the interests at stake in illuminating metaphors. I shall explain the framework and the similarities and differences with Rawls in more detail in Chapter 11. In this Chapter, I shall present the principles I consider relevant to the crypto problem. I shall define the principles I choose, first the fundamental and constitution-related principles (6.2.1), and next the more practical and technical principles (6.2.2). I conclude by indicating the way in which I shall draw upon these principles in the following chapters, and how I aim at balancing them in Chapter 11 (6.3).

6.2. A set of principles

Principles should be self-evident. It does not matter where they come from or who defends them: they explain themselves. It must only be argued why they are relevant to the problem at issue. Instead of analyzing various likely sources for finding principles (for instance, the constitution, human rights treaties, principles for legislation, various definitions of principles for a crypto policy), I shall simply present the principles I consider relevant, and argue why they are relevant to addressing the crypto controversy.

6.2.1. Fundamental principles

Fundamental principles concern basic human rights. These rights have to be respected by everyone, in all circumstances. They can sometimes be infringed upon, but only if the reason is sufficiently compelling; only competing basic human rights can legitimize such infringements. It is clear that a solution to the crypto problem should respect the basic human rights, although it may be less clear what rights are at stake. In my view, there are four rights that play a role, three of them dealing with civil and political rights (1a-1c), and one with social and economic rights (1d). Another useful distinction is between individual (1a-1b) and collective (1c-1d) human rights (some privacy lobby groups have a tendency of forgetting the latter).

Principle 1a. The right to privacy, including confidential communications

The right to privacy is based on what Judge Cooley has called the right "to be let alone" [Warren]. It is an increasingly important right: individualism is at an all-time high, and information is becoming all-important. In the information society, privacy centers on informational privacy, the right to keep your information to yourself and share it with those of your own choice.

The right to privacy is recognized in many constitutions and human rights treaties; e.g., the ECHR reads: "Everyone has the right to respect for his private and family life, his home and his correspondence." It is not absolute, but an infringement can only take place if it is necessary in a democratic society for national security, law enforcement or the economic well-being of a state. Thus, a state can enact legislation authorizing the police to wiretap, to read correspondence, or to use other means to gather privacy-sensitive information, under strict conditions meeting the requirements of subsidiarity and proportionality.

Cryptography is one of the best tools to safeguard the confidentiality of communications and to protect stored information. A crypto policy therefore naturally has to take into account the right to privacy, including the right to confidential communication.

Principle 1b. The right to a fair trial

The right to a fair trial is one of the assets of a society which advocates the rule of law. It is recognized in article 6 of the ECHR, and it has been elaborated in the case-law of the European Court. Among its many manifestations are the privilege against self-incrimination and the presumption of innocence, which are relevant to the crypto conflict because of the option of asking suspects to hand over encryption keys or to decrypt possibly incriminating ciphertexts themselves (Chapter 8).

Principle 1c. The rule of law, including the right to freedom from crime

Every theory of law somehow tries to argue for the primacy of law over power. It means that the law is primary, not the people in power who implement the law, nor those who break the law. The rule of law is a fundamental principle in our society; as long as 'the law' is a just law, and it is respected by those in power, the benefits for society are evident. Since no society has solely perfect citizens, criminal law and criminal justice have to be part of any law system. I shall not go into the general and complex aspects of criminal justice; I am mainly concerned about one aspect of criminal justice, namely that cryptography enables people to effectively escape law enforcement. The right to freedom from crime is part and parcel of the general rule of law, and it is in this sense that I shall mainly use this principle.

The rule of law means, first, that a society should try to prevent crimes, and, second, that, committed crimes should be redressed, usually by prosecuting their perpetrators. It is under this heading that I will range the law-enforcement concern about cryptocriminals: if cryptography enables some criminals to escape prosecution altogether, the principle of the rule of law is violated. That is a strong argument for infringing other fundamental rights - it is essentially here that 'the balance' has to be struck. This also means that other fundamental rights can only be breached as long as the infringement to the rule of law by cryptography is countered (that is, annulled, or at least significantly weakened). In other words, solutions to the crypto problem must help law enforcement catch criminals: the solution must be *effective*.

Principle 1d. The right to economic development

The right to economic development is of a different order than the previous. Still, it is a fundamental right enshrined in human rights law, primarily the International Covenant on Economic, Social and Cultural Rights. The more dependent economies become on information, the more important information security becomes for society. It is therefore relevant to the crypto debate, since cryptography is a primary tool for information security. Solutions to the crypto problem must take into account its effects upon the economy. The principle is related to the internationality principle (see below). Solutions that are not compatible on the international level tend to jeopardize the national economy: they will scare away companies to more crypto-friendly countries.

6.2.2. Less fundamental principles

There are other principles which are important to the crypto problem. They are less fundamental than basic human rights, in the sense that they should be fulfilled as far as possible, but they need not be maximized at all costs. Human rights can only be preceded by other human rights, and other principles can not override human rights.

Principle 2a. A solution must be workable

It almost goes without saying that if you choose a solution to a problem, the solution must be workable. Almost - for this principle is sometimes attached less importance by the legislature when it stresses the symbolic value of a law: even though a law can not be enforced, it may be important to have it because, for instance, it deters people. (Penalization of spreading computer viruses is arguably symbolic in that sense.)

The main thrust of the principle that a solution must be workable is that it is *implementable*: which means that it must be possible to implement it in real life, and that those who have to live up to the solution must be able to comply with it. Besides, it should also be *enforceable*, which means that there must be a way to ensure that the solution is lived up to.

The second component, enforceability, is not absolute: hardly any legislation is completely enforceable. However, there must be a minimum level of ensuring that the solution is carried out in practice. Where the minimum lies, depends rather on the situation - speed-limit legislation is (and generally can be) only enforced by sample controls, whereas hostage-taking has a near-total level of enforcement (in the sense that everything possible is done to prevent or to punish hostage-takers). Enforceability also relates to those who are to enforce the solution: there must be ways to ensure that those who implement and control the solution do that in a just way, compatible with the aim of the solution and with other rights and duties. In this sense, enforceability of legislation also means that government and other public officials are controlled, e.g., that they do not stop cars during a speed-limit control in order to check for drugs smuggling, or that they do not use excessive force in an attempt to free hostages.

The first component, implementability, I tend to regard as rather absolute. If part of a solution can not be implemented, it should not be part of the solution, and if this unimplementable part is inextricably related to the solution as such, the solution is seriously flawed. Likewise, if there are situations in which the solution is not observable, the solution should be altered. With legislation, and particularly with criminal law, it can not be the case that there are legal consequences (particularly punishments) attached to something which someone cannot do. Of course, this is a matter of principle: a solution must be observable *in principle* in all cases in which it can be reasonably thought to be relevant, which is not to say that all persons will always really be able to comply with it.

Principle 2b. A solution must be internationally compatible

For two reasons, the crypto problem is an eminently international problem. First, the information society, of which cryptography is a vital part, is essentially a global society with blurred national borders. Second, serious crime is increasingly cross-border crime, with criminal organizations consisting of several nationalities and cooperating with partners in delivery or supply countries. Therefore, any solution to the crypto problem must make sense in an international context. That does not mean that the same solution should be implemented worldwide, but it does mean that a soloist solution which disregards the international nature of the problem is likely to be counter-productive.

Principle 2c. A solution must be technologically sustainable

The rise of the information society has posed problems for laws that are technology-specific, for instance, the power of the police to wiretap telephone 'conversations' (which excludes facsimile messages), the constitutional protection of 'letters and telegrams' (which may not cover e-mail messages), and the criminal provisions on damaging or stealing property (which do not cover data). Whereas most of such laws have been or are being adapted to the information age, the lesson to draw is to think carefully over the substance and wording of laws, and try and make them as sustainable in light of technological developments as possible.

If a solution to the crypto problem is to withstand the tooth of time (for at least, say, ten years), it must abstract from the technology. After all, modern cryptography has been around for only thirty years, and the field is still developing rapidly. A solution must assess how future developments in cryptography and its applications may impact on its lasting efficacy.

Comparison with the OECD principles

How do the OECD principles for a crypto policy compare to the principles I consider relevant? Note that the OECD 'guidelines' are broader in scope, dealing with crypto policy at large. They are also relevant to a policy for a digital signature (or public-key) infrastructure, and they mention national-security interests on a par with law-enforcement interests. My concern is only to devise a crypto policy to meet law-enforcement interests. Also note that the OECD principles are not serially ordered: no principle has priority over others, and they should be implemented as a whole.

The first set of the OECD principles (trust, free choice, market-driven development, and standards), and the principle of liability, relate to principle 1d, the right to economic development: all these principles define that a policy must satisfy the information-security demands of the information society. They also relate partly to principle 2c, technological sustainability. The fifth principle, privacy, and the eighth principle, international cooperation, are the same as my principles 1a and 2b, respectively. The sixth principle, lawful access, relates to principle 1c, the rule of law, as far as lawful access by government authorities is concerned. Lawful access by others I do not consider relevant to my problem. Liability, the seventh OECD principle, is partially covered by principle 2a, enforceability, since liability should be addressed to make sure that crypto users – and law-enforcement agents – can observe the policy (this is mainly relevant to key-recovery solutions, see Chapter 7).

my principles	**OECD principles**
1a privacy	5 privacy
1b fair trial	(1 trust, 6 lawful access)
1c rule of law	(1 trust, 6 lawful access)
1d economic development	1 trust, 2 free choice, 3 market-driven, 4 standards, 7 liability
2a workability	(3 market-driven, 4 standards, 7 liability)
2b international	8 international cooperation
2c technological sustainability	(3 market-driven, 4 standards)

6.3. Outline of the framework

In the following chapters, I shall describe four optional directions (and one non-direction) for addressing the crypto problem (to call them 'solutions' would be too optimistic).[3] I derive these options from the survey of crypto regulations in Chapter 5, and I present them in their logical order of 'police-friendliness'.

- One can *ban cryptography*. This is really not an option. (Chapter 6½)
- If one cannot prohibit cryptography, the police will want to access the keys that cryptocriminals use. By building in some form of *law-enforcement access to keys* in cryptographic products, the police ensures *beforehand* that they can decipher suspect ciphertexts. (Chapter 7)

3 I presume that cracking crypto, although possible in some cases, is insufficient to deal with the problem in general (see 4.5.3), and hence not an option to consider.

- If it turns out that building in law-enforcement access to keys is not possible, the police will have to get the keys *afterwards*. That is, if they encounter encrypted communications or stored data, they can *demand people to decrypt or to give the key*. (Chapter 8)
- If accessing keys (either beforehand or afterwards) is infeasible, the police really has a problem. They will not be able to read encrypted data. In that case, they will have to look for *alternative investigation measures* which do not depend on data that can be encrypted. (Chapter 9)
- Ultimately, if all optional directions have more negative than positive overall consequences, then one can (consciously) decide to do nothing: the *zero option*. (Chapter 10)

I shall describe the how and why to these options, define pros and cons, and relate them to the principles outlined above. In each chapter, I will define the most viable options within each direction, arguing on the basis of the principles. This will give one or two (locally) optimal options for each direction. For clarity, I will conclude each chapter by crudely simplifying the analysis and presenting a table that illustrates how the options match the principles.

Then, the major work will have to be done in Chapter 11. I will define the relevant representative groups (law-abiding crypto users, businesses, law enforcement, suspects). Then, I will argue for the ordering of the principles as I outlined above. By dropping the veil of ignorance over the representatives, and by taking the perspective of the least-advantaged group, I will compare the options, and see which option arguably best reconciles the interests at stake.

Chapter 6½. Outlawing cryptography

If cryptography is outlawed, only outlaws will have cryptography.
(Phil Zimmerman)

When a state has a problem, its most natural reaction is to outlaw its cause. For instance, if a particular society considers it wrong to kill people, it establishes a general ban on murder. If a government thinks that it is wrong to kill, but that it may be useful for itself, it creates an exception for itself only (the death penalty). Or if a society considers it good to kill someone if it is the best option given the circumstances, it may allow a generic exception under strict conditions (euthanasia, self-defense). Or even, a society may consider it appropriate for individuals to kill in specific cases (vendetta, suttee).

Prohibiting activities which have only - or mainly - negative implications is easy. The few legitimate exceptions may be addressed by granting generic licenses or individual licenses. With actions that have good sides as well as bad sides, it becomes more difficult to create a general ban. And if an activity is generally good, but has a few bad effects as well, a general prohibition with licenses for the legitimate uses is twisting round exception and rule.

Prohibiting is only an option if the negative implications of the contentious issue significantly outweigh the positive sides. With cryptography, that is not the case: it has a crucial role to play in the information society, and the negative effects of criminal (ab)use of crypto in no way outweigh its benefits. Outlawing cryptography (with licenses for certain (government-friendly) crypto types or individuals who might need it) is simply not a real option, and that is why this chapter is not a real chapter.

However, the idea of a crypto ban has actually occurred to some governments (even to the Dutch government, which one would have expected to be more sensible), and mandatory government-accessible crypto is still advocated in several government circles. It therefore seems wise to go at least briefly into the main arguments against a ban on cryptography.

If a ban on cryptography is to aid law-enforcement, the aim will be to make sure that people do not use encryption, or that they use only cryptography that provides for law-enforcement access (mainly through access to keys, which I call 'LEAK' - Law-Enforcement Access to Keys, see Chapter 7). The ban may be all-encompassing, or it may allow certain types of cryptography to be used, for instance, weak cryptography or LEAK-enabled crypto (mandatory LEAK). It may target the manufacture, trade, import, or use of non-LEAK cryptography. It could also allow non-LEAK crypto use for specific applications (such as banking) or for users that will not hamper law-enforcement (such as the government itself).

But whatever the kind and scope of the ban or mandatory LEAK legislation, if its aim is to ensure that the police can continue to understand wiretaps and computer files obtained through a search, one must assess how the ban helps law enforcement (6½.1), and how it affects the security and privacy of citizens and the economic implications for society at large (6½.2).

> SECRET
>
> NEED FOR A NATIONAL POLICY:
>
> o Although the export of encryption products within the United States is controlled, its domestic use is not regulated. A policy is needed which embodies national legislation, which:
>
> - o Affords legitimate users of cryptography protection which their adversaries cannot defeat.
> - o Insures that cryptographic devices and systems are capable of real-time decryption by law enforcement.
> - o Prohibits cryptography that cannot meet the standard enumerated above.
>   - o An exception will, of course, exist for the protection of classified National Defense Information.
>
> SECRET
>
> Obtained by the Electronic Privacy Information Center under the Freedom of Information Act
>
> 22

Figure 6½.1. Page from an FBI presentation on encryption policy, discussing the need for a prohibition of non-LEAK cryptography. Obtained by the Electronic Privacy Information Center. [source: EPIC]

6½.1. A crypto ban does not help the police

A crypto ban is not enforceable. First of all, strong, non-leak cryptography will continue to be easily available to criminals, especially (but not only) to those with some resources. After all, strong cryptography abounds nowadays, and is still continuing to spread. In practice, a government can never make sure that all the present crypto software and hardware are destroyed. Those criminals who do not yet have a crypto program, may easily avail themselves of an old copy – banned cryptography would simply become an interesting black market. Moreover, simple yet effective crypto algorithms are described in handbooks, and they are fairly easy to implement.[1] Easiest of all, you can download good cryptography from the Internet. Even if one considers it realistic (which it is not) that all 'sensible' countries would outlaw cryptography, 'crypto havens' would emerge, and crypto-anarchist communities would, out of principle, love to cater to crooks and criminals through the Internet. A crypto ban will simply not be able to deny easy access to strong, non-LEAK crypto.

A second argument why a crypto ban is not enforceable, is that it is hard to monitor. Obviously, the police cannot check all computers and diskettes for the presence of banned cryptography. Monitoring encrypted communications is likewise a considerable challenge. Where monitoring public roads for speed-limit offenses is hard to keep up on a reasonable scale, monitoring electronic highways for crypto-use compliance on any scale will be even harder. The amount of traffic is enormous, and the monitoring would have to be automated in some way. Now this is problematic, given the diversity of formats and programs used – it is not easy to distinguish off-hand and automatically between encrypted data and other collections of bits and bytes (see sidebar on next page). The only way a knowbot (a robotic piece of software which automatically performs a pseudo-intelligent task) could distinguish between 'legal' data (encrypted or not) and illegally encrypted data, is to monitor headers or pre-fixed formats.[2] Such traffic monitoring would only be practical if the bulk of communications traffic used distinguishable headers or formats, and this is quite unlikely to achieve in the current international situation. Even then, the ever-resourceful crypto-anarchic community would develop programs which use illegal crypto while producing acceptable headers or formats that would fool the knowbot monitors; such programs would easily find their way to cryptocriminals. The police will lose the monitor race from the beginning.

Apart from general automated enforcement, a case-by-case monitoring would also often be fruitless. There are well-known ways to escape it. Steganography (see 3.1.8) can hide ciphertext in seemingly innocent data. This is not practical in all cases, but a crypto ban could spurt opponents (and there are many opponents in the cryptographic community) to devote their efforts to develop more sophisticated and practical systems of steganography. Moreover, a crypto ban would push criminals to start using steganography, even when they would not otherwise consider the effort worth while. Although, in principle, the police may often be able to unmask steganography, this is resource-consuming and not practical on a large scale. Moreover, apart from steganography, there is a much easier way to escape enforcement: use superencryption. Cryptocriminals will first use an illegal crypto system (which, as noted, is easily accessible) and then encrypt the ciphertext with a legal crypto system.

---

1 "Talent for hire is easy to obtain. A criminal party could easily hire a knowledgable [sic] person to develop needed software. For example, an out-of-work or underemployed scientist or mathematician from the former Soviet Union would find a retainer fee of $500 per month to be a king's ransom." [NRC, 269]

2 For a possible way of monitoring a LEAK-compliant crypto infrastructure, see [Verheul 97a]. With such a system, there are still easy ways to comply with the required format while not giving law enforcement access to keys (cf. Chapter 7).

What is a plain text?

a plaintext
Eleven plaintexts and one ciphertext – look for the seven differences.

a plain text? (fragment from 'Finnegan's Wake' by James Joyce)
My chart shines high where the blue milk's upset. Forgivemequick. I'm going! Bubye! And you, pluck your wark, forgetmenot. Your evenlode. So save to jurna's end! My sights are swimming thicker on me by the shadows to this place. I sow home slowly now by own way, moyvalley way. Towy I too, rathmine.

a poem (fragment from 'Oote' by Jan Hanlo)
Da da demband
Demband demband dembrand dembrandt
Dembrandt Dembrandt Dembrandt
Doe d doe d doe dda doe
Da do do do da do do do
Do do da do deu d

a Cree text (from 'Wapahke', http://arpp.carleton.ca/cree/story/wapahke.html)
Kihtwam paspapi, mikwac isa Kiwitinohk Piponiwi Mitawiwina epimipathitamiwahki ekwa isa kitha ekanawiskwahtawiin. Mitataht niyananosap akihtasowina piko eka kita mitawaniwahk ekwa mwac chiskwa awina esapwahahk. Kamihkwaspisochik isa esapohtawipathihocik, Nohta! ekwa isa ika enawihtakosit okanawiskwahtawew, mwac isa ayayin ikota, tapwe isa mihtatamwak kichiwitamawinakanak, nitohtawike matotaskwaw, tanite ayayin eitwecik, kinitawenimitinanisa eisi matotaskwaw.

a Chinese text (big-5 transcription, in ASCII)
Ãö©ó°ê»Ú¯S³j²ÕÂ´--²{ªp©M¼Æ|r¥H¤Î¥|¬°«OÅ@¤HÅv©Ò°µªº¤u§@iC³Ì·sªºÂù¤ë¥Zªº°ê»Ú¯S³j²ÕÂ´³q°T³q °T--¥H«eªºÂù¤ë¥Zªº°ê»Ú¯S³j²ÕÂ´³q°T (¯Â¤å|rÀÉ®×)iC

a Chinese text (in sijiao haoma transcription)
2368 1129 0364 6221, 1073 0502 0207 0117, 8096 1421 0433 2978, 0364 0482 2607 0171

a PGP public-key fingerprint
0DA4 14B8 EDA1 C226 E0E4 449A AE54 0D39 9825 EF38

a PGP ciphertext (fragment)
qANQR1DBwU4DvxKJpNLmeGUQCAC5kzFTqf3PS+SG/OwGfBiqY+/mmFbRBA+rQeui3gokRolIDAizhmK9sh/jTip
/XKP5RsDevAF+UojsIqz7dmD8u4NeTgBni0NtHoRXXxrYiMYrfoWy5Awxrnz3lncelogvxeW4HE3c/1IhqUfyw3yh4s
7LRflloON4ilXc

a PGP signature
iQA/AwUBNCAOO65UDTmYJe84EQL8xACdG6OMwlaM9Gzqsh24HXKm0GQrndAAoJIRh79ED4xhdCvm5icQDq+w
SOOi
=Qq9E

a crypto program (Diffie-Hellman in perl, by Adam Back)
```
($g,$e,$m)=@ARGV,$m||die"$0 gen exp mod\n";print`echo
"16dio1[d2%Sa2/d0<X+d*La1=z\U$m%0]SX$e"[$g*]\EszlXx+p|dc`
```

a GIF image (in ASCII)
³ ¿ ¿ ¿¿ ¿¿ ¿ ¿¿ÀÀÀ□□□ÿ ÿ ÿÿ ÿÿ ÿ ÿÿÿÿÿ!ù , :ðÈI«½ ¥' º[×q•6vAP…Í± …:‰\' U¿1 K¶Ø PÈM · ®P*â „_æIH`®ØJ !þï

a WAV sound (fragment in ASCII)
f``dfkkppqtsqrqvv}y□†□^‵——□š ¤¢¥|¥¨«©"ƒ|ztc`T^^iglqs}y|uuphjjst}ƒˆ‴›™œœ ¥££¢¥¨«—,ã|{e`OW`h ebkrx~yvuzuopnttƒƒˆ□•šœ□œ□¢¤¢ XWVfhkgqr~}}wy}vtpnuy…,‡Œ•šš›—š□Ÿ□›□Ÿ¨ªš,|||jgTT\gkfihtz|xs yyvupqs□„„†□"™œš—œ □□œŸ§§"†□,|rk]_cikkkluy{xwxxzyxzãˆ‰□

Mandatory LEAK and constitutional rights

Mandatory LEAK systems are often claimed to infringe constitutional rights disproportionately. Especially within the cypherpunk community, one often hears the argument that people have an (intrinsic) right to encryption. The argument often centers around the freedom of speech: people argue they have the right to say anything they want in any way they like. The argument fails, in my opinion, to recognize that the freedom of speech primarily addresses speech content, not the medium used for conveying the speech. Newspapers can refuse letters to the editor out of space considerations, and people hardly argue this infringes their right to freedom of speech. If you cannot publish your opinion in the *New York Times*, you spread a leaflet, target the radio, or publish a newspaper yourself. Freedom of speech only addresses the medium of speech in that everyone must have an *adequate* means of expression (not *any* means to one's choice). Prohibiting newspapers altogether may well be compatible with freedom of speech, if there remain sufficient other means of expressing one's opinion to a similar effect, and if it is a proportional measure.

I would argue that likewise, there is no fundamental 'right to encryption' through freedom of speech. If you cannot use the particular encryption system you want for communicating your views, use another medium – a crypto system that *is* allowed, communication in person, or, why not, a Kwakiutl courier. Also, remark that freedom of speech safeguards the possibility of making your opinion *public*, whereas encryption is used to keep your opinion *private*. Even if LEAK schemes were built-in in a significant portion of people's communications media (e.g., in web browsers and operating systems), and people would thus be more or less obliged to use them, this would not infringe upon their freedom of speech: they can still express their opinion – the fact that law-enforcement agencies could access this opinion does not alter this. Therefore, I do not think that mandatory crypto systems in general infringe upon the freedom of speech.

The US First Amendment may be more extensive than the Dutch understanding of the freedom of speech, but it can well be argued that mandatory LEAK does not infringe the First Amendment either, as Robert Litt, principal associate deputy attorney general, has aptly done in Congress [Litt]. His argument only falters with two possible infringements. First, mandatory LEAK may unduly restrict the ability of cryptographers to exchange crypto source codes (cf. the *Bernstein* decision). This, to me, seems a minor infringement one might consider proportional, given the major concerns at stake. However, the other potential infringement Litt does not adequately refute: the potential chilling effect of mandatory LEAK on free speech. People may feel restricted to communicate over a LEAK infrastructure. Litt rejects this with the argument that LEAK does nothing more than preserve the current capability of wiretapping, which, the court has decided, does not 'chill' free speech. There may, however, be good arguments to see the chilling effect of a LEAK infrastructure as larger than that of a wiretap-enabled telephone network. Communications patterns are changing with the advent of the information society, and larger parts of private life are taking place online. Therefore, the fact that governments could access these extended patterns of communications might ultimately have a chilling effect on free speech. This is not an argument that people in the Netherlands would consider valid, but in the US, it may hold more strength.

The 'right to encryption' has more to do with the right to confidential communication. This constitutional right is part of people's right to a private sphere (e.g., art. 17 ICCPR, art. 12 UDHR). The right to confidential communications implies that people must be able to choose adequate protection measures for safeguarding confidentiality. Thus, if governments consider making LEAK schemes mandatory, they have to ensure the system is secure against unlawful eavesdropping. Moreover, inasmuch as the LEAK system allows law-enforcement agencies a wider access to people's communications than they currently have, this ability must be established by formal law after a careful balance of the concerns involved. For the moment, as long as governments cannot guarantee the security of LEAK systems [cf. Abelson 97], one can argue they cannot make them mandatory. In the US, the Fourth Amendment protects reasonable expectations of privacy by prohibiting unreasonable searches. A LEAK infrastructure need not harm this expectation, if proper conditions for law-enforcement access are enacted. [Litt]

One could also suggest that obliging people to escrow their private keys infringes the privilege against self-incrimination. After all, you oblige people to give the police the means to gather evidence against them. For several reasons, the argument does not hold. First, the right to non-self-incrimination pertains to suspects, whereas a mandatory LEAK system is a general measure targeting citizens at large; people depositing their keys do not do so in a capacity of criminal suspect. Moreover, the concern protected by the privilege against self-incrimination is that the truth be found in criminal proceedings (see 8.5). Now, requiring people to use means that enable law-enforcement agencies to gather evidence does not threaten the fact-finding process, as people are not forced to give evidence itself. After all, people may refrain from using the LEAK system; they are not in any way obliged to use it for communicating incriminating evidence. There are plenty of parallels, for instance in the tax-law requirement of keeping verifiable books: this also is a requirement that creates the possibility for law enforcement to gather evidence, while it does not concretely push people to hand over incriminating evidence. The same arguments imply that mandatory LEAK does not infringe the Fifth Amendment. (See Chapter 8 for an analysis of the privilege in relation to demanding decryption.)

Knowbots and human monitors will regard the message as legal, until they decrypt it and find it contains another layer of encryption underneath (or is it an exotic image format, or perhaps Chinese big-5?). Of course, the monitors will seldom decrypt 'legal' messages, and the bulk of the 'illegal' messages will go unnoticed.

In conclusion, a crypto ban is unenforceable, and even if it were enforceable – in the sense that prohibited crypto use could be monitored – cryptocriminals could still easily escape notice. Illegal crypto use will only be noticed when it is too late: in a search, or after a wiretap. This suggests that it may be better (or rather, less bad) to restrict the ban to these situations: one could consider penalizing crypto use when this obstructs a criminal investigation (in particular, a search or a wiretap); the effects are the same for criminals facing investigation, but at least for law-abiding citizens, crypto use will be legal. There are objections to a prohibition of crypto use that obstructs investigation as well, but it may be an option to consider (see 8.7 – this non-chapter only deals with non-options).

6½.2. A crypto ban does hamper good guys

Whereas most criminals will not be affected by a crypto ban, most law-abiding citizens will be. In the information society we are building, the vast majority of the public will be affected in two ways: individually, and collectively.

First, if cryptography is banned, would-be crypto users (and who would not be a crypto user in the information society?) face extensive security and privacy threats. This is also the case if they are allowed to use LEAKing cryptography. Any LEAK system weakens the security of cryptography (by definition, since an extra access feature for law enforcement creates new opportunities for attacks, such as bribery or counter-infiltration, and in practice, because the systems are more complex and thus may introduce new security leaks): the risks of LEAK cryptography are fundamental and significant [Abelson 97] (cf. Chapter 7).

A second possible effect of a ban of non-LEAK crypto on law-abiding citizens is that the balance between citizens and their government may turn significantly in favor of the government. Taking the pre-digital era as a reference point, the rise of information and communications technologies is affecting this balance in two ways. Most notably, cryptography allows citizens to effectively escape government's scrutiny on a scale formerly impossible, which adds weight to the citizens' level of power. On the other hand, ICT also allow new monitoring techniques (cf. Chapter 9), and the increasing registration of all levels of public life and of many levels of private life gives the government considerable powers over the citizen. These countering developments mean that the digital era does not necessarily alter the precarious balance between government and citizens. However, were non-LEAK cryptography to be banned, the balance inexorably moves towards the government. Whereas this is not an immediate threat in countries with good governance (in many countries featured in Amnesty International's yearly report, one should consider this a threat), no government can ensure that powers will not be abused by future governments, as history has sadly shown so often. A LEAKing crypto infrastructure can be established with many checks and balances, but once the infrastructure is there, future abuse is easy and unavoidable once a government turns crooked. Law-abiding crypto users could become future Winstons, desperately looking for a corner to escape Big Brother's persecution.

Finally, a crypto ban will also lead to a collective, economic backlash, since international trade will significantly be obstructed if companies cannot communicate or trade securely (cf. Chapter 3). If the ban is not enforced on an international level (comprising at least the G7, but preferably the OECD and ASEAN), companies in a crypto-banned country will have a hard time staying alive in the information society, since international traders will prefer secure transactions without foreign governments' access. Indeed, they may decide to move to another, more crypto friendly country, causing damage to the economy of the crypto-banning country. Now, worldwide consensus on a crypto ban is nowhere to be reached; the OECD principles do not rule out mandatory LEAK in explicit terms, but the wording is strong enough to suggest that an international crypto ban or mandatory LEAK is not an option.[3] Moreover, even apart from global competition, the costs for implementing a LEAK infrastructure are huge. All current software and hardware containing cryptography must be replaced, throwing away all investments in current information security. Also, the costs of maintaining a LEAK infrastructure are higher than those of maintaining a strong, non-LEAK infrastructure. Lastly, it seems undesirable that corporations who will comply with the crypto ban (and thus have more costs and less security) will be at an economic disadvantage with respect to businesses who use illegal strong cryptography (which, as noted, is hard to monitor and punish).

In short, a crypto ban has very serious consequences for law-abiding citizens. It poses a significant threat to privacy and information security, and it severely obstructs the development of the information society. It may also pave the way for future governments with less noble intentions to do away with privacy altogether. Finally, a national crypto ban will lead to a severe economic backlash.

6½.3. Conclusion

The conclusion of this non-chapter is short and simple. The gains of a crypto ban or of mandatory LEAK for law-enforcement are dubious at best, and more likely low to non-existent: it does not pose serious problems for criminals to use strong cryptography. The losses of a crypto ban for individuals, businesses, and the information society, on the other hand, are certain and large. There is no way to achieve any balance between these effects. It is, as Phil Zimmerman – ever the rhetorician – has suggested, like reverse chemotherapy: it kills the benign cells, while it leaves the malignant cells intact.

Banning cryptography or mandating LEAKing crypto systems is simply not an option. We had better move on to real chapters with real options.

---

3 "Government controls on cryptographic methods should be no more than are essential to the discharge of government responsibilities and should respect user choice to the greatest extent possible." [OECD 97, principle 2]

Chapter 7. LEAKing through the Public Key Infrastructure

The people involved in the crypto debate are all intelligent, honorable and pro-escrow, but they never possess more than two of these qualities at once.
(Kenneth Neil Cukier)

If the government cannot outlaw cryptography, they will somehow have to get access to outlaws' crypto keys. The most convenient way to get access to keys is to ensure *beforehand* that law enforcement will be able to retrieve any key used by a cryptocriminal. Therefore, it is an attractive option to build in some feature in crypto systems which allows the government to access any key used. Systems with built-in Law-Enforcement Access to Keys will LEAK the tell-tale plaintexts to the police.

Since mandating LEAK systems is not an option, governments can look at ways to stimulate the development and use of *voluntary* LEAK products. The Clipper chip, the first instance of a LEAK scheme, was such a product. It has been criticized and refined, and it was followed by other schemes, all in an attempt to keep criminals leak information through law-enforcement wiretaps. The schemes follow up on the necessity of establishing Public Key Infrastructures (PKIs) – data recovery could be a prime feature of a PKI. Indeed, the private sector also considers data recovery useful, to prevent data from being irretrievably lost if someone loses the key with which they are encrypted. The difference is, however, that the private-sector need concentrates on retrieving stored data, whereas law enforcement mainly focuses on using LEAK systems to access encrypted communications; so, the systems and private and public concerns need not be the same.[1]

Ever since the Clipper chip, key escrow (or, more generic, data recovery) has been hotly debated. Law-enforcement officials have hailed the depositing or recovery of keys as a solution to the cryptocriminal problem, and privacy advocates have condemned it as an Orwellian measure. The crypto debate here has its heyday.

In this chapter, I shall describe a generic Public Key Infrastructure, and indicate the position of key deposits in PKIs (7.1). Then, I go into the general nature of LEAK systems. There are, in fact, two kinds of LEAK systems and infrastructures. The first kind is targeted at establishing a secure information infrastructure for law-abiding citizens, albeit one that does not give criminals an advantage over law-enforcement. Preventing criminal abuse is the common focus of the LEAK features in this infrastructure. The second kind are LEAK

---

1 "[T]he requirements of a government and the requirements of the commercial world and individual users are very different in this regard, so different that, in fact, there is little overlap between systems that address these two problems." [Abelson 97]

systems which aim at solving the problem of criminal use of cryptography as such, which means that the LEAK features should not only prevent criminal abuse of this infrastructure, but also prevent criminals from using non-LEAK crypto systems at all. (7.2)

Next, I describe the three main techniques in crypto systems that allow law-enforcement access to keys or plaintext. First, crypto systems can be separated into signature systems and confidentiality systems (7.3). A signature algorithms, such as the Digital Signature Standard, that can not be used for confidentiality is not a proper LEAK system, but it will help law enforcement in narrowing down the amount of encrypted material they should investigate. Second, key-escrow or key-deposit schemes 'leak' information by giving law enforcement access to private or session keys (7.4). Third, key-recovery systems (which provide 'encapsulation' of session keys) work through the sending along of information which a law-enforcement agent can access, without the need for depositing private keys (7.5). Throughout, I confine myself here to voluntary LEAK systems, since mandating the use of such systems is not an option (Chapter 6½).

In order to assess the value of these proposals, I describe several issues that have to be taken into account before a government can decide to stimulate LEAK schemes (7.6). Then, I will define the particular options that emerge from this direction, and assess how they match the principles for addressing the crypto conflict. I end with a first conclusion on the viability of these options (7.7). Since this chapter draws heavily on descriptions of public-key cryptography, readers less-versed in the technology may want to reread sections 3.1.3 and 3.1.6 first.

7.1. Public Key Infrastructures

Public-key encryption is a necessary tool in the information society. In a networked society, in which many parts of daily life are handled over public communication networks, people need encryption to communicate securely. Especially if people do not know each other, cryptography can establish the necessary confidence between communicating partners.

Widespread use of public-key encryption, however, requires an infrastructure. Public-key encryption relies on public keys, and people must be assured of the authenticity of a public key if they are to trust the encryption process. Therefore, Public Key Infrastructures (PKIs) must be set up, which perform several functions essential to public-key encryption. A PKI consists of parties who offer trusted services, such as key certification, key distribution and revocation, time-stamping, and data recovery. Depending on the service offered, the trusted party may be called a Certification Authority (CA), a Key Escrow Agent (KEA), or a Data Recovery Agency (DRA). The overall term for these parties is Trusted Third Parties (TTPs).[2]

---

2 The Infosec *Code of Practice and Management Guidelines for Trusted Third Party Services* of October 1993 defines a TTP as "an impartial organisation delivering business confidence, through commercial and technical security features, to an electronic transaction. It supplies technically and legally reliable means of carrying out, facilitating, producing independent evidence about and/or arbitrating on an electronic transaction. Its services are provided and underwritten by technical, legal, financial and/or structural means." [Castell]

In this chapter, I shall use the generic term TTP or, where a specific function of the TTP is stressed, CA, KEA, or DRA.

Key management is the central object of a PKI. First, users have to *obtain* private-public key pairs. Either they can generate key pairs themselves, or they can receive them from a Key Distribution Center. Then, they need to have the public key *certified*, so that everyone can see that the public key is authentic. One way of certifying keys is to create a horizontal 'web of trust', in which everyone signs the keys of persons whose key they know or trust to be correct. PGP uses such a certifying structure. Assuming a friend's friend to be a friend, one can trust keys of people one does not know, but there has to be a chain between communicating parties. For large user groups, especially internationally, such a horizontal

Terminology

Clipper chip	chip for the Escrowed Encryption Standard, proposed by US government in 1993, providing government access through a LEAF; died somewhere in 1996
data recovery	all-encompassing term for retrieving the plaintext of encrypted data if the key for decryption is not available, through key escrow, key recovery, or plaintext recovery; the TTP providing data recovery can give private keys, session keys, or plaintexts
DRA	Data Recovery Agency, TTP which provides data-recovery services
GAK	Government Access to Keys; outdated term for crypto systems that allow a government (law enforcement or national security) to access crypto keys or plaintext; although outdated, still useful as a generic term
KEA	Key Escrow Agent, TTP which provides key-escrow services
key backup	storing a copy of a private (or supersymmetric) key, either internally ('self-escrow') or externally ('escrow')
key deposit	synonym for key escrow
key escrow	generic term for providing government (and authorized-user) access to keys by having people deposit their private (or supersymmetric) keys with a TTP
key encapsulation	synonym for key recovery as used in this book
key management	the process of key generation, key certification, certificate distribution, and certificate revocation, may also include key deposit or backup; used in the OECD 'guidelines' as a potential euphemism for key recovery (which suggests that, once 'key recovery' becomes tainted with negative implications, 'key management' may replace it as the next generic term for GAK)
key recovery	originally a term for a crypto system which provides LEAK by having people tag along to messages a recoverable session key rather than deposit their private keys; is increasingly used, however, irrespective of the technology, as a generic term for LEAK and a replacement for 'key escrow' which has become a too negative term; I use it in the original sense: recovering session keys
LEAF	Law-Enforcement Access Field; data unit sent by Clipper chips which enables the Clipper TTPs to decrypt the message; sometimes also used in other key-recovery systems
LEAK	Law-Enforcement Access to Keys: law-enforcement part of GAK; I use this as the generic term for key escrow and key recovery for law-enforcement purposes (Law-Enforcement Access to Data would be more correct, but LEAK seems the more appropriate acronym)
TTP	Trusted Third Party; a trusted, independent organization which offers cryptography-based services that enhance the reliability of electronic data interchange and storage, such as key certification, distribution, revocation, and time-stamping; the term includes Certification Authorities, Key Escrow Agents, and Data Recovery Agencies

structure may not be practical, leaving aside the issue of having to rely on people's responsibility in certifying keys. The alternative is to create a vertical, hierarchical certification structure, in which a top-level certification authority (or root CA) certifies other certification authorities (CAs), who in their turn certify other CAs and users. PEM uses such a certification structure. Its certificates conform to the ITU X.509 standard for public-key certificates. PEM's top CA is the Internet Policy Registration Authority. [Schneier, 577-584]

In such a hierarchical certifying structure, if users generate the keys themselves, they have to send the public key (securely!) to a Certification Authority, who will check their identity and issue a certificate with the public key and appropriate personal information. Depending on the required security level of the certificate, people may have to go to the CA in person and show a passport or identity card – after all, the certificate is the basis for trust in all subsequent communications, and so the CA must be really convinced of the identity of the user. Alternatively, the encryption hardware or software of the user may have built-in automatic key generation and secure communication with the encryption producer or CA to obtain a certified public key. The CA will provide the user with a key certificate, which is usually valid for a specified period.

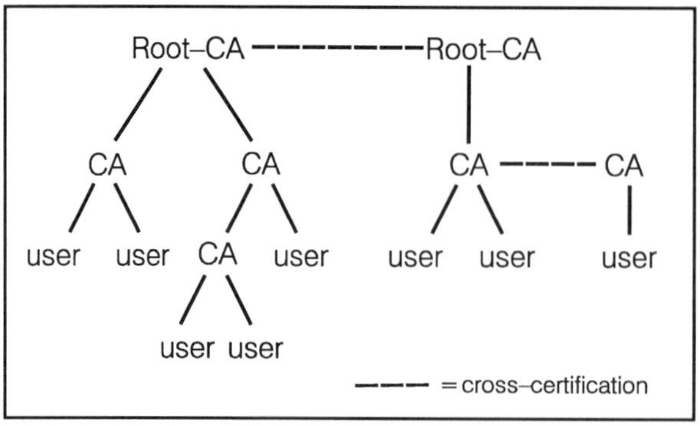

Figure 7.1. A Public Key Infrastructure

Once the users have a key pair, they will *publicize* the public key. They can send the key certificate to potential communicators, have it listed in the telephone directory, publish it on their Website, and mention it in their e-mail signature. However, this may not be enough for businesses, such as information and service providers, who wish to be widely known to, for instance, potential customers. For this, they can use a Key Distribution Center that maintains a directory of public keys. Also, the CA may have a list of the keys it has certified. As more and more CAs and KDCs go online, people will have increasing difficulty in tracing where to find a public key. Thus, some centralization of the public-key distribution process is inevitable. World Wide Web servers with advanced search engines may be a good solution.

The counterpart of key certification is key *revocation.* After all, private keys can be compromised – through carelessness, theft, or because the validity period has expired. Together with key distribution lists, CAs or KDCs will therefore maintain key revocation lists. After revocation or expiry, certificates can be deleted, but the CA must keep a copy in order to resolve potential later disputes, for instance, over a contract signed before revocation.

Now, if Alice wants to communicate with Bob, she looks up his public key in some directory. To check its authenticity, she will verify the CA's signature. This requires her to be sure of the CA's public key. Consequently, she will have to verify CAs' keys until she comes to the top of the CA hierarchy, the top-level CA. This will likely be a national or international trusted body, whose public key is generally trusted, for instance, because it is widely published on television, in the newspapers, and by government bodies. Before people use public keys, they should first check whether the key is still valid.

Key certification, distribution, and revocation are the basis of any PKI. Additional services may be offered for specific user groups. In commercial transactions, for instance, the date and time on which a document is sent may be crucial. For this, TTPs can offer time-stamping services. Alice sends a message to Trent, who adds the date and time he received the message and signs the whole with his private key; Trent can either forward the message to addressee Bob, or return the time-stamped message to Alice. This function is comparable to traditional notary services.

The crypto family revisited

Alice and Bob continue communicating extensively with each other, as usual with Eve eavesdropping. Criminals Carol and Dave are trying to frame them, and so, Leah, the law-enforcement agent who is monitoring Carol, is also intercepting Alice's and Bob's communications. Sometimes, Alice lives abroad, and Leah may require assistance from Leonard, a foreign law-enforcement official. In this chapter, Alice and Bob will use the public-key infrastructure for their communications; they sometimes require the services of trusted third party Trent. Also, they will often deposit their keys with a Key Escrow Agent, Dorothy (or, in a foreign country, Dorotea). A guest appearance is made by Polly, an (unfortunately corrupt) policewoman.

(The use of Dorothy for the canonical key-escrow agent was proposed at a SAFE meeting, 1 July 1996, at Stanford, crediting professor Dorothy Denning as a fervent advocate of law-enforcement access to keys in the US at the time; her position on the desirability of data recovery, however, is more subtle – she considers this a direction worth exploring but not mandating [Denning 97c].)

Another notary function which may be relevant in PKIs is data recovery. Users of cryptography may worry that they lose access to information, either because they lose a (private or symmetric) key, or because someone else who encrypted the information is no longer willing or able to decrypt it. After all, people get ill or die suddenly, and employees may run away to a competitor. Disgruntled employees can even encrypt essential information to blackmail the employer. Users, most often businesses, will therefore want to have a backdoor. Data recovery can be provided in a variety of ways: backing up plaintexts in a central department, storing the keys on a diskette in a safe, or have a TTP keep a copy of the private key. A TTP can be in-house or external, for instance, a Chamber of Commerce or an industrial organization. Such a Data Recovery Agency will provide access to authorized people when they need it. Data recovery will generally only be required for information storage. In communications, session keys are used, which can be discarded after the session has ended or, in case of e-mail communications, after decryption of the message.[3] Since data recovery for crypto users is mainly meant for storage purposes, it is different from other PKI services: key certification and distribution are needed for communication and information transport, not for storage.

A PKI, then, is a hierarchical structure of CAs and, possibly, DRAs. The information society will consist of several PKIs, for instance one or a few commercial PKIs, a government PKI, an academic PKI,[4] and a non-profit PKI. Root CAs may cooperate (inter)nationally and cross-certify each other, thus merging PKIs. Too many PKIs may

3 One potential exception may be when a company (e.g., a call-center) wants to listen in on its employees, for instance, to check compliance with secrecy rules, or for audit purposes; in this case, the management could require session keys to be stored for later checking. [cf. BSC]

4 In the Netherlands, one of the first PKIs to be set up was a SURFnet PGP infrastructure, initiated late 1996. SURFnet is the Dutch academic network.

confuse people, and weaken their trust in the system. Perhaps governments themselves should set up a single, overall PKI, and issue citizens with a smart card containing a certified multi-purpose private-public-key pair. In any case, because of the importance of PKIs in the information society, governments must create a legal framework for TTPs to operate. Issues such as liability and preconditions for participation in the PKI must be addressed.

7.2. Public Key Infrastructures and LEAK

One of the issues to be addressed in a legal PKI framework is law-enforcement access. Many governments are looking at TTPs and PKIs as a potential way to solve the law-enforcement problem of cryptography. In particular, in the case of data recovery, law-enforcement agencies could access private keys or plaintexts through a KEA or DRA, provided they have a court warrant.

However, one must distinguish between a PKI set up for information security, and a PKI established specifically for law-enforcement needs. The first will be established through private-market forces, following the information society's need for a PKI to ensure communications security. The second, however, is pushed by the need for law-enforcement agencies to monitor suspects, and will consequently be shaped quite differently.

These two divergent PKI goals in fact address two problems. The first problem is related to establishing a good information security infrastructure, including a PKI – I shall call this the 'security problem'. The second problem is criminal use of cryptography to thwart law enforcement – this is a 'law-enforcement problem'. The problems are intertwined, inasmuch as solving the first problem may increase the second problem: criminals may use a robust information security infrastructure to escape law-enforcement scrutiny. Therefore, in solving the first problem, one must try and prevent criminals from profiting from the PKI. Trying to prevent abuse in a security PKI, however, is different from solving the overall problem of criminals profiting from encryption. A security PKI may look at its effects on law enforcement as (only) one of the conditions to take into account, whereas a law-enforcement-triggered PKI is entirely focused on securing law-enforcement's need for information gathering.

The difference between a security PKI and a law-enforcement PKI has been underestimated by governments. This can be seen in two of the main initiatives for setting up a government-stimulated PKI. First, the *US Key Management Infrastructure* (KMI) initiative, launched in May 1996, proposed a PKI with private-sector TTPs (see 5.3.8). These TTPs would certify public keys, perform the usual key-management services, and also serve as key-escrow agencies. The draft proposal [IWGCP] lacked detail and clarity, but it seemed to presume that a security PKI would naturally incorporate key escrow as a way to solve the law-enforcement problem. However, the KMI initiative was hardly further developed, and the effort to produce a Federal Information Processing Standard for the KMI was still unsuccessful in mid-1998 when the Technical Advisory Committee "encountered some significant technical problems that, without resolution, prevent the development of a useful FIPS. There are unresolved conflicts among some requirements." [Davidson] The TACDFIPS-FKMI continues its work on requirements for key-recovery products as of August 1998.

The other main proposal for a PKI was (or is) the *European Union's ETS initiative*. This likewise started as a proposal for a public-key infrastructure that would not hamper law enforcement by incorporating some form of key escrow (see 5.2.2). The first draft proposal implied that private keys would be deposited with KEAs: "the law enforcement authorities can then apply to the TTP for access to the targeted individual's private encryption key without his knowledge or cooperation." Indeed, "the use of TTPs also potentially solves the legal interception problem." [SOG-IS] Since 1997, however, the ETS initiative has turned away from ensuring law-enforcement access, focusing instead on a digital-signature infrastructure. The European Commission's Communication of October 1997 [COM(97) 503] suggests that key escrow will not be chosen as a key feature of an ETS public-key infrastructure.

Both these developments show that the initial idea that combining a security PKI with key escrow that would solve the law-enforcement problem turned out to be mistaken. The features of both kinds of PKI are apparently hard to reconcile.

The discussion on crypto policy is thus hampered by the lumping together of the security and the law-enforcement problems. In this chapter, I will distinguish between LEAK systems that aim at preventing criminal abuse of the PKI (a security infrastructure) and LEAK systems that aim at solving the law-enforcement problem by ensuring that criminals only use LEAK cryptography.

7.3. Non-confidentiality cryptography

Despite the urgent need for setting up a Public Key Infrastructure and setting standards to enhance the international use of cryptography, efforts for standardizing cryptography and international initiatives for PKIs have been sparse. This is for a large part due to the national-security and law-enforcement concerns and consequent export regulations. As soon as economic policy initiatives are proposed to develop cryptography standards and to stimulate crypto use, state security and law-enforcement officials begin to protest, arguing their interception abilities should not be jeopardized.

This deadlock situation has a few exceptions, notably authentication-only systems and financial applications. Digital signature standards can serve a large part of the information security need in the information society, while they need not hamper law enforcement or intelligence. In particular, the US government standardization body NIST has developed a Digital Signature Algorithm (DSA), to be used in a Digital Signature Standard (DSS) [NIST 94]. (Actually, the algorithm was more or less developed by the NSA, as NIST has reluctantly admitted.) The DSS is meant for securing authenticity and integrity of electronic communications and documents. It was devised so that it would not be able to serve confidentiality purposes. Therefore, governments could readily accept it as politically uncontroversial, and potentially, the DSS could become a worldwide standard. Likewise, systems specifically designed for financial applications are relatively uncontroversial. Thus, for instance, the Secure Electronic Transactions (SET) system has been developed for secure online payments; since SET cannot be used for confidentiality encryption in general, it is not harmful to law enforcement.

In this section, I shall use the DSA to illustrate the option of stimulating the use of non-confidentiality crypto.

7.3.1. Working of DSA

The DSA is based on discrete logarithms (closely related to algorithms by Schnorr and ElGamal) and can be used for signature generation and verification. If Alice wants to sign a message, she uses DSA to generate a signed message digest. The algorithm first hashes the message with the Secure Hash Standard and uses Alice's private key (and some publicly known parameters) to produce two 160-bit numbers which serve as the message signature. Bob can verify the signature by inputting the received message, the received signature, Alice's public key and identity (plus the parameters); the DSA then verifies whether the received signature is a valid signature by Alice on the received message. Note that the public key and the parameters should be certified for Bob to know he is using Alice's real and correct public key.

There was significant criticism of the DSA when it was published for comment. One drawback is that it is slow – slower than RSA – in verifying; the signing is rather quick. In fact, DSA was specifically tailored for use in smart cards: signing by a smart card should take little time, and verifying will generally be done by a more powerful terminal. Still, many companies had invested in RSA products, and a discrete logarithm algorithm would not be compatible with many of their products. The reason NIST gave for not using RSA was that it wanted a secure standard to be distributed worldwide on a royalty-free basis. As RSA is patented, this would hamper straightforward worldwide acceptance. As it is, the DSA faces patent claims anyway, since the algorithm used is closely related to ElGamal and, more importantly, Schnorr. ElGamal is not patented, but it is supposed to fall under the Diffie-Hellman patent (which expired in 1997); the patent on Schnorr's algorithm runs until 2008. The situation remains unclear, and DSA has not seen ready acceptance. Currently, the main DSA users are ANSI, the US government, and Shell.[5]

The other main objection to DSA was its initial fixed key length of 512 bits. This was raised to a more flexible 512 to 1024 bits, making the standard secure for some time to come. Allegations of insecurity or potential trapdoors (allowing the NSA to forge signatures) stem from distrust in the NSA and may be far-fetched. A potential security problem, however, is that it is possible for crooks to implement a version of the DSA which leaks information on the user's private key [Schneier, 535]. Indeed, although the algorithm is secure, it depends on the implementation whether this security is maintained. Therefore, one should only accept DSA hardware or software from trusted manufacturers.

7.3.2. Subversive use of DSA

Contrary to the claim that DSA can only be used for authentication purposes, certain implementations can be used for *confidentiality* encryption. Schneier gives an example of

---

5 "Mindful of the difficulties in dual use encryption technology, it has been announced that Shell operating companies will use the Federal Information Processing Standard 186, Digital Signature Standard. This decision takes the least line of resistance. Enterprise partners are encouraged to follow the example." [Mansfield]

how you can ElGamal encrypt a 160-bit block by three subsequent DSA 'signatures'; decryption goes likewise. RSA encryption with DSA is even easier, according to [Schneier, 490-491]. This possibility is given when the implementation does not require fixed lengths of the public parameters. Encrypting with DSA is not efficient, but still - Alice and Bob might use it for exchanging session keys or public-key certificates, provided they have one common secret ElGamal key. Therefore, although it does not really solve the key-management problem for them (they still have to agree on a common secret key), it may be a way to exchange session keys in a hidden way. (To detect this, wiretapping agents should check the signatures and notice they are invalid; still, this would not prove that a message is being exchanged through the signature.) So, law enforcement may still have a problem with DSA.

Another potentially subversive use of the DSA is exchanging *subliminal messages*. This is a form of steganography in which the signature contains a message - but only for someone who knows it is there and has the right key. Indeed, according to Simmons, the DSA "provides the most hospitable setting for subliminal communications discovered to date." [Simmons] The DSA uses a random number for each signature, to be generated by a random number generator. However, if Alice chooses a particular number for this (say, a 160-bit conspiring message), and if Bob knows her private key, he can recover the subliminal message from the signature using this private key. So, they may exchange session keys or short messages, while seemingly communicating on trivial subjects. For this to really work, they should randomize the subliminal message with a One-Time Pad, as the number used for signing should be random, and so they should share a secret text string as well. In all, it is not an efficient way for criminals Alice and Bob to communicate, but it may be a very effective way of fooling Leah.[6]

The use of DSA for encrypting messages can be prevented by requiring DSA implementations to use fixed-length parameters. Still, law-enforcement should be aware that signatures can be used for exchanging subliminal messages. The possibility of subliminal messages is perhaps inherent to digital signature algorithms. They might be prevented by 'failsafe' encryption [Kilian], but that would likely require too much overhead and yield too little effect, considering the marginal risk of criminals exploiting this gap. Except, of course, when crypto use in general is banned or severely restricted - that would make it more interesting for criminals to start exchanging a lot of innocuous messages with smart signatures.

7.3.3. Assessment of DSA

Now, to what extent could DSA address the security and the law-enforcement problems? First, it seems the DSA could present a considerable part of the security infrastructure needed. If users have a good system for assuring information authenticity and integrity, a significant part of their information security need is addressed. Although abuse by criminals

---

6 You can also communicate subliminally in DSA without sharing a secret key, but that yields only one bit per signed message, making it more impractical, although, perhaps, still useful for criminals who know they are being wiretapped.

of the DSA is possible, it is inefficient and requires criminals to share secret keys anyway; since criminals have regular access to easy-to-use and robust cryptography, they will not need to exploit DSA gaps. Therefore, the DSA could pose a useful albeit partial solution to the security problem. Still, a PKI must be built on top of it, as users need to be assured of public keys. So far, there is not a certification infrastructure for DSA keys, and as long as patent claims hover over DSA, international standardization bodies may remain reluctant to develop a DSA PKI.[7]

Once separate programs are readily available for either signing or encrypting information, people will use the crypto tool needed for the application. Thus, only confidential and sensitive messages will be encrypted; messages for which only authenticity and integrity must be assured will only be signed. Currently, many of the latter messages are also encrypted, either because the program easily combines the two together, or because encryption is used as a way for ensuring integrity. The more messages are encrypted, the harder it is for law-enforcement to pick out the messages they need. Especially for crypto systems built-in in the information infrastructure, it is advisable that non-confidentiality crypto is used where only authentication and integrity are required. Likewise for crypto products offered to the user market, non-confidentiality crypto is one way of fulfilling security needs without making law-enforcement problems worse. Such products offer enough prevention of abuse (the potential uses of DSA for encrypting or for exchanging subliminal messages are inefficient and not useful for criminals) to make them a good solution to a part of the security problem. It is only part of the security solution, since it does not address the confidentiality needs of the information infrastructure.

Clearly, separate digital signature products solve only a very small part of the law-enforcement problem: they do not target criminals using confidentiality encryption. Their only advantage for law enforcement is that they may be used more readily in communications with the upper world. Especially in business crime, such cryptography could be used more regularly, making communications transparent to law enforcement. It does not target organized criminals or computer criminals, since they will happily continue to communicate and store data encrypted with confidentiality crypto.

There is one caveat. Once there is an infrastructure for digital signatures, including public-key certificates, the key-management problem for criminals is solved as well. They can use DSA public-key certificates to ascertain they are talking to the right person, and then use the key, not for DSA, but for ElGamal encryption or Diffie-Hellman key-exchange (cf. 7.7.1). Since the development of some sort of PKI is inevitable in the information society (see 3.1.6), this is an unavoidable consequence. To what extent this is problematic depends on the ways the law-enforcement problem is addressed in general. If governments want to retain law-enforcement capabilities through access of (private or session) keys, the potentiality of digital signature public keys for facilitating confidentiality encryption must be taken into account.

---

7 Meanwhile, companies have to set up their own key-management infrastructure; Shell, for instance, has apparently done so. This assures secure internal (intranet) communications, but it leaves external communications unaddressed.

7.4. LEAKing through key deposits

7.4.1. LEAK techniques

Several governments have taken initiatives to address the security problem through law-enforcement access to keys – key escrow, key recovery, key encapsulation, data recovery. For precision's sake, I will use the following *terminology*. The term key escrow is generally used to indicate the depositing of a key with a (trusted third) party. This is similar to the well-established practice of source-code escrow: the source code of software is deposited with a trusted third party because of an agreement between (private) parties, in order to allow the receiving party to recover the escrowed source code once the providing party is no longer able to live up to the contract. Similarly, a party could escrow crypto keys in order to assure access to encrypted data in case the key is lost. Remark that, contrary to source-code escrow, the one who deposits and the one who can claim the deposited material are the same. I will use the terms key escrow and key deposits interchangeably. Key deposits are only relevant for private keys (in case of public-key encryption) or symmetric (key-encrypting) keys. The terms escrow and deposit are more correct to refer to deposits with third parties. In the case of self-escrow (a company deposits a key with an internal unit), the term key backup is more appropriate. The overarching term for providing access to plaintexts of encrypted data is *data recovery*.

Data recovery can be performed by two different techniques.[8] The first is *key escrow*. Suppose Bob has deposited his private key with Dorothy, a Key Escrow Agent. Alice sends a message to Bob, and Leah wants to access the message. She can do this is three ways. First, Leah can ask Dorothy to give her Bob's private key. In that case, Leah can read all messages sent to Bob, be they from Alice or from Carol, in the past and in the future. This is the most rigorous form of data recovery. Remark that to read a message sent by Alice, Leah has to access *Bob*'s private key. A second option is that Leah asks Dorothy to give her the session keys of the messages she wants to read. Dorothy can decrypt the session keys with Bob's private key and hand them over to Leah. This is data recovery through session keys, which is less rigorous, as it only gives Leah access to specific messages. The third option with key escrow is for Dorothy to decrypt the messages herself and give them to Leah. This amounts to more or less the same as giving the session keys to Leah, the only difference being that Dorothy can read the message as well, and Leah must trust Dorothy not to cheat.

The second technique for data recovery is *key recovery* or, as it has been recently termed, *key encapsulation*. With this technique, Bob does not deposit his private key. Instead, within each message Alice sends to Bob (or vice versa), she includes a small information unit that contains the *session* key encrypted with the public key of Dorothy. Thus, the session key is 'encapsulated' in the message, in such a way that only Dorothy can access it. Because the message is not sent to Dorothy, however, she can only retrieve the session key if Bob or

---

8 I confine myself to the techniques that realize data recovery through accessing the decryption keys. Data recovery may also be accomplished by backing-up the plaintext, for instance by storing a print of the plaintext in a safe.

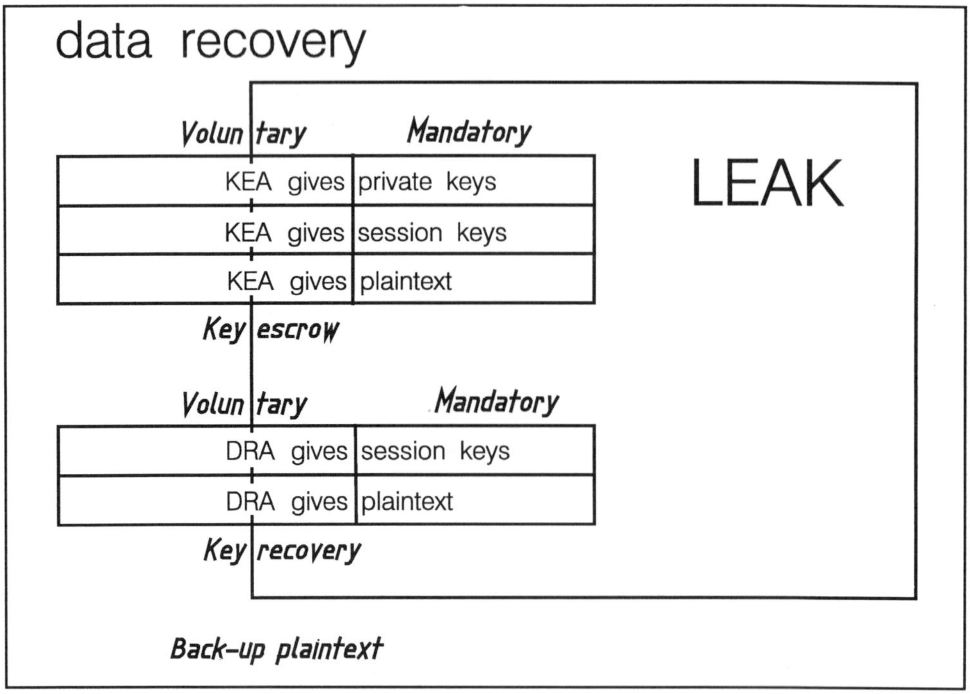

Figure 7.2. A taxonomy of data recovery

Leah bring the message to her. Dorothy can then give either the session key or the plaintext to Leah. Note that I will use 'key recovery' in this specific sense, contrary to the tendency to use it as an overarching term for LEAK itself.

Both techniques also work for retrieving *stored files* encrypted by Alice. Alice can deposit her private key with Dorothy (key escrow) if she uses asymmetric encryption. Often, Alice will only use symmetric encryption (she does not have to exchange a key). In that case, she may for safety's sake encrypt the symmetric key with her own public key ('self recovery') or with the public key of Dorothy (key recovery). Alternatively, she can symmetrically encrypt the symmetric keys with a 'super' key, which she can deposit with Dorothy. Such measures address her own need for data recovery.

Related to these different techniques of data recovery, I shall distinguish between various sorts of Trusted Third Parties. TTPs that hold keys in deposit, I shall call Key Escrow Agents (KEAs). Parties that provide a data-recovery service (either to users or to law enforcement) will be termed Data Recovery Agencies (DRAs). In the following, I describe the various proposals in this terminology, although I shall indicate what terminology the proposals use themselves as well.

7.4.2. Escrowed Encryption Initiative

Since 1993, the US government has taken various initiatives to address the security problem and/or the law-enforcement problem (the distinction has not always been clear). The initiatives were termed escrowed encryption, Key Management Infrastructure, and data recovery in the various proposals. Opponents have consistently dubbed new proposals in terms of Clipper, the chip that first implemented escrowed encryption: Clipper I, II, and III. Clipper is dead now, but its short life provides an excellent example of how key escrow works (or does not work) in practice.

The first proposal was the Escrowed Encryption Initiative (EEI) involving an Escrowed Encryption Standard (EES) [White House]. The EES was first implemented in the Clipper chip, and thus the initiative is generally known as the Clipper initiative. The essence of the EEI was to provide law-abiding citizens with a good encryption system that does not hamper law enforcement: "The U.S. key escrow encryption technology emerged from an effort to make strong, affordable encryption widely available in a way that would not be harmful to national security and public safety." [Denning 94]
The EES was meant for secure communications; it was implemented in the Clipper chip for voice encryption, and in the Capstone chip for data encryption.

The Clipper chip was a tamper-resistant device which used the Skipjack algorithm, a symmetric crypto system designed by the NSA. It used an 80-bit key and was consequently much stronger than DES to resist a brute-force attack. Many details of the EES were classified until recently; the algorithm Skipjack was declassified in June 1998. An external panel of experts concluded in 1993 that there is no significant risk that Skipjack will be broken through a brute-force attack in the next thirty years or that it can be broken trough a shortcut method of attack [Brickell]. Thus, the EES is, one assumes, a strong crypto system.

The EES provides LEAK. Every chip has a built-in unique key, that is deposited in two parts with two agencies (initially, NIST and the Treasury Department's Automated Systems Division; in the Clipper II initiative, also private bodies were allowed as KEAs). Suppose Alice and Bob want to communicate securely through EES. Their EES chips exchange a session key for each communications session. Before the session starts, each chip sends a Law-Enforcement Access Field (LEAF), which contains the chip's unique identity number, the session key encrypted with the chip's unique key, and a checksum for checking the validity of the LEAF. The LEAF is encrypted with a common family key (a built-in key in a family of EES chips). Only if the receiving chip validates the LEAF will the chip decrypt the ensuing communications session; both chips have to validate the LEAF.

If Leah taps Alice's phone, she notices that Alice is using an EES chip. The intercepted message is then routed through a law-enforcement decryption device, which decrypts the LEAF, identifies Alice's chip, requests the two key parts of Alice's chip's unique key with the two key-escrow agencies, and decrypts the intercepts after reception of these two key parts. The entire process is online and supposed to be opaque: it is essentially a black box which performs the process online without interference of law-enforcement officials. Thus, Alice's key is supposed to be destroyed by the box once the wiretap warrant expires.

The Clipper chip has only been implemented in the AT&T 3600 Telephone Security Device. Government bodies could use it for sensitive, non-classified

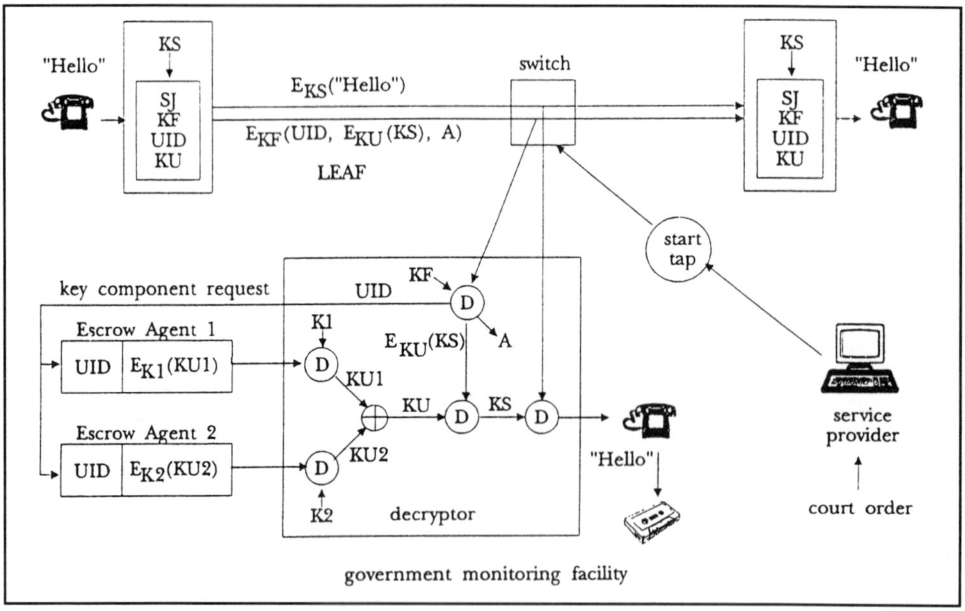

Figure 7.3. The Escrowed Encryption Standard and its LEAK system [source: Denning 94]

information. The public did not queue up for obtaining EES-enabled phones (nor did government bodies, for that matter). The main objections to EES were a suspicion of NSA backdoors, objections to the LEAK feature, and doubts about the standard being classified – the algorithm could not be reviewed publicly, and although the panel of experts concluded that the strength of the algorithm did not depend on its secrecy, the panel had only limited time for their review. With the declassification of Skipjack in June 1998, cryptographers have only just begun to cryptanalyze the algorithm. Therefore, Skipjack has not proved resistant to attacks in the way DES has withstood public scrutiny for over twenty years.

By 1997, the government acknowledged the failure of Clipper. In February 1997, the Department of Defense decided to remove the controversial key-escrow system from the Fortezza cards (which incorporate the Capstone chip) used on the Defense Message System [O'Hara], and in August 1997, the National Security Agency canceled its development of the Fortezza architecture altogether [Fritsch].

Defeating the LEAF

As the EES is only implemented in tamper-proof hardware (a chip or a PCMCIA card), law-enforcement access is supposed to be at all times assured – one cannot tamper with the LEAF. Or can one? Matt Blaze has 'attacked' a protocol failure in the EES [Blaze 94]. Blaze identifies two possible attacks. The first is when two rogues conspire to disable the LEAF feature. For instance, when Alice and Bob set up a communications session, they can feed a self-generated LEAF into the chip rather than the LEAF of the other's chip; in some operation modes, this will allow decryption of the session, while there is no LEAF being sent along the line, leaving Leah powerless. This LEAF defeat is easy to implement with

PCMCIA cards – little more than a software modification to the legal system is needed; moreover, as Blaze notes, such 'patches' to defeat the LEAF may be exchanged through the Internet quite easily, so that basically any rogue could install it.

A more general and more fundamental attack is a unilateral attack, as this enable rogues to use the EES without law-enforcement access in everyday communications with law-abiding people. Alice can search for acceptable, 'valid' LEAFs for a given session key. As the validation of the LEAF involves only a check of the 16-bit checksum component, Alice may try about 2^{16} random LEAFs to find an acceptable one (she can try them on her own chip to see which ones the chip accepts). The receiving chip will be fooled into thinking it is a valid LEAF, but Leah will not find the LEAF helpful, as it is a random number. In this way, Alice can communicate securely without giving access to law enforcement. However, the trial is effected at the expense of performance; according to Blaze, it is not realistic for real-time voice conversations, but it may be useful for facsimile or data communications.

To counter the attack, Blaze suggests that either the entire standard should be revised, or the LEAF should be adapted to allow a larger checksum at a slight cost to law-enforcement's capability of real-time decryption. According to Blaze, the NSA intended to incorporate features to discourage these attacks in future versions of the EES.

One may argue whether these attacks 'defeat' the EES. On the one hand, the EES is not meant for rogues, it is meant for law-abiding citizens (or so the government claimed). Rogues who want to escape law-enforcement scrutiny can use strong encryption anyway, so they need not bother manipulating the EES. On the other hand, the EES was specifically designed to ensure law-enforcement access, and so, defeating the LEAF feature in a way defeats the purpose of the EES. Whether the attack is a real threat to law enforcement essentially depends on the context the EES is used in. If the EES had flourished widely, as was apparently the government intention, the risk of rogues wanting to use it would have grown, as they will have to communicate with law-abiding citizens and with the government as well (for instance, the chip could be required for online tax declaration). Then, it would have been more attractive to develop and spread LEAF-defeating software, and then the wide proliferation of EES chips might have posed a problem to law enforcement. In a way, then, success of the chip would have led to its failure.

Frankel and Yung have described a spoofing attack [Frankel], in which criminals Carol and Dave could use Alice and Bob's EES chips to provide them with valid LEAFs; this would make the communications between Carol and Dave appear to be normal conversations between Alice and Bob. This way, Carol and Dave could frame Alice and Bob. However, the spoofing attack does not seem practical, and the authors rather easily assume users can spoof messages.

Software key escrow

The EES had to be incorporated in tamper-proof hardware to protect the classified algorithm Skipjack from reverse engineering and to prevent people from writing a Skipjack implementation without the LEAF function. This hardware requirement encountered resistance from the business community, not only because it prevented experts from analyzing Skipjack, but more so because hardware is not practical for all purposes. In general, software implementations of cryptography are more flexible, cheaper, and can be updated more easily.

Clearly, the EES can not be converted into software. However, Trusted Information Systems has proposed a software variant that has the same features as the EES [Balenson]. Their 'parallel Clipper' proposal only differs from the EES in that it is software-only, it uses publicly-known algorithms, and it uses public-key encryption to encrypt the LEAF (the EES encrypts the LEAF with the symmetric Skipjack using a common family key). For the rest, the system functions similarly. Two private-key parts are escrowed with KEAs, and each program has a unique identifier and a unique key which are transmitted in the LEAF. Leah, intercepting a message, can send the LEAF to each KEA to recover the session key. Enforcement of the wiretap warrant limits is effected by having the KEAs communicate automatically with Leah through symmetric encryption; for each wiretap warrant, Leah and the KEA agree upon a secret key with which all communications between them is encrypted. The moment the warrant expires, each KEA destroys this secret key, so that they can not read Leah's subsequent requests for decrypting LEAFs under that warrant.

> **Temptations for Polly**
>
> The attack on the Clipper software might be interesting for a policeman joining hands with a rogue, assuming the gains are high. In an, admittedly exotic, cheating scenario, Polly, a 'tempted policeman' may be for sale. She could collaborate with criminal Carol to intercept an extremely confidential message worth a large sum of money, say a message containing the business strategy of multinational Alice being sent to branch Bob. Polly could intercept the encrypted message, forward it to Carol, who would sign it and resend it to Bob, the original addressee. Now Polly, having a court-order to wiretap Carol, intercepts the message and brings it to Dorothy, asking her to decrypt it. Dorothy verifies Carol's signature, checks that the message was sent within the time-limits of the wiretap warrant, decrypts the message using Bob's private key, and gives it to Polly, who runs away with it to Carol, wealth and Barbados.

Unilateral abuse of the LEAF feature is discouraged by having a receiving program validate first whether a correct LEAF was included; only if this was done correctly will the program decrypt the message. Contrary to the EES, the software variant checks the entire LEAF rather than only a checksum, which invalidates Blaze's checksum-guessing attack.

The authors note one potential threat. Carol could modify the software so that it records Alice's program identifier and public key. If Carol uses this for her own communications, Leah can read Carol's messages, but she would do this through using Alice's private key. Thus, Leah would be able to also read all Alice's messages within the warrant limit for wiretapping Carol. Obviously, users would not be too happy with this possibility. Such abuse could be discouraged through extensive auditing of the law-enforcement decryption process, and through significant integrity checks built-in in the software. Obviating such integrity checks should be possible only through reverse engineering the software and extensively modifying it, which would require such an effort as not to be interesting to potential cheaters, the authors argue.

7.4.3. Royal Holloway's international TTP scheme

A notable problem with key-escrow schemes is international cooperation. Suppose Alice from Argentina wants to communicate with Bob in Britain. Suppose their private keys are deposited with Dorotea and Dorothy, respectively. Now if Alice sends a message to Bob, law enforcement can only retrieve the message with the help of Dorothy in Britain.[9] If Leonard is an Argentinian law-enforcement agent monitoring Alice, how is he going to get Bob's private key? He would have to resort to a request to Dorothy for assistance. This requires bilateral agreements, and in any case, mutual legal assistance is a time-consuming process not compatible with prompt decryption.

A study group from Royal Holloway University, London, has developed an international KEA scheme (or, in their terminology, TTP scheme) to address this issue [Jefferies]. They devised a scheme based on the Diffie-Hellman key-exchange prot-ocol[10] for confidentiality purposes (authentication features would require additional measures). Every user is associated with a (national) KEA, say Dorotea for Argentinian Alice and Dorothy for British Bob. All pairs of KEAs share a common secret key, say $\text{key}_{\text{ArgBrit}}$ for Dorotea and Dorothy. Alice has a private and a public send key (which may be common for many KEAs, depending on the parameters chosen). Moreover, she has pairs of private and public receive keys, one for each (foreign) KEA with whose users she may want to communicate. All users have such pairs of send keys and receive keys. Bob's receive key pair for communicating with Alice is generated from his identity and the shared secret $\text{key}_{\text{ArgBrit}}$. Thus, both Dorothy and Dorotea can generate this key pair, and Dorotea can generate Bob's private receive key without cooperation from Dorothy.

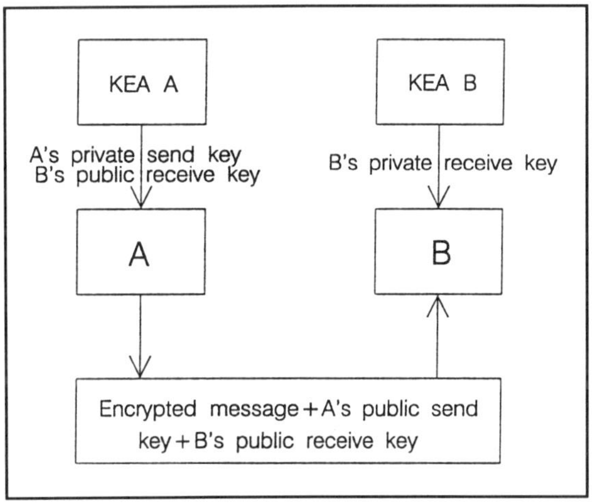

Figure 7.4. The Royal Holloway KEA scheme for one-way encrypted communications

Now if Alice wants to send a message to Bob, she requests Bob's public receive key from Dorotea. She uses this and her private send key to generate a (longer-term) shared key (with which, for instance, she can encrypt session keys for communicating with Bob). She uses the (longer-term) shared key to send a message to Bob, along with her public send key (as certified by Dorotea), and Bob's public receive key. Now Bob, upon receiving this message, can see which of his private receive keys he needs (that is why Alice must include his public receive key) and he generates the same (longer-term) shared key using this private receive key and Alice's public key. Now he can decrypt the message.

9 The EES solves this problem through requiring both sender and receiver to send a LEAF message. This is, however, impractical for one-way traffic.

10 In Diffie-Hellman, Alice and Bob can establish a shared secret key through exchanging only public numbers (depending on random numbers, generated for each session). Alice computes the shared key with Bob's public number and her own private number, Bob does this vice versa. The protocol ensures that the resulting keys are the same. Eve cannot construct this shared key, for she does not know Alice's or Bob's private number. Diffie-Hellman is based on the discrete logarithm problem.

If Argentinian Leonard is intercepting Alice's messages, he need not go to Britain to obtain Bob's private receive key. He goes to Dorotea, and asks either for Bob's private receive key (which, remember, Dorotea can generate herself from the shared secret $key_{ArgBrit}$) or for Alice's private send key: both are sufficient to reproduce the session key. Alternatively, Leah in Britain, who is monitoring Bob's communications, can obtain the same session key be requesting Dorothy to give her Bob's private receive key. (Dorothy does not know Alice's private send key, so Leah can not request that.)

The Royal Holloway authors suggest two options for sophisticating this protocol. First, key splitting may be incorporated, either in Micali's way (see 7.4.4), or in a way suggested in the paper. This splitting variant is rather rigid – it requires all KEAs associated with Alice and Bob respectively to share common secret keys. Second, as the receive keys are in principle fixed and lasting, they suggest the receive keys may be changed automatically once in a while. This would allow for more security, and it could present a method of enforcing time limits on wiretap warrants. For instance, if the receive keys were changed daily, the KEAs could provide Leah with only the daily receive key rather than a longer-term receive key. A disadvantage of this is that Alice must request Bob's public receive key each day she wants to communicate with him.

The Royal Holloway scheme has attracted considerable attention (pushed by the UK government, which lobbied ETSI to make it a standard), and it presents the only serious proposal for international cooperation to date. This I consider its prime – if theoretic – advantage. Another advantage the authors mention, namely that no key directories are required since Diffie-Hellman is used, seems less relevant, as key directories should not pose a significant problem for an international key management infrastructure.

However, the advantage of allowing domestic KEAs to recover session keys comes at the cost of several disadvantages. First, there is some overhead involved in the information required for communication. Alice must request public receive keys for any person she wants to communicate with. In principle, she can store this public receive key for later use, but this is not possible in the time-limited variant. As long as there is one KEA per country, the scheme is transparent enough, but if you allow more (commercial, private-sector) KEAs per country, and particularly if you allow key splitting with various KEAs, each KEA will need a large amount of shared secret keys, which requires considerable international cooperation and key management. Another problem is that a KEA possesses Alice' private send key. This feature is not necessary for the scheme to work at all, but it is required to make the scheme work smoothly (if Dorotea does not have Alice's private send key, she must compute separately the session key for all people with whom Alice is communicating, which requires considerable overhead and may slow down law-enforcement decryption). To prevent Dorotea from being able to forge messages from Alice with this private send key, Alice should be required to sign all her messages (with a different key pair, obviously). Still, once Leonard has obtained Alice's private send key, he can decrypt any message sent by Alice, regardless of the wiretap limits; the option of daily changing receive key pairs makes this more difficult, but not impossible if he can access the public receive key of the sender. Thus, the Royal Holloway scheme does not really enforce wiretap-warrant bounds.

A graver disadvantage is the availability required of the KEAs. The paper initially targets one-way communications, such as facsimile or e-mail, but claims the scheme can be easily transformed for two-way communications, such as the telephone. However, this requires the KEAs to be online, as users will generally not know beforehand with whom they will want to communicate. This pertains in particular to (online) shopping and business contacts. Also, in the daily-changing receive keys variant, this will involve considerable demand on KEAs to provide clients with receive keys. This demand can be shared by allowing several KEAs nationally, but this will imply a trade-off with efficiency, as all KEAs need to share secret keys.

Ultimately, as the paper states, if KEAs are not commercially viable, then the scheme will not be viable. A major success factor of the scheme is trust. And users must have complete trust in their KEAs, who, after all, can recover all messages their clients send. Much more so, users must trust *every* KEA in the scheme, as foreign KEAs can also reconstruct their private receive keys, and so recover any message they receive. The KEA can also recover messages foreign users send to its clients within its jurisdiction. When it comes to trusting foreign KEAs, the issue will become still more problematic if KEAs will be required to aid law enforcement in decrypting communications. After all, this is one of the requirements for which the Royal Holloway scheme was developed. Now, it is highly unlikely users will have complete trust in foreign KEAs in countries where they do no trust the government. This pertains not only to 'dubious' countries, but also to countries whose intelligence agencies are suspected of aiding economic espionage. For instance, large European companies may not want to use a communication scheme if they know the US government could access their communications. Especially in a commercial environment, complete international trust in KEAs is an impossibility. The Royal Holloway will therefore not be commercially viable.

7.4.4. Add-ons

Splitting keys

One major objection of the public to the EES was the choice of key-escrow agents – they were thought to be too close to the government, and people feared they might help law-enforcement agencies even without a proper court warrant. For this reason, in September 1995, the US government announced that also independent, private-sector organizations could serve as key-escrow agencies – the so-called Clipper II initiative. They released a proposal for criteria that KEAs should meet [NIST 95], and discussed this in two meetings with business representatives. However, there was little private-sector inclination for these meetings, and the process rather withered away without clear results.

With EES, the unique chip's key is generated in a government-controlled process involving both escrow agents; thus, the escrow process is a part of the chips' manufacture. If one wants to be more flexible, and allow users to generate their own keys, the escrowing of keys is more difficult to monitor. A KEA can easily check when receiving a private key in deposit whether it corresponds to the user's public key. However, once you allow key splitting to deposit only parts of the key with separate KEAs, the checking becomes impossible, as one share of the key should not give any information on the key itself (see Chapter 3 on zero-knowledge protocols). This concern is met by the concept of verifiable secret sharing.

The idea of splitting keys and depositing them with several independent bodies has been worked out in several proposals by Silvio Micali. He has proposed 'fair' crypto systems, which according to him "strike a good balance, in a democratic country, between the needs of the Government and those of the Citizens. Fair public-key crypto systems guarantee that: (1) the system cannot be misused by criminal organizations and (2) the Citizens mantain [sic] exactly the same rights to privacy they currently have under the law." [Micali]

Fair cryptography makes use of verifiable secret-sharing techniques. It allows a user to split his key into two or more parts and deposit each share with a KEA (Micali uses a fixed number of predesignated trustees). Each KEA individually verifies whether he received a valid share of the right key and reports to a certifying authority. The CA hands out a public-key certificate if all shares have been escrowed correctly. Through the key splitting, the user will be more confident that the escrowed key will not be unduly disclosed or compromised, while he can not abuse the system to deposit worthless key shares. The key can be retrieved by putting the shares together. It is also possible to use a threshold scheme, in which a certain minimum number of key shares will suffice to recover the key.

For key-escrow schemes, fair cryptography is flexible, and attractive from a privacy point of view. Alice may, for instance, deposit key shares with a court, her parents, a friend, her employer, a non-profit organization, a commercial KEA and a government KEA, and require any four out of these seven agents to cooperate to retrieve her key. Abuse by colluding of KEAs or through bribery is unimaginable. Moreover, if Alice loses her key, she can always retrieve it herself, as loss of four or more key shares by the share holders simultaneously is extremely unlikely. Note, however, that when Alice sends a message to Bob, the message is protected by Bob's choice of escrow agents, not her own; this is somewhat contradictory to the privacy enhancement of key splitting.

Leah may access the key if she can produce a proper warrant to convince the KEAs (it will usually be a legal requirement for KEAs to present a key share upon court warrant). However, the more flexible the choice of KEAs for Alice, the harder it will be for Leah, especially since in general Leah will want to keep secret the fact of Alice's being wiretapped. Moreover, the requirement of real-time decryption for voice communications will hardly be compatible with a flexible choice of multiple KEAs. There is a trade-off, then, between flexibility and privacy on the one hand, and law-enforcement capabilities on the other. Government requirements for KEAs should address this trade-off.

As with key escrow in general, from the users' point of view, verifiable key splitting is only appropriate for safeguarding stored information, not for safeguarding communications.

Traceable ciphertexts

All concepts of key escrow more or less rely on the assumption that the private key needed for decryption can be identified from the communication itself. If you do not know with whose public key the message is encrypted, you can not trace the corresponding private key. In most cases, the message itself will indicate to whom it is addressed, since the routing of the data requires an addressee. It is imaginable, however, that Alice will remove all identifying information from the encrypted message prior to transport; if Bob restores that information prior to decryption, then they can use the system while escaping Leah's scrutiny. After all, Leah, not knowing the identity of the addressee, will be unable to get the message

Cryptographic warrant bounds and edge surveillance

Several cryptographers are studying LEAK protocols with additional properties. Although innovative and at times mathematically elegant, many of these proposals are far removed from judicial and political reality. For instance, Lenstra, Winkler and Yacobi have argued that a system "in which the courts can enforce the terms of a warrant will not only help preserve privacy rights, but will also enable the courts to be more liberal in granting warrants so that federal and state authorities can make better use of electronic surveillance." [Lenstra] They propose a key-escrow system which enforces wiretap warrant bounds.

Participants each day generate message components for each party they are communicating with, and these components must be sent before a communication session can start (communication may also be one-way, such as fax or e-mail). Leah, wiretapping Alice and Bob, will intercept a message and the corresponding message component (time-stamped by the network or service provider), and take it to Dorothy. Dorothy will decrypt the message component and hand over enough information for Leah to compute the session key. If Alice has cheated, however, for instance because she sent a wrong message component, Dorothy cannot decrypt the message component; instead, she will give Alice's private key to Leah. Thus, the punishment for not complying with the 'warrant-bound rules' is a greater infringement of one's privacy – Leah will be able to decrypt as many messages sent to Alice she likes, regardless of warrant bounds. The enforcement of the warrant bounds is effected by the daily changing of the message component. According to the authors, cheating with the date is not possible – at least not unilaterally (of course, the authors argue, cheating bilaterally is always possible through agreeing upon another encryption system).

The enforcement of warrant bounds is mathematically interesting, but hardly realistic or desirable. Warrant bounds are currently being enforced by the courts (through trust of the law-enforcement agencies and challenges by the defense in court) as well as by the network and service providers that technically assist law enforcement. There is no indication that this supervision does not work, and courts would very unlikely grant more warrants only because technology would curb illegal extensions of wiretaps.

The other interesting feature of the proposal is equally unrealistic: 'edge surveillance', tapping communications only between two particular suspects (rather than traditional 'node surveillance', which taps all communications from or to a particular suspect). In the vast majority of cases, the police does not know with whom a suspect is most likely to hold incriminating conversations; often, a wiretap is used just to find that out. Again, within the broad legal community, there are no voices that 'node' tapping is a problem they want to see addressed.

It seems that such proposals are triggered more by the authors' distrust of law enforcement than by a realistic assessment of judicial practice. For mathematicians, though, they provide interesting reading.

decrypted. Although this type of colluding is feasible, it is not very convenient.

Desmedt proposes a solution to this problem for the public-key encryption scheme ElGamal. [Desmedt] The idea is that for each user, particular parameters are chosen for the El-Gamal scheme. Whatever the user chooses for his private-public key pair, these parameters – and hence the user's identity – are deducible from the ciphertext the user generates. This proposal may serve as an add-on to existing proposals rather than a solution of its own, improving the LEAK factor of key-escrow schemes.

7.5. LEAKing through key recovery

The escrow systems described so far operate through deposits of keys. Apart from privacy concerns (one has to trust the KEA completely), this also raises security concerns. Deposits of valuable keys may constitute an attractive target for crooks and criminals. The risk may be lowered through the splitting of keys, but it can not be altogether eliminated (especially as the trade-off with law-enforcement capacity for prompt decryption may not allow many key shares).

7.5.1. Commercial Key Escrow

There is another variant, however, for providing law enforcement with access to session keys. Rather than depositing keys beforehand, users may send along keys which law enforcement may read, thus 'virtually escrowing' their keys. TIS has proposed such a system as an alternative to their Clipper-parallel software key-escrow system. [Balenson]

This system is more straightforward than the key-escrow systems described. It requires users to include a component in each message they send, consisting of two halves of the session key encrypted with public keys of two DRAs. A verification field ensures that the receiving program first checks whether these halves were correctly encrypted with the public keys of the DRAs, and whether the two halves indeed constitute the session key used. (Each program contains certified copies of the public DRA keys, including integrity checks.) If the verification succeeds, the program will decrypt; if not, it refuses to decrypt. Now, Leah intercepting such a message can send the message component to the two Dorothies, asking them to decrypt the LEAF components and send her back the halves of the session key. This allows Leah to decrypt the message – and only this message, as she receives the message key, not a master or private key. Although this requires much more traffic between Leah and Dorothy, it is a better safeguard for Alice's and Bob's privacy. The authors suppose that the overhead need not significantly hamper the law-enforcement process, and real-time decryption is possible, provided a powerful online channel is available between Leah and each Dorothy.

Translucent cryptography

Cryptographers are creative people, trying to find ways to solve problems with mathematics. Sometimes, they even find solutions for problems which do not exist. Bellare and Rivest, for instance, have created the problem that there is no middle way between tapping (which overhears all conversations) and not tapping (which overhears none). To provide such a middle way, Bellare and Rivest propose 'translucent cryptography' [Bellare]. It is not opaque, in that communications are entirely unreadable for law enforcement, nor is it transparent, which means that law enforcement cannot read everything they intercept either. Rather, the system allows law enforcement to read a fraction *p* of encrypted intercepts – where p is a figure between 0 and 1, to be established by parliament.

The system is comparable to TIS Commercial Key Escrow, in that messages are accompanied by components which contain the session key encrypted with public keys of DRAs. The difference is that users can choose from a range of public keys for the DRAs, and they will make this choice for each message at random. Now, the translucency is effected by the range of DRA public keys: only a fraction p of these are valid, that is, correspond to a private key that the DRA possesses. The users do not know which of the keys are valid for the DRA (and so, for law enforcement); therefore, they cannot intentionally choose bad keys.

According to Bellare and Rivest, the fraction p could be established by parliament. It could vary with applications; for instance, whereas for domestic communications, parliament might set p equal to 0.2 (allowing a relatively high level of privacy), they might require p to be 1 for international communications (comparable to current US export restrictions). Also, the p for foreign communications could vary with the country. Parliament could decide to change the fraction if the situation changes significantly, either because some terrible crimes involving cryptography have happened, or because elections were held and parties have promised their voters to set p to a particular value.

Disregarding the battle scenes in parliament ("Chairman, our party thinks p=0.38 is a good compromise for next year's tapping"), I think this is not the right question to ask. Currently, law enforcement either taps all or nothing within a certain period, and so far, no-one has claimed that this is unsubtle. Politics is used to if-then-else regulations, not to fractional thinking, and the trade-offs lie in the conditions allowing for a tap rather than in partial results. So, governments pose strict conditions under which wiretapping may be used and set limits to the *period* of intercepting, but not to the *efficacy* of wiretapping. And why should the fact that people start using cryptography alter the privacy infringement of wiretapping per se? Translucent cryptography is a beautiful solution to a non-existent problem.

Like the Clipper-parallel system, unilateral abuse is prevented by having the receiving system check for LEAF compliance. Bilateral abuse – two rogues cooperating to defeat the LEAF function – should be discouraged, but only to the extent that the effort is comparable to the effort rogues would have to take to establish another secure, law-enforcement defeating encryption channel. Since strong, freely usable cryptography is easily available, the authors think the system need not go to much trouble to prevent cooperative abuse. Integrity checks might be incorporated into the software in such a way that bypassing all these checks would require a significant effort. However, a large number of integrity checks may harm performance, and so, a trade-off must be made of the requirements of abuse prevention and user-friendliness. (The prevention of bilateral abused could be improved by adding 'binding cryptography' to the system, see sidebar, but that does not alter its (lack of) value for addressing the law-enforcement problem.)

The initial proposal for this type of key recovery assumed that the system would be input with shared session keys, both at the sending and receiving ends. Thus, Alice and Bob would need to have a secure channel anyway besides the key-escrow system. In that case, one wonders why they would bother to use the key-recovery system at all. There must be advantages to such a system, or no-one would want to use it. TIS argues that the data-recovery feature is a goal in itself for many commercial users (mainly, companies afraid of encryption stunts of employees). Here, however, they seem to fall into the trap of identifying data storage with communications – for the latter, which seems to be TIS' main application, data recovery is not needed.

In subsequent proposals, called Commercial Key Escrow (CKE) with the product RecoverKey, TIS has included a key exchange feature in the program. Thus, Alice and Bob use public-key encryption to exchange a session key, while at the same time 'virtually escrowing' this session key by encrypting it with DRAs' public keys. The key management advantages of such a system may push Alice and Bob to use this system rather than find an alternative one.

As part of the European Trusted Services project, the European Commission has stimulated a pilot project to define a key-recovery mechanism that meets both law-enforcement and business needs. This project, oddly named KRISIS (Key Recovery In Secure Information Systems), uses RecoverKey as a prototype. It has implemented a pilot infrastructure with key-recovery centers in five countries. The results of the project were scheduled for March 1998, but they were not yet available by mid-1998.

7.5.2. PGP's Corporate Message Recovery

In 1997, PGP Inc. released PGP 5.5 for Business Security. This product contains a key-recovery feature that companies can turn on, making messages sent to employees recoverable. The Corporate Message Recovery works through an attribute in Alice's self-signature that tells Bob that Alice wants messages sent to her to be recoverable. Bob can then encrypt messages to Alice and include the session key encrypted with the public recovery key included in Alice's signature. Alice can indicate whether she considers recovery desirable (so that Bob can choose to comply or not) or compulsory. The company using PGP 5.5 can thus implement a corporate policy with mandatory or optional key recovery for its employees' communications. The Corporate Message Recovery feature is not a part of other

PGP products (notably the freeware and personal-use ones). The description of the feature [Callas] leaves it unclear whether messages sent by Alice are recoverable as well, which would seem a logical part of the system.

PGP 5.5 is targeted for business use, and the key-recovery feature was incorporated to meet the business need for retrieving employees' communications; it had nothing to do with law-enforcement requirements, PGP claimed. After all, it does not provide real-time access to messages, and the key-recovery feature can be switched on or off by the corporation at will. Indeed, so PGP Chief Scientist Jon Callas wrote: "we showed it to the FBI and asked their opinion. They told us it doesn't meet any of their needs." [Callas]

7.5.3. International Cryptography Framework

Hewlett-Packard has developed the International Cryptography Framework, a higher-level crypto technology that can accommodate various crypto programs. It is not a crypto system itself, but an interface for choosing specific crypto systems. Depending on the applicable national law, it allows people to use only those crypto systems that are authorized in the country – e.g., weak cryptography, strong cryptography, or key-recovery crypto. HP's product, VerSecure, is a Crypto API (Application Programming Interface), which can choose a crypto algorithm incorporated in the chip. For the product to work, a 'policy activation token' must be inserted, which enables only those crypto systems that are legal in the country; the token expires after a year. The method was devised to meet differing national crypto policies, and thus enables a state to allow only key-recovery crypto (or only key-escrow crypto, for that matter).

7.5.4. Key Recovery Alliance

As the examples of TIS, PGP, and HP show, several companies are developing voluntary key-recovery products for varying purposes and applications, partly because of a perceived business need for such products, and partly because of the US administration's policy of stimulating key-recovery products (which are more readily exportable).

In October 1996, several interested companies formed the Key Recovery Alliance, in order to coordinate and promote the development of interoperable key-recovery systems. By mid-1998, the KRA had over 30 members. The KRA endorses the development of a global infrastructure that supports recovery of encrypted information. To this purpose, its committees have, among others, identified business needs for key-recovery services [BSC], drafted a functional model for key recovery [Matyas], and identified public policy requirements for a global key-recovery infrastructure. The overarching KRA guideline is that the market should lead the development of key recovery. "The companion to this principle is that government-designed or imposed encryption technology solutions will inevitably fail to win marketplace acceptance." [KRA] On legal issues, the KRA asks governments to establish clear liability standards for the misuse of key-recovery information, to establish clear standards for legal (government) access under conditions of due process, including accountability and auditability procedures, and to establish standards for the retention and destruction of acquired keys.

7.6. LEAKy issues

Over the past few years, several key-escrow and key-recovery systems have been proposed. LEAK schemes, however, are scarcely out of the egg – most of the schemes are only theoretical proposals that have not yet been tested in practice. Various issues loom on the horizon of a LEAK infrastructure. These have to be addressed for any LEAK scheme to be a viable option. In this section, I describe various LEAKy issues that governments should take into account if they want to stimulate voluntary LEAK. There are more issues to be resolved, but these issues are basic ones that require addressing before one can decide to stimulate LEAK in the first place.

1. Who generates the keys?
In the EEI and Royal Holloway, the private keys are generated by the KEAs.[11] This generally assures they will avoid weak keys, and it ensures that they possess the private keys to hold in deposit. It also prevents malicious users to choose keys in such a way as to incorporate a subliminal channel in the key. It requires, however, that users completely trust the KEAs. As users will have to trust KEAs anyway, the issue of key generation does not weaken users' trust. Protocols for joint key generation, such as Kilian-Leighton's [Kilian], are not relevant to key-deposit schemes.

As to key recovery, there are no private user keys involved in the LEAK process. Therefore, users can generate key pairs themselves, if they want to.

2. Who is KEA?
A significant factor in gaining users' trust will be the identity of the KEA. As the public outcry against Clipper's two initial escrow agencies shows, government bodies may not be the best choice (although this may differ per country – in the Netherlands, government bodies would be considered more acceptable). Potential KEAs are Chambers of Commerce, branch organizations, commercial enterprises, notaries, and courts. For businesses, the first three will likely generate the best trust; for individuals, NGOs, (semi-)government organizations, notaries, and courts may serve as trustworthy escrow agencies.[12] To ensure compliance with law-enforcement rules, governments will have to set requirements for

11 Royal Holloway allows users to generate private send keys themselves, but not private receive keys.
12 The Dutch association of notaries (*Koninklijke Notariële Broederschap*) public seemed in 1996 to intend notaries to operate as key-escrow agencies [Franken], but lately seems to have abandoned this idea in favor of facilitating digital signatures only.

bodies to operate as a KEA; like in the ETS, this will probably involve a licensing and certifying scheme for KEAs. There is a trade-off between user trust (allowing a flexible set-up of many KEAs) and law-enforcement effectiveness (preventing criminals to set up or to corrupt a KEA, and enabling prompt decryption).

3. Changing of keys

The security of the scheme partly relies on how often keys can be changed. Permanent keys are an attractive target for attacks, and users may periodically want to change key pairs, depending on the sensitivity of the application and the risk involved. Key-escrow schemes should therefore allow regular key changing, and users should be allowed to either request or generate a new key pair themselves. For KEAs, this means extra storage, as they will have to retain old keys for at least a certain period. Otherwise, users could easily defeat law-enforcement access by changing key pairs a few times and then re-use old keys. Also, in a search, the police could encounter files encrypted long ago.

The EES relies partly on permanent secret family keys, and each chip has a permanent built-in key. Royal Holloway is also rather rigid with its long-term send keys. Both systems therefore do not live up to the requirement of flexible key changes.

4. Interoperability

Should LEAK systems be inter-operable with non-LEAK systems? At first sight, inter-operability would enhance their use and their acceptance. However, it would make it easy for criminals to use non-LEAK systems while communicating even with law-abiding people. From the point of view of prev-enting abuse, it seems LEAK systems should therefore not be interoperable with non-LEAK systems. As this will hamper their initial acceptance and spread, governments will have to take additional efforts to convince people to use them.

Abuse by government

Even with voluntary LEAK, one should not disregard the possibility of government abuse. First, in many countries, illegal wiretapping by government agencies is widespread [DoS]. Illegal access to keys may be a similar alluring target of abuse of police officials bent on catching criminals (or human-rights activists) by hook or by crook. Related to this, access to keys will be an attractive option for intelligence agencies. A (voluntary) LEAK infrastructure might result in intelligence agencies collecting keys of their objects of interest, adding one more item to their privacy-less files.

Perhaps most threatening of all is the bleak vision of a future government mandating LEAK cryptography, since the LEAK infrastructure is there and people are already using it anyway. It seemed the US government at one time considered doing this. Documents obtained by EPIC under the Freedom of Information Act show that already in early 1993, the government considered making a Clipper-like system mandatory. A briefing document by the FBI, NSA and Department of Justice of February 1993 concluded that "Technical solutions, such as they are, will only work if they are incorporated into *all* encryption products. To ensure that this occurs, legislation mandating the use of Government-approved encryption products or adherence to Government encryption criteria is required." In the long run, once many people use the robust government-offered crypto system, those who still refrain from using it will be suspicious. Prohibiting non-LEAK crypto is then an easy step. The vision of establishing a robust security infrastructure to protect citizens, waiting until enough people use it, and then penalize the use of security measures outside of the infrastructure reminds one of Orwell's 1984.

I do not consider these concerns relevant to the Netherlands, but I do think they should be taken into account when discussing an international crypto policy based on LEAK schemes. There are simply too many countries where governments have proved themselves to occasionally or systematically disregard the law in pursuit of real or imagined threats to law and order.

Such efforts could involve requiring people to use LEAK systems in commun-icating with the government, creating financial (tax) advantages for LEAK systems, or discouraging the use of non-LEAK systems (e.g., by establishing a licensing scheme). Such efforts, however, should not tend to make the LEAK system mandatory rather than voluntary.

Interoperability is one of the major problems in an international context, given that many countries do not consider a LEAK infrastructure desirable. The EU expert meeting in Copenhagen of April 1998 noticed that small-scale LEAK pilot projects had identified significant interoperability problems with existing or emerging solutions and standards, potentially "leading to significant disadvantages for European enterprises on the global market." [Copenhagen]

5. Liability

KEAs and DRAs are vulnerable to unauthorized disclosure of confidential, sensitive data. The risks depend on the internal security of the agency and on the sensitivity of the data; they can be substantial, with potentially huge (material or immaterial) losses. If a data leak occurs, the liability should be firmly established. KEAs and DRAs, being *Trusted* Third Parties, can not totally exonerate themselves from liability (they would hardly gain customer confidence), but they can also not accept full liability if they want to be able to survive one or two security leaks. They should therefore accept some liability, and insure themselves against the associated costs. Currently, it is not clear to what extent a TTP insurance might go; if the government stimulates TTPs to provide data-recovery services, it may have to ensure that there is an adequate insurance for these services.

7.7. Assessing the LEAK options

7.7.1. Effectiveness of LEAK systems

1. Transport or storage

The private-sector need for data recovery is mainly a matter of data storage. Businesses will require back-up keys to retrieve encrypted data in case keys are lost or employees run away or die suddenly. For communications or data transport, back-up is not necessary, as these normally involve real-time decryption; a few exceptions may relate to companies that record communications for later audits, or that check communications for policy compliance.[13] If users want to store transported messages, say e-mail messages in a mail folder, this is essentially a storage matter; they can either store the messages in the clear (usually, the risk lies in the transmission, not in internal storage), or they can (re)encrypt the messages with a system which allows data recovery. The business need for data recovery will be met by voluntary, market-driven development of data-recovery services; such services may (but do not have to) include key escrow or key recovery with in-house or external DRAs. How this market will develop is unpredictable for the time being.

---

13 "Outside of specific, limited situations (...), key recovery for communicated data is not a broad-based business requirement." [BSC]

Law-enforcement searches will also benefit if people use a key-escrow system for retrieving stored encrypted data. They can take these to the KEA(s) and have them decrypted upon presentation of a warrant.

For law-enforcement purposes, however, most key-escrow and key-recovery proposals (e.g., Clipper, Royal Holloway, and CKE) have been devised to facilitate wiretapping, and thus only see to information transport. The deposit feature in these proposals, then, is a law-enforcement feature, not a feature to meet business needs, as is sometimes claimed. Voluntary LEAK will not be used by users for communications, only for storage. They may use reliable government-stimulated LEAK products if they have sufficient trust in their security and in the government not abusing the LEAK feature; however, they will only be pushed to use such systems if they have advantages over regular non-LEAK crypto. Currently, the LEAK proposals do not generate such trust or yield advantages over non-LEAK systems.

Telecoms providers, on the other hand, if they incorporate cryptography in their networks or services, will have to ensure tappability (see 4.3.1), and incorporating LEAK may be a way for them of doing this. Service providers may also offer crypto products to their clients to use as extra end-to-end protection; the requirement to ensure tappability does not stretch to require them to offer only LEAK systems, although governments could stimulate service providers to do so.

In short, voluntary LEAK will develop as a service provided to meet business needs to provide data recovery of stored data; law enforcement will be able to use this to decrypt stored data encountered in a search. For communications, LEAK systems do not serve user needs. They may be incorporated in the information infrastructure, since telecom providers have to facilitate wiretapping, but their end-to-end use by users in telecommunications seems unrealistic on anything but a negligible scale.

2. Criminals and the effectiveness for law enforcement
Organized criminal groups and computer criminals will easily have access to strong non-LEAK crypto systems, and will generally not (need to) use a government-offered LEAK system for end-to-end encryption. (And if they would use such systems, because no other crypto is near at hand, they might apply known attacks on key-escrow schemes; computer criminals and some criminal organizations can be expected to exploit technical weaknesses.) Criminals will of course use LEAK systems built-in in the information infrastructure, but they will still be free to (super)encrypt end-to-end with their own cryptography.

LEAK schemes will likely be more used by business criminals, being part of a mainly law-abiding organization (if a large part of the business or organization engages in criminal activities, it will function as a criminal organization). The same goes for ‘small’, individual criminals and for the habitually law-abiding person who occasionally hazards upon criminal side activities. They will generally communicate mainly with law-abiding citizens, and they are not likely to use superencryption.

3. Defeating the LEAK procedure
If LEAK schemes are to maintain the law-enforcement capability for gathering information, defeating the LEAK mechanism should be made difficult, at least to the extent that this costs

more than it yields. Therefore, one should consider how people can defeat the law-enforcement access feature.

First, there is the possibility of users using the key-escrow system without the law-enforcement component. Blaze's attack is an instance of this for the EES. For a voluntary EES, the attack does not constitute a real problem, since there is no significant gain for criminals. Other potential attacks to the EES, such as Frankel and Yung's, are similar in seriousness. In general, given the voluntary nature of LEAK systems and the ready availability of strong non-LEAK systems, LEAK implementations need not go to much trouble to prevent defeating. The main goal should be to make it unrewarding for criminals to fiddle with a LEAK mechanism incorporated in the information infrastructure, so that their regular use of the network and services will be LEAK-compliant.

Then, criminals may defeat law-enforcement access through superencryption: complying with the LEAK scheme, but using another form of encryption underneath the government-stimulated system. This way, criminals can exchange undecipherable messages in a LEAK-compliant way. Obviously, it defeats the judicial capacity for retrieving information. Therefore, this does nothing to the core problem of cryptocriminals; it only narrows the selecting problem for law enforcement if most users refrain from using end-to-end (super)encryption. This underlines the point that key-escrow systems are essentially systems for law-abiding citizens, for general use; they discourage use by criminals, but they should not go to much expense to prevent criminal use.

There is yet another potential use by criminals of a government-approved system.

ALICE Hi Bob, it's Alice.

(LEAH pricks up her ears.)

BOB Hi, Alice. Can you authenticate yourself?

ALICE Sure. I sign this message with my government-approved private key. Check the public-key certificate!

BOB OK, I'm convinced. Convenient that the government gives us such certificates, don't you think? Check my signature.

ALICE OK. Say, Bob, I'd like to tell you a secret, but I don't want anyone to hear. Let's use triple-DES. We can make a secret key with Diffie-Hellman. Here's a string I computed with a random number.

BOB Here's another string computed with a random number of mine.

(Both compute the shared secret key.)

ALICE mCm/gwYv8La7xVLD3kD0pYLIamHB/3z1M94UvuUqnuf+rtCVrrQ0iQaqq 1e2S.

BOB iQCVAgUBMKHjJNlislmdOLwlAQGS+gP9EVYG2vyrh71StUZza!

(LEAH turns a puzzled face at the receiver.)

In this scheme, Alice and Bob use the government-approved key-escrow system to authenticate themselves and establish a common key, which Eve nor Leah can reconstruct. Thus, the key-escrow or authentication-only system helps them to solve their key management problem. Subsequently, they can communicate with no danger of being overheard.

These two options – superencryption and publicly exchanging Diffie-Hellman keys – effectively mean that LEAK systems do nothing to prevent criminals from communicating securely even in a LEAK-compliant infrastructure. The effectivity of LEAK schemes only lies in ensuring transparency of communications; they allow law enforcement to see through the bulk of intercepted communications and to select those (encrypted or plaintext) messages that seem of interest to them.

7.7.2. The options

The options that emerge in this direction are twofold: non-confidentiality crypto products (7.3) and LEAK systems (7.4 and 7.5). There is no fundamental functional difference in key escrow or key recovery to provide LEAK; for the purposes of this book, the similar functionality of the LEAK concept outweighs the (considerable) differences in the technology and the consequences for law enforcement and users.

Development and use of such products must be voluntary. The government therefore has the option to stimulate the development and use of such products, e.g., through subsidies, using only LEAK systems itself, and encouraging self-regulation.

Option 7.1 Stimulate the development and use of non-confidentiality cryptography
The government stimulates crypto developers to make crypto systems that can only be used for safeguarding integrity and authentication, not for confidentiality. The government stimulates users, notably businesses in e-commerce, to use such products, which can be used in all layers of the information infrastructure. They mainly see to communications, not to data storage. If reliable and secure non-confidentiality systems are available, then the government may consider requiring telecoms providers who build-in authentication and integrity functions in their networks or services to use only non-confidentiality cryptography for this.

Option 7.2 Stimulate the development and voluntary use of key-escrow or key-recovery systems for data storage and for the telecommunications infrastructure
The government stimulates the development of data-recovery services that meet business needs for recovering stored data. The government stimulates users who store data in encrypted form to use these services. The government requires service providers offering data recovery to cooperate with law enforcement (by handing over private or session keys or plaintexts, depending on the circumstances) under legal warrant.

The government stimulates crypto producers to develop key-escrow or key-recovery systems for telecommunications applications, that is, products for confidential communications that allow prompt and automated law-enforcement decryption under warrant (through key deposits or tagging along recoverable session keys). The government stimulates telecoms providers who build-in cryptography in their networks and services to use such products.

7.7.3. Applying the criteria

How do these options relate to the principles for striking the crypto balance?

1a. Privacy and the right to confidential communications

Separating authentication-only from confidentiality crypto does not affect the security of confidential communications; it allows users to apply robust and reliable confidentiality crypto to the communications they want to secure. Key-escrow and key-recovery systems, however, do pose a threat to privacy and confidential communications – they are inherently less secure than non-LEAK systems. Indeed, given the infancy of LEAK systems, which have hardly been tested outside of the laboratory, one cannot for a considerable time to come rely upon LEAK systems to offer good security. Key-escrow systems pose a larger potential threat to privacy than key-recovery schemes, since they rely upon the disclosure of private keys, and therefore potentially give access to many data or communications; in principle, key-recovery schemes provide access to single messages only.

1b. The right to a fair trial

The options in this direction do not affect the right to a fair trial, except for the potential abuse of key-escrow schemes by law enforcement to falsify evidence. This can be addressed through strict guidelines for the court to assess the authenticity of the evidence, and is not a real threat to the right to a fair trial.

1c. The rule of law

The options do not affect the rule of law in general, but the effectivity of the options outlined in this chapter is to be seriously doubted. Separating authentication from confidentiality crypto helps perhaps to not make the problem worse, but it does nothing against cryptocriminals as such. It does not address the core problem of cryptocriminals bent on escaping law-enforcement scrutiny. Voluntary LEAK schemes are not effective against true cryptocriminals either – they will use the readily-available, robust non-LEAK systems. Moreover, authentication-only crypto can assist in exchanging confidentiality keys, and so, they reduce even more what efficacy there is even in stricter LEAK schemes. There is some law-enforcement comfort in voluntary business use of data recovery, but this can potentially solve only a small portion of the law-enforcement need, namely, the investigation of business crime.

The only effectiveness of LEAK systems lies in crypto systems that are incorporated in the information infrastructure, such as mail programs, browsers, and operating systems. Such programs will be regularly used, also by criminals, and if these programs allow law-enforcement to readily decrypt the regular exchanges facilitated by these programs, the selecting problem for the police will still be manageable. If mass-market crypto systems incorporated in the information infrastructure do not contain some form of LEAK, the police will not be able anymore to see through the bulk of communications which particular messages may be of interest to them, effectively rendering tapping useless.

However, LEAK-enabled crypto in the information infrastructure does nothing to prevent end-to-end encryption or superencryption, and such systems are therefore not effective at all in curbing criminal use of cryptography as such. A LEAK information infrastructure does not make problems worse for law enforcement, but it does not reduce their crypto problems either; particularly many organized criminals and computer criminals are likely to continue to use end-to-end non-LEAK encryption.

1d. The right to economic development

Stimulating the use of authentication-only crypto may enhance electronic commerce and be beneficial for economic development in general. Voluntary LEAK schemes, on the other hand, may fetter economic activities, since the cost and risks of implementing a (trustworthy) LEAK infrastructure are huge: "Key recovery systems are inherently less secure, more costly, and more difficult to use than similar systems without a recovery feature." [Abelson 97]. It is true that schemes for business data recovery may support business use of cryptography and in that respect enhance e-commerce, but such schemes widely differ from those considered by governments to address law-enforcement needs.

2a. A solution must be workable

Authentication-only crypto may be developed, but it seems a complex task to ensure that it can really only be used for authentication (see the 'subversive' uses of the DSA). LEAK systems are even harder to devise, given the complex issues and trade-offs they have to address; at present, it seems doubtful that a reliable LEAK system can be implemented which is a substantial help to law enforcement (notably by yielding prompt access to encrypted data) and which at the same time is secure enough for crypto users to consider. A group consisting of some of the most renowned cryptographers found that: "Building the secure computer-communication infrastructures necessary to provide adequate technological underpinnings demanded by these requirements would be enormously complex and is far beyond the experience and current competency of the field" [Abelson 97] – a conclusion which they repeated in their 1998 update [Abelson 98]. Moreover, the complexity of meeting data-recovery requirements is likely to introduce security flaws that affect the product's functioning; the cryptographers stated that their "experiences designing, analyzing and implementing encryption systems convince us that adding key recovery makes it much more difficult to assure that such systems work as intended." [Abelson 97]

Enforceability is not an issue, since all options are voluntary and need not be enforced.

2b. A solution must be internationally compatible

Non-confidentiality crypto is a non-contentious issue, and so, stimulating the use of authentication-only systems is something which many countries can agree upon. (The fact that some countries considering mandatory LEAK may oppose even non-confidentiality crypto because of its facilitating key exchange for subsequent confidential communications, is not an obstacle.)

Law enforcement will have to cooperate with other countries to intercept international communications and to ask for searches at foreign places. If the country relies on LEAK to investigate cryptocriminals, the question is whether this works internationally. Somehow, law-enforcement access to foreign keys should be enabled. This can be effected either through international legal assistance or through requiring keys to be escrowed within the country. In the latter case, however, this may not be sufficient, if law-enforcement decryption depends on accessing the private key of foreign addressees. The encryption protocol should specifically require LEAFs to be sent in both directions, so that the private key of the sender or the one of the addressee suffices for decryption. Otherwise, private keys of foreigners would have to be deposited as well within the country, which is an unrealistic requirement. Legal assistance is of little help here, given the generally long time (several weeks) it takes. The major obstacle to international access to keys, however, is that it will impede many users, especially businesses, to use a LEAK scheme – if they trust their own government at all, they will often hardly trust foreign governments.

For a LEAK infrastructure to work internationally, governments must agree on the desirability and functional specifications of the LEAK feature. It is highly unlikely that a considerable number of countries would be able to agree upon this, given the widely differing concerns and law-enforcement cultures. If OECD countries cannot agree on a *direction* in which to find solutions for the crypto problem, they will surely never be able to agree upon functional details of a specific direction.

Indeed, voluntary LEAK schemes do not seem a direction many countries will (or should) consider, given their small effectiveness in addressing the law-enforcement problem. I expect that the trend set by the 1997 European Commission communication [COM(97) 503], casting serious doubts on the viability of LEAK schemes, will continue. Moreover, even if countries agree on some LEAK-stimulating policy, the issue of access to foreign keys is likely to be a major obstacle to international cooperation.

2c. A solution must be technologically sustainable

The option of authentication-only crypto is to some extent technology-neutral, since it defines a functionality rather than a technology. It remains yet to be seen whether such systems are really sustainable – they yet have to stand the test of cryptanalytic time. LEAK schemes are technology-specific and depend on state-of-the-art cryptology; specific LEAK systems now developed are based on current crypto systems and protocols. Their intrinsic complexity make them less likely to be sustainable than simple, non-LEAK crypto systems. Moreover, a LEAK infrastructure is inherently based on the current information infrastructure, which is changing rapidly; it is uncertain whether it could meet major future shifts in the technology of the information infrastructure.

Table 7.1 gives a simplified illustration of how the options match the principles.

7.7.4. Conclusion

Non-confidentiality schemes are interesting for law enforcement, as they do not shield the contents of messages, and so, they may help in not making matters worse for the police. However, they do not target the real problem, which is criminals using uncrackable crypto. As such, stimulating the development and use of non-confidentiality crypto is not an option

principles / *options*	**separate digital signatures**	**voluntary LEAK**
1a privacy	+	–
1b fair trial	+	+
1c rule of law		
-effectiveness	–	–
-general	+	+
1d economic development	+	–
2a workable	±	–
2b international	±	–
2c technology-neutral	±	–
overall estimate	0	–

Table 7.1. Crypto options and principles

– *infringes principle*
± *has mixed effects on principle, infringes to a smaller extent*
+ *does not infringe principle*
0 *not applicable*

to address the crypto conflict, although it may be an interesting sidetrack for governments.

If LEAK schemes are incorporated in the information infrastructure, this may reduce the law-enforcement problem somewhat. After all, criminals today still talk over the (wire-tapped) telephone in hardly disguised incriminating language about their activities; likewise, several criminals would use the LEAK systems built-in in the information infrastructure and refrain from using another layer of non-LEAK encryption, simply because such systems are not always be possible or convenient or quickly available, or because they communicate with law-abiding citizens. However, it remains yet to be seen whether secure LEAK systems can be built at all, and international legal cooperation in a LEAK infrastructure is a major hurdle to consider.

Voluntary adoption by business of data-recovery services may help law-enforcement investigation of business crime; this works only for stored data. However, no matter how many voluntary LEAK schemes are provided, criminals will always be able to use robust, non-LEAK crypto. Voluntary LEAK is not effective in thwarting true cryptocriminals.

Assuming cryptanalysis to be infeasible, there remains only one option for the police if they want to access the encrypted data: they will have to get the key by asking the suspect for it. Alternatively, they can consider encrypted data as evidence in itself, if there are enough reasons to assume that the data contain incriminating evidence. I will analyze these options in the next chapter.

Chapter 8. Demanding decryption

Prosecutor: Did you murder your wife?
Defendant: No.
Prosecutor: Do you know the penalty for perjury?
Defendant: No, but I bet it's less than the penalty for murder![1]

As usual, Alice and Bob are crypto-communicating at their heart's content. They are conscientious crypto users, and so they do not trust key-escrow or key-recovery systems. (Bob, who is now working in a small company, only occasionally uses self-escrow for essential stored company data.) Polly is wiretapping them, as she suspects Alice of drug dealing. She is dismayed that Alice and Bob do not use key escrow - how is she now to decrypt the wiretaps? Moreover, she wants to search Alice's house and Bob's company, but she is sure to find encrypted files in their computers - and they are smart enough to use uncrackable cryptography, and not to leave keys or passwords lingering around. Polly is at her wit's end: she will have to ask Alice or Bob to decrypt the wiretaps and the files in their computers, or to hand over their keys.

Now, a demand to decrypt or to deliver keys will run into the privilege against self-incrimination. The privilege is age-old, although there is considerable lack of agreement over the bearing of the privilege. Some define it "the right of anyone 'charged with a criminal offence' (...) to remain silent and not to contribute to incriminating himself." [*Funke*] Others, however, think the privilege has been reduced by case law to a principle that no-one can be forced by imposition of a punishment to actively contribute to his own conviction, unless the law explicitly allows it [Reijntjes, 13]. Indeed, there seems to be a trend in the judgments of both the European Court of Human Rights (in *Funke* and *Saunders*) and the US Supreme Court (in *Fisher*, *Schmerber*, *Doe I & II*, and *Braswell*) to seriously restrict the application of the privilege against self-incrimination. In the Netherlands, the Dutch Supreme Court has swayed between discerning a general privilege against self-incrimination in the spirit of the DCCP on the one hand, and asserting that there is no unconditional principle that a suspect can not in any way be obliged to cooperate in the obtaining of possibly incriminating evidence on the other hand.

So, if there is such a thing as a privilege against self-incrimination, what does it mean? Does it prohibit Polly from asking Alice or Bob to decrypt? Can the legislature create a law to require suspects to decrypt, just as suspects can be forced to give blood to traffic police or to show books to tax agents? This chapter will investigate to what extent a decryption command is compatible with current case law, whether it could be created in legislation, given the privilege against self-incrimination, and if so, what kind of enforcement would be

1 A classic joke, according to [Kaufman, 468].

most appropriate. First, I will make some practical remarks on decryption and key delivery (8.1.1), and on storage and communication (8.1.2). Then, I will distinguish between suspects and non-suspects (8.2), corporate entities and persons (8.3), and statements and documents (8.4), in order to narrow down the situations in which the privilege against self-incrimination holds. I shall then give my view on the rationale behind the privilege against self-incrimination (8.5), in order to assess whether a decryption command to suspects is in principle compatible with the privilege (8.6). Then, I will present the three main options for enforcing such a command: penalizing a refusal to decrypt (8.7.1), penalizing crypto use to obstruct a criminal investigation (8.7.2), and using a refusal to decrypt as evidence that Alice did it (8.7.3). In the latter case, the 'cryptographic silence' is used to support the evidence that Alice is guilty of the alleged crime, which I shall refer to as the 'primary offense' (to distinguish it from the potential secondary 'offenses' of refusing to decrypt or using crypto to cover up a crime). I shall conclude with an assessment to what extent a decryption command meets the principles at stake in the crypto problem, and what trade-offs are at stake if a decryption command is to help Polly catch Alice (8.8).

Although the conclusion holds for the Dutch situation, I will focus on European and US case law, which define the privilege against self-incrimination. Therefore, the analysis will by and large hold for other European countries and the United States; in fact, the European and US courts seem quite close in their application of the privilege against self-incrimination.

8.1. Preliminary distinctions

8.1.1. Demanding decryption or key delivery?

If Polly asks Alice or Bob to decrypt, in order to obtain reliable evidence, Polly will have to be there when they decrypt. Otherwise, how is she to know whether an alleged plaintext corresponds to the ciphertext at stake? If she does not have the decryption key, there is no way to check the match unless she saw it happen with her own eyes. If there are many ciphertexts to be decrypted (e.g., wiretap recordings over a period of a few months), it is not convenient for Polly to attend the entire decryption process by Alice. In many ways, it is easier and more reliable for Polly to obtain the key from Alice rather than have Alice decrypt herself. The drawback, of course, of giving Polly a master or private key, is that it potentially gives her access to many more plaintexts than the ones she is authorized to retrieve – she could use it to continue to eavesdrop on Alice and Bob after the wiretap warrant has expired, or she could decrypt recordings she made before she had a warrant. As far as protecting suspects and preventing abuse by the police are concerned, it is better to ask for decryption by the suspect rather than to command delivery of keys. A good compromise would be to ask for session keys, but this may be only possible (and often impractical) with encrypted telecommunications or with privately stored files if these were encrypted with a symmetric crypto system. Another compromise is for Alice to re-encrypt the plaintext (or re-decrypt the ciphertext) before Polly's (or the judge's) eyes to get the corresponding ciphertext (or plaintext, respectively). There is no real way for Alice to cheat here, and so the resulting plaintext is reliable (as being the right plaintext, that is).

Although there is a difference in practicality and protection for the suspect, for the purpose of this chapter, the effects of a decryption command and the effects of a key delivery command are largely the same: the suspect has to cooperate, and the question is whether such cooperation is compatible with the privilege against self-incrimination. In this chapter, I will therefore often use the terms 'decryption command' and 'demanding key delivery' rather indiscriminately, and generally use the term 'decryption command' to cover both activities.

8.1.2. Decrypting stored and communicated ciphertexts

In practice, it will make a considerable difference whether Polly asks Alice to decrypt a ciphertext intercepted in a wiretap or obtained in a search. In the latter case, with *stored encrypted data*, it will generally be possible for Alice - in principle - to decrypt. After all, if she stores data on her computer, she apparently intends to make use of them at a later time, and so, it is in her own interest to be able to decrypt. Whether she uses symmetric or asymmetric crypto does not make a difference for the *principle* of decryption ability (although it may have consequences for the *likelihood* of a denial of being able to decrypt, see 8.7.1). Note that there are some ways to subvert the decryption command by decrypting to an alternative, innocent text (duress decryption, 3.1.8).

With *encrypted communications*, the ability to decrypt afterwards is less evident. For one-way communications, notable e-mail messages, Bob will usually encrypt with Alice's public key, which implies that she can - again, in principle - decrypt the message at any later time with her private key. Depending on when and how often Alice uses her key pair, she may or may not be able to convincingly argue that she cannot decrypt (particularly older) messages; e.g., when she has revoked her public key, or when she has been using a different key for some time, or when there is no evidence that she has recently used her private key, Alice's chances of convincing Polly that she can no more decrypt Bob's former messages apply. (She could also argue, less convincingly, that Bob sent her messages she was not able to decrypt in the first place; maybe Bob mistook Carol's key for Alice's, or perhaps the message was altered during transport.) So, with one-way communications, posterior decryption is in principle possible, although it may not always be likely.

With two-way communications, however, notably with telephone traffic, the ability to decrypt an encrypted conversation after it has ended will depend on the crypto protocol used. Alice's and Bob's crypto phones will have to exchange a session key before each communication. If the key is exchanged by encrypting a session key with the other phone's public key, then Polly can ask the (holder of the) recipient phone to decrypt the encrypted session key; the crypto phone may need to be specifically configured to facilitate this. However, there are also protocols (e.g., Diffie-Hellman, cf. 7.7.1) in which the session key is derived from an unrecoverable exchange or prior session key: neither Alice nor Bob can reconstruct the session key after the conversation has ended. This feature is called 'perfect-forward secrecy', which is being researched by a number of cryptographers. (Some cryptographers are even concocting schemes for 'deniable encryption': protocols in which Alice can make the ciphertext 'look like' an encryption of a different (innocuous) plaintext, which she may happily decrypt for Polly's eyes [Canetti].)

I assume that in general, it will not be feasible for Alice or Bob to decrypt past conversations. In those cases in which it may be possible, Polly can seize the crypto phone needed to decrypt, and decrypt herself; if the phone is password-protected, she may ask Alice or Bob for the password, which is similar to the case of asking Alice for the password protecting her private key. So, for the purposes of this chapter, I will concentrate on stored encrypted data and encrypted e-mail messages.

8.2. Demanding non-suspects to decrypt

Encryption by *network operators and service providers* will not be a problem: they already have an obligation to decrypt for law enforcement. According to the EU Council resolution of 17 January 1995 on the lawful interception of telecommunications, "[i]f network operators/service providers initiate encoding, compression or encryption of telecommunications traffic, law enforcement agencies require the network operators/ service providers to provide intercepted communications en clair." [96/C 329/01, requirement 3.3] The only problem, therefore, is demanding decryption from *end users*, and here we meet the privilege against self-incrimination.

The privilege against self-incrimination is codified in the ICCPR: according to article 14 paragraph 3 sub g, everyone charged with a criminal offense has the right not to be compelled to testify against himself or to confess guilty. In the United States, the Fifth Amendment protects suspects from being a witness against themselves. The ECPHR does not contain such an explicit provision, but the European Court, in the *Funke* case, has interpreted article 6 paragraph 1 of the Convention to incorporate "the right of anyone 'charged with a criminal offence', within the autonomous meaning of this expression in Art. 6, to remain silent and not to contribute to incriminating himself." As these statements show, the privilege pertains only to people charged with a criminal offense (which, in the general interpretation of the European Court, means that someone has sufficient reason to infer that he is or will be a target for a criminal prosecution. The scope of the privilege, however, is wider. Although people not charged with a criminal offense can not invoke the privilege (and, consequently, have to contribute evidence), if subsequently they are charged, compelled statements can not be used as evidence later on (at least, they could not in the case of *Saunders*).

In Dutch law, people can be required to deliver seizable things to the police, but suspects can not. (Not cooperating with such a command can be punished with up to six months' imprisonment for not complying with an official order.) Tax officials can require people to show books, and a refusal is penalized – unless they are charged with a criminal offense.[2] Also, in other specialized law areas, such as the Chemical Substances Act, everyone is required to cooperate with investigating officials and to provide them with information. Finally, the registered holder of a car license number is required to tell who drove the car in

2 The Dutch Supreme Court held that evidence obtained by commanding a suspect to deliver documents could be used in a case against him, since at the time of the command, there was not yet a criminal charge. [HR 29 October 1996]

case of a traffic offense, unless he can reasonably infer that he is being accused of having driven himself [HR 26 October 1993].

In general, then, people *not* charged with a criminal offense can be required to cooperate in obtaining evidence, even if this potentially incriminates them. In certain cases, the evidence thus obtained can not be used in subsequent criminal proceedings, although this is restricted to testimonial statements (see 8.4).

It follows that a decryption command can also be given to people not charged with a criminal offense. In Dutch law, this power was codified in the Computer Crime Act of 1993, with the proviso that the command can not be given to a suspect.[3] Compelled testimonial statements obtained in this way may not be used in subsequent criminal proceedings against the person testifying, however. Assuming for the moment that a key delivery is a privileged testimonial statement (cf. 8.4), two interesting questions can be asked in this respect.

First, can the compelled evidence be used in criminal proceedings against *other* people? Suppose Polly forced Bob to say what key he and Alice used. Since Bob is not a suspect himself, the key can be used to decrypt the wiretaps, and these can be used in a case against Alice. Even if Bob would be a suspect, and his compelled rendering of the key would violate his privilege against self-incrimination, the key might still be used against Alice anyway, as it was not she who rendered the key and it therefore did not breach *her* privilege.[4] It seems logical that it does not violate the privilege, because it is a privilege that protects suspects against incriminating themselves – it does not protect them from incriminating statements uttered by others (otherwise, where would witnesses for the prosecution be?). Therefore, the Public Prosecutor can split multiple criminal cases, so that evidence obtained from one suspect can be used in proceedings against the others.[5] Of course, if Alice and Bob use asymmetric encryption, Bob can only decrypt (e-mail) messages sent to him by Alice (and not the messages he himself sent to Alice, unless he kept a plaintext copy), but these are the most interesting messages. The only thing Bob cannot decrypt, of course, is the files stored on Alice's computer.[6]

A second question is whether an unlawfully compelled rendering of a key also

---

3 As the class of suspects is larger than the class of people charged with a criminal offense (although the boundary is somewhat fuzzy), for convenience's sake, I shall take the larger class (of suspects, that is) as a basis in this section. If a decryption command can not be given to a suspect, it can certainly not be given to someone charged with a criminal offense.

4 This argument holds for the Netherlands (the *Schutznorm*) as well as for the US. In *Couch* v. *United States*, an accountant was forced to give tax papers of his (suspect) client. This did not violate the Fifth Amendment, as no personal compulsion was used against the accused. "The Constitution explicitly prohibits compelling an accused to bear witness 'against himself': it necessarily does not proscribe incriminating statements elicited from another." The *Federal Guidelines for Searching and Seizing Computers* also suggest asking others for a crypto key or password: "Agents should consider whether the suspect or someone else will provide the password if requested. In some cases, it might be appropriate to compel a third party who may know the password (or even the suspect) to disclose it by subpoena (with limited immunity, if appropriate)." [CD, 55]

5 For this reason, it is common practice in the Netherlands to split cases against several suspects involving the same offense.

6 A problem may occur when Bob (as accomplice) wants to shield Alice. The punishment for his not complying with a decryption command (a regular three months, in the Netherlands), will in that case not be a strong encouragement for him to cooperate. See further 8.7 on this problem.

contaminates the resulting evidence: if Alice was forced to give the key to the encrypted files on her computer, is it only the key which cannot be used as evidence in court, or also the files decrypted with this key? The 'fruits of the poisoned tree' doctrine tells that evidence resulting from an illegal investigation activity can not be used as evidence in court.[7] In general, if a key delivery is privileged, then also the resultant plaintexts will be protected by the privilege.

A first conclusion is that the police can require non-suspect people to decrypt.[8] If a key delivery is a privileged testimony, the key (and generally the data decrypted with that key) can not be used as evidence in subsequent criminal proceedings against the person who rendered it; however, they may be used in proceedings against others. This can be useful in many cases, since it means that encryption by non-criminals will not hamper an investigation. Thus, for instance, if the police is authorized to demand data from banks, accountants, or notaries, the data will have to be provided in plaintext. Also, the police can require crypto service providers, in particular Key Escrow Agents and Data Recovery Agencies, to decrypt or to hand over keys; this may be possible mainly in business crime cases, if the corporation uses a data-recovery service.

8.3. Demanding suspect corporations to decrypt

Suppose Polly suspects Bob's company of tax fraud, and she wants to search the company and investigate Bob's computer. Can she ask Bob to decrypt files she finds there? In principle, corporate entities can claim constitutional rights protection. Can Bob's company benefit from the privilege against self-incrimination? The European Court of Justice decided in the case of the French enterprise *Orkem* that the European Commission "may not compel an undertaking to provide it with answers which might involve an admission on its part of the existence of an infringement [anti-competitive conduct] which it is incumbent upon the Commission to prove." Although this recognizes that enterprises do have a privilege against self-incrimination,[9] it restricts its application to an *admission* of the *existence* of an *infringement* – that is, a virtual confession. Requiring the handing over of corporate records could well be admissible, since this would not admit the existence of an offense – only of books that an investigation agent knows the enterprise must have anyway.[10] Therefore, asking the self-escrow agent within Bob's company to hand over the keys (or plaintexts) will be possible, as it is clear that he must have the keys (or plaintexts) available as corporate records.

---

7 It is possible that, having cunningly obtained the key from Alice, the police claims that in the meantime they had been running an exhaustive key search, and that it just so happened they were very lucky and 'found the key' in the first batch of trials. The unlikelihood of such a lucky find depends on the strength of the crypto system; in many cases, the judge may do away with such a claim and conclude that Polly has used a key she unlawfully obtained from Alice.

8 They can also require suspects not (yet) charged with a criminal offense to decrypt.

9 This is not so in the United States: "the corporation (...) of course possesses no such privilege." [*Braswell*]

10 The Dutch Supreme Court ruled that a command to deliver accounting evidence can also be given to suspects. [HR 29 October 1996]

Then, one should ask whether Bob himself can be called upon to decrypt. In the United States, the protection of the Fifth Amendment for persons working in corporate entities has been reduced severely. Notably in *Braswell*, the Supreme Court said that corporations cannot claim protection by the Fifth Amendment when people are required to hand over corporate records. Even if the handing over can be seen as an admission of their existence, "a custodian may not resist a subpoena for corporate records on Fifth Amendment grounds." One reason for deciding so, is a political one: "The greater portion of evidence of wrongdoing by an organization or its representatives is usually found in the official records and documents of that organization. Were the cloak of the privilege to be thrown around these impersonal records and documents, effective enforcement of many federal and state laws would be impossible."[11] This indicates two considerations: the records required are corporate, which means their existence is presupposed, and there is no claim for personal privacy for corporate records. That means that employees of a company can be forced to give these documents. Only if the employee 'is' the company himself, can he invoke the privilege: in *Doe I*, the privilege against self-incrimination could be invoked because Doe conducted his business as a sole proprietorship, and therefore acted in a personal rather than a representative capacity (and because the act of production (not the contents) was a testimonial self-incrimination). Braswell, on the other hand, was co-director, and hence subject to the 'collective entity rule', which treats corporations different from individuals. The European situation is similar in this respect, although there may be more constitutional protection in Europe and the Netherlands for employers if they can be held personally (criminally) liable for corporate offenses.

One can conclude that in Europe, employees and employers of an enterprise can only claim protection from self-incrimination if the compelled production of evidence (the *act* of producing, not the evidence) directly admits guilt to having committed an offense, or if the documents (or statements) required are private and outside the scope of the corporation. In the United States, there is no privilege for corporations, nor is there for custodians of corporate records, except when the enterprise is conducted as a sole proprietorship and the act of production is testimonial self-incrimination.

In the case of Bob and his enterprise, handing over a key cannot be supposed to be an admission of the existence of an offense. There may be a problem if the files decrypted with the compelled key turn out to be private, say, e-mail messages from Alice asking for XTC pills. In that case, one can argue that the resulting decryptions can not be used in a case against Bob (for complicity in drug dealing); as in this case, Polly was interested in tax fraud by Bob's company, this need not be a significant drawback. The main thing is that Polly can require Bob to decrypt corporate files, except when Bob conducts his business as a sole proprietorship (US) or is an executive who can be held criminally liable for corporate offenses (Europe), and the act of production would be a testimonial self-incrimination.

11 The Dutch Supreme Court, in its 29 October 1996 verdict, likewise acknowledged that the legislature can create a power to command a suspect to cooperate in specific (law) areas, given the concerns relating to the enforcement of the pertinent criminal provisions, and the special demands and problems of finding the truth in such cases.

8.4. Demanding individual suspects to decrypt

Asking whether Polly can command suspect Alice to decrypt or to hand over the key, is asking the sixty-four thousand dollar question: what kind of (possibly incriminating) compelled cooperation is compatible with the privilege against self-incrimination? The key issue here is whether the privilege concerns only oral testimony or extends also to other forms of cooperation, such as handing over keys or documents.

Dutch penal legislation seems to incline (with a few exceptions proving the rule) to a broad interpretation of the privilege, and prevent the compelled rendering of documents by suspects. The command to hand over seizable goods cannot be given to suspects (art. 107 para. 1 DCCP), nor can the command to provide law enforcement with data (art. 125m para. 1 DCCP). One exception is a specific provision enabling investigating officers to command delivery of goods for a number of specific crimes (art. 551 para. 1 DCCP), which does not refer to privileged suspects, and the Dutch Supreme Court has allowed such a command to be given to a suspect [HR 20 March 1984].[12]

The European and US courts appear to apply the privilege in a more restricted sense, covering only factual testimony. For Europe, the verdict of the ECHR in *Saunders* v. *United Kingdom* is paramount. Saunders had been compelled to testify during an administrative investigation into an alleged corporate fraud. His statements were subsequently used during a criminal trial against him, in a manner which sought to incriminate him (by calling into question his honesty and casting doubt on his version of events). The European Court considered this use of compelled statements unacceptable in light of the privilege against self-incrimination. And in doing so, it virtually restricted the privilege to using incriminating *statements*: the privilege "is primarily concerned, however, with respecting the will of an accused person to remain silent. (...) it does not extend to the use in criminal proceedings of material which may be obtained from the accused through the use of compulsory powers but which has an existence independent of the will of the suspect such as, *inter alia*, documents acquired pursuant to a warrant, breath, blood and urine samples and bodily tissue for the purpose of DNA testing."

The European Court had earlier called the rationale of the privilege against self-incrimination, among others, protecting the accused against improper compulsion by the police, which contributes to avoiding miscarriages of justice and to securing the aims of article 6 of the Convention [*Murray*, at 45]. Compelled statements may be unreliable - who knows what someone will say in fear of violence or punishment? - and miscarry justice, but a suspect cannot lie with blood or documents (that is, documents which exist at the time of the command, and which the suspect has no ability to alter).

This view of the privilege is the key to interpreting an earlier case which had caused some confusion with ECHR watchers. *Funke* was compelled by French customs officers to render bank statements of foreign accounts. The European Court considered this a violation

12 Article 551 paragraph 1 DCCP concerns a few specific crimes, such as those involving state security, migrant trafficking, child pornography, cruelty to animals, and certain offenses against public decency; in these cases, a delivery command can be given to suspects.

"of the right of anyone to remain silent and not to contribute to incriminating himself." This phrasing suggested the Court maintained a broad view of the scope of the privilege against self-incrimination: no suspect is required to contribute to incriminating himself. This would imply that many laws forcing suspects to give blood or to breathe in a breathalyser test are violating the European Convention. *Saunders* sheds light on this judgment: it is not the rendering of documents *as such* that breached the privilege, it was the fact that the officers were not sure that the documents required *existed at all*, and so, the rendering of the documents was in effect an admission by Funke that he possessed them. One can read this between the lines of the Court's phrasing of the action: "the customs secured Mr Funke's conviction [for his initial refusal to give the bank statements] in order to obtain certain documents which they *believed* must exist, *although they were not certain of the fact.*" [emphasis added] The police can command a suspect to hand over documents, but, like with blood, they must know the documents exist and that the suspect has them at his disposal.[13] Otherwise, his refusal to give them can mean two things: he does not have them, or he does not want to give them; in other words, a refusal does not give reliable evidence - you cannot draw conclusions from it.

The view that suspects can be compelled to deliver documents can also be seen in recent US Supreme Court judgments. In *Fisher* v. *United States*, Fisher's attorney was subpoenaed to hand over tax returns drafted by Fisher's accountant. The Court referred to *Schmerber*, where it had ruled that the privilege against self-incrimination only protects evidence of a testimonial or communicative nature (which, in that ruling, excluded furnishing a blood sample). Fisher's tax returns did not contain compelled testimonial evidence, as they had not been drafted under compulsion. The SC remarked that under certain circumstances, handing over documents could be testimonial and incriminating, if in handing them over, the holder would admit his possession of the documents, and if his possession was not a foregone conclusion (say, because the existence and location of the documents were known to the police from other sources). In *United States* v. *Doe*, the Court built on this decision. Doe was commanded to hand over business documents he himself had drafted. The SC considered these documents not to be privileged through their content (he had not drafted them under compulsion), but stated that the *act of producing* them could be testimonial; in this case, it was, since "the act of production would compel respondent to 'admit that the records exist, that they are in his possession, and that they are authentic.'"[14] Whether the *contents* of a statement are testimonial in nature, was defined in *Doe II*. Doe was ordered to write an authorization for foreign banks to disclose information. According to the Court, this was not testimonial, since the authorization did not disclose factual statements. The privilege only protects a suspect from forced disclosure of 'the contents of his own mind'; the statement (oral or written) must relate, implicitly or explicitly, a factual assertion or disclose

13 It seems the protection against self-incrimination in the United Kingdom is broader: 'a man is not bound to provide evidence against himself by being forced to answer questions *or produce documents*'. [Reijntjes, 60]

14 Compare the ECHR *Saunders* ruling: "some of the applicant's answers were in fact of an incriminating nature in the sense that they contained admissions to knowledge of information which tended to incriminate him", and as such, they could not be used as evidence.

information.[15] One can conclude from these verdicts that the privilege only prohibits the compelled writing or uttering of factual statements, as well as the compelled handing over of documents if this act itself admits the holder's possession, and if his control over the documents can not otherwise be proved.[16]

Now, this case law gives Polly some reassurance. If Alice has stored her key on a diskette or a smart card, and if Polly is certain of its existence and Alice's possession of them, she can summon Alice to deliver it – at least, in the United States she can, and also in European countries, according to the European Court's decision in *Saunders*. In the Netherlands, article 107 paragraph 1 DCCP, however, prohibits Polly from commanding delivery from suspects.[17]

But what if Alice has learnt her key by heart, or has stored and password-protected it, as will mostly be the case? Can Polly ask Alice for the key or password? Here, we meet the border line of the privilege: is a key or password testimonial? That is, is it part of someone's 'integrity of conscience', or is it comparable to a physical key? One can think of a cryptographic key as equivalent to a physical key to a door. There is one fundamental difference, however: the physical key exists outside of the holder's mind, and the police can – in theory – find it by searching well, even if the holder does not cooperate. The courts in that case allow a delivery command for non-testimonial evidence: if the evidence exists outside of the will of the suspect, and its existence and the suspect's possession are clear from other sources, then the police can command delivery (in a way, this is a service to the suspect, as it may save her a ravaging of the house). With a cryptographic key or password, this is different: it does not (have to) exist outside of Alice's mind, and if Alice does not give it, there is no way the police can find it. Although – theoretically, there is: an exhaustive key search. As pointed out in section 3.1.5, this is not realistic in most cases. However, the fact that there *is* an alternative to find the thing looked for, however impractical, may be an argument to convince a court that a command to give a key or password is valid. (Mark that this is, in fact, a paradoxical conclusion: you may only use a power when there are alternatives.)

Compare the distinction Judge Stevens made in his dissenting opinion in *Doe II* (note 9), essentially unchallenged by the majority: "He may in some cases be forced to surrender a key to a strongbox containing incriminating documents, but I do not believe he can be compelled to reveal the combination to his wall safe – by word or deed." The Court considered the compulsion at issue (the authorization) to be "more like be[ing] forced to surrender a key to a strongbox" than like revealing the combination to a safe. The fundamental difference seems to be that of mind versus matter: the key to a strongbox exists anyway, whereas giving a combination to a safe reveals a person's knowledge, and thus is

---

15 Judge Stevens dissented, arguing that the authorization statement was privileged, as "by executing the document, petitioner admits a state of mind, a present-tense desire." "But can he be compelled to use his mind to assist the prosecution in convicting him of a crime? I think not. (...) The forced execution of this document differs from the forced production of physical evidence just as human beings differ from other animals." (219)

16 Another privileged act is when the handing over of documents authenticates them. [*Andresen* v. *Maryland*]

17 Only in the case of article 551 paragraph 1 DCCP could Polly demand delivery, which will not be possible in many crypto cases.

testimonial. In that respect, a safe combination is like a crypto key or password. A minor difference between a safe combination and a crypto key is that it may be easier to prove earlier knowledge of a crypto key than knowledge of a safe combination. If Alice has signed a document (very) recently with her key, which can be proven if she has a public-key certificate, this is strong evidence that she holds her private key (and remembers the password). She may claim to have just forgotten it when the police arrived, but this is rather too convenient to be convincing. I equate a crypto key or password with a safe combination rather than a strongbox key. If the police can argue that Alice holds the key or knows the password, to the extent that Alice's knowledge is a foregone conclusion, then *Doe I* suggests that a key delivery command is legal. In general, it may be a (too) hard task for the police, however, to make Alice's disposal of the key or password a foregone conclusion (compare 8.7.1). By and large, *Doe*'s 'foregone conclusion' is the same requirement as *Funke*'s, namely that the police must be sure of the fact that the documents exist and that the suspect has them available; therefore, this conclusion holds for both the US and Europe.

Like demanding key delivery, demanding Alice to decrypt will also often fall within the present scope of the privilege against self-incrimination. Although police agents can compel suspects to allow the taking of a blood sample or to give a writing sample, this is not giving testimonial evidence, as the integrity of conscience is unimpaired, and the evidence exists outside of the will of the suspect (handwriting is a characteristic of a person, and so she cannot intentionally falsify it, as experts can attest). Should Alice decrypt a document, then she would testify to knowledge of the key, and this is as testimonial as handing over the key or password itself.

Overall, then, Polly does not have much foothold for commanding suspects to deliver a key or to decrypt, as current case law stands. Only if she can show that Alice's knowledge of the key is a foregone conclusion, can she demand decryption.

8.5. The rationale behind the privilege against self-incrimination

Given the conclusion that, under current case law, a decryption command to a suspect will generally be obstructed by the privilege against self-incrimination, what are the options for the legislature to specifically create such a command? In drafting the 1993 Computer Crime Act, the Dutch legislature explicitly created a decryption command only for non-suspects, ostensibly respecting the privilege against self-incrimination. With the decision to withdraw the proposed article from the draft Computer Crime Act II to demand suspects to decrypt, this starting point was reinforced. In the US, federal-government computer search and seizure guidelines imply that encryption keys and passwords may be protected by the Fifth Amendment.[18] However, is the privilege fundamentally contrary to a decryption command, or is it only currently considered disproportionate to allow the command to be given to

18 "In some cases, it might be appropriate to compel a third party who may know the password (or even the suspect) to disclose it by subpoena (with limited immunity, if appropriate)." [CD, 55] The 'limited immunity' indicates that the password may be privileged under the Fifth Amendment.

suspects? Would it be acceptable to somehow infringe upon the privilege against self-incrimination? As the privilege is not absolute, one may investigate its margins. This requires deeper scrutiny into the background of the privilege against self-incrimination: what is its rationale?

There are various viewpoints on the rationale of the privilege against self-incrimination. Historic interpretations tend to stress the humanity principle: "in the end, is it not the point that we think it inhumane, and so we reject this ethically, to force someone to contribute to his own misfortune? Do we not think that every citizen has to right to protect himself – even if this harms truth-finding?" [Reijntjes, 18] In a way, the privilege shields the police from being tempted to force someone to give evidence, and this protects suspects from torture and inhuman treatment.[19] However, this historic explanation is not satisfactory to pinpoint the kernel of the privilege. If it is unethical to force someone to contribute to his misfortune, we should ban other forms of compelled cooperation that have gradually slipped into our legal systems, such as taking blood samples, doing line-ups, giving writing samples, or, indeed, delivering documents. Giving blood can be as devastating to a suspect as a confession of guilt, yet we allow the first while rejecting the latter. Humanity is not the all-encompassing reason of the privilege.

Others have discerned a privacy component to the privilege against self-incrimination. Notably in the US, the Fifth Amendment is often related to the Fourth, which protects people from unwarranted searches and seizures. Since the Fourth is aimed at protecting privacy of the home, the Fifth can also be seen as protecting the privacy of the mind. According to a recent decision, *Pennsylvania* v. *Muniz*, the Fifth Amendment privilege reflects "our respect for the inviolability of the human personality and of the right of each individual 'to a ... private life.'" [quoted in Sergienko][20] This contrasts sharply with Justice O'Connors concurring opinion in *Doe I*: "the Fifth Amendment provides absolutely no protection for the contents of private papers of any kind." [*Doe I*, at 618] It is hard to see that the Fifth Amendment protects the privacy of one's mind if it does not protect the privacy of (some of) one's papers. In European case law, there is little evidence to suggest that the privilege against self-incrimination is meant to protect suspects' privacy. In *Murray*, the Court stated that the privilege contributes to the "avoidance of miscarriages of justice" and the securing of the aims of article 6 of the ECPHR – that is, not the goals of article 8 ECPHR on privacy. And if compelled delivery of documents the suspect was not compelled to write by the police (a diary, for instance) is compatible with the privilege against self-incrimination, there is little privacy protection in the privilege.

Another attempt at explaining the reason of the privilege has been to distinguish between passive suffering and active cooperation; several people have suggested the privilege protects only the latter. This would explain why someone can be forced to give blood, but

19 In *Murphy*, the Court articulated seven purposes of the privilege against self-incrimination, including "unwillingness to subject those suspected of crime to the cruel trilemma of self-accusation, perjury or contempt" and "our fear that self-incriminating statements will be elicited by inhumane treatment and abuses".

20 Sergienko notes: "This statement is difficult to reconcile with interpretations of the Fifth Amendment providing no protection for existing documents."

not to provide a testimony. Indeed, the system of the Dutch Code of Criminal Procedure seems to suggest such a distinction: a suspect must allow his clothes or body to be searched, but he cannot be compelled to deliver goods or information. The Dutch Supreme Court has once phrased the privilege thus: the principle that a suspect – safe in exceptions provided in law – cannot be compelled to *actively* cooperate with something which can lead to his conviction [HR 1 October 1985, emphasis added]. People favoring the distinction have been forced, however, to make some distorted attempts at fitting allowable 'passivities' into the framework: one can, for instance, hardly define someone being forced to change clothes and to take part in a line-up as cooperating passively. More importantly, the distinction has little explicative value to pinpoint the reason behind the privilege. The Dutch Supreme Court has perhaps arrived at the same conclusion; in later case law, at least, it reverted to its general wording of the privilege, leaving out mention of 'active' cooperation.

In my view, there is a more plausible interpretation to the privilege against self-incrimination than humanity, privacy, or activity. Its *raison d'être*, as I already have implied in 8.4, is the *reliability* of evidence. Compelling someone to provide evidence can lead to unreliable evidence, if the suspect can alter the evidence, if he is too frightened by the imposing police to tell the truth, or if he simply does not know the answer. That is why the European Court speaks of avoiding miscarriages of justice.[21] Schalken has argued the case for this interpretation convincingly:

> "In that vision, which remains close to the text of article 14 paragraph 3 sub g ICCPR, which prohibits unwilled self-incrimination by testimonies, a compelled violation of the *freedom of statement* by the suspect is central. One can maintain that this relates to the reliability of the evidence. In that approach, it becomes visible that, as the method of finding the truth becomes less reliable, the significance of the privilege against self-incrimination increases. (...) The reverse then also holds: as the method of research yields more reliable evidence, the force of the privilege against self-incrimination decreases. In that sense, one can maintain that the principle, contrary to what is defended in the literature (...), is not incompatible with breath analysis and blood samples for drink-driving checks and DNA testing. The information which can be gained on this basis is available and unequivocal. The safeguards needed with this type of investigation are aimed at both safeguarding the meticulousness of the procedure with a view to the reliability of the evidence, and at ensuring that other principles are met, such as the principle that the finding of truth can not be served in another way and that therefore there are no reasonable alternatives (subsidiarity) and the principle that the gravity of the violation of the suspect's rights, in particular the right to safeguarding the integrity of the body and privacy, must be proportionate to the gravity of the offense to be solved (proportionality). The concern that the constitutional and conventional rights of the suspect aim to protect must, with humanity as the lower limit, be traded off with the concern that is at stake in a violation of those rights." [Schalken]

I consider this the most adequate description of the rhyme and reason of the privilege against self-incrimination. If the information asked from the suspect is available and unequivocal, the privilege plays no significant part. If the information is not (necessarily) available or if it can be equivocal, the privilege shields the suspect from having to give it or the judge from

---

21 Judge Martens, who dissented in *Saunders* because he considered the Court to interpret the privilege too broadly, concurred in this respect: "since there is a not negligible chance that statements made under pressure may be unreliable, the rationale of the immunities under discussion comprises – as the Court put it – the avoidance of miscarriages of justice."

being able to use it as evidence.[22] This is almost only the case when someone is forced to give testimonial statements. This view of the privilege takes into account the humanity principle (as a lower limit), and it explains the distinction between 'passive' and 'active' cooperation, which, in fact, is a distinction between non-cheatable and cheatable cooperation.[23] At the same time, it explains both the relative reluctance of the legislature to infringe the privilege and the relative ease of the courts to allow infringements. The legislature has so far found little occasion to create general powers that infringe the privilege, given the subsidiarity principle: they have only done this with blood samples for drunk-driving testing (after all, this is the only way to prove drunk driving, in a neutral, verifiable way), and with DNA testing for serious crimes (punishable with eight years or more) and a small number of violent crimes. The courts have restricted the scope of the principle much more in specific cases, as the circumstances of a particular case allow a much sharper application of the subsidiarity principle. In particular, material "which has an existence independent of the will of the suspect" can be obtained from a suspect through the use of compulsory powers (*Saunders*), because it is available and it can not be altered.

8.6. Is it possible to create a law demanding decryption?

Now, can a law authorizing decryption commands be compatible with the privilege against self-incrimination, if the privilege is primarily aimed at safeguarding the reliability of evidence? Let me first look at handing over a decryption key. Obviously, if Alice gives Polly 'the' key, it either works or it does not. If it works, i.e., if the result of decryption with the key is a reasonable plaintext, then it must be the right key. Only if Alice used a One-Time Pad (OTP) to create a dummy message, she may not hand over the right key, but a fake dummy key (see 3.1.8). If Alice decrypts with a OTP, then, it is wise for Polly to be suspicious (who, after all, uses OTPs these days?), and Alice may have to explain how she generated the key (which should be a random stream at least as long as the message itself). If Alice has prepared herself well, she may get away with it, but generally, dummy decryption will not be practical or convincing.

The evidence of the key, then, is reliable. Safe for the cumbersome option of creating dummy messages with double keys, Alice can not cheat with the key. Like blood or breath, it exists outside of her will. The same holds for a password she gives to release a key stored on a smart card or hard disk: it works or it does not. Therefore, the evidential value of a delivered key is highly reliable, and consequently, a command to deliver a key or password

---

22 Compare article 76 paragraph 2 of the English Police and Criminal Evidence Act 1984: "If, in any proceedings where the prosecution proposes to give in evidence a confession made by an accused person, it is represented to the court that the confession was or may have been obtained (...) in consequence of anything said or done which was likely, in the circumstances existing at the time, to *render unreliable* any confession which might be made by him in consequence thereof; the court shall not allow the confession to be given in evidence against him". [emphasis added]

23 As A.J. Marx put it in 1934: "It is something very different to let words cross one's lips, with which one incriminates oneself, than it is to cooperate in an examination that allows objective conclusions, which can equally well be in favor of the suspect as against him." [quoted in Ansmink, 428]

Voices for demanding decryption

The option of addressing the crypto problem by giving the police the power to demand decryption, or to shift the burden of proof, has proponents in several countries.

The Delegation of *Australia* to the OECD December 1995 Ad Hoc Meeting, for instance, noted that "the law on self-incrimination may need to be reviewed", since "the person served with a search warrant requiring decryption of his or her information may, conveniently 'forget' the key." [Australia, 7] When the report was discussed at the meeting, *Denmark* "offered the observation that in some circumstances the Danish courts will shift the burden of proof to the defendant if he does not provide certain kinds of evidence that is within his control." [Baker 96] Indeed, Danish scholars Andersen and Landrock have proposed that "a principle of 'reversal of proof' should apply in cases where three conditions [are] met: first, circumstantial evidence suggests that a person is guilty of an offence. Second, there is a substantial likelihood that the defendant has encrypted information that might provide evidence of guilt. And third, the defendant is in a position to decrypt that information and thereby free himself of any allegation, but decides not to." [Andersen, 348]

The *UK* Labour Party, before governing, opposed key escrow. Instead, they said, "the only power we would wish to give to the authorities, in order to pursue a defined legitimate anti-criminal purpose, would be to enable decryption to be demanded under judicial warrant." [Labour] Two *Belgian* senators have likewise proposed such a power. To "prevent that certain people refuse to give the key or to cooperate with the judiciary," they propose heavy criminal sanctions, because "if the person does not want to hand over the key, the judiciary has no evidence whatsoever against him and he can go free." Therefore, they propose a maximum of five years' imprisonment for those who are able to assist in decryption yet refuse to do so. [Bribosia] The *Irish* framework for cryptography policy states that "legislation will be enacted to oblige users of encryption products to release, in response to a lawful authorisation, either plaintext which verifiably relates to the encrypted data in question or the keys or algorithms necessary to retrieve the plaintext. Appropriate sanctions will be put in place in respect of failure to comply." [DPE]

The *Dutch* Data Protection Authority, in a 1998 letter to the Minister of Internal Affairs, expressed its alarm at the obligation to deposit keys that the Minister was apparently (still? again?) considering. The Data Protection Authority greatly preferred the system of requiring people to decrypt, as initially proposed in the draft Computer Crime Act II. [Registratiekamer 98]

is, in principle, compatible with the rationale of the privilege against self-incrimination.

The same is valid, grosso modo, for demanding the suspect to decrypt herself. As Polly will not be satisfied with a plain message just because Alice tells her it is the plaintext of the encrypted file at issue, Alice will either have to decrypt it before Polly's eyes, or she will have to re-encrypt the plaintext (or redecrypt the ciphertext) before Polly's or the judge's eyes to get the corresponding ciphertext (or plaintext, respectively). There is no real way for Alice to cheat here (with the same proviso when she uses a One-Time Pad), and so, the resulting plaintext is reliable (as being the right plaintext, that is; the contents may still be unreliable, of course). Therefore, in principle, a command to decrypt is compatible with the privilege's rationale.

In this respect, delivering a crypto key or decryption is comparable to furnishing a blood sample or a writing sample. The difference, however, is that with the latter, it is a foregone conclusion that the suspect is *able* to comply. With delivering a key or decrypting, one can not take for granted that someone can comply.[24] This is, I think, the crux for generally holding that revealing a safe combination is privileged: the act shows knowledge of the combination, and this is testimonial. Only if knowledge of the combination is a foregone conclusion, then, one can argue, the privilege does not hold. If one is to explore the margins

24 This, in my view, is the essence of *Funke*: if the customs officials *had* been sure of the fact of the documents' existence, they *could* have ordered their delivery. Since they were not sure, the order was unlawful.

of the privilege against self-incrimination, it is this issue that seems to be crucial. If the ability to comply is not a foregone conclusion, then the reliability of the evidence decreases – not when the suspect complies, but when she refuses. After all, a refusal can mean either inability or unwillingness, and if there are no compelling arguments that it is unwillingness, one cannot draw a conclusion from the suspect's refusal to comply. One can echo Schalken here: if there is less evidence that the suspect is able to decrypt, the significance of the privilege against self-incrimination increases; as the evidence that the suspect knows the key or password increases, the force of the privilege decreases.

Therefore, legislation granting an explicit power to demand decryption from suspects is compatible with the privilege only insofar as there is strong evidence that the suspect is able to decrypt or give the key. That is more or less the same conclusion I arrived at from examining case law: only if Polly can show that Alice's knowledge of the key is a foregone conclusion, can she demand decryption. I conclude that, in principle, creating a power to demand decryption from suspects is compatible with the privilege against self-incrimination, making explicit what is already possible under current case law (except in the Netherlands), with the condition that there must be strong or even compelling evidence that a suspect is able to comply.

8.7. How to enforce a decryption command

For a power to command decryption or key delivery to be effective, the legislature must create an incentive for the suspect to cooperate. After all, Polly can always kindly *request* Alice to decrypt – and Alice can kindly refuse to do so. If the refusal does not somehow reverberate upon Alice, she will of course not cooperate (unless to discharge herself). What kind of pressure can the legislature use to incite Alice to cooperate? There are three ways of doing so. First, penalize the refusal – just as currently a refusal to obey a legal order is punishable with up to three months' imprisonment. A second, similar, option is to penalize the use of encryption 'to obstruct an investigation', or (if there is enough evidence) to consider crypto use an aggravating circumstance, and consequently give Alice a higher sentence if she refuses to decrypt. A third method is to use the refusal to cooperate as evidence in the primary case: if Alice does not want to decrypt, she apparently has something to hide, and the encrypted file may be thought to be incriminating. This would make it easier for the judge to convict Alice given an insufficient amount of plain(text) evidence: the burden of proof is thus somewhat shifted. In this section, I will analyze the merits and drawbacks of these options, and see to what extent such legislation seems compatible with the privilege against self-incrimination and the presumption of innocence.

8.7.1. Penalize a refusal to cooperate

Penalizing a refusal to cooperate with a lawful order is often used to support the force of such an order. For instance, in Dutch law, if someone called to appear as a witness or interpreter in a court proceeding intentionally fails to comply with the consequent legal duties, he can be punished with up to six months' imprisonment. The same can happen to someone who intentionally refuses to hand over a document which is supposed to be forged.

In fact, there is a general penalization of a refusal to cooperate with a lawful order – for up to three months (art. 184 DCC).

One can therefore well consider using this incitement to enforce a decryption command. However, the threat of three months in prison will not be a serious consideration for Alice, if by obeying the command and uncovering incriminating plaintext, she would risk going to prison for many years. (This was a major gap in the initially proposed extension of the decryption command to suspects in the Computer Crime Act II: it proposed no specific enforcement, and so, if Alice refused to decrypt, she could only get three months in prison.) The punishment for not decrypting and the punishment for the primary offense must somehow be proportionate.

With drunk driving, the legislature has chosen the simplest solution. If you refuse to breathe or give blood, one may safely assume your blood was brimming with alcohol (or why would you refuse to cooperate?), and thus it is acceptable to punish a refusal to cooperate with the maximum punishment that is possible for drunk driving. A difference with a decryption command, however, is that with drunk driving, the primary offense of the suspect is obvious and one-dimensional, and the punishment only depends on the amount of alcohol in one's blood. That makes it reasonable to give someone the maximum punishment in case he refuses to cooperate (this works in effect as a burden-of-proof reversal), and the suspect can exonerate himself by complying. A crypto case, on the other hand, is not one-dimensional. Often, the plaintext is needed to determine just which offense the suspect committed (trafficking soft drugs? or hard ones? or participating in a criminal organization? Forgery? or tax fraud?), and the corresponding maximum punishments may vary considerably. More importantly, a breath or blood test is the only way to prove drunk driving – there are simply no alternatives; this makes it easier for the legislature to punish a refusal to cooperate, as otherwise the offender would easily go unpunished. With decryption commands, however, there may be sufficient other ways to gather evidence (often, there will be other sources of evidence, and, at least theoretically, the police can first try practical attacks on the ciphertext, e.g., guess the password); an encrypted file can never, I imagine, be the single source of evidence of a crime. It is true that in those (few) cases in which the encrypted files are the objects on which the evidence hinges, a refusal to decrypt will block the case. However, unlike with a breath or blood test, to penalize the refusal as such with the maximum punishment for the primary offense seems contrary to the subsidiarity principle. After all, the fact that the breath or blood test is the only way to provide evidence makes it possible to equate a refusal to cooperate with the primary offense; with encrypted files, the refusal to cooperate blocks only part of the investigation, which implies, in my view, that it cannot be equated with the primary offense.

So, in penalizing a decryption refusal, it is not that easy to find a proportionate punishment. Can one set a general maximum of, say, twelve years on a refusal to cooperate with a decryption command? The burden of proof would be all the more heavy on the prosecution as the punishment for non-cooperation is larger: the proportionality principle demands that the relationship between crime and punishment should be proportionate, and to send someone to jail for over ten years for the subsidiary offense of not complying with a legal order is easily disproportionate – unless there be overwhelming evidence that the encrypted file is incriminating, that it is the only missing link for proving a very serious offense, and that the suspect can decrypt it. In that case, I do not see a reason why the suspect could not be easily convicted for the primary offense (compare 8.7.3: if the evidence is that strong, common sense will lead the judge to gain the conviction that the suspect is guilty).

The problem, then, is finding a middle way between a low punishment (which is little incentive to cooperate, and therefore ineffective) and a high punishment (which lays an almost impossible burden of proof on the prosecution). In Belgium, parliamentarians Bribosia and Maximus have proposed a law to set a punishment of maximum five years on a refusal to cooperate with a decryption command. Their proposal lacks detail (it does not indicate, e.g., whether the command can be given to suspects, although the aim of the proposal indicates it could), but they do explain the (relatively high) punishment:

> "The information in the encrypted messages could yield him a conviction. If the person does not want to give the key, the court has no evidence at all against him, and he can go free. By providing for a heavy penal sanction, one wants to incite the citizens to cooperate." [Bribosia] [25]

Is five years an acceptable middle way, though? It seems high enough to incite many people to cooperate. Indeed, it virtually creates a Prisoner's Dilemma situation in which a suspect can choose between the certainty of five years on the one hand, and the risk of either a potential higher sentence or freedom on the other. It seems an interesting game theory question just at how many years the turning point lies between non-cooperation and cooperation for the average Prisoner.[26]

Criminal justice is not game theory, however. A sentence of five years for a simple refusal to decrypt a particular document is high enough to lay a heavy burden of proof on the prosecution. Not only should the prosecutor make a reasonable case for the document being incriminating and a missing link in the evidence of the primary offense,[27] but he must also give evidence that it is in the suspect's power to comply with the order. This is one of the crucial issues at stake in any proposal to command decryption.

There are several arguments that may support a claim that Alice knows her passphrase. For instance, if Alice has (very) recently signed a message (which can be proven with her public-key certificate), it shows that she knew her passphrase recently, at least for her private signature key. If she uses this same key also for confidentiality encryption (which, although

---

25 Unfortunately, the proposal goes on to say: "With the system of 'random' keys, it can of course happen that the person who sent or received it can no longer decipher it (the judge should surround himself with experts who can tell). That does not, however, prevent the person involved from knowing the contents of the message by heart." I am afraid this indicates Mme. Bribosia and Mme. Maximus have not thought over their proposal well; even if criminals have such good memories, would they be naive enough to tell the police? Or would the MPs have them go to jail for not knowing the messages by heart?

26 An interesting issue is that with a high punishment for the refusal and with sufficient evidence that the ciphertext is a missing link in the evidence, the fact that the suspect refuses to decrypt will almost certainly imply that the ciphertext is indeed seriously incriminating. Consequently, the police could try a brute-force attack on this particular ciphertext – they might buy a Cray supercomputer specifically for these cases, or set up a distributed attack using all police computers' idle time.

27 I disregard the option of creating a general criminal sanction on a refusal to decrypt for the police regardless of an investigation. It is too close to prohibiting cryptography as such, which I do not consider acceptable (Chapter 6½). Compare 8.7.2.

not advisable, is a common practice with, especially, PGP users), then Polly will have a good case. Another supporting argument is that it seems illogical for Alice to keep encrypted data on her hard disk if she cannot decrypt them anymore. Indeed, a natural prerequisite for using cryptography for stored data in the first place is the future ability to decrypt. Especially with recently encrypted files, one can suppose that Alice will (or should) remember her passphrase.

On the other hand, Alice can use a whole range of retorts against the claim that she knows the passphrase. For instance, she can claim that she is backing-up some encrypted files for Carol, or that she downloaded from a news group some obscure but interesting-looking file which she subsequently forgot. With files having an old date, she can claim that they were encrypted with some key she has not used for a long time (remark that Alice can anticipate this by setting back the computer clock by five years before storing the encrypted file), and that she simply does not bother cleaning her hard disk every once in a while. Or she might suggest that it is a file in an exotic word-processing format someone once sent her for comment.[28] Most of these claims are not particularly probable, but depending on the circumstances, they may be sufficiently convincing (or rather, they may not be sufficiently unconvincing) to argue that indeed, Alice is not able to decrypt. Especially the claim that the file was encrypted a long time ago with a key pair no longer in use can be convincing, I think. For the kind of criminals at issue here, storing incriminating information on a durable diskette or hard disk, there is ample opportunity to anticipate a decryption command with such a retort.

The question whether someone is able to decrypt could to a certain extent be answered by using a legal concept known as *Garantenstellung* ('vouching'). The concept is used in German law to determine liability for an offense of omission. If someone has legally 'vouched' for protecting something specific, or for protecting against a specific threat, he will be liable if he omits preventing damage resulting from the threat. The 'vouching' is determined from the person's (legal) position or from earlier acts. For instance, a close relative living in the same house will be criminally liable for not saving someone from death by starvation, because by his relationship he 'vouches' for protecting the life of his relative. A neighbor does not (legally) vouch for this and cannot therefore be prosecuted for criminally negligent homicide. Another example is the liability of land owners for waste disposal: if a land owner does not remove waste deposited on his land by third parties, he

---

28 Cypherpunks often like to suggest that a suspect can claim that she is just keeping long strings of random data on her hard disk. This argument will not convince any judge – unless perhaps the suspect is a cryptographer or a compulsive mathematician.

may be prosecuted for endangering the environment through waste disposal; his position as owner of the land implies that he vouches for protecting the land from polluting waste [Schmitz].

The concept of *Garantenstellung* could be transposed to suspects failing to decrypt.[29] If by her position or former acts, Alice has 'vouched' for 'protecting' the encrypted data, she can be held liable for not decrypting: her position or acts imply that she ought to be in the position to decrypt, whether or not she can in reality. In some cases, the prosecution can use this line of reasoning, if it can prove that Alice holds such a position. For instance, if Alice is the information manager or computer expert of a criminal organization, she vouches for her decryption capability by her position. More in general, if circumstances imply that Alice is in a position in which she ought to be able to decrypt, the burden of proof will be on her to argue why she is not able to; if she cannot argue thus, she will be held liable for having incriminating ciphertexts. Such a 'vouching presumption' can be used to assign the burden of proof of decryption capability. A *Garantenstellung* may help in a few cases, in particular with well-organized and automated criminal organizations, and with certain computer criminals.

However, if the claim that Alice ought to be in a position to decrypt is to lead to a conviction for refusing to decrypt, the standard of proof should be high. There should be compelling evidence that Alice's position is such that she has 'vouched' for being able to decrypt in the future. Absent such evidence, the judge will have to weigh the arguments of the prosecution and of the defense why Alice is or is not able to decrypt. In many cases, I think, Alice will have to be given the benefit of the doubt if she claims she no longer uses the key pair at issue.

Apart from this proof issue, there is another, more fundamental argument against the approach of convicting people for refusing to decrypt. Penalizing refusals to cooperate with legal orders are *instrumental*: they are not reprehensible in themselves, but they serve to ease investigation. If Alice is a criminal, we want her to be punished for her crimes. Penalizing a refusal to decrypt is an alternative way to punish Alice – if we cannot get her at the front, we catch her at the backdoor. It may have the same effect when it comes to keeping Alice out of society for a while, but it gives less satisfaction to our sense of justice: her crimes go unpunished (or she was even innocent in the first place). Instrumental penalization may be practical in some cases (such as drunk-driving tests), but it inflates the moral justification of criminal justice. In this case, the (potential) effect of penalizing a refusal to decrypt seems simply too small to justify such inflation.

8.7.2. Penalize cryptocriminal use

A similar way to incite a suspect to obey a decryption command, is to penalize crypto use if this hampers investigation. The issues at stake here are largely similar to penalizing a refusal to decrypt, but the proof issue may be significantly easier for the police. Consider Mr. Salabiaku, who was convicted for drugs *smuggling* merely because he *carried* them. He

29 This, of course, is very different from the German application of the concept; by transposition I mean that one might apply the line of reasoning rather than the legal circumstances.

might have acquitted himself if he had explained how he came to carry the drugs, but he did not. In fact, he had been warned by a customs official not to take the suitcase he came to collect, for there was reason to suspect it contained drugs. Still, Salabiaku had taken the suitcase and, without opening it, had walked through customs. After his arrest, he was prosecuted for smuggling drugs, as the French customs law said that possession of drugs in such a case means smuggling. Only if the defendant establishes a case of 'force majeure beyond his control' can the defendant exculpate himself. The European Court argued that the presumption of guilt in this law was not irrebuttable, as there were enough safeguards built-in through case law to allow someone to argue force majeure (and people had been given the benefit of the doubt by the courts). The French court had shown "scrupulous respect for the presumption of innocence", as it had acquitted Salabiaku of the *criminal* offense of importing narcotics, giving him the benefit of the doubt, and only convicting him for the *customs* offense of smuggling. In the latter, it had not automatically resorted to the presumption of guilt laid down in the law, but had inferred from the fact that Salabiaku had not heeded the customs official's warning that there were no arguments to rebut the evidence.

The Salabiaku case shows that it may be possible, under certain conditions, to "penalize a simple or objective fact as such, irrespective of whether it results from criminal intent or from negligence". The main conditions are that in the application of the law, there must be sufficient safeguards to maintain the rights of the defense, notably a practical chance for the defendant to argue against the presumption of guilt, a chance which the courts must explicitly give him. A caveat is that in Salabiaku, a customs law was involved, with according subject matter (it is difficult for customs officials to prove smuggling, but easy to prove possession).

Still, the case suggests an interesting analogy to the crypto question. Can a state penalize the possession of a ciphertext as such, with an acceptable defense if the suspect decrypts? There have been several proposals to this effect, notably from US senators and representatives. Three bills discussed in 1997 contained provision to this effect. The Security And Freedom through Encryption (SAFE) Act of Rep. Goodlatte, e.g., would criminalize crypto use with the intention to cover up a federal felony; Senator Leahy's bill, the Encrypted Communications Privacy Act, would penalize the use of encryption in furtherance to a felony, if the encryption is intended to obstruct investigation; and senators' Kerrey, McCain, and Hollings Secure Public Network Act contained a similar provision. The Ashcroft and Leahy E-PRIVACY Act of 1998 would also criminalize the use of encryption to conceal 'incriminating' communications or information during the commission of a crime. All these proposals are ultimately intended to ease proof issues: if Alice threatens to get away with insufficient evidence for a criminal offense because she has used cryptography, you catch her instead for the crypto use. It seems to me that this does not solve the proof issue, because, if there is not enough evidence to prove a criminal offense, how can you prove crypto use 'to cover up the felony'? You either lower the requirement of proof for the offense (which is the burden-of-proof reversal of section 8.7.3), or you penalize crypto use irrespective of a presumed crime.

The latter is an option, but it is not an attractive one. It means that, in principle, everyone who uses cryptography is potentially acting criminally, which he can only undo if he cooperates with a decryption command. That is dangerously close to criminalizing cryptography as such, which, as I argued in Chapter 6½, is absurd. Moreover, if the penalization is intended to encourage suspects to cooperate with a decryption command, the same problem of the punishment as in section 8.7.1 holds: if it is too low, no criminal will cooperate, whereas a high punishment is disproportionate – and the middle way seems the worst rather than the best of both worlds.

One would have to resort, then, to a more restricted offense, say, criminalizing crypto use only if this obstructs the investigation of a crime, regardless of the intention. This is a straightforward provision, which does away with the issues of proving the ciphertext is incriminating and a missing link in the evidence of the primary case.[30] Decrypting on command (or having used key escrow) can be an affirmative defense, to make rebuttable the presumption of guilt inherent to the provision. There remains, however, the familiar problem of the maximum punishment: three months? The maximum of the (presumed) offense under investigation? The arithmetical mean of these?

Again, my main objection to such a provision is that it is instrumental, creating an offense of something which is in no way reprehensible in itself. If it really helped in easing investigation, one can be willing to accept this. I am skeptical, however, as to the efficacy of such a provision. If it is applied carelessly by the courts, the prisons will fill up with innocent crypto users who forgot their keys. The risks of catching the wrong 'criminals' can only be strictly limited if the provision is applied by the courts with scrupulous respect for the rights of the defense. In that case, however, if the courts are sufficiently lenient in accepting a defense for a refusal to decrypt (e.g., if Alice argues she no longer uses the key, or that decrypting would infringe her privacy, and if she can make this plausible), it will not often lead to a conviction. The same remarks about the *Garantenstellung* (see 8.7.1) apply here: it will only be in a few cases of well-organized and computer crime that the prosecution can argue that Alice is in a position in which she ought to be able to decrypt.

There is yet another, similar option: use a refusal to decrypt to raise the punishment for the primary offense. Sentencing guidelines or an aggravating circumstance in a penal provision may provide that if there are encrypted data the suspect refuses to decrypt, the punishment to the offense is to be increased with a certain percentage of the maximum punishment. This does nothing, however, to solve the law-enforcement problem, since in this case, there should be sufficient evidence in the primary case anyway to convict the defendant, regardless of the encrypted data. Therefore, I do not consider it an option.[31]

---

30 There remains the issue of proving it is ciphertext rather than random noise, something which expert witnesses for the prosecution and for the defense have to fight out, and which seems doable. See 8.7.3.

31 Also remark that it is already the case that the course of action adopted by the defendant during the proceedings is a factor in determining the punishment. A cooperative defendant may be given a somewhat lower sentence than an obstinately obstructive defendant. Remaining silent to all questions, although it is a fundamental right of the defendant, may thus be weighed by the judge if it amounts to a 'negative attitude': once a judge has concluded guilt, no legal rule prevents the judge from taking into account a 'negative attitude' in determining the punishment. [HR 18 December 1984]

8.7.3. Reverse the burden of proof

Their silence was by politicians used,
Their teeth opened with phrase, their puppet heads
voided comic balloons: their speaking death
Supposed his debt, and gave him much advice.
(Howard Nemerov, Who did not die in vain)

Rather than punish someone for refusing to decrypt or for criminal crypto use, one can also use the refusal or the ciphertext as evidence that Alice has something to hide - and thus convict her of the primary offense. Here, the privilege against self-incrimination meets the presumption of innocence: no-one can be supposed guilty until proven so in a legal procedure - something which the prosecution must prove (art. 6 para. 2 ECPHR). One cannot reverse the burden of proof for the suspect to prove her innocence. On the other hand, there is no absolute prohibition of a shift in the burden of proof, as *Salabiaku* attests, and silence can sometimes be used as evidence. This section investigates the use of 'cryptographic silence' as evidence in the primary offense.

If Polly asks Alice to decrypt, and Alice refuses, can the judge use this as evidence that Alice is hiding something incriminating, and consequently, infer that Alice has done it? There is some case law on the use of silence as evidence, and I shall accordingly treat a refusal to decrypt as remaining silent on a certain question. The right to remain silent is not absolute, in the sense that silence would never be usable against the suspect. Such, at least, is the view of the European Court, which in *Murray* - in a rare pun - notices that "established international standards in this area, while providing for the right to silence and the privilege against self-incrimination, are silent on this point." From this silence in international standards, they infer, "if the evidence against the accused 'calls' for an explanation which the accused ought to be in a position to give that a failure to give any explanation 'may as a matter of commonsense allow the drawing of an inference that there is no explanation and that the accused is guilty'." Murray was asked to explain his presence in the house where an IRA hostage had been held, and his silence on this point - after several warnings that his silence could and would be used as evidence against him (in accordance with an exceptional Northern Ireland law) - was taken by the courts as evidence that he could not acquit himself. The European Court allowed this, "having particular regard to the situations where inferences may be drawn, the weight attached to them by the national courts in their assessment of the evidence and the degree of compulsion inherent in the situation." Moreover, the Court considered the following circumstances:

- there were appropriate warnings as to the legal effects of remaining silent,
- there was a prima facie case against the accused,
- the evidence 'called' for an explanation,
- the trial judge had a discretion whether an inference should be drawn from the silence,
- the judge had to explain the reasons for the decision to draw inferences, and this decision was subject to appellate review.

Local precedents for reversing the burden of proof

Although the Dutch Supreme Court does not allow using silence as evidence, there are precedents for laws that reverse the burden of proof. In several General Municipal Ordinances (GMO), carrying subversive stuff is taken as an indication of guilt until proven otherwise. For instance, in Wassenaar, it is forbidden to carry false keys, rope ladders, lanterns, or any burglary tools on the road at night; the prohibiting does not apply when it is made plausible that the carrying of the tools does not happen with the aim of burgling (art. 134a GMO Wassenaar, see HR 7 June 1977). Likewise, Groningen proscribes carrying glue, paint, tar, chalk, or any other coloring or dying substance in public at night, unless the carrier makes a reasonable case that these goods are not meant for illegal sticking or graffiti (art. 17 GMO Groningen, see HR 13 December 1977).

Contrary to the European Court, the Dutch Supreme Court does not incline to allow using silence as evidence. In a recent case, the DSC adhered to the principle that a refusal to testify cannot in itself be used as evidence [HR 19 March 1996, *NJ* 1996, 540]. The Court, however, did go on to say that such a refusal may have consequences in court, for instance, when the defendant puts forward a 'Meer & Vaart' defense, i.e., a defense that gives an explanation which is compatible with the evidence but which contradicts the alleged offense. In this case, the defendant had, out of her own accord, provided an alibi for the time of the murder. When the alibi proved false, she refused to explain why she had construed the alibi without being asked. The Court of Appeals inferred from this construing of a false alibi that she must have known when the murder had been committed, and, consequently, that she had done it. The Supreme Court did not allow the use of this inference, as the Court of Appeals had used the defendant's silence as evidence that the alibi was false and intended to cover up the truth, and as it had used this falseness as evidence that she had committed the murder. However, the Supreme Court would have allowed, it implied, using silence to reject a defense which would, for instance, have explained her presence on the spot at the time of the murder without her having committed the murder (e.g., because she had an appointment with the neighbor). If such a defense is put forward, the court must explicitly explain why it rejects this explanation – and a refusal of the defendant to answer questions related to this defense *can* be used by the court to argue that the defense does not hold.

The difference between *Murray* and the Dutch silence case, then, is the *use* of the silence: the European Court allows its use under specific conditions as direct evidence of the offense, whereas the Dutch Supreme Court only allows it to refute a specific defense from the defendant.[32] But is this difference so fundamental as it looks at first sight? If one considers the verdicts carefully, it may turn out that there is a difference in approach rather than in essence.

The Murray case was a specific one, dealing with a peculiar Northern Ireland law that allows drawing inferences from silence in specific circumstances. The European Court did not review the law, but only its application to Murray. The main question was whether there

32 A more recent case seems to go further than this in allowing silence as a basis for the proof. The failure of a defendant to explain how he came to possess a bus card stamped at the place and time of the offense was considered a reason on which to base the proof that it was the suspect who had committed the offense, since the bus card supported the claim of witnesses that they recognized this particular suspect. Not explaining something which supports a basis for the proof, can thus apparently be used to confirm evidence that establishes guilt. [HR 3 June 1997]

was enough evidence to establish a 'prima facie case',

> "i.e. a case consisting of direct evidence which, if believed and combined with legitimate inferences based upon it, could lead a properly directed jury to be satisfied beyond reasonable doubt that each of the essential elements of the offence is proved".

And in each particular case, "the question is whether the evidence adduced by the prosecution is sufficiently strong to require an answer." In his dissenting opinion, Judge Walsh argued for more evidence to make a prima facie case:

> "In a criminal prosecution the burden of proof of guilt beyond reasonable doubt always rests on the prosecution. Therefore a prima facie case means one in which the evidential material presented by the prosecution, if believed and not rebutted, is sufficient in law to establish the guilt of the accused."

This seems more in line with the reasoning of the Dutch Supreme Court, which prohibits using silence to contribute to establishing guilt.

So, just what is a 'prima facie' case? In the view of the European Court, it is a case with a lot of evidence, perhaps not entirely sufficient to prove guilt of itself, but which, if supplemented with common-sense inferences based upon it, would be sufficient to prove guilt. In the view of the Dutch Supreme Court, like in Walsh' view, a prima facie case is directly sufficient to prove guilt. Does that mean that the Dutch Supreme Court rules out common-sense inferences? No – a Dutch judge can use his observation and common sense to gain an inner conviction of the defendant's guilt. The difference is that he does not (have to) say so: he merely lists the evidence, and concludes guilt; in the Murray case, the court explicitly mentioned its 'common-sense' inference. It may really be a matter of open versus hidden, or explicit versus implicit, use of evidence, hence the stress of the European Court on the fact that in Northern Ireland, "where trial judges sit without a jury, the judge must explain the reasons for the decision to draw inferences and the weight attached to them. The exercise of discretion in this regard is subject to review by the appellate courts."

I think the main difference between the European Court and the Dutch Supreme Court's views is not so much the amount of evidence needed to establish a 'prima facie' case, but rather the way the evidence is presented. A prima facie case is a case in which there is virtually enough evidence to conclude guilt. There may be just a hairline missing for an obvious conclusion of guilt – and common sense is used to bridge this hairline's gap, be it explicitly or implicitly.

If this assessment is correct, then both the European Court and the Dutch Supreme Court would allow the use of silence as evidence, since common sense tells us that something is rotten if someone remains silent when circumstances cry out for an explanation. The conditions for using silence, however, are severe. The other evidence must be enough to base a common-sense conclusion of guilt upon, the defendant must not have been (unduly) pressured to testify,[33] and the evidence must 'call' – or, I would say, 'shout' – for an explanation the defendant is unwilling to give.

There remains, then, little room for using silence, but still, it is some room. There are three stages of judging whether evidence is sufficient – evidence must conform to the

---

33 In *Murray*, the European Court concluded that Murray had not been unduly pressured *because of* the fact that he had been able to remain silent, an *ex post* inference that would hardly meet a logician's approval.

minimum legal rules,[34] it must have been obtained legitimately, and it must convince the judge that the suspect did it. Cryptographic silence can be used in the last stage: to strengthen the judge's conviction. It can not be used in the first stage of making evidence conform to the minimum legal rules, as these are already sufficiently weak: one witness testimony together with some independent evidence which supports part of the charge will suffice. Using silence to supplement the minimum legal rules would constitute a radical change in Dutch criminal procedure law. Moreover, in the problem at issue, the evidence will almost always be legally sufficient to meet the minimum rules; the key issue is whether the evidence convinces the judge.

So, the refusal to decrypt or deliver the key might be used as (supporting) evidence that Alice did it, but only if:

1. there is enough other evidence against Alice that, combined with her refusal, allows a common-sense conclusion of guilt,[35]
2. Alice has not been pressured by Polly to give the key (echoing the European Court, if she does not give it, she has apparently not been unduly pressured),
3. the ciphertext at stake must 'call' for an explanation, and
4. there is enough evidence that Alice is able to decrypt.

I shall refer to these as the 'Murray conditions'.

The fourth condition (that Alice 'ought to be in a position to decrypt') requires considerable supporting evidence, and may lead to complex arguments in court (compare 8.7.1); it may, however, require less argument than in penalizing a decryption refusal, since 'ought to be in a position' is more objective and general than a 'foregone conclusion' that Alice knows the key. Can one say that, in general, someone using cryptography 'ought' to remember the key, and thus lay the burden of proof with Alice to argue that she did forget it? Yes, one can, but Alice will have several ways to argue that in this particular case, she – alas – does not know the passphrase (see 8.7.1). Here, the *Garantenstellung* (see 8.7.1) seems the best device to assign the burden of proof whether Alice is able to decrypt. If the prosecution shows that Alice is in a position in which she has 'vouched' for a decryption ability (notably, because she is the information manager of a criminal organization, or because she is a very experienced in encrypting crucial information), then the burden of proof is on Alice to argue why she cannot decrypt. Note that it will not be often the case that Alice 'vouches' by her position or her person for a decryption ability.

The third condition will likewise not always be easy to meet. Does the fact that Alice has encrypted her stored files and her e-mail messages 'call' for an explanation? If Alice has encrypted her hard disk or diskettes, she may assert she is just cautious with information security, having read stories in the newspapers of burglars stealing compromising diskettes even from public prosecutors. In the case of a few encrypted files on an otherwise plaintext diskette or hard disk, Alice may be called upon to explain their presence. "I just don't want

---

34 Dutch criminal procedure law has a few minimum rules to which evidence must conform: a conviction cannot be based solely on the basis of one witness, nor on the sole basis of a confession, nor on the basis of only anonymous statements.

35 Note that this is stronger than Andersen and Landrock's condition of circumstantial evidence (see sidebar in 8.6).

my daughter to see these dirty pictures" may not be the smartest answer, as in that case, the police could request (not command) her to decrypt to acquit herself – if Alice refuses that, the court can refute her 'Meer & Vaart' explanation of the encrypted files. She may resort to explaining the ciphertext as her innermost private diary, in which case Polly must have strong reasons to ask her to decrypt (private letters are not to be delivered, unless there is evidence that they are related to the crime); and here, Alice will have a somewhat stronger (though still not very convincing) case arguing her refusal (her privacy is her inner sanctum). If Alice is smart, she will use a disk encryptor to bypass the necessity of having to explain why some files are encrypted where others are not.

There is also the point of proving something *is* in fact a ciphertext, rather than random garbage. With recorded communications, Polly will be hard put to argue that it is a ciphertext: if she missed out one or two bits, or if she did not start the recording at the exact beginning of the conversation (and this is not easy with recording bits), the result will be garbage and not a ciphertext. How is she to argue that the recording is a ciphertext? With e-mail messages, it may be more viable to argue it is a ciphertext, especially if a header announces an encrypted message. The same holds for stored data. In these cases, it is logical to ask the sender or holder what the random data are doing there – you normally do not keep random garbage on your hard disk, let alone send it to someone. There may be possible explanations (e.g., using a random stream to generate crypto keys, or to research properties of random data), but at least the presence of random bits in an e-mail message and on a data carrier 'call' for an explanation, and generally Polly will be able to make a good case that these random data are, in fact, ciphertexts.

Then, as many have suggested, there is the chance that smart criminals will use steganographic means to 'hide' encrypted files on their computers. Alice may hide a ciphertext in images or sound files, and then Polly has a hard task in arguing that the files contain hidden data (she can, see Chapter 4, but it requires a lot of investigation, and a convincing expert witness). And if Alice stores some fifty encrypted dirty pictures on her hard disk, which she – reluctantly, being a good actor – decrypts on Polly's command, there is a good chance Polly will disregard the fifty-first ciphertext; or she may fail to investigate whether the decrypted dirty pictures contain hidden data. Alice may even encrypt some "mildly incriminating dummy messages" to decrypt before Polly's eyes, in order to hide the really incriminating texts (as Schneier claims, a pair of Israeli spies once did this [Schneier, 228]). Although Polly can always find out in principle, I think the options for Alice are broad, and if Alice is determined, she will fool Polly. This is not to say that Polly will always fail – not all criminals are that smart or prepared. There may be sufficient cases in which the presence of encrypted files on a computer calls for an explanation the suspect is unwilling to give. And in that case, this refusal may be used in court as supporting evidence, provided the other conditions are met.

The question that remains is whether Polly will be satisfied with this option. If the use of cryptography as such (with e-mail or a hard disk encryptor) is not sufficiently uncommon to call for an explanation, which I think will often be the case, it is only the presence of a few encrypted files on a computer or diskette that may call upon a suspect to explain why they are there. For criminals who are aware of this problem, there are options to blur the existence of incriminating ciphertexts. It is the less prepared and less wary criminals that may be caught with inexplicable ciphertexts – this may well be the largest part of the criminal society, if you consider how many criminals have incriminating conversations over the telephone. Still, the other conditions for using the ciphertext as supporting evidence hold: there must be a prima facie case against Alice, and there must be considerable evidence that Alice ought to be able to decrypt (which may be difficult if Alice has not 'vouched' for her decryption ability).

And this brings me to the ultimate question here. If there is enough evidence to make a prima facie case, which means that using common sense is enough to base guilt upon this evidence, then what is the extra evidential value of a refusal to decrypt? It may add to a judge's conviction of guilt, but it can hardly co-establish it. With current law and case law, a refusal to decrypt may bridge the (hairline's) gap between strong evidence and sufficient evidence, but the *Murray* conditions for using this explicitly are so heavy that this will only work in few cases in practice.

To alter this, and be more lenient in using silence as supporting evidence than current case law allows, does not seem acceptable to me. The above use of silence as evidence has explicitly explored the margins of the right to remain silent, and if one crosses that border, the presumption of innocence is violated. In my view, *Murray* leaves the presumption of innocence intact:[36] it is like adding a weight to a pair of scales so that the scales only just remain in the same fixed position (namely, where the defendant is presumed innocent). If one adds just a milligram more, the scales start to move, and a portion of the burden of proof is referred to the defendant. One could decide to allow that for criminal-political reasons, but in my opinion, the presumption of innocence is at the core of criminal justice, and it can not be scaled down without undermining the credibility of the rule of law. One can also, of course, expect the European Court to turn down a significant burden-of-proof shift as a violation of the presumption of innocence.

8.8. Assessing the decryption command

8.8.1. The decryption command in current law

A decryption command can be given to network and service providers, to non-suspects, and to people working in corporations (except when they conduct the business as a sole proprietorship (US) or when they are liable as executives for corporate offenses (Europe), and if the act of production is testimonial). Self-escrow agents within corporations (and, of course, external escrow agents) will be useful to obtain keys or plaintext; the current punishment for not complying with a decryption command can be considered adequate for inciting them to cooperate, as they have little reason not to. The option of demanding non-suspects to decrypt can also be useful in organized crime cases, or in other cases involving various suspects, as Bob can be required this way to provide evidence against Alice. Here,

36 "Nor can it be said, against this background, that the drawing of reasonable inferences from the applicant's behaviour had the effect of shifting the burden of proof from the prosecution to the defence so as to infringe the principle of the presumption of innocence." [*Murray*, at 54]

however, the punishment for not complying may be too low to incite accomplices to co-operate.

When it comes to asking suspect Alice to decrypt, the privilege against self-incrimination starts to assert itself. Polly can command her to deliver a stored key or a smart card with the key, if she knows Alice possesses it, but generally, this will be passphrase-protected. The key issue is whether Polly can ask Alice for the passphrase (or for the key, if she knows this by heart). Case law of both the European Court and the US Supreme Court suggests that such a command can be compatible with the privilege against self-incrimination, provided that the police can argue that Alice is able to decrypt, to the extent that Alice's ability is a foregone conclusion (in *Funke* terms: the police must be sure of the fact that Alice can decrypt). This will be possible in few cases.

Currently, therefore, there is not much room for Polly to demand decryption. When one investigates the options for the legislature to create a specific power for the police to demand decryption, the rationale of the privilege against self-incrimination suggests that, in principle, such a power can be compatible with the privilege: it provides reliable evidence (the passphrase or key either works or it does not). However, the same *Funke* requirement should hold, namely, that there is compelling evidence that Alice is able to decrypt. Case law, then, has already explored the borders of the privilege against self-incrimination; the legislature can only make this explicit, but can hardly extend beyond this in light of current law. For the purpose of this book, I shall assume that a decryption command can be given to suspects under these strict conditions. The real issue at stake is how the legislature plans to enforce this command: these are the options to consider.

8.8.2. Options for enforcing a decryption command

Together with a power to demand decryption, the legislature should create an enforcement of this power, as otherwise Alice will kindly refuse to cooperate. There are three major options for inciting suspects to cooperate.

Option 8.1 Penalize a refusal to decrypt

The legislature penalizes a refusal to obey a lawful command, given in the investigation of a serious crime, to decrypt stored encrypted data and encrypted one-way communications. This is a special clause overruling the general criminal provision of refusing to cooperate with a legal command. The legislature must determine the maximum punishment for the refusal after careful consideration of the trade-off between effectiveness and the rule of law; it should be high enough to incite (serious) criminals to decrypt, yet be low enough not to create an insurmountable burden of proof for the prosecution to show that the data are incriminating and that the suspect is able to decrypt; nor should it be a disproportionate punishment for forgetting a crypto passphrase. It can be a fixed maximum, or it can be related to the maximum punishment for the primary offense.

The legislature may at the same time consider extending the power to demand decryption to be given under less strict circumstances (than the *Funke* requirements), i.e., with less than aggravating evidence in the primary offense, or with less than strong evidence that the encrypted data are incriminating for the primary offense.

The legislature can consider extending the provision to cover encrypted two-way communications, if it turns out that technology allows users in principle to decrypt after the communication has ended.

Option 8.2 Penalize crypto use if this obstructs investigation
The legislature penalizes having stored data in encrypted form if this obstructs a specific investigation of a serious crime. The suspect can exonerate himself by decrypting. The legislature must determine the maximum punishment for the encountered crypto after careful consideration of the trade-off between effectiveness and the rule of law; it should be high enough to incite (serious) criminals to decrypt, yet be low enough not to create an insurmountable burden of proof for the prosecution to show that the data are incriminating and that the suspect is able to decrypt; nor should it be a disproportionate punishment for forgetting a crypto passphrase. It can be a fixed maximum, or it can be related to the maximum punishment for the primary offense.

The legislature can consider extending the penalization to cover sending or receiving encrypted e-mail. Likewise, the legislature can consider extending the provision to cover encrypted two-way communications, if it turns out that technology allows users in principle to decrypt after the communication has ended.

Option 8.3 Shift the burden of proof
The legislature enacts a law stipulating that the refusal to decrypt stored encrypted data or encrypted e-mail encountered during the investigation of a serious crime can be used as incriminating evidence in the case. The conditions for the judge to use a decryption refusal as evidence are the Murray conditions:

1. there is enough other evidence against the suspect that, combined with her refusal, allows a common-sense conclusion of guilt,
2. the suspect has not been pressured by the police to give the key;
3. the ciphertext at stake must 'call' for an explanation, and
4. there is enough evidence that the suspect is able to decrypt.

The legislature can consider weakening these conditions, notably the fourth and, to a less extent, the first and third, after a careful consideration of the trade-off between effectiveness and the presumption of innocence.

The legislature can consider extending the provision to cover encrypted two-way communications, if it turns out that technology allows users in principle to decrypt after the communication has ended.

8.8.3. Applying the criteria

How do these options relate to the principles for striking the crypto balance?

1a. Privacy and the right to confidential communications

The options do not as such infringe the right to privacy: everyone can use as much crypto as they want. It is only when Alice becomes a target for investigation and when there is considerable evidence against her, that she may have to decrypt and reveal privacy-sensitive information. For a law-abiding Alice, this will occur rarely, and if it happens, she may not be too particular about her privacy if she can thus exonerate herself. (I assume there are good safeguards for Polly to deal with the decrypted information.) The very rare case that law-abiding citizens would be required to decrypt privacy-sensitive information they would not want the police to see, is of too little weight to take into account. (Besides, in such a case, Polly could also allow Alice to have a notary decrypt the information and notify Polly whether it is what she is looking for or not.) In general, then, the right to privacy is not infringed.

The right to privacy might be infringed, however, when the stipulations for the decryption command and the penalty for refusing to decrypt are significantly weakened. That is, if the command can be given when there is less than strong evidence in the first place, or when the decryption command can be given for less serious crimes, the chances for (law-abiding) Alice to have to decrypt privacy-sensitive information will be higher. If the likelihood of law-abiding citizens eventually facing a decryption command becomes such that one can speak of a strict liability when they use cryptography, then (and only then) privacy is at stake. It might lead to people reconsidering the use of cryptography ("What if the police barge in and ask me to decrypt, what if I forget my key?"), which could lead to an infringement of their privacy. Note that the hypothetical case of the police asking law-abiding citizens to decrypt is unlikely, even with weakened conditions for allowing a decryption command; it is more likely to occur in business surroundings, but there, people have considerably less expectation of privacy. Even strict liability for crypto use would not quickly lead to an infringement of privacy.

Comparing the three options, the first two may be considered somewhat more privacy-threatening in the graver versions: if there are comparatively weak conditions for allowing a decryption command and for convicting someone for not decrypting, the question of strict liability will come up more easily. With reversing the burden of proof, strict liability is less privacy-threatening, since there must always be sufficient evidence in the primary case (in other words, weak conditions can only apply to claiming ability to decrypt, not to circumstantial evidence in the primary case); law-abiding citizens would not consider such a measure a reason to use less cryptography.

1b. The right to a fair trial

Where the privilege against self-incrimination and the presumption of innocence are at stake, the right to a fair trial may be infringed, even severely. As long as the decryption command and the sanction for not complying with it remain within the limits set by case-law (*Funke*, *Saunders*, and *Murray* in Europe, *Doe II* and *Schmerber* in the US), the right to a fair trial will be safeguarded. In that case, however, the decryption command will hardly be effective: it will only be applicable in very few cryptocriminal cases, and smarter criminals have good opportunities of anticipating a decryption command with convincing retorts.

If the decryption command is to be more effective, by raising the penalty on not complying, the right to a fair trial may be infringed. Since current case law has, as I have argued, already explored the limits of the privilege against self-incrimination and the presumption of innocence, it is likely that all three options do infringe the right to a fair trial to some extent. It will depend on the modalities of the option whether the infringement is small or rather severe. For instance, if a low punishment is set for refusing to decrypt or having crypto that blocks an investigation, or if the Murray conditions are adhered to, the infringement will be small (i.e., one could expect the European Court of Human Rights to condone the law if it is sufficiently shown by the government to be necessary in a democratic society). On the other hand, if a relatively high punishment is chosen (for instance, five years) to incite criminals to decrypt, or if the Murray conditions are weakened to shift the burden of proof, the infringement will be significant. Obviously, there is a trade-off between effectiveness and the right to a fair trial.

Of the three options, the burden-of-proof reversal is the most threatening to the right to a fair trial. The presumption of innocence is a more fundamental right for the defendant than the privilege against self-incrimination; the latter safeguards finding the truth rather than the rights of the defendant as such. Depending on the conditions under which a refusal to decrypt can be counted as evidence in the primary case, the infringement of the right to a fair trial range from significant to severe.

1c. The rule of law

As noted, there is a key trade-off between effectiveness and the right to a fair trial (and, less so, between effectiveness and privacy). As such, the rule of law is affected in two ways. If a strong enforcement of a decryption command is chosen, this means more effectiveness and thus, better prosecution of crimes, which is an important benefit for the rule of law, but at the same time, it means an infringement of one of the most important rights safeguarding the rule of law itself. If a weaker enforcement is chosen, compatible with current case law, the effects are reversed. Of course, this is a trade-off that pervades criminal justice: the legislature always has to balance the rights of the defendant with the need to prosecute crimes and convict criminals.

One of the difficulties in the present case is that the legislation would be targeted at serious criminals, who are mostly premeditating, calculating people apt to anticipate police activities. Notably when they store incriminating evidence, one can expect them to be more careful of possible police monitoring than when talking over the phone. If a criminal uses cryptography to hide incriminating evidence, he is likely to be aware of the possibility that the police may one day ask him to decrypt; thus, he can anticipate this by, for instance, using many different key pairs or setting back the clock of his computer (or, perhaps, using a duress escape). This could mean that a decryption command would work least of all with the most serious criminals the legislation would precisely aim at; it may turn out to work in practice only with minor, less serious criminals. Of the three options, reversing the burden of proof under weaker Murray conditions would be best targeted at catching the most serious and calculating criminals (especially if one takes into account a *Garantenstellung*). It is also better compatible with the rule of law in that the criminals are convicted for the primary offense they are charged with, not for instrumental 'crimes'. In any case, the decryption command will not work in many cases in practice, since it would only be allowed as a last resort to finalize the evidence; one can assume that in many cases, the encrypted data will only be part of the overall evidence, and there will not be sufficient evidence that these particular encrypted data are incriminating and necessary for the final evidence. Thus, the expected effectiveness of the options is, at best, not great (unless one chooses a really severe enforcement that does away with the rights of the defendant altogether).

Another aspect is the potential 'stepping stone' effect of this legislation. Infringements of the privilege against self-incrimination and burden-of-proof reversals are rare in the Dutch law system (as in most law systems). Penalizing a decryption refusal or obstructive crypto use will set another precedent for instrumental penalization and allowing an infringement of the privilege against self-incrimination. Using a decryption refusal as evidence, even under Murray conditions, would be a unique step in Dutch criminal procedure: so far, silence or refusals to cooperate have never been (explicitly) allowed to be used as evidence in criminal cases. It could be a first step on a slippery slope that can ultimately lead to a downfall of the presumption of innocence altogether.

1d. The right to economic development

The right to economic development is not at stake. Indeed, the market would welcome these options as leaving crypto manufacture, sale, and use unharmed, thus reinforcing information security and electronic commerce.

2a. A solution must be workable

The options can fairly easily be implemented: guidelines for the police and courts under which conditions they can give a decryption command and how they should deal with delivered crypto keys and decrypted evidence would suffice. The only difficulty for the legislature in implementing the two first options is to find an acceptable and effective punishment for not decrypting. As I argued above (8.7.1), it will be hard to choose a punishment that is high enough to incite serious criminals to cooperate, yet low enough not to create insurmountable proof issues for the police. These proof issues may be the only problem for the police in enforcing the options in practice. Especially with the third option, the Murray conditions require them to find sufficient arguments that the encrypted data are incriminating and, often more difficult, that the suspect is able to decrypt.

2b. A solution must be internationally compatible

The international component is one of the advantages of these options. Obviously, the options can be implemented in national legislation, regardless of what other countries are doing. Note that the option mainly targets stored information, which will, by definition, be encountered by the national investigation agents (they have (currently) no authority to search abroad). With encrypted e-mail, it is usually only the recipient who is able to decrypt, and he may live abroad. In that case, the police can ask for international legal assistance if the recipient's country has a similar power to command decryption.

2c. A solution must be technologically sustainable

Demanding decryption is independent of the crypto technology used, and so, the options are eminently sustainable.[37]

---

37 Well – Ron Rivest recently introduced 'chaffing and winnowing'. [Rivest] This is a procedure in which Alice and Bob exchange authenticated messages interspersed with 'chaff'. That is, the message is not encrypted with a key, but intermixed with random, unauthenticated data. Alice and Bob use a common and secret authentication key with which they can distinguish the 'wheat' (the true plaintext) from the 'chaff'. Since

Table 8.1 gives a simplified illustration of how the options match the principles.

options / *principles*	penalize decryption refusal	penalize criminal crypto use	reverse burden of proof
1a privacy	±/+	±/+	+
1b fair trial	±/–	±/–	–
1c rule of law -effectiveness	+/±	+/±	+/±
-general	–	–	–
1d economic development	+	+	+
2a workable	+/±	+/±	+/±
2b international	+	+	+
2c technology-neutral	+	+	+
overall estimate	±/–	–	±

Table 8.1. Demand-decryption options and principles

– *infringes principle*
± *has mixed effects on principle, infringes to a smaller extent*
+ *does not infringe principle*

8.8.4. Conclusion

If one is to choose some kind of infringement of the privilege against self-incrimination or the presumption of innocence (the crypto problem, after all, is a serious one), I would choose the option of 'shifting' the burden of proof. Penalizing a decryption refusal (let alone penalizing 'criminal' crypto use) is an instrumental law which creates complex proof debates, and one which resorts to catching criminals the wrong way. If cryptography hampers an investigation, we want the offense at issue, not the hampering of the investigation, to be punished. 'Shifting' the burden of proof is in some way compatible with the presumption of innocence, but only if several – severe – conditions are met. Most notably, there must be strong evidence against Alice (more or less a prima facie case), her refusal to decrypt must call for an explanation, and there must be evidence that Alice is able to decrypt. Moreover, she may not be unduly pressured into cooperating, e.g., through threat of violence (humanity is a lower limit here).

In choosing an enforcement variant, two major trade-offs have to be made. The first is

authentication keys should be exempt from delivery to the police (or otherwise the police could easily forge evidence), Polly cannot demand Alice or Bob to deliver the authentication key. She can ask them to 'winnow' the ciphertext, but she has no way of knowing whether Alice or Bob provides her with 'wheat' or 'chaff'. The scheme thus resembles a duress code.

effectiveness versus proportionality. In penalizing a refusal to decrypt or 'criminal' crypto use, the punishment for the refusal must meet the middle between a low punishment that is ineffective (it will not incite serious criminals to cooperate), and a high punishment which, if it is not to be disproportionate, is ineffective as well (it creates an insurmountable burden of proof for the prosecution). A similar trade-off has to be made by the court if the refusal is to be used as evidence in the primary case: the lower the burden of proof on the prosecution to show that Alice is hiding incriminating plaintexts, the less evidential value will her refusal to decrypt have.

The other trade-off is more fundamental: *effectiveness versus the rule of law*. Using a refusal to decrypt as evidence is only possible in the few cases where there is already almost enough evidence (a prima facie case), and there is considerable evidence that the ciphertext at stake contains incriminating evidence that Alice is unwilling, although able, to decrypt. That is, if the current level of protection of the rights of the defense is to be maintained, the decryption command will not be very effective. To make it more effective would mean to cut down this protection, by shifting the burden of proof somewhat to the defense – more than the courts have allowed in recent case law. Here, the presumption of innocence is at stake; a real burden-of-proof shift does not seem to be compatible with the ECPHR.

Can one trade-off effectiveness with the rule of law? On the one hand, one can point out several cases in which the courts have allowed infringements of constitutional rights for criminal-political reasons – think of *Braswell* and *Murray*. On the other hand, one can argue that these cases have *explored* the borders of the rights at stake rather than *crossed* them; as I have indicated, *Braswell* is compatible with the rationale of the privilege against self-incrimination of providing reliable evidence, and *Murray* is compatible with the presumption of innocence.

I incline to defending the latter point of view. In current case law, the privilege against self-incrimination and the presumption of innocence have perhaps been narrowly interpreted, but their essence has remained intact. Were one to violate their essence, the constitutional courts would likely not tolerate this – the more so, as the effectiveness to be expected of an enforceable decryption command is not high anyway. If one is to maintain at least some respect for constitutional rights, notably the presumption of innocence, the same problem emerges which currently hampers the decryption command: how to show that Alice's ability to decrypt is a foregone conclusion? A *Garantenstellung* may help to prove this, but arguing that a particular suspect has vouched for the ability to decrypt by her person or former acts seems possible in a limited number of cases. Moreover, if one is to raise the potential punishment for refusing to cooperate, there must be more and stronger evidence in the primary case to meet the proportionality principle. And was not the evidence in the primary case insufficient *because* there was cryptography around? Here, we enter a vicious circle: Polly needs the plaintext to gain evidence that Alice committed a crime, and she needs evidence that Alice committed a crime in order to allow her to command Alice to decrypt and get the plaintext. That is not solving the problem. Creating a specific power that allows Polly to demand decryption, and enforce this with a penalization or a burden-of-proof shift, will not help her really more than her current ability to demand decryption if she can show that Alice is able to decrypt – a hard enough task for sure. In short, the effectiveness of this option can not be considered substantial.

In the Netherlands, Polly does not currently have this ability, and she will likely not get it in the (near) future, considering the removal of the proposed power to demand suspects to decrypt from the draft Computer Crime Act II. Interestingly, however, given the restrictions on the privilege against self-incrimination that the European Court seems to allow, the Dutch legislature *could* enact the withdrawn decryption-command proposal (overruling the current prohibitions to give a decryption command or a smart-card delivery command to suspects). To enforce the proposed provision, the legislature might consider allowing a burden-of-proof 'shift' when the police encounter a ciphertext, under strict Murray conditions. This may help to catch criminals, but if the presumption of innocence is to remain intact, the Murray conditions will be so severe that it will help in only few cases. In most cases, then, Polly will just have to leave the ciphertexts as they are, and look elsewhere.

Chapter 9. Alternative investigation measures

You read the clicking keys as gibberish
Although they strike out sentences to sense.
So in the fluttering leaves, the shoaling fish,
The continuum nondenumerable and dense,
Dame Kind keeps rattling off her evidence.
(Howard Nemerov, Analogue)

If the police want to read encrypted data, they can either crack them or try and get the key. Cracking, as pointed out in Chapter 4, will be difficult and, in many cases, impossible. Accessing the key will then be the only option. However, Chapters 7 and 8 show that accessing the key beforehand (through LEAKing) or afterwards (through demanding decryption) is wrought with problems. Perhaps, then, the police will just have to leave the encrypted data as they are – unreadable, unfathomable, beyond access.

Rather than sit down and despond over the hardships of modern crime fighting, the police can move on and try other ways of finding information on crime and criminals. After all, wiretapping and computer searches are not the only ways to catch criminals. If modern technology hampers their work, why could it not help the police in other ways? Directional microphones have become strong enough to listen in on conversations taking place hundreds of meters away in a building, and bugs prove a good way of direct eavesdropping.[1] Electromagnetic radiation from a computer screen can be tapped from a house next-door.

Moreover, other legal investigation measures may be considered. The police can infiltrate a criminal network, and gather first-hand information in person. Or, if suspect Alice refuses to decrypt, why not ask accomplice Bob to testify against her in return for some impunity? Ultimately, if no new sources of information can be found, the police can re-examine the data they already have; here, data-warehousing and data-mining techniques may help in ordering the overwhelming amounts of information that roam around in police files – and in the public domain – to find information needles in data haystacks.

Of course, such investigation measures are disputed – even if they are technically feasible, there are major legal obstacles to overcome: such measures threaten people's privacy and the rule of law, and Big Brother looms large on the horizon of extended observational investigation measures.

This chapter deals with such alternatives to wiretapping and computer searches. I use

---

1 Note that in the US understanding, 'wiretapping' covers intercepting (voice and electronic) telecommunications as well as bugging ('oral interception'). In the Netherlands, wiretapping only covers intercepting telecommunications. Bugging, or, more general, oral interception, has until now not been allowed for law enforcement. Therefore, it is a topic in this chapter as an alternative investigation measure.

'alternative' in the sense of 'another way' to gather information, possibly as a supplement, rather than as a strict replacement of wiretaps or computer searches. Of course, there are many ways to gather information. In this chapter, I describe five measures which may to some extent serve to fill the information gap caused by cryptocriminals. There are doubtless other measures that can function as supplementary sources of information; the five measures described here serve as examples of ways in which to look for other powers:

- *technical* measures that are *closely related* to wiretaps and computer searches (direct eavesdropping (9.1) and intercepting electromagnetic radiation (9.2));
- *legal* measures to gather information on criminal organizations (infiltration (9.3) and crown witnesses (9.4)); these are *further removed* from wiretaps and computer searches but may provide similarly useful information in organized crime cases; and
- a *technical* measure dealing with information management in general, *unrelated* to wiretaps and computer searches (data mining (9.5)).

For each measure, I shall indicate in what situations it may be useful, what sorts of crimes may be involved, and what is its relation to cryptography, in order to assess to what extent it may be regarded as an 'alternative' to tapping or searching. For every measure, I will describe the legal issues involved: is it currently allowed or being considered, or is it imaginable in light of the investigational culture? I will conclude with a definition of what alternative investigation measures may be considered options to address the crypto conflict, and assess how they relate to the principles (9.6).

As this chapter is meant as a source for inspiration rather than a final, exhaustive analysis of investigation measures, it touches upon the legal issues involved and is not an in-depth analysis. Its main intention is to show that there are other ways of investigating, if tapping and searching computers are rendered useless through encryption.

Like in Chapter 4, the analysis in this chapter focuses on the Dutch situation when it comes to assessing whether a particular measure can be considered viable – after all, this depends to a large extent on the national culture of criminal investigation. For other countries, the assessment may yield a different result; therefore, I will include some information on the situation in other countries.

9.1. 'Direct eavesdropping'

> *"The antennae!" said Legrand, who seemed to be getting unaccountably warm upon the subject; "I am sure you must see the antennae."*
> *(Edgar Allan Poe, The Gold-Bug)*

Before Alexander Bell, people only talked to each other in person (well, sometimes through tom-toms, smoke signals, or optical telegraphs), and the police could only listen in on them by standing close to them. With the advent of (long-)distance communications, people increasingly converse without seeing each other – or the police who is listening in. In fact, with the telephone, the police gained an eavesdropping method which was safer and more secure than before. Now that encryption hampers eavesdropping in between, the police may have to resort to the old method of listening in: at the edge, near one of the telecommunicating partners, or directly at 'face-mail' conversations.

9.1.1. Description

'Direct eavesdropping' is the monitoring and recording of communications with technical means – directly where the communication takes place.[2] One can distinguish three types:

1. listening in on and recording a conversation in its direct presence;
2. listening in on and recording with a directional microphone;
3. placing bugs.

The borders between the types are fuzzy, but there is a clear difference in practicality.

Recording a conversation *directly* is quite feasible when it is done by one of the interlocutors (consensual monitoring). By carrying a small tape recorder in one's pocket, one can record conversations in public or, more interesting still, in private. This has been done several times by informants or undercover agents. [Traa, 175] Recording a conversation may also occur in public, for instance, near people sipping a beer on a terrace, or talking on the corner of the street. A (plainclothes) policeman sitting near the suspect(s) can record the conversation at the next table with a device he carries in a suitcase or briefcase. In practice, for the time being, it seems to be of little value, according to W.J.A. Paulissen, former leader of the Core Team South: "If you're there, you catch snippets of a conversation at an adjacent table. Why not try as a policeman to catch those snippets? (...) Looking back, it all looks rather amateurish. It didn't work, then. So, at a given point, we stopped." [Traa, 176]

Directional microphones are more stealthy. They are potentially strong enough to overhear conversations at a distance of several hundreds of meters, even across walls; often, however, there is too much background noise to distinguish anything useful. "I have never seen such a thing work. They have never been able to prove to me that this is doable for our kind of work. It is nice in a forest, when it's very quiet, for the birds, but I don't think you can use a directional microphone in a city like Amsterdam." [A. Kloosterman, observation detective, in Traa, 177] Indeed, paranoid criminals may employ disrupting devices to thwart this kind of eavesdropping: "It appears from recent press releases that some professional criminals protect themselves from directional microphones

2 The Dutch legislature uses a slightly different classification. It describes the power to record confidential communication with technical means, which apart from bugs and directional microphones, also covers scanners.

with an 'acoustic noise generator': a small box that fills the room with electronic noise that thwarts all eavesdropping techniques." [23047, nr 5, 8] On the other hand, given the fact that many criminals speak in hardly disguised language over the phone, even while they can expect being wiretapped, many criminals will not take precautions. A study on interception in the US found that in 80 per cent of the cases involving direct eavesdropping, incriminating conversations were recorded. "The experts consulted by us on this point confirmed this estimation [that criminals only seldomly take precautions against eavesdropping], and added that a large part of the people arrested had, also according to their own statements, felt absolutely secure." [Böttger, 14] Through their size, directional microphones can only be used in certain circumstances, when they can be placed stealthily somewhere next-door or in a car – they are not the kind of device you carry with you in the street.

Placing *bugs* may be more useful; experience in the US shows that it is a valuable way to gather information [Böttger]; think of what people may say in a parlor or a sleeping room. Bugs can transmit or record conversations quite clearly (for instance, when placed in a telephone, a lamp, or a cockroach), and they can also transmit or record computer activity (keyboard strokes and mouse clicks). Placing bugs requires breaking into the suspect's premises to place them, and so, there is a risk of being discovered and alarming the suspect.

9.1.2. Situations, crimes, and encryption

Direct eavesdropping centers on overhearing conversations. It is a measure directed at communications, both in person and through telecommunications. Thus, it is especially relevant to investigating criminal organizations, who have a high communication need (see 4.1.1). The police can use it to quickly gain knowledge on how the organization functions and who are involved. It will therefore be important in the early investigation stage. The initial Dutch law proposal from 1993 on direct eavesdropping specifically introduced a 'proactive' stage as a focus for direct eavesdropping. Indeed, the reason why direct eavesdropping was proposed, was the "increase in serious crime, the hidden way in which it functions and the technological developments, through which especially organized crime is able to communicate without using the public telephone, and thus out of reach of the telephone tap. Intensive communication is of great importance for these kinds of crime." [23047, nr 6, 9]

Also in other forms of serious, 'non-organized' crime, direct eavesdropping may be relevant [23047, nr 12, 8]. It was (illegally) used, for instance, in the investigation of a violent murder. A drug addict who lived at his mother's was suspected. During two days, their conversations were recorded from the house next-door, from which it appeared that the boy was not involved in the murder. [Traa, 176] Bugging, for which locations have to be entered to place bugs without the owner's consent, can be considered in offices, as well as in houses and cars of (serious) organized criminals. Bugging may therefore be especially relevant to investigating organized crime and business crime.

However, not only conversations can be recorded, but also keyboard strokes. Thus, e-mail messages, passwords, letters, private notes et cetera can be recorded. Although keyboard strokes are not directly interpretable, it is possible to derive the contents of someone's typing activity after close scrutiny of someone's typing pattern in one or two days (it helps if you know the language being typed). Thus, one might transcribe keyboard strokes if enough strokes are captured. One should not overestimate this possibility, though. It requires the recording of many key strokes, intensive study of the pattern, and therefore is very resource-consuming. Moreover, with the increasing use of Windows programs and the consequent increasing use of the mouse, investigating keyboard strokes may become increasingly difficult (I estimate that retracing and interpreting mouse movements is harder than interpreting keyboard strokes). Still, in some cases, bugging the keyboard can yield plaintext of messages or files before encryption; it may even yield passwords that protect encryption keys (most encryption programs store private keys on a hard disk or chip card with password protection).

Contrary to wiretapping, direct eavesdropping is not hampered by cryptography. Indeed, where end-to-end cryptography hampers wiretapping because it takes place *between* the two ends, direct eavesdropping takes place *at* one end, before the speech is being encrypted (or after it is decrypted). This was one of the main reasons for the Minister of Justice in 1993 to propose direct eavesdropping as an investigation measure: "The increase in serious crime, together with the more hidden way in which it operates, necessitates submitting this proposal. What is more, also the technological developments unfortunately urge this. (...) Already at this moment, and certainly in the near future, the technological developments allow entertaining communication out of reach from the judiciary and police. The possibility to have advanced cryptology is an example of this. The competence now proposed can to a certain extent serve as a replacement for the decreasing possibilities to intercept telecommunications." [23047, nr 3, 2-3]

In all, direct eavesdropping is a good alternative to wiretapping.[3] It yields the same kind of information (people's conversations), albeit in somewhat different circumstances: it focuses on personal conversations in private or public. Telecommunication may also be recorded, which will yield only one half of the conversation, but this need not be a serious drawback. However, direct eavesdropping can not replace the wiretapping of facsimile or e-mail messages; it is only a logical alternative to wiretapping conversations. Given the difficulty of interpreting recorded keyboard strokes, and, what is more, the fact that computers contain a lot more information than what is typed in the interception period, it is less effective an alternative to the search and seizure of stored information.

9.1.3. Legal status in the Netherlands

Direct eavesdropping is currently not allowed for law enforcement, but it will likely be in the near future when the draft law on special investigation powers is enacted (it is, incidentally, already legal for the Dutch National Security Service). Despite its being illegal, the police has used direct eavesdropping several times a year. [Traa, 329]

With the introduction of the power to tap phones in the late 1960s, direct eavesdropping for law enforcement was also discussed. At the time, it was considered too grave an

3 Indeed, some investigating officials have noticed a shift in criminals' communication behavior: "We saw that criminals didn't talk over the phone with each other, but traveled all over the country to meet each other. We even had a case in which someone traveled to Luxemburg to chat with someone on the corner for ten minutes, and then returned." [W.J.A. Paulissen, former team leader Core Team South, quoted in Traa, 175]

infringement of privacy. The Explanatory Memorandum to the tap law explicitly stated, however, that the result of the balance of interests involved could shift due to an increase in, particularly, serious and organized crime [23047, nr 3, 1-2]. Apparently, by the early 1990s, the time had come to rebalance the interests, and the proposal to allow direct eavesdropping was submitted: the developments in serious and organized crime and in cryptographic technologies were now seen to necessitate the measure. The parliament took its time discussing the proposal, and with a view to the discussion on investigation methods resulting from IRT-gate, the proposal got stuck somewhere in the First Chamber.

In 1997, it was reintroduced in the draft law on special investigation methods [25403, nrs 1-2]. This law allows the recording of confidential communications with a technical device. The power may be used when there is probable cause of a crime which allows pre-trial detention and which forms a serious threat to the legal order. Moreover, it must reasonably be necessary for the investigation. There is no requirement that the suspect should be a participant to the communication. The placing of bugs is allowed in non-public places; there are stricter conditions for placing bugs or otherwise recording communication within homes. The order for recording communications requires a warrant of the examining judge; it can be given for a period of four weeks, and can be extended every four weeks. Undercover agents recording conversations in which they themselves participate also require a warrant, although it is considered less privacy-infringing (the suspect should be aware of the possibility of talking to an undercover agent, and so, he has less expectation of privacy than is the case with stealth recording through bugs or directional microphones). The same power is allowed when there is not (yet) probable cause for suspecting someone of a specific crime, but when there is a reasonable presumption that he is involved in the scheming or committing of organized crimes.[4] In this case, only communications in which the person involved (the 'suspect') participates may be recorded.

The law pays specific attention to the evidentiary value of recorded conversations. Since the recording (in case of a bug) takes place outside the view of the police, there should be guarantees that the recordings cannot be hampered with. Moreover, background noise has to be filtered out, and so, the tapes have to be upgraded by specialists. This entire process has to be auditable to allow the defense to challenge the evidence. Specific procedures and technical requirements, to be outlined in an Order in Council, will see to it that the process of recording and upgrading is done in a transparent, verifiable way.

The term confidential communications indicates the private exchange of messages between two or more persons, for instance, a private conversation, a private e-mail message, non-public radio traffic, and even the use of an ATM; it does not, however, cover entering data in a personal computer. Therefore, if it is expected that a computer is not used for communication (notably, if the computer is not attached to a network), direct eavesdropping is not allowed. Still, it may incidentally happen that a bug records data (typing a personal letter, talking in oneself, dictating a letter) at which the power is not targeted; the

---

4 The Minister of Justice abandoned the 'proactive stage' approach of the earlier proposal. In her opinion, the stage in which you suspect someone of scheming or committing organized crimes and the stage in which you suspect someone of a specific crime overlap. It is the focus of the investigation (organized crime versus investigation of a specific crime) which matters, not the various stages, which are chronologically diffuse.

Explanatory Memorandum is not clear whether such data can be used as evidence or not. [25403, nr 3, 35-6]

With the possible exception of undercover agents recording conversations, direct eavesdropping is an extremely privacy-infringing measure. Especially in homes, people expect complete privacy – it is the only place where one can be completely oneself, and where one can rely on not being intruded upon. Whereas the 1993 Dutch proposal for direct eavesdropping allowed bugging in homes (under severe restrictions [23047, nr 3, 7]), the draft law on special investigation powers initially ruled out eavesdropping in homes. The Minister of Justice considered the privacy within homes to be too sacred. However, after criticism from the police, the Council of State, and Parliament on the dubious effectiveness of the measure if it were not allowed in homes, the Minister granted the power to eavesdrop in homes if this is necessary for the investigation of a crime that is punishable with at least eight years [25403, nr 8].[5]

9.1.4. Situation in other countries

In *Germany*, direct eavesdropping is allowed to a certain extent. The German states allow preventive eavesdropping to avert danger; the preconditions for this differ per state [see Kutscha]. Although this power is limited to prevention, the German Federal Court has decided, in a controversial case, that information gathered from preventive eavesdropping can be used for a criminal investigation [*NJW* 1996, 405].

There has been a heated debate in Germany to what extent direct eavesdropping can be used for criminal investigation [see, e.g., Seifert, Ostendorf]. Germany distinguishes between 'small' oral interception (recording of a conversation by an undercover agent) and 'big' oral interception (bugs and directional microphones). With the *Law to Fight Drug Dealing and Other Forms of Organized Crime* of July 1992, a power was introduced to intercept and record not-publicly spoken words with technical means. The conditions are similar to the conditions for tapping phones, and it can be used only if other measures are useless or considerably more difficult. Although this indicates a broad power, it excludes eavesdropping within houses, as this was rejected in an earlier draft. It was generally accepted that the German constitution would have to be amended to allow direct eavesdropping in houses. In 1997, the debate started anew with the draft *Act on improving the fight against organized crime*. The law was enacted in May 1998, allowing direct eavesdropping in homes, after the constitution had been amended to that effect in March.

In the *United States*, bugging is a common practice. A survey of interception in the US between 1987 and 1992 [Böttger] found bugging to have been used in 567 of 4,935 cases involving interceptions (11,5 per cent).[6] Much more than wiretaps, bugging took place in offices (40.4 per cent); 18.6 per cent involved bugging in houses, and 38.7 per cent elsewhere (cars, hotel rooms, and others); compare this to wiretaps, which involved houses

---

5 MP Vos has proposed an amendment to lower this to five years, since she considers direct eavesdropping within homes to be preferable over infiltration.

6 The survey split the cases in wiretap, bugging, electronic communications, and combinations thereof. In the following, I mention the figures for wiretap only and bugging only, in order to show the differences between the two.

in 66.9 per cent, 14.9 per cent in offices, and 11.5 per cent elsewhere. Bugging yielded more irrelevant conversations than wiretaps (7.2 per cent of the conversations were incriminating in bugging, 20.5 per cent in wiretaps), but it involved far less people being overheard (26.5 persons per bugging case, versus 138.1 persons per wiretap case). Therefore, bugging is in some respects less privacy-infringing than wiretaps (less people are overheard, relatively often in offices), but more so in other respects (more irrelevant private conversations are recorded, and people have a higher expectation of privacy when talking in private than when talking over the phone).

As to its efficacy, bugging yielded incriminating conversations in 80.9 per cent of the cases (95.3 per cent with wiretaps), but the percentage of cases which led to arrests or convictions is much lower: 29.6 per cent arrests and 20.4 per cent convictions (compared to 46.7 per cent arrests and 33.1 per cent convictions with wiretaps). Despite these relatively low figures, it did turn out that once an interception led to an arrest, many more arrests or convictions followed (8 to 15 on average), which indicates that wiretaps and direct eavesdropping are especially efficacious measures for prosecuting (organized) groups. Setting off the number of people being overheard against the number of convictions, the ratio for bugging (17.1:1) is more favorable than wiretapping (44.7:1) or the combined use of wiretaps and bugs (77.5:1), but it is apparently somewhat less effective than wiretaps.

The survey concluded that bugging is only seldom authorized by judges in the US. It gave as reasons for this the fact that trespassing to place a bug constitutes a significant risk, that a specially high percentage of irrelevant small-talk is overheard (which makes it time-consuming), that the bugs can be discovered, and that judges are required to authorize only the least privacy-infringing measure.

9.1.5. Conclusion

Direct eavesdropping is to a certain extent a good alternative to wiretapping, particularly as it is not hampered by encryption; it will likely soon be introduced in Dutch law. In particular, undercover agents can record conversations, and directional microphones may be used to a certain extent, although they are technically not always usable, and they may only be used to eavesdrop on in-house conversations in very grave cases. Bugging seems to be the best option – the US survey shows that it is a serious alternative to wiretapping telecommunications. However, although in some ways less privacy-infringing than wiretapping, bugging is in many ways a grave infringement of people's privacy; for that reason, in the Netherlands, it will only be possible in houses in the investigation of the most serious crimes, contrary to the US. Overall, bugging is less efficient than wiretapping in general: it can not record facsimile messages, and, given the risks of detection and its being time-consuming to sift out all the small-talk, will have to be used more sparingly. Still, it yields the same kind of information as wiretapping, which makes it the most direct alternative to record criminal conversations.

9.2. Tempest monitoring

Brave new world
(Shakespeare, The Tempest)

Computers can do more than you think – they may even do more than you want. Computer screens allow you to see what you do, but they also emit radiation which allows others to see the same. This 'gift' of free electromagnetic radiation is a feature of all computer screens and peripherals, although the intensity (and therefore, the potential for eavesdropping) varies with the technology used and the age of the screen. The technology for eavesdropping on electromagnetic radiation I will indicate with TEMPEST: Transient ElectroMagnetic Pulse Emanation Surveillance Technology. I derive this acronym from the standard which the US has developed for computer technology that is sufficiently shielded against electromagnetic eavesdropping. The standard was termed TEMPEST, an acronym[7] for Transient ElectroMagnetic Pulse Emanation STandard. I will use the acronym in the broader sense to refer to the technology of eavesdropping; where I refer to the shielding standard, I shall term it the TEMPEST standard.

9.2.1. Description

Although TEMPEST has been around since the 1950s, the dangers of electromagnetic radiation became more widely known when Wim van Eck, a Dutch engineer working at the research laboratory of the Dutch PTT, published an article in 1985[8] – which was immediately classified by the US government. Indeed, TEMPEST is clouded in secrecy, and the US makes a consistent effort to keep TEMPEST-related information secret. Enough information is extant, though, to get a picture of the possibilities of this technology.

Computer monitors (or Video Display Terminals) use an electron gun to fire electrons at the screen, which cause pixels to fluoresce. The electron beam scans across the entire screen many times per second. When the beam fires, it causes a high voltage emission of electromagnetic radiation (all electronic devices emit such radiation, but for the purposes of this chapter, reconstructing the contents of computers is by far the most interesting application). This electromagnetic radiation travels across considerable distances, and wires and cables may serve as an antenna, extending the emission range; also, power cables may serve as conducts of the emission. Now, with the proper devices and some technical knowledge, someone from a distance can pick up the radiation and, with synchronization, reproduce the original signal on a TV or computer screen. To get a clear signal, one may need sophisticated devices, but these are generally available – the sophistication required depends on the distance from which you pick up the radiation. Note, however, that modern computer screens have generally much lower emission rates, and secret monitoring may therefore only

7 Or perhaps it is not – the US government denies it being an acronym, and says it was a code word without a particular meaning, according to [McNamara 98].

8 The article [Eck] was intentionally incomplete, as admitted in a sequel 'Electromagnetic Eavesdropping Machines for Christmas?' [*Computers & Security* No. 4 (1988)], but even so, others were able to replicate the results of van Eck's experiments.

be practical with somewhat older computer products.

Although laptop computers, which use a different screen technology, are better shielded from electromagnetic radiation eavesdropping (laptop LCD monitors emit less radiation than computer CRT monitors), it could be possible to eavesdrop on laptops as well: the fact that there are TEMPEST-certified laptops available indicates that there is a risk. [McNamara 98]

What is more, cables emit radiation as well. Peter Smulders, an Eindhoven University of Technology researcher, has experimented with eavesdropping on RS-232 cables (which, e.g., link computers with modems) and concluded that data "transmitted along an RS-232 cable connection may be vulnerable to interception at a distance. Eavesdropping experiments showed that RS-232 data signals can be intercepted several metres away from a target system, even when a shielded data cable is used. (...) [A]lthough the separation distance at which interception is possible is limited to several metres, in many circumstances eavesdropping can be done without attracting attention." [Smulders] Like cables, power lines or metal (e.g., water) pipes can also transmit radiation. It seems, then, that with the proper technology (which Smulders claims to be relatively cheap), one can eavesdrop on what is transmitted between, say, a computer and a modem. Given the fact that many programs block passwords on the screen (typing stars instead of the password), eavesdropping on cables (which, of course, do transmit the password in the clear) is a valuable addition to the surveillance of monitors.

One (possibly biased and rather hollering) reporter recounts a TEMPEST expedition in Manhattan: "The World Trade Center was fertile. It afforded open parking areas nearby with millions of glass windows to snoop... we were most successful snooping the lower floors from the street. We borrowed a friends office at mid-tower in the south building and were able to view CRT's [computer screens] in the north building easily. We headed east towards the New York Post newspaper offices and read the latest news off their monitors (which was printed the next day). We headed north towards City Hall and NYPD Police Headquarters. Guess what? They're not TEMPEST certified either... Neither is the United Nations" [and so on, Jones]. Although difficult to estimate the real value of this snooping enterprise, it does seem to indicate that very few companies and institutes have sufficiently protected themselves.

Indeed, equipment certified as conforming to the TEMPEST standard is expensive and can only be acquired with government approval. Apart from these TEMPEST-certified devices, there are ways to shield computers and peripherals yourself. The measures traditionally involve encapsulating the device or the room in enough metal to block radiation – building a Faraday cage around the computer or in the room will do the trick. Such measures are cumbersome and can be expensive, and one may assume only the paranoid will take the trouble to implement such measures. After all, a risk analysis will show there are other likely ways in which information may be gathered more easily than through TEMPEST monitoring. Recently, however, Markus Kuhn and Ross Anderson have proposed more cost-effective software solutions to shield against TEMPEST attacks; in particular, they propose a font which hardly reduces text quality for the user, but which filters out the text on a TEMPEST-eavesdropping monitor. [Kuhn]

9.2.2. Situations, crimes, and encryption

TEMPEST will be used to recover information that is processed on computers – stored files, e-mail messages, or web browsing. It may therefore be a good tool for the police to investigate organizational crime, which almost by definition makes plenty use of computers. The fact that most offices contain several computers is, surprisingly, not a drawback: TEMPEST monitoring easily distinguishes between computers; only when two computers consist of exactly the same components from the same manufacturers from the same batch, and no component has been updated in any way, will the radiation characteristics be similar [Seline], and this is rarely the case.

Likewise, it could be used to catch computer criminals 'on the spot', such as hackers or spreaders of illegal information, but as this requires suspecting someone in particular, this will mainly be effective for obtaining evidence, not for investigating a case. As to organized crime, it depends on the kind of criminal organization involved whether TEMPEST monitoring is an effective investigation measure – not all criminal groups use computers to communicate or to store incriminating information.

Since TEMPEST reproduces what the computer user sees on his screen, it will not be hampered by encryption: the user will type in plaintext before encrypting it, or will decrypt messages. To capture passwords (that protect encryption keys or access to the computer), in most cases, reproducing the screen will not help, since all except outdated operating systems shield ********* on the screen. Monitoring the cable will capture passwords or keys, but this generally requires a smaller distance – often, the adjoining room or, perhaps, building – and will therefore be somewhat less practicable. Monitoring screens can take place from a considerable distance, and may therefore be done from a mini van or from a building across the street.

9.2.3. Legal status in the Netherlands

TEMPEST has hardly been discussed in legal circles in the Netherlands; the only reference I know of is in the parliamentary documents of the Computer Crime Act. The Explanatory Memorandum states that the provision prohibiting the technical interception of digitally transmitted data (art. 139a DCC) also covers the interception of 'residuous radiation' emitted by computer devices [21551, nr 3, 17]. Therefore, TEMPEST monitoring is in principle punishable in the Netherlands.

To estimate whether the police could use it as an investigation measure, one must consider whether there is an analogous power that can be interpreted as including TEMPEST monitoring. Since it is a privacy-infringing measure, it requires explicit legislation; a potential power may not be interpreted extensively as including TEMPEST monitoring.

The potential analogous powers that come to mind are intercepting telecommunications (wiretapping), observation with technical means, 'recording of places', and direct eavesdropping. The power to *wiretap* can not include recording electromagnetic radiation, as the radiation is not transmitted across the public telecommunications infrastructure. *Observation with technical means* is a new power included in the draft law on special investigation powers; its goal is to observe persons or goods, and cameras or video recorders may be used. However, no communication may be recorded. As recording electromagnetic radiation from a computer monitor will often involve communication, I would not interpret 'observation' as a power that includes TEMPEST monitoring.

The same goes for the *'recording of places'*, a (new) power that aims at assessing whether a place contains illegal goods or traces; technical devices (say, cameras or video recorders) may be used for recording the traces, but no conversations may be recorded. Although one could suggest that TEMPEST monitoring is a way of securing traces (or to assess whether a place contains illegal information, such as child pornography), the casual nature of a 'peeping operation' is contrary to the systematic monitoring of a computer; moreover, the computer may also involve conversations or communications. Using the power of a peeping operation to record electromagnetic radiation would be *détournement de pouvoir*.

TEMPEST monitoring is most similar to *direct eavesdropping*, which is the recording of communications with technical means. The wording of the power was altered from 'conversations' to 'communications', in order to include a broader range of data traffic. Even if the law is interpreted as to include the recording of what someone is doing on a computer (see 9.1), the Explanatory Memorandum only mentions tape recorders, bugs, and directional microphones. Apparently, the Minister has not thought of recording electromagnetic radiation – TEMPEST is nowhere mentioned in the draft law on special investigation powers. Since investigation powers should be narrowly interpreted,[9] the extension of direct eavesdropping to include TEMPEST monitoring is a step too far.

I conclude that the Dutch police is not allowed to use TEMPEST monitoring. Creating such a power is certainly possible, and given its similarity to direct eavesdropping, may also be considered realistic, or even desirable. It would help the police, as a useful supplement to using directional microphones. The indication that most computers are not shielded against TEMPEST monitoring suggests that the police could really benefit from such a power. On the other hand, it is one more power that severely infringes people's privacy, and one may well argue that the present range of investigation powers should be enough, the more so as the accumulation of various privacy-infringing measures can constitute an extra infringement.

9.2.4. Situation in other countries

Canada, in its Criminal Amendment Act of 1985, specifically included a reference to the use of electromagnetic devices to access computer data, which shows the intent to penalize the use of TEMPEST equipment. [Seline]

There are no countries that I know of that specifically authorize the police to use TEMPEST monitoring. Whether they are allowed by extensive interpretation of similar powers, depends on the national situation. In a case study with arguments pro and con the opinion that TEMPEST monitoring is illegal in the US (as an interception of an electronic communication, and/or as a violation of privacy by intrusion upon seclusion), Timothy Rabel quotes an interesting analogy: US police may use thermal imagers to detect

---

9 Which is not to say that they always *are* narrowly interpreted. HR 8 November 1988, NJ 1989, 667 (search in rectum) interpreted the power to do a body search (literally: search 'on' the body) to include the power to do an internal investigation (search 'in' the body, in this case, the anus), which is a rather extensive interpretation.

temperature changes on the surface of objects (excessive heat from a building may indicate marijuana cultivation). In *United States* v. *Penney-Feeney*, the "court held that the heat was not a protected communication but a byproduct or 'heat waste' in which the defendant could not expect privacy, similar to abandoned garbage and odors from a suitcase." [Rabel] On the other hand, the Court of Appeals for the 9th Circuit ruled in *United States* v. *Kyllo* that an infrared scanner which records heat patterns is not merely recording 'waste heat', but may also offer information on intimate activities, and therefore violates the Fourth Amendment if used without a warrant. Although one could argue that electromagnetic radiation is a 'byproduct' or 'data waste' that does not warrant an expectation of privacy, the information leaked through data waste is more privacy-sensitive than heat waste information, and it seems likely that it is an infringement of privacy protected by the Fourth Amendment.

Although there are allegations that intelligence agencies have applied TEMPEST monitoring, I know of no cases of law-enforcement agencies recording electromagnetic radiation.

9.2.5. Conclusion

TEMPEST monitoring is an interesting option to retrieve data processed by computers. It is currently illegal for the police (at least, in the Netherlands), but the legislature could consider creating a power to this effect. One may be optimistic about the expected results of TEMPEST monitoring, although it would not be practicable in many cases: it can only target cases in which people use computers to process significant data, and it requires proximity to the premises. Still, the police could benefit from it as a supplement to data interception and direct eavesdropping. The fact that it is not hampered by cryptography and that it may sometimes yield encryption passwords or even keys makes it a valuable alternative. However, the infringement of privacy is considerable, and the legislature should conscientiously trade-off the expected benefits with the fact that it is one more power that many people would feel to be part of Big Brother's Brave New World.

9.3. Infiltration

Technical measures, such as direct eavesdropping and TEMPEST monitoring, may yield valuable information, but they remain passive and are not very flexible to follow a criminal organization. In certain cases, it may be more effective for the police to simply approach the organization in person - undercover, needless to say. Through infiltrating a criminal organization, the police can see who is involved in what activities and, if they notice incriminating activities, can directly write their observations down in an official report. This yields another kind of information than wiretaps and computer searches, but it will be equally valuable for the prosecution.

9.3.1. Description

Infiltration is defined by the Dutch draft law on special investigation powers as "participating in or assisting a group of persons planning or committing crimes, under the direction of the public prosecutor for the sake of investigation" [25403, nr 3, 28]. It

encompasses many activities: long-term infiltration, pseudo-purchase (the 'buying' by the police of prohibited goods), pseudo-sale, operating a front-store (a fake company which offers services to criminals), controlled delivery (helping to deliver prohibited goods, in order to arrest the buyers and sellers on the spot), and 'controlled delivery' (allowing prohibited goods to be marketed). Infiltration can be done both by (undercover) police agents and by (law-abiding or criminal) civilians.

Infiltration, or more in general, undercover policing, is an accepted practice in most Western countries, where it has been used at least since the early 19th century. In the Netherlands, chief inspector Waldeck may have been the first undercover agent, operating in the Hague around 1846; he gained the confidence of a gang of counterfeiters, and thus assured the arrest of the core culprits. [Frielink, 9] Towards the end of the century, the practice of *agents provocateurs* investigating – or rather provoking – alcohol crimes was heavily debated, until they were checked in 1889 by a circular from the Minister of Justice ruling that no investigating officer should provoke crimes. Undercover agents again gained public attention in the 1970s, when the increasing investigation of drug crimes provoked new means of investigation – the US Drugs Enforcement Administration (DEA) seems to have introduced the practice of infiltrating drug crime groups in the Netherlands. [Frielink, 19] Despite concerns over the lawfulness of the practice, it was institutionalized in the 1980s with training for infiltrators and the establishment of pseudo-purchase teams.

Practice has proven infiltration to be an effective tool in the investigation of organized crime (and, to a lesser extent, serious business and non-organized crime): it is "increasingly seen as an efficient and even necessary strategy to combat major crime problems" [Fijnaut, 1]. It has been used in all its manifestations by the Dutch police, notably long-term infiltration and pseudo-purchase [Traa, 232-274]. Indeed, the Dutch combination of public confidence in the police, lenient judges, and the generally accepted concern over serious organized crime seem to create "an optimal climate for covert policing." [Klerks, 105]

Still, several risks are involved. As police chief Welten has put it: "As far as I am concerned, every infiltrator is definitely somewhat criminal. Perhaps you can be both reliable and criminal, but that is a contradiction which I can not really manage." [quoted in Traa, 242] There is always a risk that the infiltrator is corrupted by the criminals whose company he is keeping, he may play a double role, or leak information to the criminals. He may even get so much used to the luxury of fast cars and fancy lifestyles, that after the termination of the infiltration, he 'goes native' and continues his criminal activities, this time not bothered by supervision of the public prosecutor. Besides the risk of corruption, there is always the risk of the criminal organization exposing the undercover agent and retaliating upon him – or his family. Infiltrators thus have to steer between the Scylla of being credible to the criminals, which means committing crimes, and the Charybdis of being reliable to the police, which means keeping clean from unwarranted criminal activities – a hard task, for sure.

Then, there are practical difficulties. To diminish the risks for undercover agents, they should be specially trained police agents. The costs and time for training and for executing infiltration operations are significant. Also, there are organizations which no qualified police agent can enter because of cultural or language requirements, and some organizations are extremely closed to outsiders. In those cases, only a civilian close to the culture of the group could infiltrate. Apart from higher risks of corruption, civil infiltrators are less 'steerable' than police agents, and the judiciary cannot really control their criminal activities. Another problem is that civilians cannot write official reports (for court evidence in the Netherlands); they have to report to police officials, so that the incriminating reports are second-hand. In any case, the reliability of a civil infiltrator will be a prime target for the defense in court. A legal problem closely related to undercover investigation is the fact that in many cases, the undercover agent will want to remain anonymous (out of fear of retaliations, or because the police wants to remobilize him) – and the legal status of anonymous witnesses is still contentious.

9.3.2. Situations, crimes, and encryption

Obviously, one can only infiltrate groups, not single criminals. Therefore, infiltration is an investigation measure eminently targeted at organized crime. Its goal can be to delineate a criminal organization; it can also be used to gather evidence against specific suspects. It is in no way hampered by encryption, and, as such, it is a good alternative to wiretapping in the investigation of organized crime.[10] To a lesser degree, it can replace or supplement evidence-gathering through searching computers – the evidence undercover agents can provide is generally quite different from evidence stored in a computer; in some cases, it may yield similar circumstantial evidence, but in most cases, the testimony of undercover agents cannot replace evidence of stored data. Still, evidence-gathering is also a valuable asset of infiltration.

Although undercover agents have the reputation to only infiltrate in criminal organizations, they are also deployed to investigate other crimes committed in groups. Thus, infiltration can be used in business crime cases, notably to investigate corruption and large-scale fraud; indeed, it has been used "against the most (...) unlikely of targets (...) to find corruption among police, prison officials, prosecutors, defense attorneys and even judges

10 Indeed, Simmelink argues for the similarity between wiretapping and infiltration: "The parallels between both investigation measures are the secret character of the state behavior and the breaking of the confidential character of the communication, enabled by a technical act (with telephone conversations) and by an investigation agent operating undercover (with infiltration). (...) The essence of both investigation measures is, after all, the same; in both cases, the state 'eavesdrops' in a devious and secret way." [Simmelink, 46]

and legislators." [Fijnaut, 24] The Dutch legislature also recognizes opportunities for infiltration in serious forms of non-organized crime (e.g., in murder cases), and for investigating certain forms of computer crime – for instance, online infiltrating a network of persons exchanging digital child pornography [25403, nr 3, 28-9]. In most of these cases, the infiltration can replace to a certain extent the gathering of information by wiretapping or by computer searches.

9.3.3. Legal status in the Netherlands

Infiltration has been allowed for a long time without an explicit legal basis. The practice of undercover agents in the 1970s was condoned by the courts; the landmark 1979 *Tallon* decision formulated the main requirement for undercover agents: they should not lead the suspect to other acts than he already intended to do. Besides this 'Tallon criterion', the principles of subsidiarity and proportionality also seemed to be requirements posed by the Supreme Court [Frielink, 27]. Following a study into opinions within the police and judiciary on the subject, the Minister of Justice released a report [19328, nr 1] in 1985 with conditions under which he considered infiltration acceptable. These were somewhat stricter than the case-law requirements, and included mandatory prior approval by the prosecutor and supervision by the chief detective. Also, the Minister preferred only specially trained police officials to be deployed. These constraints on infiltration were finally laid down in guidelines issued by the Public Prosecutor in 1991.

The practice of infiltration without an explicit legal basis has been contentious, because the investigation measure may infringe the constitutional right to privacy (and therefore would require an explicit legal basis), and also because the committing of crimes by undercover agents does not seem to be authorized outright by the legal grounds for exemption from criminal liability [Frielink, 35-72].

There is disagreement whether and to what extent infiltration infringes the privacy of people participating in a criminal organization. The European Court did not find a privacy infringement in the *Lüdi* case: "Mr Lüdi must therefore have been aware from then on that he was engaged in a criminal act (...) and that consequently he was running the risk of encountering an undercover police officer whose task would in fact be to expose him." Frielink argues that privacy is not at stake, mainly because infiltration involves purely business contacts [Frielink, 55]. In case of more structural infiltration, however, which usually involves activities far exceeding criminal business contacts, the privacy of suspects may very well be at stake. As the Dutch Minister of Justice states: "with infiltration, in certain circumstances, the privacy of the people involved can be at stake" [25403, nr 3, 30].

Following the recommendation of the Van Traa committee to create an explicit legal basis, the draft law on special investigation powers introduces specific powers for infiltration and pseudo-purchase. These are not only allowed for investigating specific crimes, but also for investigating organized crime more in general (in particular, to infiltrate a group which is suspected to scheme or commit crimes). Contrary to the Van Traa recommendation, the proposed law allows for civil infiltrators, if undercover police agents can not be appointed for the task. They sign a contract with the prosecutor regulating their rights (including an indication of the crimes they may commit) and duties. In extremely exceptional cases, even criminal civilians may be appointed to infiltrate (although they may not commit any crimes without prior written authority by the public prosecutor, a somewhat unrealistic demand). Infiltration is allowed only for serious crimes (for which pre-trial detention is possible) which can pose a serious threat to the rule of law. The safeguards include the constraints posed by case law (including the Tallon criterion and the principle of subsidiarity), and pay attention to the control and supervision by the public prosecutor.

9.3.4. Situation in other countries

During the 19th century, infiltration became an accepted investigation measure in Western Europe. It was only gradually accepted in the United States, but in the course of the 20th century, it turned into a major investigation tool in the US – at the time when in Europe, it had become highly suspect after the experience with Soviet and Nazi covert policing. By the 1970s, the US practice gradually (re)influenced European practice, with the war on drugs and the advent of (political attention for) organized crime, and covert policing "again became routine European police activity" [Fijnaut, 15].

In most countries, there is a similar 'Tallon' requirement that the police may not provoke crimes, although its scope and the consequent proof issues differ per country [Frielink, 142-143]. In *Germany*, for instance, the case law on whether the undercover agent has 'considerably influenced' the suspect seems to indicate that undue influence is not easily assumed by the courts: there is considerable room for an infiltrator to 'steer' an action [Frielink, 117]. US courts judge whether the undercover agent has 'entrapped' the suspect, and they decide this mainly on the basis of the behavior and the past of the suspect (thus, for example, undercover agents can be more 'provocative' towards suspects with a criminal record than towards 'unwary innocents') [Frielink, 119].

The extent of infiltration also differs per country. In the *United States*, since the early 1980s, there have been about 400 FBI undercover investigations a year [Fijnaut, 13], whereas *Canada* has proportionally less undercover investigations – perhaps, as Brodeur notes, because Canada uses interception of communications about twenty times more, relative to the US, and because drug cases are much less important in Canada [Brodeur, 77-8].

9.3.5. Conclusion

Infiltration is an effective measure in the investigation of organized crime, as well as in certain other cases of crimes committed by groups, such as large-scale business crime, corruption, and online kid-porn exchange. Police undercover agents – or, in exceptional cases, civil infiltrators – can lay bare the structure of a criminal organization or gather evidence against the group committing or planning crimes. Infiltration does, however, involve high risks – both to the infiltrators (facing unmasking and retaliation) and to the rule of law (if the infiltrators are corrupted by the criminal environment and 'go native'). Long-term infiltration also involves high costs for training police specialists.

To a considerable extent, infiltration is a viable alternative to wiretapping, untroubled by encryption. It will generally yield somewhat different information – the undercover agent will not observe all conversations, if only because he is physically bound to being in one location at a time. Still, he can provide information and evidence on the structure of the criminal organization, and in that respect, infiltration is a good alternative to wiretapping in the early stages of an investigation. However, it requires considerably more effort and time, and it involves higher risks for the police. Therefore, infiltration can never replace wiretaps entirely. Although yielding different information than computer searches, infiltration is also important for evidence-gathering, and in that respect, it may fill some of the gaps in cases where encryption blocks computer searches and seizures.

9.4. Crown witnesses

> *ROMAINE. But you do not understand at all.* I *knew he was* guilty.
> *(Agatha Christie, The witness for the prosecution)*

9.4.1. Description

If the police does not succeed in pushing outsiders into a criminal organization, they may resort to pulling insiders out of the organization and have them testify against their (former) accomplices. As nothing works for nothing (especially with criminals), the police will have to offer the insiders considerable benefits: protection from retaliation and reduction of a sentence. Thus enters the crown witness: someone who in return for judicial advantages provides essential testimony against serious criminals.

Generally, the police finds evidence against many people participating in a criminal organization, but often, these are only lower people executing higher orders – the bosses remain conveniently veiled behind the curtains which no wiretap, directional microphone, or even undercover agent can readily draw. Crown witnesses know the core of the organization and can pinpoint the responsible top. They can therefore be a primary tool in prosecuting criminal organizations, and especially the top thereof.

Whereas a crown witness is generally associated with criminal organizations, he may also feature in certain business crime cases, notably in major fraud schemes of otherwise (supposedly) respectable enterprises. The evidence provided is of a different kind, however, than books or computer files that show direct evidence of a fraud. In the general business crime case, the police may not have to use the commercial crown witnesses as a last resort because other investigation measures can provide sufficient evidence. Only with the most serious cases of business crime would the crown witness be an option; in those cases, one can probably speak of the business as a criminal organization as such. Therefore, in this chapter, I will treat the crown witness as a character in organized crime cases only.

What makes this measure extra appealing is the fact that, contrary to most investigation measures, criminal organizations can hardly take counter-measures: they can only prevent people from defecting through severe intimidation. The police can parry this intimidation with a trustworthy, effective protection scheme. To be sure, the success of having crown witnesses relies on the efficacy and reliability of this protection program. Since the witness has defected from a criminal organization to the police, the organization will try its utmost to retaliate: silence the witness, preferably through killing him, or else through killing his kin or dear.[11] Therefore, the state must not only protect the witness, but also his (close)

---

11 The reaction of the Italian mafia to the first *pentiti* ('penitents') was to try to kill them. Then, they tried to discredit the pentiti system by 'infiltrating' with false penitents. When this did not work, the mafia resorted again to killing the penitents. [Manunza 94, 64]

relatives, for a long time. (In areas where family ties are very close, such as Calabria in Southern Italy, a protection program may involve over a hundred family members!) In most cases, this will mean that the witness and his or her close relatives will move to another (part of the) country and assume a new identity. (The Netherlands being the small country that it is, real protection can only be sought abroad.) The costs of such a program are therefore considerable – not only financially, but also psychologically. It is clear that states can only afford a limited number of crown witnesses, if they can attract them at all. (Note that with criminal business organizations, the use of violence against traitors may be less natural, and so, a witness protection scheme may be less necessary.)

Although several countries stage crown witnesses in criminal proceedings, typically in organized crime cases, the character remains controversial. After all, although a crown witness can provide evidence and insights into a criminal organization which no other investigation measure can match, who is to say that he – a criminal, for sure – speaks the truth? And does not the fact of reducing punishment for some criminals undermine the very essence of criminal justice – punish the same crimes with the same punishments, and punish according to the amount of guilt?

Many of the drawbacks and doubts can be addressed in a careful statutory regulation of the way in which crown witnesses may be staged in criminal cases [Asbeck]. The disputed reliability of crown witness testimonies is not a serious problem. Judges will view their statements with extra caution (judges always assess witness reliability, and they will naturally be more wary with crown witnesses), and they will check their information with other evidence (a conviction should never be based on crown witness evidence alone). Thus, in Italy, the law demands independent supporting evidence for crown witness statements. More importantly, crown witnesses have every reason to cooperate: if their statements are found to be false, their sentence reduction will be reviewed, and they may also be prosecuted for perjury or calumny. Moreover, government protection will stop, and they will be at the mercy of the criminal organization they defected – in many cases, this means certain death. Experience in Italy shows that legislation and case-law have developed an adequate set of guarantees for the reliability of crown witnesses [Manunza 98].

However, there are more fundamental arguments against crown witnesses. The state protection program can turn against itself if the crown witness commits new crimes with the help of his new identity (see [Abadinsky, 490] for examples of such wayward witnesses). Also, it seems contrary to the (Dutch) criminal system to bargain with criminals about punishments, although, in practice, this is happening frequently in, generally, less grave cases. A more fundamental argument is the fact that punishment should be related to the amount of guilt of the perpetrator – reducing punishment for reasons that have nothing to do with the crime in itself is detrimental to the credibility of the legal system. Although these objections can be met to a reasonable extent by having a judge evaluate the deal in court according to clearly established criteria (subsidiarity and proportionality for one), which makes the procedure controllable and transparent, there will always remain an amount of inequality before the law: similar crimes may be punished differently according to a perpetrator's accidental testimony in another case. This is inherent to any regulation involving crown witnesses, and must be accepted if the benefits are considered to be significant enough for the prosecution of organized crime.

9.4.2. Situations, crimes, and encryption

Although someone suspected of a crime may in principle know something about any other crime or criminal, most people consider a crown witness to be someone testifying against an organization in which he himself participated – it will therefore concern organized crime. Given the fact that allowing crown witnesses potentially undermines the credibility of the entire criminal procedure, it will only be allowed in serious organized crime cases, and then only as a last resort. The judiciary can only consider adopting a crown witness, if there are no other ways left to investigate and prosecute a criminal organization.

Crown witnesses appeared on the criminal stage in several countries in the 1970s, mainly in terrorism cases – in Germany and Italy, they were found to be virtually the only way to penetrate closed extremist groups. Later, they were used also in kidnaping and drug cases, and in other forms of serious, organized crime. In Italy, crown witnesses (called 'cooperators with the judiciary') are now mainly used in mafia cases. In the United States, the witness protection program is used in cases involving organized crime, drug trafficking, other serious federal felonies, state offenses similar to the federal categories, and certain civil and administrative proceedings in which a testimony may jeopardize a witness [Shur, 67]. In Belgium, Denmark, and Germany, the crown witness plays a part in drug trafficking cases. [Tak 94b, 147]

Evidently, encryption does not hamper crown witnesses. On the contrary, it is a valuable tool in the protection program, which often involves complex procedures for letting the witness-with-a-new-identity communicate with the beloved ones of his former life.

9.4.3. Legal status in the Netherlands

In 1983, the Ministry of Justice issued guidelines for deals with criminals. These involved procedures and guidelines for the prosecutor to 'bargain' with criminals, but they did not touch upon crown witnesses. A witness protection program was introduced in 1993, which can be used in organized crime cases and matters of life and death; in exceptional cases, a change of identity can be part of the program. Case law has accepted a crown witness in a few cases,[12] although opinions differ on the extent to which these decisions okay crown

---

12 The most important case is Hof Amsterdam, 30 January 1998, in which key statements by crown witnesses Karman and Abbas were used to convict Johan V. 'the Stammerer'. The Court considered the statements reliable, in particular because they were detailed and consistent, supported by other evidence, and because the defense had had ample opportunity of examining the witnesses. The Court did, however, lower the sentence of 'the Stammerer', because the Public Prosecutor was not authorized to promise Karman that if he were convicted, they would not execute his sentence. Other cases that involved statements by people who had been promised judiciary advantages were so 'a-typical' that the term crown witness is perhaps not justified. [HR 15 February 1994 and HR 19 March 1996, *NJ* 1997, 59]

witnesses in general. The Van Traa committee counseled against immunity for crown witnesses, mainly because they thought it too grave a measure, given the fact that organized crime does not threaten democratic institutions in the Netherlands. However, the Public Prosecutor updated the guidelines on bargains with criminals in early 1997 to include crown witnesses: under the conditions of proportionality, subsidiarity, openness, and review during trial, the prosecutor can promise the testifying criminal to demand a lower punishment against him or to alleviate the execution of his punishment. Such bargains require prior evaluation by the top of the Public Prosecutor.

The Minister of Justice agreed that crown witnesses are a valuable investigation measure, and started drafting legislation in 1997. After considerable reflection, a legislation proposal was approved by the Council of Ministers in April 1998 and sent to the Council of State for advice. By July 1998, it had not yet been submitted to parliament. The draft law allows – with extreme reticence – 'pledges to criminals' in very serious cases, punishable with at least eight years' imprisonment. The conditions are similar to those of the Public Prosecutor's guidelines. The pledge is subject to review by an examining judge, and a court can only reward the crown witness for his cooperation by reducing his prison sentence by at most a third, or by replacing part of the prison sentence by a fine. Moreover, the law stipulates that no-one can be convicted on the basis of crown witness statements alone.

9.4.4. Situation in other countries

The *United States*' Federal Witness Protection Program, meant for criminal insiders who are at risk because they cooperate with law enforcement to provide evidence against other criminals, has been effective since the 1970s in combating organized crime. According to one of its directors, "without the Program the convictions of tens of thousands of high-ranking members of major organized crime groups throughout the United States could not have been obtained." [Shur, 69] Between the early 1970s and 1994, over 6,300 witnesses and over 7,950 family members were taken up in the protection program. *Canada* made extensive use of crown witnesses ('delators') between 1972 and 1986, but the testimony of one delator that the police had incited him to present false evidence led the Supreme Court in 1988 to imply that "the use of paid delators tended to bring the administration of justice into disrepute" [Brodeur, 80].

In *Italy*, reward regulations were introduced in the late 1970s and early 1980s for collaborators with the judiciary in terrorism and kidnap cases. The regulations were extended in the early 1990s to cover drugs and mafia cases as well. At the same, a witness protection program similar to that in the US was introduced. By March 1994, 668 witnesses and some 3,000 to 4,000 family members had been taken up in protection programs. [Manunza 94, 53] It is considered an essential, effective, and reliable tool in combating various forms of organized crime and, in particular, the mafia. In *Germany*, in the early 1980s, a crown witness regulation was introduced for drug trafficking cases, which allows the judge to decrease punishment of a member of a criminal organization who provides information on drug crimes; the suspect need not necessarily testify in court, and so he need not be a 'crown witness' proper. The regulation was used over 500 times in the first year and a half of its existence. [Tak 94b, 66] It was followed by a 1989 crown witness law for terrorism cases, in which a crown witness can be indemnified from prosecution or given a lower punishment.

The law contributed to gaining insight in the organization and strategies of terrorist groups, and confirmed the correctness of earlier convictions of RAF terrorists. Although the law was at first heavily debated, notably because it is contrary to the German principle of legality which requires the prosecutor to prosecute all crimes, the debate has cooled down since its establishment. [Tak 94b, 148]

9.4.5. Conclusion

Crown witnesses can be valuable in prosecuting organized crime, as they give essential insight into the core and top of criminal organizations; they may also sometimes be useful in the most serious cases of business crime. They provide to some extent an alternative to wiretaps, and less so to computer searches (the information turnout is comparable to infiltration in this respect). Although their statements must be viewed with caution, there are enough guarantees that crown witnesses provide reliable statements – it is in their own interest. Since the system of crown witnesses may undermine the essence of criminal justice (punishing crimes in proportion to people's guilt), it is a legally controversial measure. This, together with the practical problems and high costs involved, means that crown witnesses may only be staged in a very limited number of cases. Whether a state allows crown witnesses at all is a matter of criminal politics: balancing the benefits of combating organized crime in a way unparalleled by other investigation measures with the drawbacks of a potentially less credible criminal justice system and the costs involved. Several countries, notably the US and Italy, have decided in favor of the crown witness, and their experience so far seems to be favorable within the context of their legal systems. A Dutch draft law would also, under strict conditions, clear the way for crown witnesses.

9.5. Data mining

Of course! How could Carol have known Alice was reading 'The witness for the prosecution' if she hadn't spoken with her in two weeks? It must have been her who killed Alice... In the last pages of whodunits, the detective often puts together several separate information pieces (carefully hidden by the novelist) to deduce who did it. The answer was there all along, only you did not see it earlier. Combining data can give you new information, and this is the essential principle of 'data mining'. If the police fails to retrieve new pieces of data, they can resort to smart techniques to re-examine the data they have – and the police have loads of data: much more than they have information. Data warehousing and data mining can be useful tools for the police to supplement their news-gathering activities. It is not a genuine investigation measure, but more an information management tool. In that respect, it can hardly be considered an 'alternative investigation measure'. I will discuss it nonetheless, since a better information management may also serve to improve the information-gathering results by the police in general.

9.5.1. Description

Data mining is a relatively new technology used mainly by enterprises for marketing purposes. Over the past few years, *data warehousing* has risen as a necessary first step for the data mining process. This refers to building (ultra)large data bases in such a way that they can be searched by more or less intelligent tools. A data warehouse (often built up of smaller 'data marts') is a collection of basic data, such as personal data, postal code data, telephone traffic data, and buyer and seller data. *Data mining* is the technique to retrieve information from such data bases – not the basic information, but 'added-value' information. Until recently, only more or less trivial queries were used to retrieve information from data bases. Nowadays, smarter technologies, such as neural networks, visualization techniques, and genetic algorithms, are emerging, which search in a more intelligent way. The entire process is best referred to as 'knowledge discovery in data bases' (KDD): "the non-trivial extraction of implicit, previously unknown and potentially useful knowledge from data" [Adriaans, 5].

The process of KDD typically involves the following steps: building a (large) data base, selecting data to search, cleaning, enriching, coding, mining, and reporting. That is, about 80 per cent of KDD concerns preparing the data. Cleaning is important, because often, a significant percentage of data in a data base is polluted (double entries, outdated data) – and the basic rule in KDD is 'garbage in, garbage out'. After cleaning, the data can be enriched by adding new data, such as the average house price per postal code or car registry data. Coding (redefining data into mutually comparable digital data) is necessary to enable efficient searches. The mining process will then yield new data, which can be evaluated and used. The entire process is often recursive, and several steps will interact.

9.5.2. Situations, crimes, and encryption

There are a lot of data around, in uncountable data bases. For the police, several data bases are interesting to explore for data mining purposes: police registries, intelligence registries, municipal, social security, and car license registries, public data bases (such as Chamber of Commerce or land register data), private-enterprise data bases (such as subscription data or buyer information), and commercial data bases (marketing data, user or buyer profiles), et cetera. Of course, not all of these data bases can be accessed or used forthwith for law-enforcement purposes, but in principle, data marts that can be used for building a law-enforcement data warehouse abound.

What is more, the police can gather new data themselves to build the data warehouse. For instance, the police can collect telecommunication traffic data for a certain period on a (large?) number of telephone connections, or they can scan the air to record pager traffic data, or perhaps they can scan Internet connections for e-mail messages containing certain words or codes. (See 9.5.3 for a discussion whether this is legally acceptable.) In Germany, for instance, the intelligence service (*Bundesnachrichtendienst*) regularly scans the international telecommunications transmitted over the air on key words to pick out 'suspect' messages (this is called electronic *Rasterfahndung*). [Pfeiffer]

After collecting several data sources, data mining can help the police in two ways. First, mining a warehouse may yield interesting patterns or profiles, e.g., of people convicted for drug dealing or murder. Second, such profiles may be used for tracing suspects. The German intelligence service has apparently combined air flight data with holiday house renting data, since terrorists were found to be avid flyers and to rent holiday houses in winter. Persons who matched both properties were consequently good targets for further investigation. Such profiling and matching techniques have also been used lately by Dutch IRTs to conduct 'phenomenon investigation', that is, screening certain sectors of society on their criminal behavior or, conversely, examining criminal processes on general characteristics. Once 'phenomenon investigation' yields profiles of suspect behavior, data bases can be mined to match persons or organizations.

Such profiling and matching techniques will yield a certain number of potential suspects – one should always bear in mind that matching a profile can never be equated with possible criminal behavior (a German scholar may well like to fly to quiet Pacific islands in summer and spend his winters on the Lueneburger Heide in order to write scholarly books). These techniques therefore do not constitute investigation; rather, they can be indicated as 'prevestigation' – the stage preceding actual investigation of a crime or criminal group. Prevestigative profiling and matching can be useful in examining individual or organizational fraud, or for examining criminal group structures. It can yield persons who merit further study or keeping an eye on.

The second use for the police is in the stage of investigation proper. The converse use of profiling and matching is to start with someone suspected of certain criminal behavior, and to use KDD to see whether he matches a profile associated with such behavior. If he does, this will serve to reinforce the suspicion – it could even be used (with proper reserve) as supporting evidence. Also, the combination of a concrete suspicion with additional data gathered, such as telephone traffic data, can lay bare possible group structures. Finally, the police can match data bases with personal data that match specific characteristics of the suspect. For instance, one can compare a data base with all owners of a red Volkswagen in Hamburg with a list of Hamburg customers who have payed their electricity bills in cash (as terrorists seem wont to do). Germany has a specific investigation power that regulates such automatic comparing of data bases for investigation purposes (called *Rasterfahndung*).

9.5.3. Legal status in the Netherlands

'Phenomenon investigation' may use KDD to screen a sector of society on suspicious behavior, but the use is limited through data protection laws. Both the Dutch Police Registries Act and the Dutch Data Registries Act (and the future Data Protection Act) apply to using and merging data bases for law-enforcement purposes. Although not all data bases contain personal data, many of the data somehow relate to persons (e.g., through address information or telephone numbers), and especially the merging of distinct data bases may create personal data if they do not already contain them. If the goal of the data mining process is profiling (which is the case, e.g., in 'phenomenon investigation'), the data can be anonymized (or, if desirable, pseudonymized through encryption, cf. 3.2.3) to avoid data protection obstacles. If the goal, however, is to match a profile with a data base to find (potential) suspects, anonymizing can not be used; in these cases, the goal-binding principle of data protection law will generally prohibit data mining, as most data bases are not built for such purposes. On the other hand, law-enforcement agencies may create data bases themselves, e.g., of telephone traffic data or pager scans, but in that case, the recording of such data must be compatible with criminal procedure law, and the police will require approval by the public prosecutor or the examining judge to gather such data.

In the meantime, the Ministry of Justice has discovered the potential of data mining. In its policy document *Legislation for the electronic highway* of February 1998, it proposes research on data mining as an investigation measure. It would be allowed only in case someone is suspected, during an exploratory investigation, or in the investigation of organized crime where there is not a concrete suspicion. The trade-off with privacy must carefully be addressed, and the law should at all times specify whether the police can do occasional searches on a person, or whether they can use data mining at large. [25880, nrs 1-2, 197]

9.5.4. Conclusion

In all, KDD may be an effective tool for law enforcement: in prevestigation to yield material to start a criminal investigation, and in the early stages of criminal investigation to lay bare potential criminal structures, and to match suspects with known criminal profiles. Data mining is generally allowed as far as it is targeted at profiling, and provided data protection law is taken into account. If it is targeted at matching and finding potential suspects or supporting evidence for known suspects, data mining may only use data bases created for the purpose.

Evidently, data mining will never be a major tool in itself, as it must be used in conjunction with other information-gathering techniques. In this sense, it can never replace wiretaps or searches, and as such, it is not a proper alternative if these measures are rendered powerless through encryption. It may be a supplementary tool, however, to compensate for the loss of new information as wiretaps and searches yield less and less information through increasing encryption use. Obviously, KDD itself is never hampered by encryption, as it uses plain data.

9.6. Assessing the alternative investigation measures

9.6.1. The options of alternative investigation measures

Looking at the five investigation measures outlined in this chapter, what are the options relevant to the crypto problem? First, one must distinguish between, on the one hand, investigation measures that are already allowed or will most likely be allowed in the near future (direct eavesdropping and infiltration), and, on the other hand, measures that are currently or may shortly be allowed in only a limited number of cases (crown witnesses and data mining) and measures which are not allowed at all (TEMPEST monitoring). Policy options of course can only address the latter: allowing new measures or significantly widening the application of restricted measures. Thus, only TEMPEST monitoring, crown witnesses, and data mining would be considered options. The other measures (direct eavesdropping and infiltration) should rather be taken as part of the context in addressing the crypto problem.

Second, one must distinguish between measures that are more or less natural alternatives to wiretapping and computer searches (direct eavesdropping and TEMPEST monitoring), and measures which are far removed from the traditional measures hampered by cryptocriminals. In this sense, only direct eavesdropping and TEMPEST monitoring can be considered 'options' to address the crypto problem; the other measures hardly relate to the crypto problem at all. Cryptocriminals are only one of the arguments in the broader debate over infiltration, crown witnesses, and data mining. If such powers are enacted for other reasons than cryptocriminals, they may have the side effect of making the crypto problems for law enforcement less acute, but this will never be their main purpose.

Combining these distinctions, only TEMPEST monitoring would emerge as an option to address the crypto problem. However, I think that other – relatively minor – partial options also merit being taken into account. With direct eavesdropping, assuming that the current law proposal is enacted, one can consider lowering the conditions for eavesdropping within homes. With infiltration, one cannot, I think, lower the conditions for allowing it (it can by definition only be used in serious organized crime cases). It might be considered an option, however, to extend its scope and to use it in more cases (in other words, the option is to apply the principle of subsidiarity less strictly in applications for an infiltration warrant). Likewise, one may consider allowing crown witnesses in more cases than only the exceptional cases for which they are now envisaged. Data mining, however, remains too far removed from the crypto problem to consider it an option for the purposes of this book. It is an interesting tool for the police to research, and if it is employed, it must be taken into account when judging the overall potential of the police to gather information.

Thus, I arrive at the following options.

Option 9.1 Allow (more) direct eavesdropping, in particular within homes
(I assume here that the draft law on special investigation powers will be enacted; thus, the police has the power to eavesdrop directly, and they can use this power within homes only in cases involving crimes punishable with at least eight years.) The legislature lowers the conditions for allowing direct eavesdropping within homes, for instance, to crimes for which pre-trial detention is allowed (roughly, crimes punishable with at least four years). The legislature can also consider allowing direct eavesdropping for non-communications, i.e., for non-networked computers, talking in oneself, and the like.

Option 9.2 Allow TEMPEST monitoring
The legislature creates the power for the police to eavesdrop on electromagnetic radiation emanating from computers, under conditions similar to those for direct eavesdropping.

Option 9.3 Allow infiltration in more cases
The courts are more lenient in granting permission to infiltrate. The government provides extra money for training and protection programs for undercover agents. The legislature can consider dropping the subsidiarity condition for civil infiltrators (according to the draft law on special investigation powers, a court can only give permission for a civil infiltrator if it is not possible to employ a police infiltrator).

Option 9.4 Allow crown witnesses
If the law proposal on pledges to criminal witnesses is enacted, the legislature lowers the conditions for staging a crown witness (i.e., allows it in more than only the most serious and exceptional cases). Or, if the proposal is not enacted, the legislature reconsiders enacting it in light of the crypto problem.

9.6.2. Applying the criteria

1a. Privacy and the right to confidential communications

Options 9.1 and 9.2 substantially infringe privacy. Especially if the powers are allowed to eavesdrop within homes, the privacy infringement is severe – perhaps more severe than the privacy infringement of wiretaps. After all, people know that what they say over the phone can in principle be overheard (if only because one occasionally encounters others on the line). Currently, people have a complete expectation of privacy on what they say within their home (which is precisely why the Dutch Minister of Justice at first did not want to allow direct eavesdropping within homes). Moreover, it is not only what people say in their house, but also what they do that can be overheard: what music they listen to, when and how long they take a bath, and perhaps even what they write in their electronic laptop diary. TEMPEST monitoring can only intercept computer activities, and as such is less privacy-infringing overall; on the other hand, some computer activities may be more privacy-sensitive, such as writing personal letters, or surfing the Internet.

One can argue that the chance that a law-abiding citizen is the victim of a direct eavesdropping operation is small, and so, the expectation of privacy within the home would not be significantly altered by granting the police this power. After all, a similar development has taken place with the phone: people at first were cautious in trusting its confidentiality, whereas nowadays, most people are not particularly worried that their phone conversations can be overheard, particularly since the (Dutch) police is not known to do extensive (illegal) wiretapping. With direct eavesdropping and TEMPEST monitoring, public feeling may go the same way. On the other hand, one can also argue that the powers of direct eavesdropping and TEMPEST monitoring are perceived as more threatening powers, perhaps because they are closer and more direct – think of the specter Orwell has raised by putting two-way screens in 1984's homes. Especially in countries where the government has shown itself not to be very particular about citizens' rights, such powers are extremely threatening. My feeling is that direct eavesdropping and TEMPEST monitoring are significantly privacy-threatening (even in the Netherlands where people generally trust the government), in particular in view of the rapid development of surveillance technologies.

Infiltration is much less privacy-threatening. In some cases, law-abiding citizens may meet undercover agents under sensitive circumstances, but the chance that this infringes their privacy is remote (much more so than with direct eavesdropping). With crown witnesses, privacy is not at stake.

1b. The right to a fair trial

Provided that the evidential value is safeguarded (legislation or regulations should define standards of care for the gathering of evidence) and carefully assessed in court, none of the optional measures need infringe the right to a fair trial. With infiltration, one could argue that the testimony of an undercover agent may not always be refutable; the defense may be at a disadvantage to challenge the reliability of the evidence. The same goes, in principle, for crown witnesses. This concern can be addressed by the judge in paying particular attention to assess the reliability of the undercover agent or crown witness. Still, using evidence from undercover agents or crown witnesses may be somewhat detrimental to the rights of the defense if they have insufficient opportunity to question the witness themselves.

1c. The rule of law

As to *effectiveness*, all measures hold promise. Direct eavesdropping, especially bugging, is an effective investigation measure that can to a certain extent replace wiretaps. It is not usable in all cases, since it is confined to a specific location and it involves a risk of discovery; therefore, it cannot be used in quite as many cases as wiretaps. TEMPEST monitoring can yield the same kind of information as wiretaps or, to some extent, computer searches, but it can be used in far less cases, since it requires close proximity; moreover, there are rather strong technical limits to what can be retrieved with this measure. Infiltration and crown witnesses are also effective investigation measures, perhaps more so than direct eavesdropping, but their use is restricted to the more (or most) serious cases of organized crime. As alternatives to wiretaps and computer searches, they cannot really be considered effective as such, since they yield quite different information and are limited to organized crime (and the most serious cases of business crime) only. As options to address the crypto problem, then, their effectiveness is limited.

The *rule of law in general* is at stake because the first three options are extensions of intrusive observation powers. If enacted with the proper checks and balances, such powers need not infringe the rule of law – in the Netherlands, I expect that such powers would not be abused by law enforcement, at least not to the extent that the rule of law is threatened. (In countries with a less supervised role for government, one must consider whether allowing such powers does not give a blank check for government surveillance.) Infiltration may be somewhat more threatening to the rule of law than direct eavesdropping or TEMPEST monitoring, since it involves a risk of corruption. As to crown witnesses, this measure does infringe the rule of law considerably: it negates the principle of punishing according to guilt and of punishing similar cases in similar ways, and it allows criminals to get away with a minor punishment.

1d. The right to economic development

The right to economic development is not at stake, since all options leave crypto use unharmed.

2a. A solution must be workable

The technology for direct eavesdropping and TEMPEST monitoring is available, but it has its limits in practice – directional microphones may not work if there is a lot of background noise, and TEMPEST monitoring requires close proximity; bugs are good enough, but they require breaking into places and may be discovered. Thus, these options can be implemented, but only to a certain extent. The same holds for crown witnesses: they can be staged only if there is someone available within the criminal organization and if there is a reliable protection program. Infiltration seems the best implementable, although it requires considerable costs.

None of the options are without risk of abuse. Bugs and directional microphones may be employed without a warrant, an undercover agent may go native, a crown witness may not keep his part of the bargain (for instance, by not telling the whole truth). The courts will supervise this, but their enforcement of the powers may leave gaps for abuse. At least, the measures at stake are less enforceable than wiretaps or computer searches, since these require the cooperation of third parties (telecom operators and house owners) who can also see to it that the power is used according to the law. Therefore, the enforceability of the options is not optimal.

2b. A solution must be internationally compatible
Investigation measures are rooted in national investigation culture, and so, these options can well be implemented on a national scale, regardless of what other countries do. Only with infiltration, there might be a problem if in the investigation of an international criminal organization, an undercover agent gathers evidence against citizens of countries in which infiltration is not allowed. Since most countries allow infiltration, this need not be a significant problem.

2c. A solution must be technologically sustainable
Direct eavesdropping is defined in a functional, technology-neutral way, and thus is technologically sustainable. TEMPEST monitoring is more dependent on state-of-the-art technology, and developments in computer screen and peripherals technology may significantly limit the viability of this measure; it does therefore not seem very sustainable. Infiltration and crown witnesses, of course, are eminently sustainable from a technological point of view.

Figure 9.1 gives a simplified illustration of how the options match the principles.

options / *principles*	**direct eavesdropping**	**tempest**	**more infiltration**	**crown witnesses**
1a privacy	–	–	+	+
1b fair trial	+	+	±	±
1c rule of law				
-effectiveness	±	±/–	±/–	±/–
-general	±/+	±/+	±	–
1d economic development	+	+	+	+
2a workable	±	±	+/±	±
2b international	+	+	+/±	+
2c technology-neutral	+	±/–	+	+
overall estimate	±/–	–	±	±/–

Table 9.1. Alternative investigation measures and options

– *infringes principle*
± *has mixed effects on principle, infringes to a smaller extent*
\+ *does not infringe principle*

9.6.3. Conclusion

Various investigation measures, unhampered by encryption, can to a certain extent replace or supplement wiretapping and computer searches. Direct eavesdropping, especially bugging, is a natural alternative to wiretapping, which can record plaintext conversations. Likewise, TEMPEST monitoring may reproduce a computer screen, and thus reveal information someone is sending or storing before encryption (or after decryption); it may also retrieve passwords which protect cryptographic keys. Both measures have practical shortcomings, however, and, more importantly, pose a severe threat to people's privacy.

Infiltration and crown witnesses may be employed to gather first-hand information from within a criminal organization, and as such, are well tailored to laying bare the structure of a criminal organization and to gather incriminating evidence. Thus, they are alternative information sources to wiretaps and computer searches in organized crime cases. Both infiltration and crown witnesses involve high personal risks, and they may undermine the credibility of the rule of law. They can therefore be used only sparingly.

Data mining for profiling and matching criminal behavior is not a proper alternative to wiretapping or computer searches, and thus not an option.

All measures more or less infringe constitutional rights or undermine the system of law itself; only the option of extending infiltration need not seriously infringe the constitutional rights involved. Moreover, their effectiveness to fill the information gap caused by crypto-criminals is limited. So, there must be strong arguments in favor of them to balance their negative implications, if one is to choose one of these options to address the crypto problem.

Since these measures are part of a larger debate on investigation measures, one can hardly argue pro or con only on the basis of the crypto debate. There may be other compelling arguments for allowing direct eavesdropping in homes, for infiltrating more, or for staging crown witnesses. In the context of this book, however, I cannot take into account the broad issues involved in discussing these investigation powers. I will therefore abstract from the general debate, and argue whether one or more options should be considered only on the basis of the crypto problem, disregarding other reasons for choosing (or rejecting) them. This may be artificial for the legislature, but it is helpful for the argument in this book – it is the only way to compare this direction with the other optional directions.

Whether the fact that encryption increasingly hampers wiretapping and computer searches is strong enough to choose one of the options (and thus, to infringe constitutional rights) depends on several factors, notably the number and kind of cases in which the police uses or is dependent on wiretaps or computer searches, the extent to which uncrackable encryption is encountered in such cases, and, not the least, the national investigation culture and the nature of constitutional protection in a country. One must also take into account the effect of the *combination* of new investigation powers, which can pose additional threats to constitutional rights, in particular to privacy. Implementing several new powers that each help to partly diminish the crypto problem for the police could well lead us one step forward and three steps backwards, into the world of 1984. Privacy is not a salami to be continually sliced down. Whether the crypto problem is big enough to cut another slice of more investigation powers, can only be determined in an integrated analysis of the crypto dilemma, including the other optional directions, which I will attempt in Chapter 11. But first, I will discuss a final option: deciding not to choose one of the options discussed so far.

Chapter 10. The zero option

Doing nothing is often doing something. The effects of failing to act can be just as serious as the effects of acting. In some cases, the effects of neglect are even considered grave enough to be punishable, e.g., not filling in your tax returns form, or not throwing the lifebelt you are standing next to when someone shouts to you "Help! I can't swim!" while slowly submerging. The same holds for the government: some situations call for action, and if the government fails to act, it is seriously remiss. On the other hand, a failure to act can sometimes also be a conscious decision, for instance, because the time is not yet ripe for action, or because one expects the problem to solve itself.

In the crypto case, the situation calls for action: cryptography is spreading rapidly, and ever more criminals will use it in the near future, so that criminal investigation will be seriously hampered. However, inaction is an option to take into account as well, given that the options to (actively) address the problem all have their flaws. It is at the extreme end of the spectrum of 'solutions', which has at its other extreme the banning of cryptography (Chapter 6½). In a way, it mirrors a crypto ban, with by and large reverse effects for society as a whole, i.e., the loss for law enforcement is significant, but the benefits for the information society at large are also significant. Therefore, inaction *is* an option to consider.

10.1. The zero option

Option 10. Decide to do nothing
The government decides not to take specific measures to regulate cryptography and not to take additional measures aimed at securing future information-gathering powers specifically to redress the decreasing effectivity of wiretaps and computer searches caused by crypto use.

One of the advantages of this zero option is that it is clearly feasible and technology-neutral - one need not analyze the *how* of this option. It is the *effects* that matter in assessing its desirability.

What are the consequences of doing nothing for law enforcement? If the government refrains from taking measures to ensure the future effectiveness of wiretaps and computer searches (or to establish alternative measures instead), the continuing spread of cryptography will inexorably hamper investigation (compare Chapter 4). Regardless of whether the government stimulates crypto use (for instance, through establishing a national public-key infrastructure), cryptography will soon be widespread and used by the vast majority of information society citizens. It will be built-in in major computer e-mail programs, web browsers, and operating systems, ensuring that virtually all electronic communications will be encrypted in the near to middle future. However, telecom providers are obliged to provide for tappability, and so, the building in of cryptography in the information infrastructure need not hamper law enforcement. Crypto phones and crypto facsimile machines will become more widely available, although not necessarily everyone will use one (criminals, for that matter, will not hesitate to buy them). The market will provide standards for all kinds of crypto products, just like PGP became a de facto standard for private e-mail encryption in the middle 1990s. As the US National Research Council concluded in 1996: "the widespread nongovernment use of cryptography in the United States and abroad is inevitable in the long run." [NRC, 300]

For wiretaps, this development would mean that the police will not be able to get at the content of all electronic communications. The effectiveness of voice wiretaps will slowly but surely decrease (particularly since electronic communications will to a certain extent replace current voice communications), although it will not become immediately pointless. In the longer term, however, say, in ten to twenty years, the police might have to forget about wiretapping to retrieve the content of communications altogether. Still, traffic analysis will always be possible. Indeed, to quote the Minister of Justice when she defended Dutch wiretap policy: "wiretapping concerns much more than only the contents of the conversation. *Regardless of applied cryptography*, the tap will remain useful." [25533, nr 5, 137, italics added]

Moreover, not all criminals would use cryptography, just as nowadays not all criminals are careful what they say over the phone. It may depend for a considerable part on the future development of the communication infrastructure to what extent end users will widely employ cryptography as an add-on, or whether the security features of the communication infrastructure will be considered adequate by the vast majority of information citizens (including the less wary or over-self-assured criminals), just like they trust the telephone network today. In the former case, wiretapping would become virtually useless, but in the second case, it would likely still retain some effectiveness, albeit less than today.

Likewise, computer searches will become increasingly difficult. Although programs for file encryption will not spread so quickly as communications crypto products, they will be provided for by many operating systems. Moreover, word-processor programs, which currently use weak encryption, may shift to stronger encryption, and may build in a feature for automatic file storage in encrypted form. Disk encryptors will soon be efficient enough to encrypt the hard disk continuously, without any trouble to the user. This suggests that, like wiretaps, computer searches will become ever less effective, and may in the long term be of little use at all. With stored encryption, there will always remain chances of finding passphrases written down, and cryptanalysis and practical attacks will be more viable to crack stored encrypted data than they are with encrypted communications. (Note that there is not a severe time constraint like in wiretapping, which allows more opportunities to investigate practical attacks (see 4.5.3)). However, computer files will become more pervasive in the near future, as ever more people are using computers for daily affairs as well as business. The importance of computer searches will therefore increase in relation to physical searches. The possibility of cryptanalysis or a lucky passphrase find may not outweigh the increasing importance of stored encrypted data. So, even if there remain some chances of decrypting encrypted files found in a search, overall, law-enforcement searches will be crippled by cryptography.

There is another side to the effects of doing nothing, however. The spread of cryptography will also help law enforcement, because it will protect the information society. One of the beneficent uses of cryptography is its ability to prevent information crimes, such as computer crime, economic espionage, and counter-measures by criminal organizations to eavesdrop on the police (see 3.2.2). In this respect, law enforcement will benefit from inactivity by the government to restrict the use of cryptography. One cannot say that this positive effect 'balances' the negative effects of cryptography for law enforcement, since the effects are disparate, but even so, governmental inaction has its advantages for law enforcement as well.

The positive effect for law enforcement holds, of course, all the more so for the information society at large. It will benefit from the growing use of cryptography by all layers of society, in all layers of the information infrastructure. Given the necessity of cryptography to safeguard information security, not restricting crypto use may be deemed vital to the development of the information society (see 3.2). Indeed, the unrestricted market development of robust crypto systems without complicated and risky LEAK features will reinforce information security and privacy protection, while refraining from implementing legally controversial decryption demands or investigation measures respects fundamental tenets of the rule of law.

10.2. Applying the criteria

The zero option does not infringe privacy and the right to confidential communications, the right to a fair trial, the rule of law in general, or the right to economic development. Indeed, it is by and large beneficent for these principles, since the unrestricted, market-driven development of cryptography and crypto use will promote the information society. Needless to say, the zero option is also workable, internationally compatible, and technologically sustainable.

However, the zero option does infringe one fundamental principle: the effectiveness of the rule of law, in particular the principle that crimes must be punished. Crypto use will increasingly hamper investigation, and so, more criminals will escape justice.

Figure 10.1 gives a simplified illustration of how the zero option matches the principles.

principles / *options*	**zero option**
1a privacy	+
1b fair trial	+
1c rule of law -effectiveness	 –
-general	+
1d economic development	+
2a workable	+
2b international	+
2c technology-neutral	+
overall estimate	±

Table 10.1. Zero option and principles

- – *infringes principle*
- ± *has mixed effects on principle, infringes to a smaller extent*
- \+ *does not infringe principle*

10.3. Conclusion

If nothing is done, law enforcement may lose two valuable investigation tools. Wiretaps (for content) and, to a large extent, searches will be ever less effective; in the middle to long term, they may even become largely useless, depending on the future development of the information infrastructure. On the other hand, the continuing spread of cryptography helps law enforcement in that it will prevent information crimes. For society at large, a decision by government to do nothing on the crypto problem will have many benefits in terms of robust information security. The zero solution is therefore a viable option – but it must be a conscious decision by the government after a careful balance of the consequences of this and other options, not a failure to take a decision.

Chapter 11. Reconciling interests

The proofreader nodded, 'You see, you cannot draw lines and compartments, and refuse to budge beyond them. Sometimes you have to use your failures as stepping-stones to success. You have to maintain a fine balance between hope and despair.' He paused, considering what he had just said. 'Yes,' he repeated. 'In the end, it's all a question of balance.'
(Rohinton Mistry, A Fine Balance)

The crypto conflict is a clash of legitimate interests. Privacy and information security conflict with law enforcement and national security; individual interests conflict with collective interests. I have reviewed several options to address the crypto problem for law enforcement: law-enforcement access to keys, demanding suspects to hand over keys, alternative investigation measures, or doing nothing at all. All options have positive and negative sides for differing concerns; there is no option which is a uniformly optimal solution.

Perhaps the key issue at stake is the question who controls the power to safeguard information. If cryptography is widespread, it will be the users who can protect their information – against crooks as well as against their government (which, in some countries, may occasionally coincide, for that matter). If crypto use is restricted, through promotion of LEAK crypto or through penalizing crypto use 'in furtherance of a crime', it will be the government who can wield the power to decide which information may be protected, and which information must be revealed. The delicate balance between government and citizens is at issue here. In a society where information becomes ever more important, this is a key issue indeed. This balance of power between government and citizens is intricately related to the balance in the crypto controversy. And so, we arrive at the ultimate question: how must we balance the interests of information security and privacy with the concern of law enforcement? How do you choose the option, or combination of options, that best reconciles the interests at stake?

I look at *A Theory of Justice* by Rawls as a source of inspiration. Rawls addresses the problem of social justice, which differs from the crypto problem (a part of criminal justice), but his methodology offers good clues for addressing the crypto conflict. In this chapter, I shall first describe the methodology of Rawls (11.1). Then, I shall explain how his problem differs from mine, and indicate what parts of his argument I will use (11.2). I will work out these points for the crypto problem (11.3). Then, I will apply this to the Dutch situation, and see what option or combination of options may be considered to best reconcile the conflict of crypto interests in the Dutch situation, given the assumptions outlined (11.4). I will also roughly indicate how the same procedure might be applied to the situation in the US (11.5). Finally, I will reflect on the outcome and the procedure followed (11.6).

11.1. Rawls and social justice

In *A Theory of Justice* (1971), John Rawls follows a long line of social philosophers to present a theoretical view of how a just society functions, or rather, should function.[1] Rawls aims at defining a set of principles for the major institutions of society (e.g., the organization of the political system, and the distribution of material wealth). Having an essentially contractarian point of view, he uses the mental construct of a contract that everyone in society enters into to create these institutions. He defends this position against the other major school in social philosophy, utilitarianism, which holds that the organization of society is aimed at creating the largest overall benefit for the largest number of people.

Rawls follows a fascinating thought experiment to construct his contract theory. Suppose people have to decide upon the major institutions of society. Let there be representative groups to decide this. Let them be in the 'original position', a hypothetical construction of a situation in which people are in a position to make an informed and just decision. To prevent personal circumstances and prejudices from influencing the decision (e.g., rich people would choose purely capitalist institutions, whereas poor people would choose socialist institutions, simply because these are better for themselves, not necessarily for society), we drop a veil of ignorance over the people: they do not know to which group they belong in real life (but they may know the relevant theories or facts of society necessary to make the decision). Thus, they will make an impartial decision and choose an organization which is the best for society at large.[2]

However, what is good for society at large is not necessarily good for all its groups: if the rich get twice as rich while the poor get somewhat poorer, society at large may be better off, but not the poor. Rawls assumes that people will choose principles that benefit the least advantaged group. After all, if they turn out to belong to that group once the veil of ignorance is lifted, they want the principles to ensure them an acceptable minimum level of liberty and wealth. The want to avoid the risk that the basic principles they choose will worsen the position of the least advantaged. Moreover, Rawls assumes that improvements for the least advantaged benefit the more advantaged as well (or at least will not make them worse). Therefore, he argues, the people in the original position will choose the least advantaged group as the perspective from which to make the decision. Thus, the rules should be chosen in such a way that the outcome will be preferable for the least advantaged group.

In simplifying the problem, Rawls makes several assumptions. The most important assumptions relevant here are:

- strict compliance: all members of society participate in the process and will comply with the outcome;

---

1 This section is only a description of *A Theory of Justice*, not an indication of relevant issues transposable to the crypto conflict. The differences will be outlined in 11.2.

2 "The veil of ignorance makes possible a unanimous choice of a particular conception of justice. Without these limitations on knowledge the bargaining problem of the original position would be hopelessly complicated." [Rawls, 140]

- pure procedural justice: the problem does not allow one to judge the result from an objective criterion (material justice); rather, it is a problem that has a just outcome if the process has been followed correctly; in pure procedural justice, a correct procedure leads by definition to a just outcome;[3]
- the problem is tailored for a 'maximin' solution: people will choose the solution in which the worst possible outcome is the least bad, that is, they want to maximize the minimum they will get;[4]
- liberties can be effectively exercised and freedoms enjoyed; having a set of liberties which you cannot exercise is not very helpful, and someone may in that case agree to less liberties if this will enable him in future to better exercise his liberties; Rawls assumes that in a long-term perspective, the liberties will be exercised [Rawls, 151-2].

Having outlined the original position and the assumptions, Rawls advances two principles which, he argues, people would choose as the primary principles to guarantee just institutions of society. He also defines a priority rule which says that the first principle takes precedence over the second.

> "First Principle
>
> Each person is to have an equal right to the most extensive total system of equal basic liberties compatible with a similar system of liberty for all.
>
> Second Principle
>
> Social and economic inequalities are to be arranged so that they are both: (a) to the greatest benefit of the least advantaged, consistent with the just savings principle, and (b) attached to offices and positions open to all under conditions of fair equality of opportunity.
>
> First Priority Rule (The Priority of Liberty)
>
> The principles of justice are to be ranked in lexical order and therefore liberty can be restricted only for the sake of liberty. There are two cases: (a) a less extensive liberty must strengthen the total system of liberty shared by all; (b) a less than equal liberty must be acceptable to those with the lesser liberty. (...)
>
> General Conception
>
> All social primary goods – liberty and opportunity, income and wealth, and the bases of self-respect – are to be distributed equally unless an unequal distribution of any or all of these goods is to the advantage of the least favored." [Rawls, 302-303]

As one can see, these principles are highly abstract: they define a theoretic 'concept of justice' which needs to be implemented in 'conceptions of justice'. Rawls' major concern is with this abstract concept of justice. The thrust of his argument is that if a conception of justice follows the principles of justice, it is a just conception. Thus, for instance, capitalist

---

3 Compare this to criminal justice, which is imperfect procedural justice, as exemplified by a criminal trial. "The characteristic mark of imperfect procedural justice is that while there is an independent criterion for the correct outcome, there is no feasible procedure which is sure to lead to it." [Rawls, 86]

4 For instance, if people can choose between living in the US, where they can become very rich but also very poor, or living in the Netherlands, where you can never get as rich as fast as in the US, but where you will never get as poor as many in the US either, with a maximin strategy, they will choose the Netherlands. Rawls cites three characteristics of problems tailored for a maximin solution [Rawls, 154]:
- it is difficult or impossible to judge the likelihood of one or the other outcome;
- the person choosing has a conception of good which makes him care little for gaining more than the minimum he is sure to get by following the maximin rule;
- the rejected alternatives have hardly acceptable outcomes.

and socialist institutions could both be just conceptions, as long as they satisfy the rules of the concept of justice (whether they do depends for a large part on the information available in the original position on the particular society and the positions of the various groups therein).

Particularly important in Rawls' reasoning is the (first) priority rule. There is a lexical or serial ordering between the principles of justice. This means that a prior principle should be satisfied first before one can turn to the next principle. First and foremost, people have the right to liberty, which can only be restricted for the sake of other people's right to liberty. Material advantages for some (or for many) can not justify infringements of liberty of others. The system must be such that the total set of liberty is the largest possible; this total amount can be restricted only if it strengthens the system as such (e.g., society may be more stable if everyone gives up some liberty to allow law enforcement to catch those who undermine society), and the liberties may be distributed unequally only if this benefits those least advantaged.

11.2. The crypto conflict and criminal justice

Finding a framework to reconcile the conflicting interests in the crypto conflict differs significantly from finding rules to define social justice. The crypto problem is part of criminal justice, which, as Rawls notes himself, is quite a different area. For one thing, the assumption of strict compliance is negated in criminal justice, which deals by definition with people who will not play by the rules. Therefore, in choosing rules, you will have to take into account the effect of there being certain people who will not abide by them. Also, the level of abstraction differs: Rawls addresses the philosophical problem of social justice in the most abstract sense, whereas the crypto conflict calls for solutions in practice on a much lower level of abstraction – essentially, it is finding a solution within the context of criminal justice, not justifying criminal justice as such.

Still, there are many elements in Rawls' methodology that appeal to me and which I consider usable in describing how one can reconcile the interests in the crypto conflict. Defining an original position in which representative groups have to decide upon rules or criteria behind a veil of ignorance is a helpful way of presenting the problem in an impartial way. From this framework, with the device of the perspective of the least advantaged group, one may argue for a more detailed solution, that is, deciding which option best reconciles the conflict of interests. The ordering principle is of primary importance here, and posing a lexical ordering between, first, fundamental rights and, second, appropriate but less fundamental principles is an appealing simplifying device. This lexical ordering is of primary importance to solve a problem of justice: fundamental rights can only be infringed because of other constitutional rights, and only if they are satisfied can one look at less fundamental (or more materialistic) principles.

In the crypto conflict, it is not the case that improvements for the least advantaged group will also improve the situation of those better advantaged – improving the legal protection of suspects may decrease the freedom from crime of law-abiding citizens, and vice versa. However, the perspective of the least advantaged group is a useful device – indeed, it is at the core of justice itself. One of the basic tenets of justice is to protect the weak from the strong: "law cannot be impartial in its function of regulating order: it will have to take sides with the powerless, with those placed under custody, with those who are most threatened to be overpowered." [Peters, 13] Therefore, the least advantaged group can be regarded a key device in judging conflicts of interest in criminal justice.

In presenting this analysis, I look at the problem from a Dutch perspective, since I do not consider a supranational joint approach realistic (see 1.3.1). This Dutch perspective implies several assumptions. For one, I am not extremely concerned about abuses and excesses by the police or by the threat of a police state; despite the bad example of IRT-gate, I consider in general that there is such a level of rule of law in the Netherlands that we can adequately deal with such excesses. The Dutch generally have a fairly high level of trust in their government.[5] I am concerned about privacy, given the process of individualization taking place on the one hand, and the increasing push of commerce and the government to infringe upon informational privacy on the other hand. Another assumption is the level of crime in the Netherlands, which, although ostensibly serious, is not particularly alarming. There is a considerable level of organized and business crime, but this does not presently threaten the rule of law or the stability of society. The concern is to check growth of crime rather than to significantly decrease it. Lastly, a basic assumption is the aim of the Dutch government to make the Netherlands an information gateway to Europe: the Netherlands wants to be at the forefront of the information society, which implies that information security is of crucial concern.

11.3. Description of the problem

11.3.1. The original position

Into the original position, I input the relevant information on the present-day information society, cryptography, and cryptocriminals.[6] We are in a process of establishing a society in which information is one of the most valuable goods. Information security therefore is crucial, and cryptography is a necessary tool to achieve this. Cryptography may soon be built-in in the information infrastructure. If telecoms providers build in cryptograph, they have to ensure its decryptability to comply with wiretap obligations.

There is a considerable level of crime, in particular organized crime; business crime and computer crime are also of concern. The smarter and more sophisticated criminals, notably the organized and computer-literate ones, are increasingly using state-of-the-art technology

---

5 Having read many Amnesty International reports, I know this is a strong assumption. In most other countries, indeed in several Western European countries, the risk of police abuses should be considered (much) more serious.

6 "The notion of the rational and impartial application of principles defines the kind of knowledge that is admissible." [Rawls, 200] The crypto problem is a legislative rather than a constitutional or philosophical problem, and so, the participants to the crypto conference have much more information on the particulars of their society than Rawls allows those in the original position to have when they choose principles of justice. [See Rawls' four-stage sequence, 195-205.]

to escape the scrutiny of law enforcement. Cryptography is a tool they have just discovered, and are likely to use more in the near(er) future to shield their communications (particularly e-mail) end-to-end and to protect their stored data. The police can crack and attack encrypted data to some extent, notably through practical attacks against weaknesses in crypto use, but a considerable part of the ciphertexts will remain inaccessible to them.

The police has several investigation powers: search and seizure, wiretapping, and infiltration, for instance. Soon, they will most likely also be able to use direct eavesdropping and other special investigation powers, and perhaps, in a few cases, crown witnesses.

In this setting, I organize a conference in Noordwijkerhout with representatives of relevant parts of society. They have to decide upon a crypto policy that reconciles the interests of privacy and information security with the interest of law enforcement. They have all necessary information at their disposal, including the extent to which cryptography hampers law enforcement. The conference will have to answer the following question: how can and should the Dutch government address the problem that the use of strong cryptography by criminals poses to law enforcement, taking into account the legitimate needs to use cryptography in the information society?

11.3.2. Representative groups and their veil of ignorance

Attending the conference are:

- Alice, a law-abiding crypto user,
- Bob, a business crypto user,
- Polly, a law-enforcement official, and
- Suzie, a suspect.

Also attending, as a listener, is Carol, a crypto-using criminal and delegate of a criminal organization. She has an interest in the crypto policy to be established, but she will not play by the rules which will be decided here. Carol therefore has no voting right, but she is attending the conference as a naturally interested observer, sitting in the gallery. Note that the crypto industry is absent. They have an interest in the conference, of course, but this is not of the same order of magnitude as the interests of Alice and Bob, which are more fundamentally at stake than the interests of a minor part of industry (cf. the lexical ordering of the principles at stake).

The attendants have names and functions, but in the process of resolving the issue, they will not know who they are. We drop a veil of ignorance over the conference table, so that not even the attendants themselves know which group they represent.[7] (The veil does not

7 More generally, "any knowledge that is likely to give rise to bias and distortion and to set men against one another is ruled out." [Rawls, 200] The veil of ignorance does allow a lot of information on the particular details of the crypto problem, but not about how each participant is positioned in the information society. Thus, it ensures impartiality.

cover the gallery – the ones around the table know they are not Carol; in reality, they may be Suzie, however.)

The academics are absent from the conference. Since they devised the procedure to ensure a just outcome, they do not need to participate in the process. The veil of ignorance ensures an impartial decision: "It enables us to say of the preferred conception of justice that it represents a genuine reconciliation of interests." [Rawls, 142]

11.4. The crypto policy conference

11.4.1. The least advantaged group

The first agenda item is to decide which is the least advantaged group. The conferees will want to do this, because they do not know to which group they belong in real life. If they happen to be the least advantaged person in the information society, they will want the crypto policy to have taken seriously into account the consequences for them. Indeed, the worst possible outcome of some of the options for some of the representatives are very grave: Suzie might face long-term imprisonment if the burden of proof is radically shifted, if she is innocent but forgetful; Alice might lose her online privacy if she is forced to deposit her keys; Bob may have to move his company if his business has to comply with national key-recovery rules which are not implemented internationally. This is a strong argument for treating the crypto dilemma as a maximin problem: the participants will want to maximize the minimum they will get in any situation. To ensure this, they will decide the problem from the perspective of the least-advantaged representative. Another, more fundamental, reason to choose a least advantaged group is the central tenet in law to protect the weak from the strong.

Who is the least advantaged? Not Bob, who is quite powerful – his IT business is booming indeed. One might think for a moment that Polly is a candidate for the least advantaged position, but the threat of cryptography to the entire level of catching criminals is not high enough for Polly to be greatly disadvantaged. The worst outcome for her – doing nothing and seeing wiretaps and computer searches become much less efficacious – still leaves her with many investigation measures, and with many (although not all) criminals to catch.

The choice, then, is between Alice and Suzie. Suzie has a considerable level of protection in the Netherlands (although this is somewhat being eroded for the sake of crime-fighting), and in the Dutch system of a moderately inquisitory trial, the interests of the suspect are more or less balanced with those of the prosecution. The option least favorable to Suzie, enforcing a decryption demand with a penalization of a decryption refusal a or burden-of-proof reversal, will alter this balance, but not fundamentally so. If the option is to be compatible with constitutional protection of suspects as ensured by the ECHR and the case-law of the European Court, the right to a fair trial is safeguarded, and so, Suzie has less to lose than Alice.

So, Alice really represents the least advantaged group. She may suffer privacy infringements through alternative investigation measures and through restrictions in the use of cryptography, and in the unlikely event of her being suspected of a crime, she might suffer grave consequences if she has been careless or forgetful with her crypto keys and passwords. So, the conferees decide to judge the problem from the perspective of Alice.[8]

11.4.2. Principles and ordering rules

Next on the agenda are the defining of principles and adjudication rules. After some brainstorming and discussion, the conferees agree upon a set of principles (cf. 6.2). After some discussion over the ordering of the principles, they present the principles as following.

1a. The right to privacy (including confidential communications)
1b. The right to a fair trial
1c. The rule of law (including the right to freedom from crime)
1d. The right to economic development
2a. Workability (implementability and enforceability)
2b. International compatibility
2c. Technological sustainability

The lexical ordering between fundamental and less fundamental principles is natural, because the fundamental liberties at stake take precedence over other considerations. Human rights can only be infringed because of other human rights. This means that the conferees will make a decision primarily on the basis of the human rights involved. The other principles play a less decisive role, mainly when two competing options cannot be clearly decided on the basis of the primary principles.

Within each set, the ordering is less evident. The human rights of the first set are interrelated and interdependent; no human right takes precedence over others (the right to life does, but that is not at stake). It "is important to recognize that the basic liberties must be assessed as a whole, as one system. That is, the worth of one liberty normally depends upon the specification of the other liberties, and this must be taken into account in framing a constitution and in legislation generally. While it is by and large true that a greater liberty is preferable, this holds primarily for the system of liberty as a whole, and not for each particular liberty." [Rawls, 203]

Each human right has a primary interested party: Alice for the right to privacy, Suzie for the right to a fair trial, Polly for the rule of law, and Bob for the right to economic development. This is not to say that these rights are only important for their primary interested parties – all human rights pertain to all people. However, the argument for choosing the least advantaged group does suggest to order the rights according to their primary interested party. Therefore, the conferees order the rights as pertaining to Alice (1a), Suzie (1b), Polly (1c), and Bob (1d), that is, from weak to strong. This (sub)ordering is not lexical: options should balance the principles 1a-1d rather than satisfy the first principle, the right to privacy, to the maximum extent. It does indicate, however, a certain weight attached

8 On a European level, one may address the problem by allowing a change in the protection of suspects as an option, that is, in fact, changing the European Convention for the Protection of Human Rights and Fundamental Freedoms. This is not realistic (nor desirable) at present. If one were to do so, one should probably consider Suzie the least advantaged person, since she has much to lose in that case. This would be a different conference, though, with a European crypto policy on the agenda rather than a Dutch crypto policy.

to the principles, so that, other things equal, a higher principle will have more weight.

The ordering in the second set is less important, since the principles matter less. It seems logical to first look at whether an option is workable in the first place, before you look at its viability in the international context or its technological sustainability. Given the strong international component of the crypto problem, international compatibility is a more valuable asset than technological sustainability. One might say that a state has more control over technology than it has over the policy of other states (the US may be an exception here).

In deciding upon this ordering, the conferees have chosen the following adjudication rules.

1. A solution should satisfy the set of human rights principles to the maximum extent possible. Only if this rule is indecisive, the second set of principles should be taken into account.
2. Within each set of principles, higher principles have more weight than lower principles, other things equal.

11.4.3. Selecting the options

In the afternoon, the conferees survey the available options. Discarding right away the non-option of a crypto ban, they briefly discuss all options, ranging from cryptographic measures, demanding decryption, and alternative investigation measures to the zero option. They define the options as follows.

Option 7.1 Stimulate the development and use of non-confidentiality cryptography

The government stimulates crypto developers to make crypto systems that can only be used for safeguarding integrity and authentication, not for confidentiality. The government stimulates users, notably businesses in e-commerce, to use such products, which can be used in all layers of the information infrastructure. They mainly see to communications, not to data storage. If reliable and secure non-confidentiality systems are available, then the government may consider requiring telecoms providers who build-in authentication and integrity functions in their networks or services to use only non-confidentiality cryptography for this.

Option 7.2 Stimulate the development and voluntary use of key-escrow or key-recovery systems for data storage and for the telecommunications infrastructure

The government stimulates the development of data-recovery services that meet business needs for recovering stored data. The government stimulates users who store data in encrypted form to use these services. The government requires service providers offering data recovery to cooperate with law enforcement (by handing over private or session keys or plaintexts, depending on the circumstances) under legal warrant.

The government stimulates crypto producers to develop key-escrow or key-recovery systems for telecommunications applications, that is, products for confidential communications that allow prompt and automated law-enforcement decryption under warrant (through key deposits or tagging along recoverable session keys). The government stimulates telecoms providers who build-in cryptography in their networks and services to use such products.

Option 8.1 Penalize a refusal to decrypt

The legislature penalizes a refusal to obey a lawful command, given in the investigation of a serious crime, to decrypt stored encrypted data and encrypted one-way communications. This is a special clause overruling the general criminal provision of refusing to cooperate with a legal command. The legislature must determine the maximum punishment for the refusal after careful consideration of the trade-off between effectiveness and the rule of law; it should be high enough to incite (serious) criminals to decrypt, yet be low enough not to create an insurmountable burden of proof for the prosecution to show that the data are incriminating and that the suspect is able to decrypt; nor should it be a disproportionate punishment for forgetting a crypto passphrase. It can be a fixed maximum, or it can be related to the maximum punishment for the primary offense.

The legislature may at the same time consider extending the power to demand decryption to be given under less strict circumstances (than the *Funke* requirements), i.e., with less than aggravating evidence in the primary offense, or with less than strong evidence that the encrypted data are incriminating for the primary offense.

The legislature can consider extending the provision to cover encrypted two-way communications, if it turns out that technology allows users in principle to decrypt after the communication has ended.

Option 8.2 Penalize crypto use if this obstructs investigation

The legislature penalizes having stored data in encrypted form if this obstructs a specific investigation of a serious crime. The suspect can exonerate himself by decrypting. The legislature must determine the maximum punishment for the encountered crypto after careful consideration of the trade-off between effectiveness and the rule of law; it should be high enough to incite (serious) criminals to decrypt, yet be low enough not to create an insurmountable burden of proof for the prosecution to show that the data are incriminating and that the suspect is able to decrypt; nor should it be a disproportionate punishment for forgetting a crypto passphrase. It can be a fixed maximum, or it can be related to the maximum punishment for the primary offense.

The legislature can consider extending the penalization to cover sending or receiving encrypted e-mail. Likewise, the legislature can consider extending the provision to cover encrypted two-way communications, if it turns out that technology allows users in principle to decrypt after the communication has ended.

Option 8.3 Shift the burden of proof

The legislature enacts a law stipulating that the refusal to decrypt stored encrypted data or encrypted e-mail encountered during the investigation of a serious crime can be used as incriminating evidence in the case. The conditions for the judge to use a decryption refusal as evidence are the Murray conditions:

1. there is enough other evidence against the suspect that, combined with her refusal, allows a common-sense conclusion of guilt,
2. the suspect has not been pressured by the police to give the key;
3. the ciphertext at stake must 'call' for an explanation, and
4. there is enough evidence that the suspect is able to decrypt.

The legislature can consider weakening these conditions, notably the fourth and, to a less extent, the first and third, after a careful consideration of the trade-off between effectiveness and the presumption of innocence.

The legislature can consider extending the provision to cover encrypted two-way communications, if it turns out that technology allows users in principle to decrypt after the communication has ended.

Option 9.1 Allow (more) direct eavesdropping, in particular within homes

(I assume here that the draft law on special investigation powers will be enacted; thus, the police has the power to eavesdrop directly, and they can use this power within homes only in cases involving crimes punishable with at least eight years.) The legislature lowers the conditions for allowing direct eavesdropping within homes, for instance, to crimes for which pre-trial detention is allowed (roughly, crimes punishable with at least four years). The legislature can also consider allowing direct eavesdropping for non-communications, i.e., for non-networked computers, talking in oneself, and the like.

Option 9.2 Allow TEMPEST monitoring

The legislature creates the power for the police to eavesdrop on electromagnetic radiation emanating from computers, under conditions similar to those for direct eavesdropping.

Option 9.3 Allow infiltration in more cases

The courts are more lenient in granting permission to infiltrate. The government provides extra money for training and protection programs for undercover agents. The legislature can consider dropping the subsidiarity condition for civil infiltrators (according to the draft law on special investigation powers, a court can only give permission for a civil infiltrator if it is not possible to employ a police infiltrator).

Option 9.4 Allow crown witnesses

If the law proposal on pledges to criminal witnesses is enacted, the legislature lowers the conditions for staging a crown witness (i.e., allows it in more than only the most serious and exceptional cases). Or, if the proposal is not enacted, the legislature reconsiders enacting it in light of the crypto problem.

Option 10. Decide to do nothing
The government decides not to take specific measures to regulate cryptography and not to take additional measures aimed at securing future information-gathering powers specifically to redress the decreasing effectivity of wiretaps and computer searches caused by crypto use.

Now, the participants to the conference indicate how each option matches the principles, and on this basis, they categorize the options as an option to consider (category I), not an option (category II), or an option which does not address the problem (category 0) (cf. Chapters 7-10). For each direction, they define the local optimum: the best option *within* the direction. Also, they look at the effectivity of the option in relation to the kind of crime (organized, business, or computer crime), and they assess whether it targets transported or stored encrypted data. They simplify their analysis in two hand-outs (see Tables 11.1 and 11.2 on the following pages).

Within the cryptographic direction (cf. the analysis in 7.7.3 and 7.7.4), they argue that to separate digital signature cryptography from confidentiality crypto is viable, but they note that it does not really address the core problem; it may help in not making matters worse for law enforcement, but it does nothing to address true cryptocriminals. (It may assist criminals in exchanging keys, but since outlawing cryptography is not an option anyway, that is no argument against this option.) Since it does not infringe human rights (indeed, it may be a stimulus to economic development), the conferees decide right away that this is something the government can consider implementing, and they refer it to their colleagues who are developing a digital-signature infrastructure policy.

The other option in this direction, voluntary LEAK through key deposits or key recovery, they discard after ample consideration, as not being effective in addressing the problem. They are threatening for Alice and Bob because they involve security risks, and do not really help Polly, because (smarter) criminals will not use them. Two partial LEAK applications may help the police, however. First, LEAK systems may be a way for telecoms providers to meet their obligations of ensuring the tappability of their networks or services if they decide to build-in cryptography. The conferees note that this potential use is in fact already covered by the general wiretap cooperation requirements (see 4.3.1), and so, they need not consider this an option to address the crypto conflict – if telecoms providers use encryption, they must ensure decryptability, and if they do not use encryption, they do not pose a law-enforcement problem. The second positive contribution of voluntary LEAK is the use of data-recovery services by businesses for stored data. The conferees note that the effectiveness for law enforcement of such schemes is quite limited, since it targets only stored data in business crime. In fact, for these particular cases, the police already has sufficient powers to retrieve stored data: practical attacks to crack ciphertexts are of considerable value here (see 4.5.3), and the police can usually command business people to decrypt (see 8.2 and 8.3). So, additional stimulation of data-recovery services does not really provide extra help to the police; the government can leave it to the market to take care itself of the business need for data recovery.

Next, the participants review the direction of demanding suspects to decrypt (cf. Chapter 8). They agree that penalizing a refusal to decrypt is preferable to penalizing crypto use which hampers investigation, since the latter does not ease the proof issues it is supposed to target (the primary offense should still be proven without the ciphertexts, otherwise a con-

principles / ***options***	separate digital signatures	voluntary LEAK	penalize decryption refusal	penalize criminal crypto use	reverse burden of proof	direct eavesdropping	tempest	more infiltration	crown witnesses	zero option
1a privacy	+	–	±/+	±/+	+	–	–	+	+	+
1b fair trial	+	+	±/–	±/–	–	+	+	±	±	+
1c rule of law -effectiveness	–	–	+/±	+/±	+/±	±	±/–	±/–	±/–	–
-general	+	+	–	–	–	±/+	±/+	±	–	+
1d economic development	+	–	+	+	+	+	+	+	+	+
2a workable	±	–	+/±	+/±	+/±	±	±	+/±	±	+
2b international	±	–	+	+	+	+	+	+/±	+	+
2c technology-neutral	±	–	+	+	+	+	±/–	+	+	+
overall estimate	0	–	±/–	–	±	±/–	–	±	±/–	±
ranking	0	II	I	II	I	I	II	I	I	I

Table 11.1. Options matching principles

– *infringes principle*
± *has mixed effects, infringes to a smaller extent*
\+ *does not infringe principle*

0 does not address the problem, refer elsewhere
I option
II no option

viction for criminal crypto use cannot itself be proven). Penalizing criminal crypto use is therefore not an option.

They have some difficulty in choosing between the former option and reversing the burden of proof. Looking at the effect on Alice, the main difference is that penalizing a decryption refusal under weaker conditions is somewhat more privacy-infringing, since it puts a strict liability on crypto use (which may prevent people from using crypto as extensively as they would otherwise do). This liability is less in the burden-of-proof reversal, since the probable-cause requirement will better shield law-abiding Alice against investigations in which she would have to decrypt (cf. the analysis in 8.8.3, particularly under 1a and 1c, and 8.8.4). On the other hand, the penalization of the refusal to decrypt is somewhat more effective, for the same reason (more criminals will be convicted because of the lower proof requirement, albeit it not for the primary offense). From Alice's point of

options and measures / *applicability*	separate digital signatures	voluntary LEAK	penalize decryption refusal	penalize criminal crypto use	reverse burden of proof	direct eavesdropping	tempest	more infiltration	crown witnesses	zero option	wiretapping	computer search	crack/ practical attacks	ask others to decrypt
organized crime			x	x	x	x	x	x	x		x	–	–	
business crime	x	x	x	x	x	x	x				–	x	x	x
computer crime	–		x	x	x	–	x	–			x	x	–	
transport/ alternative to wiretapping	–	x		–		x	–	–	–		x			
data storage/ alternative to computer search		–	x	x	x		–		–			x	x	x

Table 11.2. Applicability of options and measures

x *applicable to a substantial degree*
– *partially applicable*

view, penalizing a decryption refusal catches criminals the wrong way, and might sooner lead to catching the wrong criminals than a burden-of-proof reversal risks doing. Indeed, reversing the burden of proof under weaker Murray conditions is better targeted at catching the most serious and calculating criminals (especially if one takes into account a *Garantenstellung*). Here, Alice's individual right to privacy prevails over her collective right to freedom from crime by seeing criminals convicted. The conferees therefore find that the burden-of-proof reversal is the local optimum of this direction. They note, however, that the effectiveness of this option is, at best, not great.

Next, the conferees look at alternative investigation measures (cf. Chapter 9). The conferees assume that the law on special investigation powers is enacted, and thus, that direct eavesdropping is allowed under strict conditions. Comparing the option of more direct eavesdropping (i.e., weakening the conditions, within homes) with TEMPEST monitoring, they agree that the latter is technically more problematic and less practical, and that it will in general be less effective than the former. In fact, they feel that TEMPEST monitoring would be so little effective in practice, that it can not outweigh the privacy infringement on the basis of the crypto problems for law enforcement.

Reviewing infiltration and crown witnesses, they discuss their respective merits for the fundamental principles; infiltration is somewhat more privacy-infringing, whereas crown witnesses are more detrimental to the general principle of the rule of law. On the other hand, the difference in privacy infringement is negligible, since the likelihood of such an infringement is very small in any case; Alice will not adjust her expectation of privacy if she knows that the police will use more infiltrators. Since infiltration is more effective than crown witnesses (they can be used in more cases), Alice would prefer that, although she does not want to discard the option of crown witnesses altogether – they may work in other cases than infiltration.

In the tea break, Bob mentions the subject of data mining. The others feel that it is a fascinating technology with a large potential for law enforcement, but they agree that it is not related to the crypto problem. So, they refer it to a partner committee analyzing the information policy of the judiciary.

After the break, the participants discuss whether any one alternative investigation measure is preferable over the others. Here, they get somewhat confused. On the one hand, the two preferable options (direct eavesdropping and infiltration) are applicable in more or less the same broad categories of crime: their main application is organized crime, although direct eavesdropping may also be useful in investigating business crime (but note that eavesdropping is generally less important to investigating business crime). Also, they only provide (to some extent) an alternative to wiretapping: they can reveal what criminals talk about among themselves, and – related to that – what they do. The measures cannot be regarded as useful to replace computer searches. On the other hand, direct eavesdropping is closely related to wiretapping, whereas infiltration is far more removed from the crypto problem, and consequently, their effectiveness for the police will differ considerably. One cannot say that one measure is generally more effective than the other. It is therefore quite difficult to argue whether one can compare these options, or whether one should leave them on a par, and see in each particular case which measure is more appropriate. For the moment, then, the conferees leave the options on the agenda for further consideration and comparison with the other optional directions.

But wait, Bob suggests, what would happen if we do nothing? (Cf. Chapter 10.) Having the elegance of being a very simple option which leaves most principles unharmed, the conferees see only one drawback: it does not help solve the problem. That is a major drawback, conflicting with the principle of the rule of law; criminals should, after all, be caught. By this time, the conferees have become rather despondent over the attractiveness of the options considered so far, all of which have their negative sides, and so, they are not yet convinced that they should act at all. Thus, they keep the zero option as one to consider as well.

At the end of the day, the conferees have thus limited the problem significantly, as illustrated in the following table (see Tables 11.3 and 11.4).

options / *principles*	reverse burden of proof	direct eavesdropping	more infiltration	zero option
1a privacy	+	–	+	+
1b fair trial	–	+	±	+
1c rule of law				
-effectiveness	+/±	±	±/–	–
-general	–	±/+	±	+
1d economic development	+	+	+	+
2a workable	+/±	±	+/±	+
2b international	+	+	+/±	+
2c technology-neutral	+	+	+	+
overall estimate	±	±/–	±	±

Table 11.3. Options to consider and principles

– *infringes principle*
± *has mixed effects on principle, infringes to a smaller extent*
+ *does not infringe principle*

options / *applicability*	reverse burden of proof	direct eaves-dropping	more infiltration	zero option	wire-tapping	computer search
organized crime	x	x	x		x	–
business crime	x	x			–	x
computer crime	x	–	–		x	x
transport/ alternative to wiretapping		x	–		x	
storage/ alternative to computer search	x					x

Table 11.4. Applicability of options to consider

x *applicable to a substantial degree*
– *partially applicable*

11.4.4. Narrowing down the problem

The next day, the conferees look at the hand-out with the table of options to consider. They note that the principle of economic development is not a distinguishing criterion: all options score equally well on this principle. Therefore, they can leave it aside.

They also see that the less fundamental criteria do not yield fundamentally different results for the various options, having rather minor differences. The main difference is the workability, in particular the enforceability, which is not optimal for the burden-of-proof reversal or infiltration. In fact, the main problems of enforceability for these options have to do with the effectiveness and the rule of law: both options cannot be enforced completely, and thus not be completely effective, unless by infringing upon the rule of law (e.g., by radically shifting the burden of proof, or by using criminal infiltrators). This trade-off in enforceability, then, can be taken into account when discussing the primary principle of the rule of law. As to implementability, infiltration is less implementable because of the high costs involved, and the limited number of cases in which it is a valuable and valid investigation measure; direct eavesdropping is less implementable because of technical requirements and the risks of discovery; and the burden-of-proof reversal has implementation problems in that it is hard to trade-off effectiveness with the rule of law in specifying the conditions allowing it. So, in effect, all these implementation arguments can be taken as arguments in judging the effectiveness of these options. This way, the conferees can subsume the less fundamental principles under the fundamental principles. Indeed, the adjudication rule says anyway that the conferees should judge the problem by the fundamental principles first. So, they can leave aside the set of less fundamental principles and focus on the first set only.

This yields the following – simplified – decision table.

options / *principles*	**reverse burden of proof**	**direct eaves-dropping**	**more infiltration**	**zero option**
1a privacy	+	–	+	+
1b fair trial	–	+	±	+
1c rule of law				
-effectiveness	+/±	±	±/–	–
-general	–	±/+	±	+

Table 11.5. The decision table

– *infringes principle*
± *has mixed effects on principle, infringes to a smaller extent*
\+ *does not infringe principle*

11.4.5. The key decision

Having come this far, the conference has defined the core of the problem. Reconciling the interests in the crypto conflict really means making a decision on the basis of this table. To do this, one does not only need a perspective from which to argue for a decision, but one also needs sufficient information on which to base the decision.

It is here that rabbits are put into the hat. The perspective is one such rabbit, and another is the information one uses. These are closely related rabbits. Depending on your perspective, you extract different information from the same data. For example, suppose that cryptography hampers investigation in 20 per cent of all cases involving wiretaps, and that in 60 per cent of these cases, the investigation does not lead to a conviction. Now Bob will argue that cryptography does *not* hamper investigation in 88 per cent (80% plus 40% of 20%) of all wiretap cases, and in the 12 per cent in which it does, who says that without cryptography there would have been enough evidence anyway? Polly, on the other hand, will argue that 12 per cent of all wiretap cases is quite significant (over 400 cases a year), and, moreover, these 12 per cent will likely include the most intelligent and serious criminals, who pose the biggest threat to society. This way, one's perspective can effectively steer one's 'knowledge' and the way one interprets data.

Therefore, I argue that the perspective in judging the dilemma is tantamount, and that this is the main rabbit one puts in the hat. In my case, the rabbit is Alice. I have argued that she is the least advantaged party in the discussion.[9] Therefore, the conferees will look at the decision table from her perspective, which means that in principle, they will rate privacy higher than the effectiveness of a solution. The base-line is a level of the rule of law which Alice, the everyday crypto user, considers acceptable. She does not want to live in a society ruled by criminals; nor does she want to live in a police state. She will measure "the danger to the liberty of the representative citizen measured by the likelihood that these sanctions will wrongly interfere with [her] freedom. The establishment of a coercive agency is rational only if these disadvantages are less than the loss of liberty from instability." (Rawls, p. 241)

First, Alice remembers that all (active) options are implementable, but in a limited way: they can only solve a small part of the problem if they are not to do away with the rule of law at all. Reversing the burden of proof under Murray conditions can be successful in only a very small number of cases where stored encrypted data hamper investigation. Allowing direct eavesdropping under less strict conditions may yield extra wiretap-replacing information in some cases, but the additional value of lowering the conditions can never redress the information loss in the bulk of crypto cases. Likewise, stepping up infiltration will only yield a quite limited additional source of information for the police.

Moreover, living in the Netherlands, Alice does not currently perceive cryptocriminals as a severe threat to her living. The information she has available does not indicate that (the baseline of) the rule of law is really threatened. For one thing, serious criminals are still being convicted, and there is no indication that there is a significant market segment of criminal organizations which escapes law enforcement through cryptography.[10] Indeed, the

---

9 Note that it is the choice of Alice as the least advantaged group which is a rabbit, not the device of the least advantaged group as such.

10 The press release of the Public Prosecutor on its publication of the 1997 annual report rings optimistic about its investigation of organized crime. "Moreover, in 1997, the Public Prosecutor has successfully brought before the court the top of a number of important gangs. Besides, much attention has been paid to setting up and expanding the information position. For this, more and more varied channels are being tapped to collect (criminal) information." [OM 98]

number of cases in which cryptography is blocking cases is currently very low (4.5.2). One can expect this to increase in the future, but to what extent this will be so remains to be seen – this may for a large part depend on how the information infrastructure develops, with either built-in cryptography or with a security infrastructure that depends more on end-to-end encryption. In any case, there will always be criminals who will not use cryptography, just as currently there is a significant number of criminals who use tappable phones despite the common knowledge that they run a risk of being overheard.

Also, if Alice looks at the information available to her in the original position, she sees that the police has quite a few tools available to continue retrieving information in the course of investigation. For one thing, the police can try practical attacks to decrypt stored data, or – if the encrypted file seems important enough – they may even try a brute-force attack on a supercomputer or through a distributed attack (cf. 3.1.4-5). Current experience seems to indicate that such attacks have a significant chance of success (4.5.3). Also, in some cases, the police can command people to decrypt, notably in business crime cases when the privilege against self-incrimination does not hold (8.3), or when the business uses a data-recovery service. Alice also notes that when network and service providers use encryption, they are already required by law to provide the original signal. Besides, traffic analysis is an important part of gathering information in transport, and this is not hampered by cryptography. Then again, the police have other investigation measures at their disposal, which can satisfy some of their need for knowledge. Infiltration is a good alternative to gather information and evidence on criminal organizations, although the high costs limit its potential. Direct eavesdropping will most likely soon be allowed, even within homes for very serious crimes, and perhaps crown witnesses will appear on the court stage soon. These alternative investigation measures may to some extent replace the use of wiretaps (note that options 9.1 and 9.3 do not concern the use of direct eavesdropping or infiltration as such, but they involve lowering the conditions for their use to make them more investigation-friendly).

Judging from this information, Alice decides that the current threat of cryptocriminals is not enough to justify infringing fundamental rights by enacting one of the (non-zero) options. The blocking of computer searches can be addressed by practical attacks and by demanding others to decrypt – the potential small extra value of a burden-of-proof reversal (option 8.3) cannot outweigh the detriment to the rule of law. The decrease in wiretap efficacy can to some extent be met by other investigation measures currently allowed; the potential extra infringement of privacy and the rule of law if the conditions for such measures are weakened (options 9.1 and 9.3) cannot be justified by their marginal additional value to retrieve still a little more information.

There will no doubt be some criminals who will escape justice through cryptography in the next few years, but this does not alter Alice's view: she puts up with this in view of her privacy. Moreover, her intuitive sense of justice tells her that the rule of law would currently be more infringed by allowing burden-of-proof reversals or by having bugs or infiltrators became more pervasive. For the moment, Alice concludes to do nothing. The Dutch government should endorse the zero option as the one which best reconciles the conflicting crypto interests.

11.4.6. Looking at the future

The conference participants are aware, though, that we live in a changing world, and they will continue to closely monitor developments to see whether Alice's argument still holds. They will look at the number of investigations being definitively blocked by cryptography, and they will also continue to make assessments of the overall level of crime and of the sway criminal organizations may hold over Dutch society. Besides, Alice and Polly are avid readers of the *Staatsblad* (which promulgates legislation) and the *Nederlandse Jurisprudentie* (which publishes case law), so that they can monitor the investigation powers the police have. They will take into account whether and to what extent the police can use directional microphones, bugging, TEMPEST monitoring, infiltration, crown witnesses, data mining, and other measures that may be invented and allowed in future. If the conference participants find that cryptography indeed allows criminals to escape the police more than they care for (i.e., if the base-line of the rule of law is crossed), they will reconsider the options for addressing the crypto conflict.

Then, they will again make a list of the available options. They will leaf through the latest proceedings of the CRYPTO and EUROCRYPT conferences to see what developments there are in the cryptographic field. Perhaps, new LEAK protocols or systems are being developed which are more reliable and more secure than current proposals. Also, if the market for data-recovery services will have developed over the next few years, the conferees can see to what extent individuals and businesses are using these services. If they turn out to be quite reliable and not to pose significant security risks (which can currently not be said, because such services are yet in their infancy), they could define an option to stimulate these services, or perhaps even to make them mandatory in specific circumstances (such as today there are formal obligations for keeping books). This could mean that the participants should reconsider option 7.2 (which I do not consider likely, but for a just procedure, they must take everything into account).

The option list will, of course, still contain the decryption command options, in particular the burden-of-proof reversal, and it may comprise several alternative investigation measures – new ones, or traditional ones with weaker conditions. Depending on these options and on the positions of the various representative groups, future conferences should each time decide which is the least advantaged group. For instance, if it is seriously being considered to reverse the burden of proof under weaker Murray conditions (which likely should be done on a European level, given the protection of the ECPHR), then it may turn out that Suzie rather than Alice has most to lose. Or if cryptocriminals overwhelmingly defeat the police and future IRT gates lead to a restriction of police powers, perhaps Polly will emerge the least advantaged. I consider it unlikely that in the near to middle future the decision on the least advantaged group would lead to anyone but Alice, but it is a decision which should always be carefully made. For the time being, let us suppose that Alice will still provide the perspective to judge the problem from.

To decide which of the option is preferable to the least advantaged group, the conference participants will redefine the original position. What is the exact way in which crypto blocks the investigation? Is it mostly stored ciphertexts obtained through searches that the police cannot read, or is it end-to-end encryption that defeats wiretaps? In what stage of the investigation does the police encounter crypto? The burden-of-proof reversal is targeted mainly at stored encrypted data needed for finalizing the evidence, whereas most alternative investigation measures are more useful as a replacement of wiretaps in the earlier stages of the investigation, or, sometimes, to gather key evidence. The conference will also investigate what kinds of crime are at stake: is it mainly cryptocriminal organizations that escape justice, or is it white-collar criminals, or is computer crime soaring because of the crypto shield? Again, the exact scope of the investigation powers will be a major determinant of the original position. Depending on the definition of the original position and the perspective of the least advantaged group, the conferees can debate which option is preferable.

Currently, it is hard to predict what the conference will find in the future. Still, some judgments can be made at this stage. Enforcing decryption commands through penalizing a decryption refusal (or worse, through penalizing crypto use which hampers investigation) put a strict liability on crypto use, and it is instrumental legislation which does not lead to convicting criminals the right way. From the perspective of Alice, the law-abiding crypto user, this can hardly be desirable. The trade-off between effectiveness (convicting serious criminals who refuse to decrypt) and a fair trial (not convicting Alice if she has forgotten her key) is hard to make, as is the setting of a maximum punishment on the decryption refusal. The only viable way to enforce a decryption command, therefore, will be to reverse the burden of proof. Here, the trade-off of strict Murray conditions (ensuring compatibility with the right to a fair trial) with effectiveness will also be difficult. If a burden-of-proof reversal is to be effective in really convicting the serious criminals the option is aimed at, it can easily infringe the right to a fair trial more than the European Court will care for.

But perhaps the future will make the trade-off easier. If it turns out that the information infrastructure is a highly secure and reliable one, which Alice can trust with her confidential messages without having to encrypt end-to-end (like we currently trust the telephone system), or, more importantly, if operating systems are developed to automatically encrypt stored data in a LEAK-compliant way, so that Alice does not need to encrypt stored data herself, then a strict liability for using crypto and having to decrypt may become more acceptable. In other words, it may then be more fair to require Alice to prove that the encrypted data are not incriminating by decrypting, or, if she cannot decrypt, to argue why she used encryption in the first place. With the current confusion over crypto laws (in particular, export laws) and the rapidly changing information infrastructure, it cannot be predicted whether the information infrastructure will develop in this way. It may turn out that to realize her right to privacy and to confidential communication, Alice will have to use encryption herself, and in that case, I think reversing the burden of proof if the police encounters cryptography during an investigation is not really an option.

My feeling is that for at least several years to come, if a non-zero option is required to counter the increasing threat of cryptocriminals, the government should look at alternative investigation measures rather than at enforcing decryption commands through contentious legal constructions. It is true that a decryption command is much more closely targeted at the problem of cryptocriminals, whereas most investigation measures provide quite different kinds of information in only part of the investigation cases. Yet from the perspective of Alice, alternative investigation measures will likely be more acceptable than putting a strict liability on crypto use. This is all the more so since with stored encrypted data, the police has a considerable array of tools available to retrieve the information: practical attacks, and demanding decryption within the limits of (*Funke* and *Saunders*) case law; also, in investigating business crime (one of the important targets of computer searches), there is a larger likelihood of the business cooperating with law enforcement. The biggest future cryptocriminal threat may therefore be to wiretapping rather than to computer searches, and it will most likely be caused by organized criminals. To investigate and convict them, other investigation measures hold higher promise than reversing the burden of proof, which is problematic anyway with encrypted communications. Perhaps, then, the government will slowly have to adapt to the idea that wiretapping is not a panacea for the information need of the police, and to focus their resources on other, less crypto-sensitive, investigation measures.

11.4.7. Evaluation

At the end of the conference, the participants look back and evaluate what they have done. After defining principles and adjudication rules, surveying possible options, narrowing down the list to viable options, the conferees had to decide the core problem. Using the perspective of Alice as the least advantaged group, they found that for the time being, the zero option seems preferable. Policy makers should continue to closely monitor developments, in order to periodically readjust this decision. Depending upon the crime rate and the crypto use by criminals, and depending upon the investigation powers the police can use, a future readjustment of the policy may be to allow more alternative investigation measures to counter the possibly decreasing efficacy of wiretaps.

What the conferees have done, is to list all viable options, then to narrow these down to the best option, given the principles, information, and perspective chosen. They have also pondered upon possible future measures, in case more is felt to be needed in future, by adding other options and then readjusting the balance. The process thus resembles a multiple hour-glass, in which the sand (all possible options) is narrowed down to the best option at that time, after which the other options are again added together with new data; then, the options may be again narrowed down to the best option at the next point of time. At each point of time, the weight of the grains of sand (the data added) and the form of the glass (the perspective from which you look at the problem) steer the outcome.

11.5. Agenda for a US conference

If the conference had been held in the US, with the aim of developing a US crypto policy, would the outcome have been different? Not necessarily, although the input would have differed considerably. A good analysis of the US situation requires an extensive research which is outside the scope of this book. Here, I can only indicate what items should be researched and taken into account in addressing the crypto conflict in the US.

First of all, the assumptions for the Dutch situation are not directly applicable to the US. For one thing, the crime rate and the kind of criminals may differ; apart from organized and business crime, computer crime may be ahead of the Netherlands, considering the general lead the US has in the ICT field. Moreover, terrorism is a bigger concern in the US than in the Netherlands. In fact, the crypto debate centers as much on national security as on law enforcement, and the two will be difficult to treat as separate policy issues in the US. Also, one must consider to what extent crime in the US is threatening the rule of law or society at large.

Likewise, investigation powers differ as well. In the US, bugging has been used for quite some time, and crown witnesses have played their part in criminal proceedings. Law enforcement in the US seems less dependent on wiretapping (see 4.3.2). So, the specific problems cryptography poses to law enforcement in the US will to some extent differ from those in the Netherlands, at least in scope.

Another difference relates to the concern over police powers. The Dutch generally seem to have a higher level of trust in their government (including law-enforcement agents) than US citizens have – compare Mike Nelson's constraints for an acceptable crypto policy: "Any solution the U.S. government endorses is immediately suspect" and "No one trusts anyone" [Nelson]. Related to this is a different conception of privacy in the US: "Though it may be an overgeneralization to say our European neighbors trust governments but not corporations with their personal lives while our loyalties are reversed, to some degree this pattern is reflected in each of our laws." [Field] More in general, differences in constitutional protection in the US can lead to different weights being attached to the fundamental rights that are pivotal to the argument.

All these (potential) differences in the state of affairs imply that the input into the original position must be described differently for the US. This, of course, is a major factor influencing the outcome of the conference.

Another important agenda item in the US will be choosing a least advantaged group. I think the same representative groups should participate behind the veil of ignorance in the US conference: individual crypto users, business crypto users, law enforcement, and suspects, perhaps complemented with a national-security representative. The main factors influencing the decision which of these groups is the least advantaged are the weights attached to the various fundamental rights, the balance of power between citizens and the state, and the instruments that the various groups have to secure their powers and rights.

The principles and ordering rules I used for the Netherlands can likely be used in the US as well, perhaps with some shifting of the order of the fundamental rights within the first group of principles.

Since most alternative investigation measures I have outlined are already allowed to a certain extent in the US, the option list in the US would consist mainly of law-enforcement access to keys (which would, more generally, be government access to keys, since the national-security agencies would be the first to grasp the opportunity of accessing keys), enforcing a decryption demand, and significantly stepping up certain investigation measures, like bugging or infiltration. Of course, the zero option should be on the US agenda as well.

With these items settled, the US conferees can start debating which of the options is preferable, given the information for the original position and the least advantaged group. This will require thoughtful analysis, and the conference should take time for its decision. The procedure is in fact key to developing a crypto policy which is acceptable to all representative groups, and therefore, the conferees should carefully detail the argumentative steps they take and motivate their choices. Only with open and argued reasoning is there a chance that the still much polarized debate can be resolved in the US.

11.6. Conclusion

If the scheme as a whole seems on reflection to clarify and to order our thoughts, and if it tends to reduce disagreements and to bring divergent convictions more in line, then it has done all that one may reasonably ask. (Rawls, A Theory of Justice)

How does the outcome of the conference match, in Rawls' phrase, our considered judgments in reflective equilibrium? That the zero option is for the time being the best way (not) to act need not be surprising. That is a rather direct consequence of the rabbit I put in the hat, having chosen the average, law-abiding crypto user Alice as the least advantaged group and having looked at the various options in the original position from her perspective. It is more on the procedure that I would like to reflect: has it been a good way of reconciling the interests at stake in the crypto conflict?

There are two crucial factors in the procedure. The first is giving a good overview of the options available and judging how they meet the required principles. The second, and most important, factor is making clear which choices one makes in making a decision: how do you value the principles (that is, which adjudication rules do you use), what information do you use as input, and which perspective do you choose? These 'rabbit choices' are essential; the conjuring one performs with the hat afterwards is more show than substance. In fact, there are many ways of conjuring, but in the end, you still draw out of the hat the rabbit you used as input. Still, the conjuring matters, because it is key to making the rabbit acceptable to all interested parties.

The Rawls procedure is a good way of showing these choices and arguing for the decisions made. It has made me order the principles, and describe the information for the original position that I perceive as essential to the problem. Also, it has made me choose the perspective of the least advantaged group. The specific choices I made (the rabbits I chose) are open to discussion; I have argued for them from my point of view. The procedure is open to discussion as well, although I argue that this procedure is preferable to that used by most studies so far, which often amount to showing a rabbit and claiming this was conjured out of a hat backstage. That is not a satisfactory way to address so crucial a conflict of interests as is at stake here. The citizens of the information society have a right to know in what way their interests are balanced by the policy makers. Alice must be able to review the decision-making process, and she should be able to feel that she would indeed have made the same decision herself. Only then can she say that the outcome really reconciles her conflicting interests.

Summary

The crypto controversy. A key conflict in the information society

Noordwijkerhout (Netherlands), August 1998 – In the information society, information and, consequently, information security are growing more and more important. Therefore, there is an increasing need to employ cryptography: programs which make data inaccessible to unauthorized people. On the other hand, there is an increasing concern that criminals can use this cryptography to effectively escape the notice of police. So, cryptography produces a conflict of interests: privacy and information security versus criminal investigation. The related discussion is strongly polarized: privacy groups and law enforcement flatly oppose each other. Behold the *crypto controversy*, one of the key conflicts in the information society.

To address this controversy, I organize a three-day conference on the Dutch crypto policy, which is to answer the question: "How can and should the Dutch government address the problem that the use of strong cryptography by criminals poses to law enforcement, taking into account the legitimate interests to use cryptography in the information society?" Attending the conference are representatives of the relevant groups of Dutch society that have an interest in a just crypto policy: Alice, an average crypto user, Bob, a business crypto user, Polly, a law-enforcement official, and Suzie, a suspect (who worries about a draconian crypto policy infringing her rights of the defense). They will have to decide upon a crypto policy that reconciles the interests of privacy and information security with the interest of law enforcement.

Background

To enable the conferees to make a just decision, the organizers (Tilburg and Eindhoven Universities) have written an extensive background paper which outlines the problem and the context in which it should be seen. The paper starts with a presentation of the information society, which "will profoundly change the way we live and work", according to European Commissioner Bangemann. As information is becoming ever more important to our life and work, an information society is taking shape in which traditional borders are blurred. Media as well as market sectors converge, state monopolies on telecommunications are abolished, and electronic commerce enables customers and enterprises to do business through other intermediaries than retail shops. This society is global by nature, and national and jurisdiction borders are rapidly becoming less relevant as the Internet is booming. In this society that depends for a large part on information, the need for information security is a primary one. The confidentiality, integrity, and availability of information (the CIA of information security) must be safeguarded by a mixture of physical, organizational, technical, and legal measures.

One of the key technologies for establishing information security is cryptography, systems which use mathematical algorithms and digital keys to encipher data in such a way that only authorized people can decrypt and read them. Especially public-key or asymmetric cryptography, which was developed in the 1970s, has opened up a vast array of applications for wide-scale encryption. (In public-key cryptography, users have a key pair consisting of a private and a public key. By widely distributing the public key – which does not require a secure channel – people can safely communicate with any number of others.) Cryptography is employed to protect, e.g., telecommunications, personal data, electronic payment systems, intellectual-property rights, sensitive government and business data, and human rights. Also, cryptography can prevent crime, like computer crime and economic espionage.

A drawback of cryptography, however, is that criminals can use it to escape the notice of wiretapping and computer-searching police officers. Uncrackable crypto systems are easily available, and if criminals use them correctly (that is, if they are careful with their passphrases), they can communicate securely and store incriminating information safely without risk that the police be any the wiser. Therefore, cryptography will hamper the investigation of crime, in particular of organized crime, business crime, and computer crime. Today, the problem is not large: in the few cases that police have encountered encryption, they could generally crack it or find enough other evidence to make a winning case. However, the general expectation is that cryptocriminal use will rise significantly as cryptography is becoming ever more widely available and more user-friendly, particularly once it is built-in in the information and communications infrastructure. Since wiretapping and searching computers are important investigation measures (law-enforcement officials call wiretapping a crucial investigation technique, even if the efficacy of tapping is sometimes disputed), the threat of cryptocriminals to the rule of law is a real one. There is therefore a legitimate public interest in countering the (future) negative effect of cryptography on law enforcement. In the Netherlands, this can best be addressed in the context of the general revision of investigation measures, which is taking place as a result of the finding in the mid-1990s that investigation practice had gotten out of hand ('IRT-gate').

The problem of cryptocriminals is being studied in many countries. Some states have enacted legislation (France and Russia, for instance, have virtually prohibited strong cryptography, and the Netherlands has introduced a provision that requires people to decrypt, which may soon be extended to demand decryption by suspects as well), and some states (notably the UK and the US) have expressed a serious desire to restrict the application of cryptography to systems which leak information to law-enforcement. Most countries, however, are at a loss. The OECD have issued 'guidelines' for a crypto policy which in fact do not guide at all, and states seem to be waiting for each other to see what the emerging international direction will be. This much for the background paper, which ends on a rather desperate note: "there is a general impasse in the crypto controversy debate."

Procedure

To break the impasse, Alice, Bob, Polly, and Suzie will have to decide which option best addresses the problem of criminals using cryptography. As this is essentially a problem of balancing conflicting interests, the conference agenda follows a procedure inspired by John Rawls' *A Theory of Justice* which should lead to a result that is acceptable to all. A particular feature of this conference is that the conference room is covered in a 'veil of ignorance', which ensures that the participants do not know which position in society they themselves have in reality. Thus, although they have all relevant information at their disposal, Polly, Alice, Suzie, and Bob can not be biased by their personal preferences or the particular interests of the group they represent. This will ensure that their decision is impartial and a genuine reconciliation of interests.

The first agenda item is choosing a least advantaged group, that is, the group which has most to lose in the crypto debate, where losses are counted in terms of fundamental freedoms and not in terms of material wealth. After all, the central tenet in law is to protect the weak from the strong: "law cannot be impartial in its function of regulating order: it will have to take sides with the powerless, with those placed under custody, with those who are most threatened to be overpowered." [Peters] If there is no option which is in all respects preferable to the others, the perspective of the least advantaged group is a good device to make a decision that does justice to this central tenet. The conferees agree that, in the Dutch context, Alice represents the least-advantaged group: her privacy, including her right to confidential communications, is at stake. Alice has more to lose than Polly, who – even if wiretaps would become useless – still has various investigation measures to catch criminals, while Suzie's rights are sufficiently protected by the right to a fair trial as interpreted by the European Court (being a Dutch conference, it has to respect the European Convention for the Protection of Human Rights). And for businessman Bob, no fundamental freedoms are at stake. Therefore, the issue will be decided from the perspective of Alice, and so, the outcome must be the one which is most acceptable to the law-abiding crypto user.

Next, the conferees choose a set of principles, with which they can assess the options to address the crypto problem. They perceive four fundamental rights as essential to the crypto problem:

- the right to privacy (including confidential communications),
- the right to a fair trial,
- the rule of law (including the right to freedom from crime), and
- the right to economic development.

Besides, the conferees will also take into account the less fundamental, but still desirable principles of workability, international compatibility, and technological sustainability. Since the principles will conflict, the conferees also define an adjudication rule: a fundamental right can only be infringed for the sake of another fundamental right, and not for the sake of a desirable principle. And to decide which fundamental right carries most weight, the conferees agree that, if all else is equal, a principle higher on the list will be accorded more weight.

Optional directions

To end the first day, Bob, Polly, Suzie, and Alice start with discussing which options are viable to address the crypto conflict. They discard right away the non-option of banning cryptography, since this hampers the legitimate use of cryptography and thus seriously threatens privacy and information security, while it is not at all effective in preventing criminals from using cryptography anyway. With some brainwaving, they come up with four optional directions.

- Stimulate the use of cryptography which does not hamper law-enforcement, either because it cannot be used for confidentiality, or because it LEAKs (that is, has built-in Law-Enforcement Access to Keys).
- Demand suspects to decrypt and punish them if they refuse, by either convicting them for refusing to cooperate with a decryption command (that would be a new criminal provision), or by using the refusal as evidence in the primary case (effectively reversing the burden of proof).

These first two options are in fact the only options which ensure that the police can access crypto keys and decipher the encrypted data they gathered. If it should turn out that both these options are infeasible or undesirable, the police will have to do something else.

- Look elsewhere. Thus, one can consider using 'direct eavesdropping' (directional microphones and bugs), monitoring electromagnetic radiation (TEMPEST monitoring), stepping up infiltration, and staging crown witnesses – these are alternative ways to gather incriminating information which are not hampered by cryptography.
- Decide to do nothing (the zero option).

The second day, Polly, Suzie, Bob, and Alice discuss the merits and flaws of the options. Stimulating the development of non-confidentiality crypto does not make the problem worse for the police, but it does nothing to address cryptocriminals either. Therefore, they do not consider it an option after all. Next, reviewing LEAK cryptography (that is, key-escrow and key-recovery systems which give Law Enforcement Access to Keys to decrypt), the conferees note that the technology is yet in its infancy and that it involves intrinsic security risks. More importantly, it is not effective to catch cryptocriminals, since (smarter) criminals will not use systems which they know LEAK to the police. It is true that the police can profit from voluntary data recovery by businesses, but the development of data recovery should be left to the market.

Now, the conferees analyze under what conditions a decryption command can be given to suspects, given the privilege against self-incrimination as interpreted by the European Court in the *Funke* and *Saunders* cases. (A decryption command can easily be given to non-suspects and generally also to corporate crypto users, Bob happily notes, so that a decryption command can at any rate be given in several cases.) The privilege is not absolute, and given the *Saunders* finding that material which exists outside the will of the suspect may be demanded, the police can demand diskettes with private crypto keys to be handed over. Whether the police can also force a suspect to give the passphrase which normally protects the key is more contentious. If the police is pretty sure that the suspect is able to decrypt (in US case-law terminology: if it is a foregone conclusion that someone is able to decrypt), a decryption command is legally acceptable. The tricky issue is, however, how to enforce a decryption command: the general punishment for a refusal to cooperate with a legal order is three months, and this can not be enough to incite serious criminals to decrypt (with which they would risk many years' imprisonment). Penalizing crypto use 'in furtherance of a crime' is not an option, since it does not ease the proof issues it is supposed to alleviate. The two main enforcement options are therefore penalizing a decryption refusal with a substantial punishment (say, a few years), or reverse the burden of proof in order to allow the decryption refusal to be used as evidence in the primary case ("if you don't want to decrypt this, we assume it contains incriminating information"). Since the first option catches criminals the wrong way (one wants offenders to be punished for the offense they committed, not for 'cryptography abuse'), and since the second option is better targeted at serious criminals, reversing the burden of proof would be better to enforce a decryption command. However, if the fundamental presumption of innocence is to be respected, strict conditions must apply (consistent with the conditions the European Court defined in *Murray*), and the command will not be effective in many cases.

A general despondency now descends over the conference: perhaps there is no feasible way to ensure that the police can access crypto keys and decipher encrypted data they suspect to be incriminating. However, Suzie, Bob, Alice, and Polly realize with some relief that the police has other investigation powers to gather data, particularly since in the post-IRT-gate era, new investigation measures are being considered. The Dutch draft law on special investigation powers proposes 'direct eavesdropping': directional microphones and bugs which catch conversations (and, who knows, keyboard strokes) the moment they are spoken (or typed), before they can be encrypted. This power could be significantly extended to address the crypto problem, in particular by allowing the police to eavesdrop directly within homes. Another alternative investigation measure is intercepting electromagnetic radiation (TEMPEST monitoring), which can reproduce the contents of computer screens from an adjacent building or vehicle. Then again, there are other ways to gather information about, in particular, organized crime: one can infiltrate a criminal organization, or one can have an accomplice testify in court as a crown witness in return for a sentence reduction. The conferees realize that these legal measures, contrary to the technical measures of eaves-dropping and TEMPEST monitoring, are far removed from wiretapping and computer searches, because this yields different kinds of information. Moreover, all measures seriously infringe fundamental rights: the first two are major threats to privacy, and the last two threaten the rule of law. None of these measures, then, is an obvious solution to redress the gap in information-gathering caused by cryptocriminals. All the conferees can say at this moment, is that direct eavesdropping is more practicable than TEMPEST monitoring and that infiltration is to be preferred to crown witnesses (which is more detrimental to the rule of law).

Perhaps, then, Suzie sighs, we should do nothing at all. If the negative consequences of the options are all larger than the positive ones, perhaps that would be the best option. The one drawback of this is, of course, that it gives cryptocriminals free play. The conferees end the second day in some confusion. They have identified which options are viable to address the crypto problem: demand suspects to decrypt and reverse the burden of proof if they refuse, step up 'direct eavesdropping' and infiltration, or decide to do nothing – but they realize that not one option is really satisfying.

Conclusion
A night's rest, however, clears the mind, and the conferees start to review the options with renewed vigor on the third day. Remembering the perspective of Alice, the law-abiding crypto user, as the one to tackle the problem from, they review the options again. They note, first, that all viable options are of limited efficacy, as they can only be implemented with difficulty or in a quite limited number of cases. Also, they remember from the background paper that currently, the threat of cryptocriminals is small – hardly enough to justify serious infringements of fundamental rights. Besides, the police has many investigation powers that may help to partly compensate the information loss caused by cryptocriminals. For instance, they can use telecommunications traffic analysis (which is not hampered by cryptography), infiltration, and (soon) 'direct eavesdropping'. Moreover, in some cases, they can command (non-suspect or business) people to decrypt with a reasonable chance of success. Since Alice's right to privacy carries more weight than her right to freedom from crime (for the lower limit of the latter is not at stake in any option), the conferees must be wary with options which infringe privacy but which have a limited efficacy and a poor justification in investigation practice.

Taking everything into account, the conferees choose the zero option. They thus conclude that for the moment, the Dutch government should endorse the zero option as the one which best reconciles the conflicting crypto interests.

Future
Since everything flows, however, Suzie, Alice, Polly, and Bob realize that in the future, this policy needs to be reviewed periodically. They speculate that, once cryptocriminals do turn out to be a serious problem for the prosecution of crime, another option than the zero option may have to be chosen. The biggest future cryptocriminal threat will most likely be posed by organized criminals, and cryptocriminals will hamper wiretapping more than computer searches. To investigate and convict organized criminals, other investigation measures hold higher promise than reversing the burden of proof, which is problematic anyway in the case of encrypted communications. Moreover, from the perspective of Alice, alternative investigation measures will likely be more acceptable than a decryption-command legislation that may have the effect of putting a strict liability on crypto use. So, they feel that alternative investigation measures are preferable to enforcing a decryption command through contentious legal constructions. Perhaps, then, the government will slowly have to adapt to the idea that wiretapping is not a panacea for the information need of the police, and to focus their resources on other, less crypto-sensitive, investigation measures.

To end the conference, the participants look back and evaluate what they have done. Having defined principles and adjudication rules, surveyed possible options, and narrowed down the list to viable options, the conferees had to decide the core problem. Using the perspective of Alice as the least advantaged group, they found that for the time being, the zero option is preferable. Policy makers should, however, continue to closely monitor developments, in order to periodically review and if necessary to adjust this decision. Depending on the crime rate and the crypto use by criminals, and depending on the investigation powers the police can use, this could lead to allowing more alternative investigation measures to counter the possibly decreasing efficacy of wiretaps and computer searches.

Abbreviations

AES	Advanced Encryption Standard
ANP	Algemeen Nederlandsch Persbureau
ASEAN	Association of South-east Asian Nations
ATM	Automatic Teller Machine
BIPT	Belgian Institute for Posts and Telecommunications
BSI	Bundesamt für Sicherheit in der Informationstechnik (German Federal Agency for IT Security)
CA	Certification Authority
CALEA	Communications Assistance for Law Enforcement Act
CCA	Computer Crime Act
CCP	Code of Criminal Procedure
CKE	Commercial Key Escrow
CLSR	Computer Law and Security Report
COCOM	Coordinating Committee for Multilateral Export Controls
CR	Computer und Recht
DCC	Dutch Criminal Code
DCCP	Dutch Code of Criminal Procedure
DES	Data Encryption Standard
DRA	Data Recovery Agency
DSA	Digital Signature Algorithm
DSS	Digital Signature Standard
DTI	Department of Trade and Industry (UK)
DVD	Digital Versatile Disk
EAR	Export Administration Regulations
EC	European Commission
ECHR	European Court of Human Rights
ECJ	European Court of Justice
ECLR	Electronic Commerce & Law Report
ECPHR	European Convention for the Protection of Human Rights and fundamental freedoms
EDI	Electronic Data Interchange
EEI	Escrowed Encryption Initiative
EES	Escrowed Encryption Standard
EFTA	European Free Trade Association
EPIC	Electronic Privacy and Information Center
EPLR	Electronic Information Policy & Law Report
E-PRIVACY	Encryption Protects the Rights of Individuals from Violation and Abuse in CYberspace
ETS	European Trusted Services
EU	European Union
FIID	Fiscal Intelligence and Investigation Department
FIPS	Federal Information Processing Standard
GAK	Government Access to Keys
GII	Global Information Infrastructure
GMO	General Municipal Ordinance
GSN	General Software Note
GVU	Graphic, Visualization, & Usability Center
HR	Hoge Raad (Dutch Supreme Court)
ICCPR	International Covenant on Civil and Political Rights
ICT	Information and Communication Technologies
IDEA	International Data Encryption Algorithm
IITF	Information Infrastructure Task Force

IP	Internet Protocol
ISDN	Integrated Services Digital Network
IT	Information Technology
ITAR	International Traffic in Arms Regulation
ITSEC	Information Technology Security Evaluation Criteria
KDD	Knowledge Discovery in Data bases
KEA	Key Escrow Agent
KMI	Key Management Infrastructure
KRA	Key Recovery Alliance; Key Recovery Agency
KRISIS	Key Recovery In Secure Information Systems
LEAK	Law-Enforcement Access to Keys
MAC	Message Authentication Code
MIME	Multipurpose Internet Mail Extensions
NII	National Information Infrastructure
NIIAC	National Information Infrastructure Advisory Council
NIST	National Institute for Standards and Technology
NJ	Nederlandse Jurisprudentie
NJW	Neue Juristische Wochenschrift
NRC	National Research Council
OJ	Official Journal
OTP	One-Time Pad
PEM	Privacy-Enhanced Mail
PET	Privacy-Enhancing Technologies
PGP	Pretty Good Privacy
PKI	Public Key Infrastructure
RC4	Rivest Cipher (or Ron's Code) version 4
RSA	Rivest, Shamir, Adleman
SAFE	Security And Freedom through Encryption
SCSSI	Service Central de la Sécurité des Systèmes d'Informations (French Central Information-Systems Security Service)
SET	Secure Electronic Transactions
SIM	Subscriber Identity Module
SOG-IS	Senior Officials Group – Information Security
SSL	Secure Sockets Layer
SWIFT	Society for Worldwide Interbank Financial Telecommunications
TACDFIPSFKMI	Technical Advisory Committee to Develop a Federal Information Processing Standard for the Federal Key Management Infrastructure
TCP/IP	Transmission Control Protocol/ Internet Protocol
TEMPEST	Transient ElectroMagnetic Pulse Emanation Surveillance Technology or Transient ElectroMagnetic Pulse Emanation STandard
TFA	Telecommunications Facilities Act
TIS	Trusted Information Systems
TK	Tweede Kamer (Dutch Lower House)
TTP	Trusted Third Party
UMTS	Universal Mobile Telecommunications System
US	United States of America
VAS	Value-Added Service
WIPO	World Intellectual Property Organization
WWW	World Wide Web
XOR	exclusive or

Glossary

Glossary of terms

asymmetric crypto system	crypto system which uses different keys (a public and a private one) for encryption and decryption, and for putting and verifying digital signatures
authenticity	the property that a message was indeed sent by the purported sender
Certification Authority	TTP which offers a key-certification service (certifying that a public key belongs to a specified user)
cipher	crypto method which changes each letter or each group of letters into other letters or symbols
ciphertext	unit of encrypted data
Clipper	key-escrow initiative using the Escrowed Encryption Standard, proposed by US government in 1993; died about 1996
code	crypto method which uses a dictionary-style list of words and names coupled with an encrypted form
coercive power	investigation measure which infringes a constitutional right and which requires a basis in formal law
confidentiality	the property that data are kept secret from people who are not authorized to access them
crack	break a crypto system or an encrypted message (synonym: cryptanalyze)
cryptanalysis	breaking a crypto system or an encrypted message
cryptocriminal	criminal who uses cryptography to thwart the police
cryptography	(the making of) crypto systems
cryptology	science that studies the making and breaking of crypto systems
crypto system	implementation of an encryption scheme or algorithm
data recovery	all-encompassing term for methods to retrieve the plaintext of encrypted data if the key for decryption is not available
Data Recovery Agency	TTP which offers a data-recovery service
decryption	undoing encryption
digest	synonym for hash
digital signature	authentication method that uses public-key cryptography
duress code	crypto system which can decrypt a given ciphertext into two different, meaningful plaintexts (the original one and a fake one)
encryption	automated process of making data inaccessible to unauthorized people
extranet	intranet that is restrictedly open to external users
firewall	computer located between an internal network and an outside network that shields the internal network from external threats by allowing only authorized messages to pass
hash	short, fixed-length block of data used to prove the integrity of a message
hash function	algorithm which computes a hash for messages
information (super)highway	network of computer networks
integrity	the property that data are unaltered and complete
intranet	internal computer network that uses Internet technology
IRT-gate	Dutch scandal in 1993-1994 of unlawful police investigation practices by InterRegional Teams that investigated organized crime
key deposit	synonym for key escrow
key encapsulation	synonym for key recovery (as used in this book)
key escrow	method of data recovery in which people deposit their private (or supersymmetric) keys with a TTP
Key Escrow Agent	TTP which offers a key-escrow service

key recovery	(in this book) method of data recovery in which people tag along to messages a recoverable session key (in general usage, the term often functions as a synonym for data recovery)
knowbot	robotic piece of software which automatically performs a pseudo-intelligent task
LEAK	Law-Enforcement Access to Keys: (in this book) generic term for key escrow and key recovery for law-enforcement purposes
logic bomb	nefarious program installed on a hard disk which is triggered by a certain event, such as the advent of a specific date and time
metatags	meta-data in an Internet page which (should) indicate its contents for search engines
network provider	operator of a telecommunications network
nomenclator	crypto method which combines a code and a cipher, in use from the 15th to the 19th centuries
non-repudiation	the property of a message which ensures that the sender or receiver cannot deny having sent or received it
optical telegraph	system devised by Claude Chappe in the late 18th century for transmitting messages through a two-arm device placed on high buildings
passphrase	sophisticated version of a password
plaintext	unit of unencrypted data
private key	the part of a key pair used in asymmetric crypto systems that is to be kept secret
proportionality principle	legal principle which requires the use of an investigation measure to be proportional to the seriousness of the offense under investigation
public key	the part of a key pair used in asymmetric crypto systems that is publicly available
public-key cryptography	synonym for asymmetric cryptography
Public Key Infrastructure	framework in which Certification Authorities (and possibly Data Recovery Agencies) cooperate to provide TTP services
Rasterfahndung	investigation method which compares data bases automatically to find 'suspect' information
replevin	(order to) cease seizure
secret key	key used in symmetric crypto systems
service provider	organization which provides basic or value-added telecommunications services
session key	symmetric crypto key used only once for a communications session
spamming	sending unsolicited e-mail messages on a massive scale
steganography	(the making of) programs which hide data in other data
subsidiarity principle	legal principle which requires that the least-infringing investigation measure be used that will serve the investigation purpose
supersymmetric key	symmetric crypto key used to encrypt symmetric keys for exchange and retrieval purposes
symmetric crypto system	crypto system which uses the one and the same (secret) key for encryption and decryption
time-stamping	TTP service which establishes the date and time a message was sent
traffic analysis	analysis of data about telecommunications traffic (who called whom when from where for how long and how often)
Trusted Third Party	trusted, independent organization which offers cryptography-based services that enhance the reliability of electronic data interchange and storage
Van Traa committee	Dutch parliamentary inquest into IRT-gate, chaired by Maarten van Traa
warez	illegally copied software
XOR	exclusive or: mathematical function of adding bits (0+0 = 0, 0+1 = 1, 1+0 = 1, 1+1 = 0)
zero-knowledge protocol	cryptographic series of steps which proves that the user knows a secret without revealing any information about the secret

Glossary of legal terms (English-Dutch)

coercive power	dwangmiddel
controlled delivery	gecontroleerde aflevering
criminal financial inquest	strafrechtelijk financieel onderzoek
direct eavesdropping	direct afluisteren
examining judge	rechter-commissaris
General Municipal Ordinance	Algemene plaatselijke verordening
in flagrante delicto	op heterdaad
inquest	gerechtelijk vooronderzoek
IRT-gate	IRT-affaire
legislature	wetgever
Order in Council	Algemene Maatregel van Bestuur
peeping operation	inkijkoperatie
phenomenon investigation	fenomeenonderzoek
pre-trial detention	voorlopige hechtenis
privilege against self-incrimination	*nemo tenetur*-beginsel
pseudo-purchase	pseudokoop
public prosecutor	Officier van Justitie
search	huiszoeking
seizure	inbeslagneming
Strip 'em	Pluk ze

Glossary of laws and regulations (English-Dutch)

Act on Municipal Basic Registries	Wet Gemeentelijke Basisadministratie persoonsgegevens
Computer Crime Act	Wet computercriminaliteit
Data Protection Act	Wet Bescherming Persoonsgegevens
Data Registries Act	Wet persoonsregistraties
Decree on government-department information-security instructions 1994	Besluit voorschrift informatiebeveiliging rijksdienst 1994
Dutch Civil Code	Burgerlijk Wetboek
Dutch Code of Criminal Procedure	Wetboek van Strafvordering
Dutch Criminal Code	Wetboek van Strafrecht
Governments Accounts Act	Comptabiliteitswet
Instructions for information security within the central government	Voorschriften voor informatiebeveiliging bij de rijksoverheid
Police Information Security Regulation	Regeling informatiebeveiliging politie
Police Registries Act	Wet politieregisters
State Taxes Act	Algemene wet inzake rijksbelastingen
Telecommunications Act	Telecommunicatiewet
Telecommunications Facilities Act	Wet op de telecommunicatievoorzieningen

Glossary of organizations (English-Dutch)

Central Criminal Intelligence Agency	Centrale Recherche Informatiedienst
Chamber of Audit	Algemene Rekenkamer
Co-operation Centre Tilburg and Eindhoven Universities	SamenwerkingsOrgaan Brabantse Universiteiten
Council of State	Raad van State
Data Protection Authority	Registratiekamer
Economic Surveillance Department	Economische Controledienst
Fiscal Intelligence and Investigation Department	Fiscale Inlichtingen en Opsporingsdienst
Internal Revenue Service	Belastingdienst
National Detective Team	Landelijk Recherche Team
National Police Services Force	Korps Landelijke Politiediensten
Public Prosecutor	Openbaar Ministerie

Bibliography

The references available online are also listed on my homepage.
See <http://cwis.kub.nl/~frw/people/koops/thesis/ref.htm>.

Abadinsky — Howard Abadinsky, *Organized crime*, 4th ed., Chicago: Nelson-Hall, 1994

Abelson 1997 — Hal Abelson, Ross Anderson, Steven Bellovin et al., *The Risks of Key Recovery, Key Escrow, and Trusted Third-Party Encryption*, 27 May 1997, <http://www.crypto.com/key_study/report.shtml>

Abelson 1998 — Hal Abelson, Ross Anderson, Steven M. Bellovin et al., *The Risks of Key Recovery, Key Escrow, and Trusted Third-Party Encryption*, June 1998, <http://www.cdt.org/crypto/risks98/>

ACM — S. Landau, S. Kent et al., *Codes, Keys, and Conflicts, Issues in U.S. Crypto Policy*, New York: Association for Computing Machinery, June 1994, <http://Info.acm.org/reports/acm_crypto_study.html>

Ad Hoc — Ad Hoc Group of Crytopgraphers and Computer Scientists, *Minimal Key Lengths for Symmetric Ciphers to Provide Adequate Commercial Security*, January 1996, <ftp://ftp.research.att.com/dist/mab/keylength.txt>

Adriaans — Pieter Adriaans, Dolf Zantinge, *Data mining*, Harlow: Addison Wesley, 1996

Andersen — Mads Bryde Andersen, Peter Landrock, 'Encryption and Interception', *The Computer Law and Security Report* (November-December 1996), pp. 342-348

Anderson 94 — Ross J. Anderson, 'Why Cryptosystems Fail', *Communications of the ACM* (November 1994), pp. 32-40

Anderson 96 — Ross Anderson, Markus Kuhn, 'Tamper Resistance - a Cautionary Note', in: *The Second USENIX Workshop on Electronic Commerce Proceedings* (Oakland, 18-21 November 1996), pp. 1-11, <http://www.cl.cam.ac.uk/users/rja14/tamper.html>

Ansmink — A.A. Ansmink, 'Het meewerken van de verdachte aan zijn veroordeling en art. 29 Sv', *RM Themis* (1981), pp. 426-448

Arnbak — J.C. Arnbak, J.J. van Cuilenburg, E.J. Dommering, *Verbinding en ontvlechting in de communicatie*, Amsterdam: Cramwinckel, 1990

Aronowitz — A.A. Aronowitz, D.C.G. Laagland, G. Paulides, *Value-added tax fraud in the European Union*, The Hague: WODC, 1996

Asbeck — F.D. van Asbeck, 'De kroongetuige vanuit de visie van de wetgever', in [Tak 94a], pp. 25-36

Australia — *Australian Encryption Policy*, document to OECD Ad Hoc Meeting of Experts on Cryptography Policy, 18-19 December 1995

Baker 96 — Stewart A. Baker, *Summary Report on the OECD Ad Hoc Meeting of Experts on Cryptography*, <http://www.us.net/~steptoe/276908.htm> (accessed 14 February 1996)

Baker 98a — Stewart A. Baker, 'Review of "Privacy on the Line: The Politics of Wiretapping and Encryption" by Whitfield Diffie and Susan Landau', *Notices of the AMS* 45, No. 6 (June-July 1998), p. 709

Baker 98b — Stewart A. Baker, Paul R. Hurst, *The Limits of Trust. Cryptography, Governments, and Electronic Commerce*, The Hague: Kluwer Law International, 1998

Balenson — D.M. Balenson et al. (TIS Inc.), 'A New Approach to Software Escrow Encryption', in [Hoffman 95], pp. 180-207

Bangemann 94 — High-Level Group on the Information Society, *Europe and the Global Information Society: Recommendations to the European Council* (Bangemann Report), Brussels, 26 May 1994

Bangemann 97 — Martin Bangemann, 'A New World Order for Global Communications. The Need for an International Charter', speech at Telecom Inter@ctive '97 (Geneva, 8 September 1997), <http://www.ispo.cec.be/infosoc/promo/speech/geneva.html>

Barendrecht	J.M. Barendrecht, 'Rechtswetenschap: stoffig of inventief?', *Nederlands Juristenblad* (10 May 1996), pp. 705-714
Beaver	Donald Beaver, 'Factoring: The DNA Solution', in: Josef Pieprzyk et al. (eds.), *Advances in Cryptology – ASIACRYPT '94*, Berlin: Springer, 1995, pp. 419-423
Bekkers	V.J.J.M. Bekkers, 'The Playground of the Electronic Superhighway', in: Victor Bekkers et al. (eds.), *Emerging Electronic Highways. New Challenges for Politics and Law*, The Hague: Kluwer Law International, 1996, pp. 9-26
Beleidsadviesgroep	Beleidsadviesgroep computercriminaliteit, *Op weg naar... digitaal rechercheren. De invloed op en de gevolgen van de vergaande digitalisering van de Nederlandse maatschappij op het werk van politie en justitie*, June 1996
Bellare	M. Bellare, R.L. Rivest, *Translucent Cryptography. An Alternative to Key Escrow, and its Implementation via Fractional Oblivious Transfer*, 18 February 1996, <http://theory.lcs.mit.edu/~rivest/BellareRivest-translucent.ps>
Beth	Thomas Beth, 'Confidential Communication on the Internet', *Scientific American* (December 1995), pp. 70-73
BfW	Bundesministerium für Wirtschaft, *Info 2000: Deutschlands Weg in die Informationsgesellschaft*, February 1996, <http://www.kp.dlr.de/BMWi/gip/programme/info2000/>
Biham	E. Biham, A. Shamir, 'Differential Fault Analysis of Secret Key Cryptosystems', in: B.S. Kaliski (ed.), *Advances in Cryptology – CRYPTO '97*, Berlin: Springer-Verlag, 1997, pp. 513-525
Blaze 94	Matt Blaze, 'Protocol Failure in the Escrowed Encryption Standard', November 1994, reprinted in [Hoffman 95], pp. 131-146
Blaze 96	M. Blaze, W. Diffie, R. Rivest et al., *Minimal Key Lengths for Symmetric Ciphers to Provide Adequate Commercial Security*, January 1996, <ftp://ftp.research.att.com/dist/mab/keylength.txt>
Bonn	*Ministerial declaration* (Global Information Networks, Ministerial Conference, Bonn, 6-8 July 1997), <http://www2.echo.lu/bonn/final.html>
Böttger	Andreas Bötgger, Christian Pfeiffer, 'Der Lauschangriff in den USA und in Deutschland', *Zeitschrift für Rechtspolitik*, No. 1 (1994), pp. 7-17
Boutros-Ghali	*Secretary-General calls for effective action against 'crime multinationals' in address to conference on organized transnational crime*, Federal News Service, 22 November 1994, <http://www.alternatives.com/crime/ghali.htm> (accessed 19 July 1996)
Braun	David Braun, 'FBI Calls Privacy Extremists Elitist', *TechWire* (25 September 97), <http://www.techweb.com/wire/news/1997/09/0925fbi.html>
Breed	N.F. Breed, D.J. Out, O. Tettero, *Informatiebeveiliging. Een blik achter de schermen*, Alphen aan den Rijn: Samsom BedrijfsInformatie, 1994
Breuil	Hans Oude Breuil, *Van achterklap tot telefoontap*, graduate thesis Tilburg University, January 1984
Bribosia	*Wetsvoorstel tot opheffing van de artikelen 70bis en 95, eerste lid, 5°, van de wet van 21 maart 1991 betreffende de hervorming van sommige economische overheidsbedrijven en tot aanvulling van het Wetboek van Strafvordering met bepalingen betreffende de decryptie van berichten*, Parl. Doc. Senaat, 1-352/1, 11 June 1996, <http://www.senate.be/docs/lex/1/1-352/1-352-1_nl.html>
Brickell	Ernest F. Brickell and others, 'SKIPJACK Review: Interim Report', 28 July 1993, reprinted in [Hoffman 95], pp. 119-130
Brodeur	Jean-Paul Brodeur, 'Undercover Policing in Canada. A Study of its Consequences', in [Fijnaut], pp. 71-102
Brouwer	Aart Brouwer, 'Amerika luistert, Dossier Echelon', *de Groene Amsterdammer* (18 February 1998), pp. 14-16
Brown	Ronald Brown, Larry Irving et al., *The Global Information Infrastructure: Agenda for Cooperation*, February 1995, <http://www.iitf.nist.gov/documents/docs/gii/giiagend.html>
BSC	Business Scenarios Committee, Key Recovery Alliance, *Business Requirements for Key Recovery, Release 3.0*, 18 December 1997, <http://www.kra.org/whitepapers>

BSI	*Code of Practise for Information Security Management*, BS7799 part 1, London: BSI, 1995
Buruma	Y. Buruma, *De strafrechtelijke handhaving van bestuurswetten*, Arnhem: Gouda Quint, 1993
Cabinet	Swedish Cabinet Office Reference Group for Cryptographic Issues, *Cryptography Policy: Possible Courses of Action for Sweden*, October 1997, <http://www.ud.se/english/press/pdf_publ.htm#crypto>
Callas	Jon Callas, 'What's really in PGP 5.5?', mailing list <cryptography@c2.net>, 7 October 1997
Canetti	Ran Canetti, Cynthia Dwork et al., 'Deniable Encryption', in: B.S. Kaliski (ed.) *Advances in Cryptology – CRYPTO '97*, Berlin: Springer Verlag, 1997, pp. 90-104
Castell	Stephen Castell (ed.), *Code of Practice and Management Guidelines for Trusted Third Party Services*, Infosec 93 S2101/02 (version 1.0), 6 October 1993
CD	Criminal Division, US Department of Justice, *Federal Guidelines for Searching and Seizing Computers*, Washington, D.C., July 1994
Chandler	James P. Chandler, Diana C. Arrington et al., *Identification and Analysis of Foreign Laws and Regulations Pertaining to the Use of Commercial Encryption Products for Voice and Data Communications*, Washington: DOE Project No. 2042-E024-A1, January 1994
Charbon	F.H. Charbon, H.W.K. Kaspersen, *Computercriminaliteit in Nederland*, Den Haag: Stichting Beheer Platform Computercriminaliteit, 1990
Chor	Benny Chor, Amos Fiat, Moni Naor, 'Tracing Traitors', in Yvo Desmedt (ed.), *Advances in Cryptology – CRYPTO '94*, Berlin: Springer Verlag, 1994, pp. 257-270
Clerk	*Question orale de Mme. Bribosia à Mr. Stefaan De Clerk, Ministre de la Justice*, maintained by Olivier Bonaventure, < http://pgp.netline.be/cryptage/question-complete-bribosia.html> (accessed 11 July 1996)
Clinton	William J. Clinton, Albert Gore, *A Framework For Global Electronic Commerce*, 1 July 1997
CoE 82	Council of Europe, *Telephone tapping and the recording of telecommunications in some Council of Europe member states*, Legislative dossier No. 2, Strasbourg: Council of Europe, Legal Documentation and Research Division, May 1982
CoE 90	Council of Europe, *Recommendation No. R (89) 9 on computer-related crime and final report of the European Committee on Crime Problems on Computer-Related Crime*, Strasbourg, 1990
CoE 95	Council of Europe, *Recommendation No. R (95) 13 of the Committee of Ministers to Member States Concerning Problems of Criminal Procedure Law Connected with Information Technology*, 11 September 1995, <http://www.privacy.org/pi/intl_orgs/coe/info_tech_1995.html>
Copenhagen	*The Copenhagen Hearing April 23-24 1998. Report of Day 1*, <http://www.fsk.dk/fsk/div/hearing/first.html>
Corstens	G.J.M. Corstens, *Het Nederlands strafprocesrecht*, 2nd ed., Arnhem: Gouda Quint, 1995
Counterpane	Counterpane Systems, *Flaw in cell phone encryption identified; Design process blamed. Press Release*, 20 March 1997, <http://www.counterpane.com/cmea-press.html>
Coutorie	L.E. Coutorie, 'The Future of High-Technology Crime, A Parallel Delphi Study', in *Journal of Criminal Justice* 23, No. 1 (1995), pp. 13-27
Cukier	Kenneth Neil Cukier, 'Wide-eyed OECD delegates politely accosted by journalist', mailing list <fight-censorship@vorlon.mit.edu>, 26 September 1996
Davidson	Alan Davidson, Technical Advisory Committee, final letter to US Secretary of Commerce, 19 June 1998, available at <http://www.steptoe.com/WebDoc.nsf/Law+&+The+Net-All/All>
DB	Deutscher Bundestag, 'Recht: Über 8.000 Telefone eine Zeitlang überwacht', *WIB* 7, 23 April 1997, <http://www.bundestag.de/wib97/797259.htm.>
Denning 94	Dorothy Denning, 'The U.S. Key Escrow Encryption Technology', July 1994, reprinted in [Hoffman 95], pp. 111-118

Denning 96 — Dorothy Denning, *The Future of Cryptography*, version 6 January 1996, <http://www.cs.georgetown.edu/~denning/crypto/Future.htm>

Denning 97a — Dorothy Denning, William Baugh, *Encryption and evolving technologies as tools of organized crime and terrorism*, 15 May 1997, excerpt at <http://www.cs.georgetown.edu/~denning/crypto/oc-abs.html>

Denning 97b — Dorothy Denning, *Encryption Policy and Market Trends*, version 17 May 1997, <http://www.cs.georgetown.edu/~denning/crypto/Trends.html>

Denning 97c — Dorothy Denning, *Declaration on Encryption Policy*, 6 June 1997, <http://www.cs.georgetown.edu/~denning/crypto/position.html>

Denning 97d — Dorothy Denning, William Baugh, *Cases involving encryption in crime and terrorism*, version 10 October 1997, <http://www.cs.georgetown.edu/~denning/crypto/cases.html>

Desmedt — Y. Desmedt, 'Securing Traceability of Ciphertexts - Towards a Secure Key Escrow System', in: L. Guillou, J.-J. Quisquater (eds.), *Advances in Cryptology - EUROCRYPT '95*, Berlin: Springer Verlag, 1995, pp.147-157

DG XIII — Commission of the European Communities, Directorate General XIII, *Green Book on the Security of Information Systems. Draft 4.0*, 18 October 1993

Diffie — W. Diffie and M.E. Hellman, 'New Directions in Cryptography', *IEEE Transactions on Information Theory* IT-22, No. 6 (November 1976), pp. 644-654

Dijk — Cees van Dijk, 'Mogelijkheden om af te luisteren worden vergroot. Telefoontap heeft nog toekomst', *Algemeen politieblad* (12 September 1992), pp. 13-14

DoC — U.S. Department of Commerce and the National Security Agency, *A Study of the International Market for Computer Software with Encryption*, redacted copy, no date, <http://www.epic.org/crypto/export_controls/commerce_study_summary.txt>

DoS — U.S. Department of State, *Country reports on human rights practices for 1996 (Privacy Sections)*, January 1997, <http://www.privacy.org/pi/reports/hr96_privacy_report.html>

DPE — Irish Department of Public Enterprise, *Framework for Ireland's Policy on Cryptography and Electronic Signatures*, no date, <http://www.irlgov.ie/tec/html/signat.htm>

Duyne — Petrus C. van Duyne, *Het spook en de dreiging van de georganiseerde misdaad*, Den Haag: Sdu, 1995

ECC — Danish Ministry of Research and Information Technology, *Report by the Expert Committee on Cryptography*, April 1997, <http://www.fsk.dk/fsk/publ/1997/crypt/crypt.html>

Eck — Wim van Eck, 'Electromagnetic Radiation from Video Display Units: An Eavesdropping Risk?', *Computers & Security*, No. 4 (1985), pp. 269-286

EFF — Electronic Frontier Foundation, *EFF Builds DES Cracker that proves that Data Encryption Standard is insecure. Press release*, 17 July 1998, <http://www.eff.org/descracker.html>

Ellis — James H. Ellis, *The story of non-secret encryption*, written 1987, published December 1997, <http://www.jya.com/ellisdoc.htm>

EPIC — Electronic Privacy Information Center, *FBI Documents on Encryption*, no date, <http://www.epic.org/crypto/ban/fbi_dox/>

ETS — Commission of the European Communities, Directorate General XIII, *INFOSEC: ETS*, version 23 January 1998, <http://www.cordis.lu/infosec/src/ets.htm>

EZ — Ministerie van Economische Zaken, *Actieplan Electronic commerce*, March 1998, <http://www.minez.nl/ecom/my_html/actieplan.htm>

FBI — Federal Bureau of Investigations, *CALEA – Communications Assistance for Law Enforcement Act*, no date, <http://www.fbi.gov/calea/calea1.htm>

Field — Richard L. Field, 'The Great Mining Disaster of '99', *Electronic Banking Law and Commerce Report* (November/December 1997), republished in *Journal of Internet Banking and Commerce*, <http://www.arraydev.com/commerce/jibc/9801-7.htm>

Fijnaut — Cyrille Fijnaut and Gary T. Marx, *Undercover. Police Surveillance in Comparative Perspective*, The Hague: Kluwer Law International, 1995

Fokke & Sukke — *Fokke & Sukke webzijde*, <http://www.networld.org/~Fokke_Sukke/>

Fotis — *Testimony of James J. Fotis Executive Director Law Enforcement Alliance of America Before the Subcommittee on the Constitution, Federalism and Property Rights of the Senate Judiciary Committee*, 17 March 1998, <http://www.computerprivacy.org/archive/03171998-5.shtml>

Frankel — Yair Frankel, Moti Yung, 'Escrow Encryption Systems Visited: Attacks, Analysis and Designs', in: D. Coppersmith (ed.), *Advances in Cryptology – CRYPTO '95*, Berlin: Springer-Verlag, pp. 222-235

Franken — H. Franken, G.J.C. Lekkerkerker et al., *De notaris en het elektronisch rechtsverkeer*, The Hague: Vermande, 1996

Fraser — Barbara Fraser, *Site Security Handbook. RFC 2196*, September 1997, <ftp://ftp.isi.edu/in-notes/rfc2196.txt>

Freeh 95a — Louis J. Freeh, Testimony before the House Committee on the Judiciary Subcommittee on Crime, 30 March 1995

Freeh 95b — Louis J. Freeh, *Speech Before the International Cryptography Institute, Washington, D.C., September 21, 1995*, <http://www.fbi.gov/dirspch/crypto.htm>

Freeh 95c — Louis J. Freeh, Letter to Honorable Henry Hyde, Chairman Committee on the Judiciary, House of Representatives, 2 November 1995, <http://www.fbi.gov/archives/congress/wiretap.htm>

Freeh 96 — *Statement of Louis J. Freeh Director Federal Bureau of Investigation on July 25, 1996 before the Committee on Commerce, Science, and Transportation, United States Senate, regarding impact of encryption on law enforcement and public safety*, <http://www.epic.org/crypto/export_controls/freeh.html>

Freeh 98 — *Threats to U.S. National Security. Statement for the record Louis J. Freeh, Director Federal Bureau of Investigation before the Senate Select Committee on Intelligence*, 28 January 1998, <http://www.fbi.gov/congress/threats/threats.htm>

Frielink — P.M. Frielink, *Infiltratie in het strafrecht*, Arnhem: Gouda Quint, 1990

Fritsch — Kenneth M. Fritsch, 'Fortezza 2.0 Cancellation', 7 August 1997, message forwarded by Phil Karn to mailing list <cryptography@c2.net>, 7 August 1997

Fsk — Forskningsministeriet, 'Ingen regulering af kryptering. Pressemeddelelse', 26 June 1998, <http://www.fsk.dk/fsk/presse/260698.html>

Ghosh — Rishab Aiyer Ghosh, 'Interpol's Top Internet Crimefighter Speaks Out', *Telecom Digest*, No. 299 (2 November 1997)

GVU — *GVU's 8th WWW User Survey*, December 1997, <http://www.gvu.gatech.edu/user_surveys/survey-1997-10/>

Hager — Nicky Hager, 'Exposing the Global Surveillance System', *Covert Action Quarterly* (Winter 1997), <http://caq.com/CAQ/CAQ59GlobalSnoop.html>

Harbou — Christian Harbou, Jens Nielsen, 'Politiet står magtesløs over for kriminel data-kryptering', *ComputerWorld*, No. 35 (1995)

Hendriks — R. Hendriks, 'Recherche stroomlijnt berichtenverkeer', *Telecommagazine* (September 1996), pp. 33-36

Hoffman 94 — Lance J. Hoffman, Farez A. Ali et al., 'Cryptography Policy', *Communications of the ACM* 37, No. 9 (September 1994), pp. 109-117

Hoffman 95 — Lance J. Hoffman (ed.), *Building in Big Brother. The Cryptographic Policy Debate*, New York: Springer, 1995

Hogesteeger — G. Hogesteeger, D.A. Korving, *Bellen voor de vrijheid, Illegale telefoonverbindingen in de Tweede Wereldoorlog*, Den Haag: Stichting Het Nederlandse PTT Museum, 1990

Hruska — Jan Hruska, Sophos, *Macro viruses: problems and defences*, October 1996, <http://www.sophos.com/virusinfo/techreports/macropro.html>

HRW — Human Rights Watch, *Silencing the Net. The Threat to Freedom of Expression On-line*, 10 May 1996

Hueske — Thomas Hueske, Axel Pfau, 'Software-Versiegelung mit kryptografischen Methoden', *Datenschutz und Datensicherung*, No. 6 (1990), pp. 298-304

Hutt — Arthur E. Hutt, Seymour Bosworth, Douglas B. Hoyt (eds.), *Computer Security Handbook*, 3rd ed., New York etc.: John Wiley & Sons, 1995

Huybrechts	Luc Huybrechts, 'Het gerechtelijk afluisteren in het Belgisch recht na de nieuwe afluisterwet', *Panopticon* (1995), pp. 41-57
INRA	Eugen Ehmann, 'Opinion Poll', *Computer und Recht*, No. 7 (1997), pp. 449-450
ITSEC	*Information Technology Security Evaluation Criteria (ITSEC). Draft*, 2 May 1990
IWGCP	Interagency Working Group on Cryptography Policy, *Enabling Privacy, Commerce, Security and Public Safety in the Global Information Infrastructure*, draft paper, 20 May 1996, <http://www.epic.org/crypto/key_escrow/white_paper.html>
Jefferies	N. Jefferies, C. Mitchell, M. Walker, 'A Proposed Architecture for Trusted Third Party Services', in: *Cryptography: Policy and Algorithms, Proceedings of the conference*, Springer-Verlag (LNCS 1029), 1996, pp. 98-104
Jones	Frank Jones, *Nowhere to run... Nowhere to hide... The vulnerability of CRT's, CPU's and peripherals to TEMPEST monitoring in the real world*, 1996, <http://www.thecodex.com/c_tempest.html>
Kahn	David Kahn, *The Codebreakers. The Story of Secret Writing*, New York: MacMillan, 1967
Kaufman	Charlie Kaufman, Radia Perlman, Mike Spencer, *Network Security. Private Communication in a Public World*, Englewood Cliffs, NJ: Prentice Hall PTR, 1995
Kephart	Jeffrey O. Kephart et al., 'Fighting Computer Viruses', *Scientific American* (November 1997), pp. 56-61
Kilian	Joe Kilian, Tom Leighton, 'Fair Cryptosystems, Revisited', in: D. Coppersmith (ed.), *Advances in Cryptology – CRYPTO '95*, Berlin: Springer-Verlag, pp. 208-221
Klerks	Peter Klerks, 'Covert Policing in the Netherlands', in [Fijnaut], pp. 103-140
Kocher	Paul Kocher, *Timing Attacks on Implementations of Diffie-Hellman, RSA, DSS, and Other Systems*, no date, <http://www.cryptography.com/timingattack.html>
Komen	Dick Komen, Computer Crime Team Amsterdam-Amstelland, personal communication, 14 October 1996
Koops	Bert-Jaap Koops, *Crypto Law Survey*, version 13.0, June 1998, <http://cwis.kub.nl/~frw/people/koops/lawsurvy.htm>
KPMG 94	KPMG EDP Auditors, *Rapport aan de Ministers van Economische Zaken, Binnenlandse Zaken, Justitie en Verkeer en Waterstaat inzake de uitkomsten van het Bedrijfseffectenonderzoek Cryptografie*, Amstelveen, 7 April 1994
KPMG 98	KPMG EDP Auditors, Ministerie van Economische Zaken, Ministerie van Verkeer en Waterstaat, *Draft policy proposal concerning the Dutch policy in the field of Trusted Third Parties*, Amstelveen, 1 March 1998, <http://www.minvenw.nl/hdtp/factsheets/trust1.html>
KRA	Key Recovery Alliance, *Public Policy Requirements for a Global Key Recovery Infrastructure*, 2 September 1997, <http://www.kra.org/whitepapers>
Kristof	Nicholas D. Kristof and Sheryl WuDunn, *China Wakes. The struggle for the soul of a rising power*, London: Nicholas Brealey Publishing, 1994
Kuhn	Markus G. Kuhn, Ross. J. Anderson, 'Soft Tempest: Hidden Data Transmission Using Electromagnetic Emanations', 1998, <http://www.cl.cam.ac.uk/~mgk25/ih98-tempest.pdf>
Kuner	Christopher Kuner, 'Rechtliche Aspekte der Datenverschlüsselung im Internet', *Neue Juristische Wochenschrift-Computerreport*, No. 6 (1995), pp. 413-420
Kutscha	Martin Kutscha, 'Der Lauschangriff im Polizeirecht der Länder', *Neue Juristische Wochenschrift* (1994), pp. 85-88
LAB	*European Commission Legal Advisory Board meeting on electronic commerce / computer crime, 6-7 October 1997, Draft minutes*, <http://www2.echo.lu/legal/en/lab/971006/minutes-text.html#42>
Labour	Labour Party, *Communicating Britain's Future*, no date, <http://www.labour.org.uk/views/info-highway/content.html>
Landwehr	Hartmut Landwehr, *Online mit Jesus*, <http://www.beichte.de>
Lazarus	David Lazarus, '*Playboy* Hopes 'Watermarks' Keep Bunnies Safe', *Wired News* (30 June 1997)

Leijten	Jan Leijten, 'Afweging en de mythe van de weegschaal', *Nederlands Juristenblad* (4 April 1997), pp. 636-637
Lensing	J.A.W. Lensing, 'De evolutie van de politiebevoegdheden in het raam van de bestrijding van de ernstige, georganiseerde misdaad', *Delikt en Delinkwent* 24, No. 10 (1994), pp. 1007-1030
Lenstra	A.K. Lenstra, P. Winkler, Y. Yacobi, 'A key escrow system with warrant bounds', in: D. Coppersmith (ed.), *Advances in Cryptology - CRYPTO '95*, Berlin: Springer-Verlag, 1995, pp.197-207
Leutwyler	Kristin Leutwyler, 'Calculating with DNA. Genetic material solves mathematical problems', *Scientific American* (September 1995), pp. 18-21
Litt	Robert S. Litt, 'Prepared Statement before the Senate Judiciary Committee, Subcommittee on the constitution, federalism, and property, Privacy in a digital age: encryption and mandatory access', mailing list <cryptography@c2.net>, 17 March 1998
Lorentz	*Rapport du groupe de travail présidé par M. Francis Lorentz. Commerce électronique: une nouvelle donne pour les consommateurs, les entreprises, les citoyens et les pouvoirs publics*, 7 January 1998, <http://www.finances.gouv.fr/commerce_electronique/lorentz/>
Madsen	Wayne Madsen, 'Crypto AG: The NSA's Trojan Whore?', *Covert Action Quarterly* (Winter 1998), <http://caq.com/cryptogate>
Mansfield	N.P. Mansfield, Shell Internationale Petroleum Maatschappij B.V., *Commercial Use of Cryptography*, unpublished paper, no date
Manunza 94	E.R. Manunza, 'De bescherming van kroongetuigen in Italië', in [Tak 94a], pp. 37-64
Manunza 98	Elisabetta Manunza, Bert-Jaap Koops, 'Garanties voor de betrouwbaarheid van kroongetuigen', *Delikt en Delinkwent* (October 1998), pp. 768-785
Margherio	Lynn Margherio et al., Secretariat for Electronic Commerce, *The Emerging Digital Economy*, April 1998, <http://www.ecommerce.gov/emerging.htm>
Matyas	Stephen M. Matyas Jr., *Key Recovery Functional Model. Version 1.0*, 8 June 1998, <http://www.kra.org>
McNamara 97	Joel McNamara, *Practical Attacks on PGP*, (intended) speech to Hacking In Progress, 9 August 1997, <http://www.eskimo.com/~joelm/pgpatk.html>
McNamara 98	Joel McNamara, *The Complete, Unofficial TEMPEST Information Page*, version 30 March 1998, <http://www.eskimo.com/~joelm/tempest.html>
Micali	Silvio Micali, 'Fair Public-Key Cryptosystems', in: Ernest F. Brickell (ed.): *Advances in Cryptology - CRYPTO '92*, Berlin: Springer Verlag, 1993, pp. 113-138 (see also the version in [Hoffman 95], pp. 149-173)
Moeller	Ulf Moeller, *Kryptographie: Rechtliche Situation, politische Diskussion*, version 2 May 1997, <http://www.thur.de/ulf/krypto/verbot.html>
Mulder	Richard De Mulder, 'Wetgeving maakt technologie tot een veelkoppige draak', *Nederlands Juristenblad* (4 November 1993), pp. 1429-1430
Nash	Susan Nash, 'European co-operation in telephone tapping', *New Law Journal* (June 1995), p. 954
Nelson	*Report of the Business-Government Forum on Global Cryptography Policy, Held on 19-20 December 1995 in Paris. Annex IV -- Mike Nelson Policy Problem*, <http://www.cs.umass.edu/~lmccarth/cypherpunks/icl.txt> (accessed 10 January 1996)
Nemerov	Howard Nemerov, *The collected poems*, Chicago: University of Chicago Press, 1977
Neumann	Peter G. Neumann, *Computer-Related Risks*, New York: ACM Press, 1995
Nielsen	Leif Nielsen, 'Sikkerhed i telenettet', in [Stripp], pp. 36-37
NIIAC	NIIAC, *Common Ground: Fundamental Principles for the National Information Infrastructure*, March 1995, <http://nii.nist.gov./pubs/common-ground.txt>
NIISIF	NII Security Issues Forum, *NII Security: The Federal Role*, June 1995, <http://nsi.org/Library/Compsec/nii.txt>
NIITF	Privacy Working Group, Information Policy Committee, NII Task Force, *Privacy and the Information Infrastructure: Principles for Providing and Using Personal Information, Final Version*, 6 June 1995, <http://www.iitf.nist.gov/ipc/ipc/ipc-pubs/niiprivprin_final.html>

NIST 94 — NIST, *FIPS 186: Specifications for the Digital Signature Standard (DSS)*, 19 May 1994, in [Hoffman 95], pp. 84-86

NIST 95 — NIST, *Draft Software Key Escrow Encryption Export Criteria*, version November 1995, <http://csrc.ncsl.nist.gov/keyescrow/criteria.txt>

NIST 98 — NIST, *Advanced Encryption Standard (AES) Development Effort*, <http://csrc.nist.gov/encryption/aes/aes_home.htm>

Norway — *Status on Norwegian encryption policy*, Document to the OECD Ad Hoc Meeting of Experts on Cryptography Policy, 18-19 December 1995

NOU — *Pseudonyme helseregistre. Et lovetkast om personvern, pasientvern og helsevern*, Norges offentlige utredninger 1993:22, Oslo: Statens trykning, 1993

NRC — Kenneth W. Dam, Herbert S. Lin (eds.), National Research Council, *Cryptography's Role In Securing the Information Society*, Washington, D.C.: National Academy Press, 1996, <http://www.nap.edu/readingroom/books/crisis/>

OA — Administrative Office of the US Courts, *1997 Wiretap Report*, April 1998, <http://www.uscourts.gov/wiretap/contents.html>

OECD 86 — OECD, *Computer-Related Crime: Analysis of Legal Policy*, Paris, 1986

OECD 97 — OECD, *Cryptography Policy: The Guidelines and the Issues*, March 1997, <http://www.oecd.org/dsti/sti/it/secur/prod/e-crypto.htm>

O'Hara — Colleen O'Hara, Heather Harreld, 'DOD sinks the Clipper', *Federal Computer Week* (17 February 1997)

OM 94 — Vergadering van Procureurs-Generaal, *Openbaar Ministerie verscherpt beveiliging*, press release, 6 December 1994, <http://www.openbaarministerie.nl/archief/persberichten/pb94-0612_2.htm#top>

OM 98 — Openbaar Ministerie, *Jaarverslag Openbaar Ministerie: trendbreuk door stijging aantal misdrijven in 1997*, press release, 22 July 1998, <http://www.openbaarministerie.nl/persberi/pb980722.htm#top>

Orlowski — Steve Orlowski, 'Encryption and the global information infrastructure. An Australian Perspective', *Lecture notes in computer science* 1029 (1996), pp. 65-74

Ostendorf — Heribert Ostendorf, 'Ein Allheilmittel? Der »sogenannte Lauschangriff« auf dem rechtsstaatlichen Prüfstand', *Neue Kriminalpolitik*, No. 3 (1996), pp. 32-35

OTA — Office of Technology Assessment, *Information Security and Privacy in Network Environments*, OTA-TCT-606, Washington, D.C.: U.S. Government Printing Office, September 1994

Patijn — Alexander Patijn, 'Grondrechten en nieuwe communicatietechnologieën: de rol van de wetgever', *NJCM-Bulletin* 21, No. 5 (1996), pp. 796-806

Peters — A.A.G. Peters, *Het rechtskarakter van het strafrecht*, inaugural lecture Utrecht University, Deventer: Kluwer, 1972

Pfeiffer — Christian Pfeiffer, 'Telefongespräche im Visier der elektronischen Rasterfahndung', *Zeitschrift für Rechtspolitik*, No. 7 (1994), pp. 253-255

Pfitzmann — Birgit Pfitzmann, Michael Waidner, 'Anonymous Fingerprinting', in: W. Fumy (ed.), *Advances in Cryptology – EUROCRYPT '97*, Berlin: Springer-Verlag, 1997, pp. 88-102

Powell — Corey S. Powell, 'The Rights Stuff. Buying and selling art in a digital world', *Scientific American* (January 1995), pp. 18-19

Rabel — Timothy Rabel, 'Eavesdropping on Electromagnetic Radiation: A Violation of Federal Law and/or an Intrusion Upon Seclusion?', *Journal of Computer & Information Law* (1994), pp. 627-644

Rawls — John Rawls, *A Theory of Justice*, Oxford: Oxford University Press, 1972

Registratiekamer 94 — Registratiekamer, Letter to the Dutch Minister of Justice, 3 May 1994, reference 94.A.11

Registratiekamer 95 — Registratiekamer, Information & Privacy Commissioner (Ontario), *Privacy-enhancing Technologies. The path to anonymity*, Sdu, 1995

Registratiekamer 98 — Registratiekamer, Letter to the Dutch Minister of Internal Affairs, 9 April 1998, reference 98.A.294.01

Reid — Tim Reid, 'Hackers pillaged US files to sell secrets to Saddam', *Electronic Telegraph* (23 March 1997)

Reijne — Z. Reijne et al., *Tappen in Nederland*, WODC, Gouda Quint, 1996

Reijntjes J.M. Reijntjes, 'Nemo tenetur: een holle leus?', in: J.M. Reijntjes (red.), *Nemo tenetur*, Arnhem: Gouda Quint, 1996, pp. 9-21

Rivest Ronald L. Rivest, *Chaffing and Winnowing: Confidentiality without Encryption*, version 24 April 1998, <http://theory.lcs.mit.edu/~rivest/chaffing.txt>

Roche Barbara Roche, UK Department of Trade and Industry, 'Secure Electronic Commerce Statement', 27 April 1998, <http://jya.com/uk-ecomm.htm>

RSA R.L. Rivest, A. Shamir, and L.M. Adleman, 'A Method for Obtaining Digital Signatures and Public-Key Cryptosystems', *Communications of the ACM* 21, No. 2 (February 1978), pp. 120-126

Saxby Stephen Saxby, 'Public Sector Policy and the Information Superhighway', *International Journal of Law and Information Technology* 2, No. 3 (1994), pp. 221-254

Schalken Tom Schalken, annotation of HR 29 October 1996, *NJ* 1997, 232 m.nt. Sch

Schmid A.P. Schmid, 'Inleiding', in: *Georganiseerde misdaad. Een nieuwe bedreiging voor de samenleving, Verslag van een symposium 20 november 1993 Erasmus Universteit Rotterdam*, Driebergen: Stichting Synthesis, 1993, pp. 7-29

Schmitz Roland Schmitz, '"Wilde" Müllablagerungen und strafrechtliche Garantenstellung des Grundstückseigentümers', *Neue Juristische Wochenschrift* 1993, pp. 1167-1171

Schneier Bruce Schneier, *Applied Cryptography. Protocols, Algorithms, and Source Code in C*, 2nd ed., New York etc.: John Wiley & Sons, 1996

Schönfeld Carolien Schönfeld, 'Informatiebeveiliging bij Rijk en gemeenten', *Openbaar bestuur*, No. 1 (1995), pp. 24-27

Seifert Jürgen Seifert, 'Vom Lauschangriff zum »Großen Lauschangriff«', *Kritische Justiz* (1992), pp. 355-363

Seline Christopher Seline, *Eavesdropping on the Electromagnetic Emanations of Digital Equipment: The Laws of Canada, England and the United States*, 1989, <http://jya.com/tempest.htm>

Sergienko Greg Sergienko, 'Self Incrimination and Cryptographic Keys', *Richmond Journal of Law & Technology*, No. 1 (1996), <http://www.urich.edu/~jolt/v2i1/sergienko.html>

Shur G. Shur, 'The United States' Witness Security Program', in [Tak 94a], pp. 65-76

Simmelink J.B.H.M. Simmelink, *De rechtsstaatgedachte achter art. 1 Sv*, Arnhem: Gouda Quint, 1987

Simmons Gustavus J. Simmons, 'Subliminal Communication is ~~Possible~~ Easy Using the DSA', in: Tor Helleseth (ed.), *Advances in Cryptology – EUROCRYPT '93*, Berlin: Springer Verlag, 1994, pp. 218-232

Smith Martin Smith, 'Personnel Security', in: K.M. Jackson, J. Hruska (eds.), *Computer Security Reference Book*, Oxford etc.: Butterworth-Heinemann, 1992, pp. 417-436

Smits J.M. Smits, J. de Vries, 'Het lagenmodel: een toekomstvaste basis voor inrichting en regulering van de telecommunicatiemarkt', *Informatie en Informatiebeleid*, No. 3 (1993), pp. 48-55

Smulders Peter Smulders, 'The Threat of Information Theft by Reception of Electromagnetic Radiation from RS-232 Cables', *Computers & Security*, No. 9 (1990), pp. 53-58

SOG-IS SOG-IS, *Proposal for a Council Decision in the field of security of information systems, concerning the establishment of a Europe-wide network of Trusted Third Party Services (ETS)*, 1 November 1995

Solms Sebastiaan von Solms and David Naccache, 'On Blind Signatures and Perfect Crimes', *Computers & Security* (1992), pp. 581-583

Sophos *Data Security Reference Guide 1994/1995*, Abingdon: Sophos, 1994

Stapel & De Koning A.A. Buijens, J. van Diemen, A.S. de Winter, 'Licht', *Opsporingsleer, Stapel & De Koning. Handboek voor de politie*, The Hague: VUGA Uitgeverij B.V.

Statewatch Statewatch, 'UK: Security services reports', *Statewatch Bulletin* 5, No. 3 (May-June 1995)

Stripp Teknologirådet, Steffen Stripp (red.), *En dansk krypto-politik. Hvordan skal digitale informationer hemmeligholdes?*, Teknologirådets rapporter 1995 nr. 5, København: Teknologirådet, 1995

SWIFT S.W.I.F.T. s.c. Marketing, 'S.W.I.F.T. and Security', *Compact* (Winter 1992), pp. 8-22

Tak 94a	P.J.P. Tak (red.), *Bespiegelingen omtrent de kroongetuige*, Arnhem: Gouda Quint, 1994
Tak 94b	P.J.P. Tak, *De kroongetuige en de georganiseerde misdaad*, Arnhem: Gouda Quint, 1994
TFEC	Task Force on Electronic Commerce, *A Cryptography Policy Framework for Electronic Commerce. Building Canada's Information Economy and Society*, February 1998, <http://strategis.ic.gc.ca/SSG/cy00005e.html>
Thiesen	Henning Thiesen, 'Efterforskning af kriminalitet', in [Stripp], pp. 47-50
TIN	Tibet Information Network, 'Tourist denounced for "Bomb" Fax from Lhasa', mailing list *World Tibet Network News* <wtn-l@vm1.mcgill.ca>, 21 March 1996
TIS	Trusted Information Systems, 'Worldwide Survey of Cryptographic Products', version December 1997, <http://www.tis.com/research/crypto/crypt_surv.html>
Traa	Enquêtecommissie opsporingsmethoden, *Inzake opsporing*, The Hague: Sdu, 1996
Указ	Указ Президента Российской Федерации от 3 Апреля 1995 года, No. 334, о мерах по соблюдению законности в области разработки производства, реализации и эксплуатации шифровальных средств, а также предоставления услуг в области шифрования информации, *Российская Газета*, 68, 6 April 1995
US	*Administration Statement on Commercial Encryption Policy*, 12 July 1996, <http://www.epic.org/crypto/key_escrow/wh_cke_796.html>
Verheul 97a	E.R. Verheul, B.J. Koops, H. van Tilborg, 'Binding cryptography. A fraud-detectible alternative to key escrow proposals', *The Computer Law and Security Report* (January-February 1997), pp. 3-14
Verheul 97b	E.R. Verheul, H.C.A. van Tilborg, 'Binding ElGamal: A fraud-detectable alternative to key escrow solutions', in: W. Fumy (ed.), *Advances in Cryptology – EUROCRYPT '97*, Berlin: Springer-Verlag, 1997, pp. 119-133
Wallich	Paul Wallich, 'Meta-Virus', *Scientific American* (November 1995), p. 25
Walsh	Gerard Walsh, *Review of Policy relating to Encryption Technologies*, 10 October 1996, <http://www.efa.org.au/Issues/Crypto/Walsh>
Warren	Samuel D. Warren, Louis D. Brandeis, 'The right to privacy (The implicit made explicit)', *Harvard Law Review*, No. 4 (1890), pp. 193-220, reprinted in: F.D. Schoeman (ed.), *Philosophical dimensions of privacy: an anthology*, Cambridge: Cambridge University Press, 1984, pp. 75-103
Wayner 93	Peter Wayner, 'Should Encryption Be Regulated?, Politics, not technology, may hamstring the use of data encryption in the U.S.', *Byte* (May 1993), p. 129-134
Wayner 95	Peter Wayner, 'Picking the Crypto Locks', *Byte* (October 1995), pp. 77-80
Wayner 96	Peter Wayner, *Disappearing Cryptography. Being and Nothingness on the Net*, Boston etc: AP Professional, 1996
White House	The White House, *Statement of the Press Secretary*, 4 February 1994, reprinted in [Hoffman 95], pp. 232-234
Wright 95	Marie A. Wright, 'Protecting Information from Internet Threats', *Computer Fraud & Security Bulletin* (March 1995), pp. 6-10
Wright 98	Steve Wright, Omega Foundation, *An appraisal of technologies for political control. Working document*, Luxembourg: European Parliament – STOA, 6 January 1998, <http://jya.com/stoa-atpc.htm>
WRR	Wetenschappelijke Raad voor het Regeringsbeleid, *Staat zonder land. Een verkenning van bestuurlijke gevolgen van informatie- en communicatietechnologie*, Den Haag: Sdu, 1998, English summary at <http://www.wrr.nl/rap54_e.htm>
Wuermeling	U. Wuermeling, S. Felixberger, 'Staatliche Überwachung der Telekommunikation', *Computer und Recht*, No. 9 (1997), pp. 555-561
Zimmerman 94	Philip Zimmermann, 'Pretty Good Privacy: Public Key Encryption for the Masses', revised 31 August 1994, in [Hoffman 95], pp. 93-107
Zimmerman 96	Phil Zimmerman, 'PGP and Human Rights', mailing list <cypherpunks@toad.com>, 18 and 21 March 1996
Zysman	George I. Zysman, 'Wireless Networks', *Scientific American* (September 1995), pp. 52-55

Legislative proposals, decisions, and other parliamentary documents

Dutch

18 995 *Samenleving en criminaliteit* (Society and crime), 22 May 1985, TK 1984-1985

19 328 *Infiltratie als opsporingstechniek* (Infiltration as investigation measure), TK 1985-1986

21 551 *Wijziging van het Wetboek van Strafrecht en van het Wetboek van Strafvordering in verband met de voortschrijdende toepassing van informatietechniek (Wet computercriminaliteit)* (Change of the Criminal Code and of the Code of Criminal Procedure concerning the advancing application of information technologies - Computer Crime Act), TK 1989-1990ff

22 838 *De georganiseerde criminaliteit in Nederland* (Organized crime in the Netherlands), TK 1992-1993

23 047 *Wijziging van het Wetboek van Strafvordering in verband met de regeling van het opnemen van gesprekken met een technisch hulpmiddel* (Change of the Code of Criminal Procedure concerning the regulation of recording conversations with a technical device), TK 1992-1993ff

23 900 *Elektronische snelwegen. Nationaal Actieplan: van metafoor naar actie* (Electronic highways. National action plan: from metaphor to action), TK 1994-1995, 23 900, nr 20

24 072 *Enquête Opsporingsmethoden* (Inquest into investigation measures), TK 1995-1996ff

24 108 *Wijziging van de Wet op de telecommunicatievoorzieningen in verband met het aftappen van GSM* (Change of the Telecommunications Facilities Act concerning tapping GSM), TK 1994-1995

24 175 *Beheersing informatiebeveiliging* (Control of information security), TK 1994-1995

24 565 *Elektronische snelwegen* (Electronic highways), TK 1995-1996ff

24 679 *Aftappen van telecommunicatie, Beleidsvoornemen bevoegd aftappen telecommunicatie* (Tapping telecommunications. Policy intention authorized tapping of telecommunications), 4 April 1996, TK 1995-1996

25 208 *Inbraak bij het LRT* (Burglary at the National Detective Team), 27 January 1997, TK 1996-1997

25 290 *Informatiebeveiliging Belastingdienst* (Information security Internal Revenue Service), 7 April 1997, TK 1996-1997

25 403 *Wijziging van het Wetboek van Strafvordering in verband met de regeling van enige bijzondere bevoegdheden en wijziging van enige andere bepalingen (bijzondere opsporingsbevoegdheden)* (Change of the Code of Criminal Procedure concerning the regulation of some special powers and change of some other provisions - special investigation powers), TK 1996-1997ff

25 533 *Regels inzake de telecommunicatie (Telecommunicatiewet)* (Rules concerning telecommunications - Telecommunications Act), TK 1996-1997ff

25 880 *Wetgeving voor de elektronische snelweg* (Legislation for the electronic highway), 12 February 1998, TK 1997-1998

European

86/C160/01 *Council resolution of 9 June 1986 on the use of videoconference and videophone techniques for intergovernmental applications* (86/C160/01), *OJ* 27 June 1986

92/242/EEC *Council decision of 31 March 1992 in the field of security of information systems* (92/242/EEC), *OJ* 8 May 1992

COM(94) 347 *Europe's Way to the Information Society. An Action Plan, Communication from the Commission to the Council and the European Parliament and to the Economic and Social Committee and the Committee of the Regions*, 19 July 1994, COM(94) 347 final

COM(95) 382 *Green Paper on Copyrights and Related Rights in the Information Society*, 19 July 1995, COM(95) 382 final

95/46/EC *General Directive of 24 October 1995 on the protection of privacy with regard to the processing of personal data and on the free movement of such data* (95/46/EC), *OJ* 23 November 1995

96/19/EC *Directive of 28 February 1996 regarding the implementation of full competition in telecommunications markets* (96/19/EC), *OJ* 22 March 1996

96/C329/01 *Council Resolution of 17 January 1995 on the lawful interception of telecommunications (96/C329/01)*, *OJ* 4 November 1996

COM(96) 607 — *Draft Communication from the European Commission to the Council, the European Parliament, the Economic and Social Committee, and the Committee of the Regions – Europe at the forefront of the Global Information Society: Rolling Action Plan*, COM(96) 607

COM(97) 157 — *A European Initiative in Electronic Commerce, Communication to the European Parliament, the Council, the Econocmic and Social Committee and the Committee of the Regions*, 16 April 1997, COM(97) 157

COM(97) 356 — *Proposal for a European Parliament and Council Directive on the legal protection of services based on, or consisting of, conditional access*, 9 July 1997, COM(97) 356, provisional version

COM(97) 503 — *Ensuring security and trust in electronic communication – Towards a European Framework for Digital Signatures and Encryption*, 10 October 1997, COM(97) 503

COM(97) 623 — *Green Paper on the convergence of the telecommunications, media and information technology sectors, and the implications for regulation – towards an information society approach*, 3 December 1997, COM(97) 623

97/66/EC — *Directive of the European Parliament and of the Council of 15 December 1997 concerning the processing of personal data and the protection of privacy in the telecommunications sector* (97/66/EC)

COM(98) 50 — *The need for strengthened international coordination*, 4 February 1998, COM(98) 50

COM(98) 297 — *Proposal for a European Parliament and Council Directive on a common framework for electronic signatures*, 13 May 1998, COM(98) 297 final

COM(98) 332 — *Amended proposal for a European Parliament and Council Directive on the Legal Protection of Services Based on, or Consisting of Conditional Access*, COM(98) 332 final, *OJ* 30 June 1998

Case Law

Dutch

HR 7 June 1977, *NJ* 1978, 483
HR 13 December 1977, *NJ* 1978, 592
HR 4 December 1979, *NJ* 1980, 356 m.nt. ThWvV (*Tallon*)
HR 20 March 1984, *NJ* 1984, 547 m.nt. ThWvV
HR 18 December 1984, *NJ* 1985, 358
HR 28 May 1985, *NJ* 1985, 822 (*cocaine in kitchen cupboard*)
HR 1 October 1985, *NJ* 1986, 405 m.nt. ThWvV
HR 14 April 1987, *NJ* 1988, 515
HR 21 March 1989, *NJ* 1989, 864
HR 26 May 1992, *NJ* 1992, 753 m.nt. ThWvV
HR 26 October 1993, *NJ* 1994, 629 m.nt. C
HR 15 February 1994, *NJ* 1994, 322 m.nt. AHJS
HR 29 March 1994, *NJ* 1994, 577 (*pocket computer*)
HR 19 March 1996, *NJ* 1996, 540 m.nt. Sch
HR 19 March 1996, *NJ* 1997, 59 m.nt. Kn
HR 29 October 1996, *NJ* 1997, 232
HR 3 June 1997, *NJ* 1997, 584

Hof Amsterdam, 30 January 1998, No. 117/98 (*Hakkelaar*)

Rechtbank Amsterdam, A.D., Parketnummer 13/129018-95

European
Funke v. *France*, ECHR 25 February 1993
Kruslin v. *France*, *Huvig v. France*, ECHR 24 April 1990
Lüdi v. *Switzerland*, ECHR 15 June 1992
Murray v. *United Kingdom*, ECHR 8 February 1996
Orkem SA v. *Commission EC*, ECJ 18 October 1989
Salabiaku v. *France*, ECHR 7 October 1988
Saunders v. *United Kingdom*, ECHR 17 December 1996

US
Andresen v. *Maryland*, 427 U.S. 463, 1976
Bernstein v. *U.S. Department of State*, 974 F. Supp. 1288 (N.D. Cal. 1997) (*Bernstein III*)
Braswell v. *United States*, 487 U.S. 99, 1988
Couch v. *United States*, 409 U.S. 322, 1973
United States v. *Doe*, 465 U.S. 605, 1984 (*Doe I*)
Doe v. *United States*, 487 U.S. 201, 1988 (*Doe II*)
Junger v. *Daley*, N.D. Ohio, 1:96-CV-1723 (1998)
Katz v. *United States*, 389 U.S. 347, 1967
United States v. *Kyllo*, U.S. No. 96-30333, 7 April 1998
Pennsylvania v. *Muniz*, 496 U.S. 582, 1990
Murphy v. *Waterfront Commission*, 378 US 52, 1964
United States v. *Penney-Feeney*, 773 F. Supp. 220 (D.Haw. 1991)
Schmerber v. *California*, 384 U.S. 757, 1966

About the author

Bert-Jaap Koops (the Netherlands, 1967) studied Mathematics and General and comparative literature at Groningen University from 1985 to 1992. Besides, he did first-year examinations in Philosophy and in History of art, and he studied Italian and literature in Siena (Italy) for half a year.

In 1992 and 1993, Bert-Jaap worked for Amnesty International on a two-year project supporting local groups. From 1994 to 1998, he worked as a Ph. D. student at Tilburg University and Eindhoven University of Technology, facilitated by the Co-operation Centre Tilburg and Eindhoven Universities (SOBU). Since October 1998, he is working as a senior research fellow with the Center for Law, Public Administration, and Informatization of Tilburg University.

Bert-Jaap is editor of the Dutch *IT & Recht* magazine and of the forthcoming Dutch reference book *Recht & informatietechnologie*. He co-edited a book on *Emerging Electronic Highways*, and he has published widely, in Dutch and English, on law and information technology. His main research areas are encryption regulation, computer crime, and Trusted Third Parties.

Bert-Jaap has been an active member of Amnesty International for many years, facilitating local group activism, coordinating country work on China and Tibet, and campaigning on the Internet. His main interests are literature, classical music, visual arts, languages, and travel.

e-mail e.j.koops@kub.nl
WWW http://cwis.kub.nl/~frw/people/koops/bertjaap.htm